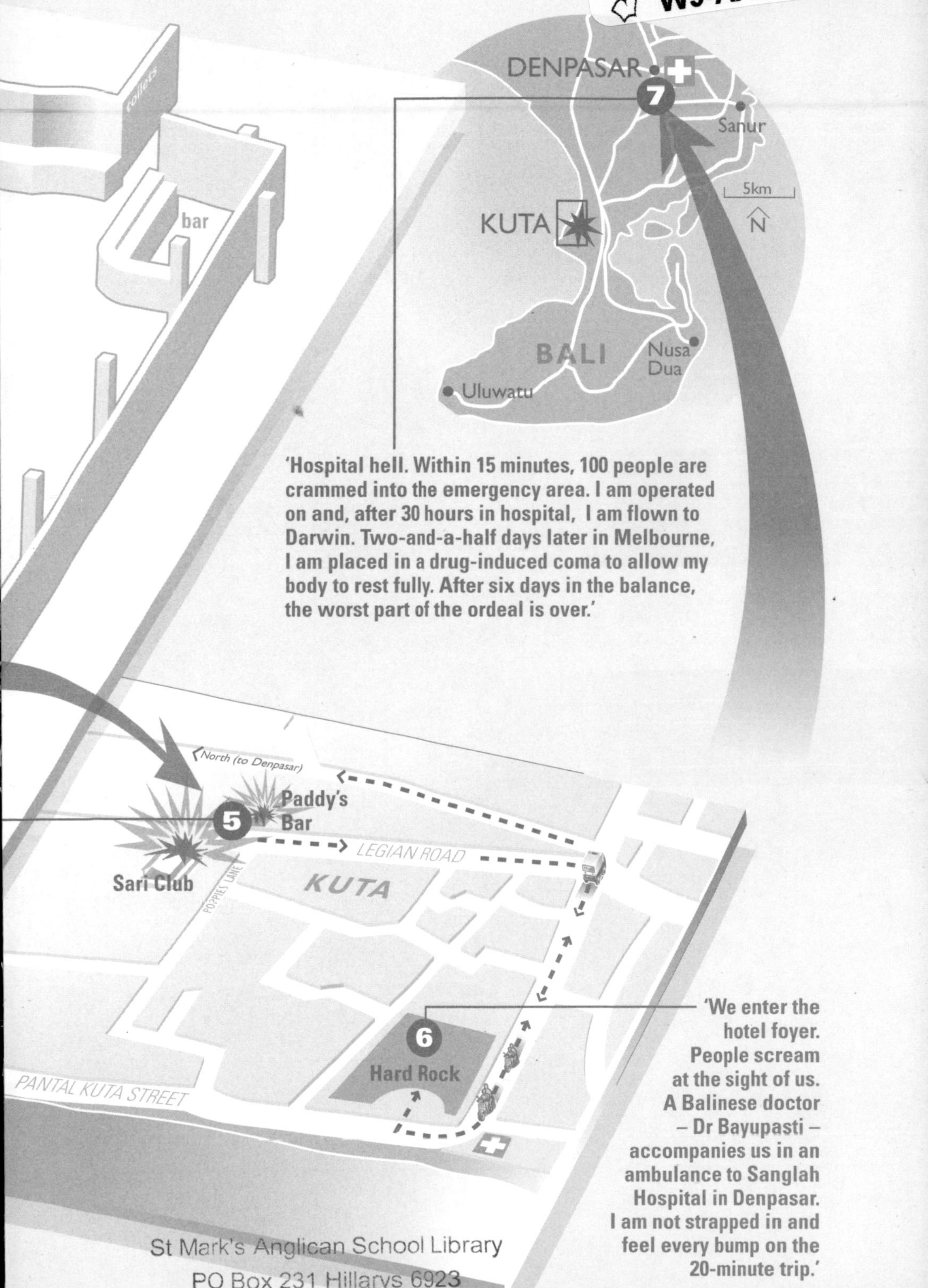

'Hospital hell. Within 15 minutes, 100 people are crammed into the emergency area. I am operated on and, after 30 hours in hospital, I am flown to Darwin. Two-and-a-half days later in Melbourne, I am placed in a drug-induced coma to allow my body to rest fully. After six days in the balance, the worst part of the ordeal is over.'

'We enter the hotel foyer. People scream at the sight of us. A Balinese doctor – Dr Bayupasti – accompanies us in an ambulance to Sanglah Hospital in Denpasar. I am not strapped in and feel every bump on the 20-minute trip.'

AFTER BALI

JASON McCARTNEY

AFTER BALI

SLATTERY
&
LOTHIAN
BOOKS

Lothian
BOOKS

Geoff Slattery Publishing Pty Ltd
140 Harbour Esplanade, Docklands 3008
www.geoffslattery.com.au

Thomas C. Lothian Pty Ltd
132 Albert Road, South Melbourne 3205
www.lothian.com.au

First published 2003

National Library of Australia
Cataloguing-in-Publication data:

Collins, Ben.
Jason McCartney: after Bali.

ISBN 0 7344 0639 8.

1. McCartney, Jason. 2. Australian football players – Biography. 3. Victims of terrorism – Australia – Biography. 4. Bali Bombing, Kuta, Kuta, Indonesia, 2002 – Biography. 5. Terrorism – Indonesia – Kuta (Kuta). I. McCartney, Jason. II. Title.

796.336092

Cover and page design by Mick Russell, Geoff Slattery Publishing
Graphics by Jo Gay
Interviews by Ben Collins, with assistance from Sean Callander, Gary Hancock, Peter Di Sisto, Bruce Eva and John Murray
Edited by Cathy Smith, Sharon Mullins and Amy Thomas

Cover photograph by Sean Garnsworthy, Getty Images
Photographs by Getty Images and the McCartney family collection
Photograph of Jason McCartney and Mick Martyn courtesy of *Bali Post*
Wedding photographs courtesy of *New Idea* and Lindsay Kelley (Instyle Studios)

Printed in Australia by Griffin Press

This book is dedicated to the innocents who lost their lives in the Bali bombings — two hundred and two people from twenty-two countries, including eighty-eight Australians, were killed on the night of 12 October 2002.

This book also recognises those of us who continue to be touched by the tragedy — the one hundred and sixty-eight Australian survivors, of which I am one, our families and support networks, and the families of those who lost loved ones.

I particularly wish to thank the volunteers and medical staff who treated me in those grim days after the bombings — I am forever in your debt.

To my wife Nerissa, whose love and constant support was the driving force behind my recovery, and my family, who have always been there for me and remained strong as ever throughout this amazing year.

And, finally, thanks to everyone who devoted their time and contributed their stories to this book.

Foreword

On the morning after Jason McCartney's comeback game (6 June 2003), his former coach, Denis Pagan, wrote the following letter to Jason. After ten seasons as senior coach, Pagan left the Kangaroos to coach Carlton at the end of 2002. The letter has been published with Pagan's authority.

Dear Jason,

As I left Telstra Dome last night, I couldn't help but to be awe-inspired by Jason McCartney, one of the most courageous people I know, and those brave, mentally tough Kangaroos.

My thoughts at 7.30 a.m. the day after have me reflecting back to our first meeting, at your residence in West Lakes and where you informed me that you were not interested in playing AFL any more and would prefer to finish up your playing days at South Adelaide.

I can remember at the time thinking, and probably selfishly so, that the Kangaroos really needed you and why wouldn't you come and play for us.

Whatever changed your mind, it was a real triumph for the Shinboners and a real addition to the unbreakable/unstoppable Shinboner spirit. You have certainly done the great 'blue and white' Kangaroos team proud.

I have always admired your spirit, your character, your mental strength and the way your parents delivered you into adulthood.

Football, and life for that matter, is not about ability and God-given talent, it is about what you do with those gifts that count. You have certainly done everything you could with yours.

Your football career, like the majority involved in the AFL, is about highs and lows, and the way you have always carried yourself through the rough times is a real credit. 1999 only exemplifies that.

As I write I think of your football oval courage, backing into packs and running, attempting to mark with the flight of the ball. I think of the way the coaches' box and its inhabitants shuddered, and we all had to look at the TV replay monitor in the back corner to see if it really happened. Your ability to do those things ranks with Glenn Archer, Anthony Stevens, Leigh Colbert, Wayne Carey, Adam Simpson and other great Kangaroos' players.

The way you have carried yourself since Bali is no surprise to many, being a role model, an outstanding Australian and a real inspiration for those who need hope to go on and have to fight to have a future. Everyone in this country admires you for that!

Jason, you are a real hero to many and as I pulled into my driveway last night I realised you were a hero to me, and to have been involved in a very small way in your life so far and to have been your football coach, is something I will always cherish.

Congratulations on a fine football career and the special way you announced your retirement. It was with great dignity, style and class and only a select few could have delivered it that way.

In whatever direction life takes you and Nerissa, I wish you both all the very best and hope your future path is fruitful, positive and happy.

Catch up for a beer and a chat one day.

Yours sincerely,

Denis Pagan

DENIS PAGAN

Contents

Foreword by Denis Pagan vii

Contributors xi

1 *To paradise* 1

2 *Terror strikes* 10

3 *Good decision* 20

4 *The hospital* 34

5 *The news gets home* 40

6 *Helping hands* 50

7 *An anxious wait* 60

8 *To Darwin* 78

9 *Back home* 87

10 *Grave fears* 94

11 *Out of danger* 111

12 *Small steps* 118

13 *Getting better* 128

14 *Walk the walk* 137

15 Home again 156

16 On the run 166

17 Falling in love 179

18 The wedding 188

19 New beginnings 195

20 Back to work 197

21 Feeling my way 211

22 Back to Bali 224

23 Biding my time 231

24 Injured … again! 238

25 Lows and highs 247

26 Farewell to footy 253

27 Justice is done 289

28 One year on 298

Letters to Jason 303

Epilogue by Ben Collins *307*

Contributors

ADAM SIMPSON — Kangaroos teammate
DR ALLEN AYLETT — Kangaroos president
ANTHONY STEVENS — Kangaroos captain 2002-2003
ARDRI VANDERHEYDEN — Nerissa's father, Jason's father-in-law
BRAD FLOOD — close mate
BRENDEN MCCARTNEY — Jason's brother, 11 months his junior
BRENT HARVEY — Kangaroos teammate
COREY MCKERNAN — former Kangaroos teammate
DAVID BONYTHON-WRIGHT — Jason's counsellor, adviser and friend
DAVID DUNBAR — Port Melbourne coach 2000–2003
DAVID KING — Kangaroos teammate
DEAN LAIDLEY — Kangaroos coach
DENIS PAGAN — former Kangaroos coach, now coach of Carlton
DI LLOYD — Kangaroos communications manager
DR BAYUPASTI — Balinese doctor who first attended Jason
DR CON MITROPOULOS — Kangaroos club doctor
DR HEATHER CLELAND — plastic surgeon and director of the Alfred Hospital's burns ward
DREW PETRIE — Kangaroos teammate
EMMA BLOWES — nurse, Royal Darwin Hospital
FIONA MCPHAIL — volunteer nurse from New Zealand
GARY NASH — friend of Jason's close mate Peter Hughes
GEOFF WALSH — Kangaroos chief executive
GLENN ARCHER — Kangaroos teammate
GORDON MCDONALD — Kangaroos physiotherapist
GREG WAUGH — close mate
HENRIETTA LAW — senior clinician physiotherapist, Alfred Hospital
IAN MCCARTNEY — Jason's father
JAN MCCARTNEY — Jason's mother
JESS SINCLAIR — Kangaroos teammate
JOHN BLAKEY — former Kangaroos teammate, now an assistant coach at Brisbane
KAREN CAREY — sister of Jason's former Kangaroos teammate Wayne Carey
KADEK WIRANATHA — Balinese businessman

LAWRIE WOODMAN — The AFL's national coaching development manager
LEANNE WOODGATE — masseur, Carlton Football Club, younger sister of Samantha Woodgate
LEIGH BROWN — Kangaroos teammate
LEIGH COLBERT — Kangaroos teammate
LEIGH HUGHES — close mate and son of Peter Hughes
MATTHEW BURTON — Kangaroos teammate
MATTHEW FEBEY — former AFL footballer with Melbourne and twin brother of Steven Febey
MEL PACQUOLA — nurse, intensive care unit, Alfred Hospital
MICK MARTYN — Former Kangaroos teammate
MIKE SHEAHAN — chief football writer, *Herald Sun*
NERISSA — Jason's wife
PAUL CONNORS — Jason's manager
PAUL HAMILTON — Kangaroos assistant coach
PETER HUGHES — close mate
PETER KENNEDY — Flight Sergeant, Royal Australian Air Force
ROBERT SHAW — former Adelaide coach, now an assistant coach at Essendon
ROBYN WOODLEY — Corey McKernan's partner
ROGER MOORE — Kangaroos physiotherapist
SAMANTHA WOODGATE — elder sister of Leanne Woodgate
SHANNON GRANT — Kangaroos teammate
SHANNON WATT — Kangaroos teammate
SIMON CREAN — Federal Opposition Leader and No. 1 ticket-holder at the Kangaroos
STEVEN FEBEY — former AFL footballer with Melbourne
STEVEN MCCARTNEY — Jason's youngest brother, five years his junior
STUART COCHRANE — former Kangaroos teammate, now at Port Adelaide
SUE DECKERT — Jan McCartney's sister, Jason's aunt
TIM HARRINGTON — Kangaroos football manager
TIM MCGILL — Australian volunteer helper and partner of Zoey Keir
TONY 'OOGY' AUSTIN — close mate
TROY MAKEPEACE — Kangaroos teammate
WAYNE CAREY — Kangaroos dual premiership captain, now at the Adelaide Crows
ZOEY KEIR — Australian volunteer helper and partner of Tim McGill

1

To paradise

Everything was so normal. An end-of-season holiday in Bali. I'd been there every October for the previous nine years after falling in love with the place on my first footy trip with Collingwood as a 19-year-old. This time though, in October 2002, my Kangaroos teammate and close friend, Mick Martyn, would spend a week there with me. Aside from footy trips, it would be the first time that we would go away together. It could just as easily have been our last.

While Mick is one of my best mates, it didn't start out that way. I had the misfortune of playing on him in my younger days at Collingwood. I was never scared on the football ground, but I knew I would be in for a torrid time when I was opposed to Mick. He was just so strong and he had that mean head that only a mother could love. He had the image of being one of the toughest footballers in the AFL — a man you didn't want to cross.

When I joined the Kangaroos in 1998, that all changed. I discovered that, underneath the huff and puff, he's a gentle giant. He has a really sensitive side and genuinely cares about people. (Try telling that to the full-forwards that he belted and man-handled over his 16-year career!)

Our friendship initially grew out of the fact that we were the club's two key defenders — Mick was the full-back, I was the centre half-back. In footy clubs, sometimes you tend to find that your closest mates are guys that play in positions near you on the ground. We were forever talking about match-ups with opposition forwards and how we could do hatchet jobs on them. We would also pair up for some extra skills work after training on Thursday nights.

But as hard as Mick has worked at his game, he loves nothing more than socialising with his mates. We'd always gravitate towards each other at social functions and on footy trips.

MICK MARTYN (FORMER KANGAROOS TEAMMATE): Jason and I struck up a friendship pretty easily. Backmen always stick together. It's important for a footy side to have a tight-knit back six and I suppose you get so used to looking out for each other and covering each other's backs on the ground, that you naturally become mates away from footy too. I've always valued his friendship. He's a good mate and he'll do anything for you.

We knew exactly what we would be getting from one another in Bali: no fuss, no pressure, just pure relaxation. We also knew the routine leading up to a Bali trip.

Traditionally, the Kangaroos best-and-fairest count, the Syd Barker Trophy, is held on a Thursday night and we leave on our footy trip the next day for five or six days. After that, we were free to do our own thing. Some blokes go home, but most go on to other places in smaller groups. Mick and I made up our minds early that our old faithful, Bali, would provide the perfect recovery from what was certain to be another last-man-standing affair on the footy trip. After all, boys will be boys.

The two-week break was just what Mick and I needed. Our football careers were in limbo. Coach Denis Pagan had left the Kangaroos to coach Carlton after two premierships and nine finals campaigns in ten seasons. Neither Mick nor I knew exactly where we stood with the new coach, Mick's 1996 premiership teammate Dean Laidley. Dean had spoken to the players as a group on Syd Barker Trophy night, but nothing was said individually. He'd only been appointed earlier that week, just days after being involved in the AFL Grand Final as an assistant coach at my first club, Collingwood, which came within 9 points of the Brisbane Lions. Dean's appointment was all very sudden. I don't think even he knew at the time exactly what he wanted to do with the playing list.

DEAN LAIDLEY (KANGAROOS COACH): When I first got the job, Jason was away in Darwin. He rang me a couple of times because he wanted to speak to me about his footy future. I said to him, 'Enjoy your holiday, go on the footy trip and we'll have a chat when you come back.'

I was going to make changes to the playing list and he probably fell into the category of 'do I or don't I?' I hadn't decided which would be the case at that stage.

The irony was that it was probably going to be between him and Mick Martyn for one spot because I wanted to give Shannon Watt a crack at full-back. I thought, 'Jason might be able to give us a bit more up forward than Mick,' so that probably gave him a real advantage.

I wasn't in the greatest situation. I'd just come out of contract after a spasmodic season in which I only played 14 matches.

With our superstar captain, Wayne Carey, leaving the club before the start of the season, I was used as a pinch-hitter at centre half-forward. Although I was far more comfortable at centre half-back, I relished the opportunity to play in such an important position. I did reasonably well in the first half of the year — I even kicked five goals in the space of two matches — but I soon found out why it is regarded as the toughest position on the ground.

I played the first 13 games but my form deteriorated and I strained a hamstring, which sidelined me for two weeks. I probably would've been dropped anyway. Predictably, I was forced to work my way back through our then reserves side, the Murray Kangaroos, in the Victorian Football League (VFL) — the feeder competition to the AFL. While I was named an emergency for the seniors three times, it was a real battle. The Murray Kangaroos had a good side — one that played finals — but it was a classic rob-Peter-to-pay-Paul scenario. If everyone was fit, we could match it with most of the top VFL sides; but if there were three or four injuries at AFL level, we could be ordinary. We even got done by 15 or 20 goals a couple of times.

The coaching staff persisted with me at centre half-forward, with limited success. It was hard work because the ball would hardly get to me some days and, when it did, it was delivered under pressure. It was frustrating when I knew what I could do in a key role at the other end of the paddock.

Getting frustrated didn't help. One day at Coburg I lashed out and cracked my opponent, former Essendon player Matthew Banks, on the jaw as hard as I could. I don't know how I didn't break it.

At times, I was in a foul mood after training, selection nights and games. The drive home was often tense. My form was average and the team was getting thumped. My career had hit a roadblock. I thought, 'What am I doing playing in the VFL? What am I doing at centre half-forward in a side that's getting thrashed when I'm needed down back?'

It wasn't just a game any more. My livelihood was at stake. I could feel it slipping away. I would be 29 before the start of the 2003 season and I'd played at three clubs. Would a fourth club give me a chance? I doubted it.

It couldn't end like this. I had to be proactive. 'Do something about it,' I challenged myself. I did. I trained harder and continued to prepare myself in the best way I knew how. Left absolutely nothing to chance. If my career was going to end, at least I would know I'd given it my best shot.

The tables turned. I got back for a senior game in round 20. The centre half-forward experiment continued. I kicked a goal but didn't set the world on fire. Back to the reserves. Denis told me later that he thought my AFL career might have been over.

Finally, the penny dropped and I returned to my familiar role in the backline.

I played in two finals with the Murray Kangaroos before we were eliminated. A consolation was that I was one of the best on ground in both games. My passion for the game returned. I knew I could still play, but I didn't know if I would be a required player at the Kangaroos. Denis knew I still had a lot to offer. But with him going to Carlton and Dean taking over as coach, I feared this vital piece of information might have been lost. I was anxious.

It wasn't all doom and gloom though. During the 2002 season, I passed 100 games for the Kangaroos. I'd played 38 games with Collingwood between 1991 and 1994, and 37 with Adelaide between 1995 and 1997. My career tally stood at 208 games, including 27 pre-season games. Not a bad effort for an 'underachiever'.

Mick won't like me saying it but my football future appeared more promising than his. He'd been a great servant of the club since he started in the under-19s with Denis in the mid 1980s. He was a dual premiership player, a dual best-and-fairest winner, a Michael Tuck Medal winner (best on ground in the pre-season Grand Final) and in 2001 was named as a back-pocket in the Kangaroos' 'Team of the Century'. He played 19 of a possible 23 games in 2002, but the writing was on the wall for him. He had been delisted and redrafted by the club the previous year, and he had turned 34 that August.

Despite the fact that Mick and Dean shared the bond of being premiership teammates in 1996, Mick was always going to struggle to be part of the plans of a new coach keen to rebuild the side and take the club into a new era.

Understandably, neither Mick nor I wanted to talk too much about footy on our overseas holiday. We knew what would confront us when we got back. Tough decisions were going to be made. We just wanted to get away from it all and forget about it for a little while, forget the world.

My wedding was also on the horizon. December 14 had been set aside as the day I would marry my beautiful fiancée, Nerissa Vanderheyden. So a holiday would certainly recharge the batteries before Nerissa and I would make the final preparations for our wedding. (I'd already arranged the venue, the photographer and the cars.)

We decided to spend five nights of the footy trip in the jazz capital of the world, New Orleans, in the USA. I'm not sure that jazz was part of the consideration, or that any of the boys even knew the names of any jazz musicians — I certainly didn't — because they were generally into Top 40 music.

Nerissa was naturally apprehensive about us going to the US, as it was only 13 months after the September 11 terrorist attacks. I was sympathetic to her concerns; I didn't want her to worry. But I believe that if you stop doing certain things because of terrorists, they win. It's that simple. This belief was to be amplified in the coming days, and weeks, and months — perhaps for the rest of my life.

Initially, I thought the US was too far to go for only five nights. But as Mick and I discovered, four nights were more than enough. We hit the cool, all-night bars and jazz joints along the famous Bourbon Street strip. We watched the sun go down, and we often watched it come up before we got off to bed. Several big nights didn't end until midday the next day, with the boys succumbing to the lure of the nearby casino. The real killer though was the footy trip rule that everybody had to meet at 5 p.m. for 'happy hour' drinks. So you'd only have four or five hours sleep, if that, and you were straight back into it again. As they say, there is no rest for the wicked.

Mick and I went hard like the rest of the boys. Maybe we were getting too old for such childish behaviour, and we paid the price. We felt very ordinary indeed. The DTs (delirium tremens) had kicked in. We decided to take a night off — almost a cardinal sin on a footy trip. We copped some ribbing from our teammates, some of whom didn't look too flash themselves. But with a flight back to Sydney the next day, we rested our weary bodies in our hotel room. It's times like those that you wonder, 'Why do I do this to myself?' It was a form of self-abuse.

DREW PETRIE (KANGAROOS TEAMMATE): A group of us had to be at the airport to fly to Las Vegas by 7 a.m. We were still pretty drunk at the time, but Jason was downstairs making sure all the boys were in the taxi and right to get to the airport on time. As we left, I shook his hand and said, 'Thanks, Jason, I'll see you back at home.' It was a while before I saw him. I'll remember that for the rest of my life.

The plan was to spend a night in Sydney with our former teammates Corey McKernan (who has since gone to Carlton), Matthew Capuano (St Kilda at the time) and a couple of other blokes who were staying for the weekend. We would then leave the next day for Bali.

While I was in the States, Nerissa suggested that she fly to Sydney to spend the night with me, just to break up the two weeks we would be apart. It was a good idea, but it presented a dilemma — one that I would have liked to have avoided. I don't think she had a premonition that something terrible was going to happen — well, not yet anyway. I think she was just missing me. I was missing her too. It wasn't that I didn't want to see Nerissa, but Mick and I had only booked one room at the hotel, and we had arranged to catch up with Corey and Caps. I'm sure Mick's wife Leah had the same feelings. It was just a short stopover and then we were going again, so I didn't want to suddenly abandon Mick. Despite the fact that Mick is big enough and ugly enough to look after himself, I had an obligation to him. I came to regret that decision. Two lessons there: (1) don't ditch your mates, and (2) think carefully before you reject an offer of quality time with the woman you love.

Sure, I felt like a mongrel, but, at the time, I made the decision and moved on. Later, when all the dust — and debris — had settled, Nerissa and I spoke about it a couple of times. We didn't dwell on it too much. While hindsight has 20/20 vision, your first instinct is usually the correct one.

NERISSA (JASON'S WIFE): I'd been worried about them going to America only a year after the September 11 terrorist attacks. But then I thought, 'Well, they're not flying anywhere within America, which is how September 11 happened.'

It was a bit nerve-racking but Jason reassured me all the time. He'd say, 'We're going to New Orleans, not New York.'

You just had to ride with it. I certainly wasn't going to stop him from going on the football trip. I'd never say to Jason, 'No, I'm not letting you do that.' I have the belief that if you stop someone you love from doing something, it can start resentment in the relationship.

I knew that Jason and Mick were going to Bali afterwards to sit by the pool and detox from the football trip. That was fine, except for the fact that I'd really wanted to go with them. Jason had taken me there for the first time the year before and I really liked it. It was a wonderful place, just so relaxing and the people are beautiful. So, initially, I was carrying on like, 'It's not fair. I want to go too.'

I also knew they had a stopover in Sydney for a night before they went to Bali. I wanted to break up the two weeks that we were going to be apart. In one of our conversations while Jason was in the States — he rang me nearly every day — I said, 'Can I meet you in Sydney? I really want to see you before you go to Bali.'

He said, 'Well, you can, but we're going to be here just a night, and we'll be sleeping.'

I'm like, 'That doesn't matter. I can just sleep next to you,' carrying on like girls do.

He said, 'Well, it's not worth it.'

I checked the prices and it was something ridiculous like $600 for one night. I thought, 'No, that's silly,' and didn't end up going. I was disappointed. Mick's wife Leah was in the same situation. She wanted to go there but it was too expensive.

It's weird looking back because there were things that sort of make sense now. For some reason, I just had to see him.

On the morning of Friday, 11 October, we flew into Sydney with about ten of our teammates. Most of the other guys had continued on in the States. We checked in at the InterContinental Hotel. One of the first things we did was go to the hotel gym to sweat out some of the alcohol we had consumed in the previous week. It was hard work. It always is when you've let yourself go for a while. We also had a healthy breakfast and I had a haircut to revitalise myself. That afternoon, we also 'checked in' with our women. I could tell Nerissa still wished she was there with me, but she'd gotten over it.

NERISSA: Jason said, 'So, what are you doing for the weekend?'

I said, 'I'm going out with the girls.' The partners of the girls that I hang around with were all away on footy trips too. I said, 'I'm not sure whether they're going out tonight, but I know they'll go out all weekend.' After all, the boys were away. I said, 'What are you doing?' I told him to have a good time and blah, blah, blah. Despite the fact that we were apart, we were both happy and comfortable, and that's how the conversation ran. I was more relaxed about him going to Bali than being in America. I asked, 'Well, when will I hear from you again? ... OK, you call me again tomorrow.' I did end up going out with the girls that night. We all stayed at the same house.

That night we caught up with Corey, Caps and a few other blokes for dinner and some quiet drinks. We slipped away at about 1 a.m. Nothing too serious because we were flying to Bali at 10 a.m. the next morning.

COREY MCKERNAN (FORMER KANGAROOS TEAMMATE): I could see that Mick and Jase were fairly weary after the footy trip. I was joking around with them, saying, 'I'm gonna kidnap you so you miss your flight.' In hindsight, maybe I should have.

We were really looking forward to arriving in Bali. We had booked in at the Hard Rock Hotel. Mick had stayed there before and raved about it. Rock bands played there, it had a great restaurant and, like most of the hotels and resorts in Bali, it had a superb pool bar. The hotel was also well-situated — right on the beach and close to the centre of Kuta, the pulse of Bali's tourism and party district. While we planned to enjoy ourselves, 'partying' was not part of our criteria. We were still tired. Our eyes must have hung out of our heads like Slinkys (you know, those kids' toys that are stretchy springs). Anyway, our sole aim was to chill out — completely. We could lie back in the jacuzzis, get daily massages and allow ourselves to be pampered by the hotel staff. It would be a tough existence. The worst things that could happen, we thought, were Bali belly, alcohol poisoning or sunstroke.

Mick and I wouldn't be on our own either. We were to meet Peter Hughes and two of his mates who I had never met before. But if they were mates of Hughesy's, they'd have to be good blokes because he's one of the best I've known. I first met Hughesy in Bali in the late 1990s when I stayed with a few of the Kangaroos boys at the Intan Hotel. The hotel has a pool bar that is open 24 hours a day, and that was a kind of meeting place for a lot of people coming home from the Sari Club at 2 or 3 a.m. Hughesy and I really hit it off in this party environment. The thing that drew me to him, like a bee to honey, was his knockabout attitude. He can fit in anywhere, talk to anyone. I don't think I've introduced him to a person that he hasn't got along with.

He's a real knockabout bloke, so easygoing. If he was any more laid-back, he'd be asleep. When I'd check out potential dates and prices for trips to Bali, I'd ring Hughesy from Jetset Travel, when I used to work there, and ask, 'What do you reckon?'

The response would always be something like, 'Mate, whatever you reckon's a good thing. Whatever suits you. Whenever you finish the footy trip. You've got my credit card number. You book it and let me know.'

PETER HUGHES (CLOSE MATE): My first impression of Jason was that he was a wild country boy having a good time. I think that's what attracted me to him; he was different to the other blokes.

I can tell the difference between a city guy and a country guy, having coached football sides in the country years ago. I went out with a country girl for eight years.

Country boys like him behave differently. Once they've had a few drinks, they're out there on their own. They don't upset anyone but they do things off the cuff, whereas guys from the city tend to be more calculating and a bit more reserved.

I remember one time at the Intan Hotel, there was a 10-foot tall frog by the side of the pool. Water would flow out of its mouth and it had a floodlight hanging off it. At three o'clock one morning, Jason climbed on top of it with the idea of jumping off it into the pool. As he jumped, he flicked the floodlight off. Immediately, I thought, 'Oh no, he's going to electrocute himself.' He was unpredictable, but very sensible too.

I was very fortunate to meet Jase. Right from the start, I could tell he was a good-natured, kind-hearted, genuine good bloke who'd do anything for anybody and talk to anyone. He respected who you were. He treated everyone the same, regardless. He reminded me a bit of myself. I'd already met Corey, Wayne Carey, Mick and a few of the boys, and from that point on it seemed the right thing to do to stay in contact. When he went back to Melbourne, he'd ring me and I'd ring him. It was one of those instant friendships.

We'd always catch up when the Kangaroos played against the West Coast Eagles or the Fremantle Dockers in Perth, or when they came over for the Perth Cup in January. Sometimes I'd go to Melbourne, which became like a second home because I went out with a Melbourne girl for a couple of years.

I'm 15 years older than these guys, so Jason was like a younger brother for me and an older brother for my son Leigh, who wasn't too much younger than him.

Before we caught up in Bali in 2002, he had really put his life together. He was playing football and trying to plan his future. He already had good qualities and morals.

I've also got a strong friendship with Hughesy's only child, his son Leigh. They're more like mates than father and son.

LEIGH HUGHES (CLOSE MATE AND SON OF PETER HUGHES): I first met Jason after a footy match that Jason played — North Melbourne versus Hawthorn — in 1998. Dad and I flew over to see the game. Dad already knew him. We clicked from the start. Since then, as a young footballer, I've always looked up to him as my idol.

He's like a big brother to me. I look up to him so much, he's almost like family. Every time I need advice on anything, he's only too happy to give it.

It's a unique thing when you meet a bloke who lives over the other side of the country and, all of a sudden, he's there for you whenever you need him.

You can tell Jason loves my old man massively and Dad loves him like a younger brother.

I'd never had a friend with celebrity status. That took about a week to wear off because he was a mate. I've met a few AFL footballers and a lot of them are just full of themselves, but Jason's so genuine and down-to-earth. There's no boundaries there at all. If you want to talk to him, you just go up and do it.

I'm really good mates with his younger brother, Steven, too. They're a good family.

Catching up with Hughesy each year was like reuniting with a long-lost brother. And each time, it was as though no time had elapsed since our last meeting. We'd slip back into the same old groove. When you've got that, you know it's a special mateship. I was assured of a good time if Hughesy was with me. It was a bond that was to become infinitely stronger.

2

Terror strikes

The start of our holiday coincided with the end of Melbourne Football Club's end-of-season trip. Peter Vardy, a former Adelaide teammate of mine who had finished his first season with the Demons, was staying on in Bali and his girlfriend was to join him. 'Vards' and I are good mates. When he first went to Melbourne at the end of 2001, he actually bunked with me for three or four months in my townhouse in Albert Park until he found a place of his own.

Another former Crows teammate, Kane Johnson, was to be there with his girlfriend. After seven quality seasons with the Crows, Kane had publicly announced his intention to return home to play with a Melbourne club. Like Mick and me, he obviously felt that a few days of relaxation in Bali would help him relax and clear his mind before crunch time.

And then there was young Steve Armstrong, one of Vards's teammates at Melbourne, who was also staying on for a couple of days. Ironically, Steve's father Gary works for Hughesy's roofing company in Perth. Small world.

While it's great to be aware of friends in the same neck of the woods, you could just as easily go there on your own. When you go to Bali at the same time every year, as I had done for nine years, you're bound to bump into some familiar faces.

The beauty of your first night out in Bali is reacquainting yourself with people that you've met there for years. It's weird because even though they might have lived near me at different times in Adelaide or Melbourne, the only place I caught up with them was in Bali. I've also run into friends over there by complete chance. But considering so many Aussies go to Bali, it's not that freaky.

I had really been looking forward to the Bali trip for a number of months but, for some reason, when we landed in Denpasar, that excitement disappeared. I didn't feel as hyped up as I had on previous trips. I was as flat as a tack. I wished we had touched-down in Melbourne instead. That way, Nerissa would have been there to take me home and I could get some sanity back into my life again. But, alas, I was 4300 kilometres away.

I reflect on it now and wonder, 'Did I know something? Was it a sign? Was my subconscious trying to tell me something?' But, unfortunately for the believers out there, the answer to each of these questions is no.

I think my indifference was simply a result of being exhausted after a week of hard drinking on the footy trip. But, in the end, I thought, 'Well, we planned this a long time ago, we have to just go and do it. We can't pull out now. We'll get there and it'll be good, because it always is.'

I started doubting this when Mick and I couldn't find our luggage. When you'd rather be somewhere else, the last thing you want is to be worrying about such things. It was just another headache to add to a week of hangovers. At least if you lose your gear in Bali you can buy some cheap stuff to get you by. That's assuming you haven't lost your wallet as well.

With a combination of relief and embarrassment, we realised that we hadn't tagged our bags properly. The last two bags that had been doing the circuit for the previous half-hour were, in fact, ours. It wasn't the greatest start to the trip, but we were sure it would be the last hiccup. What could go wrong in peaceful Bali? In hindsight, perhaps the bag saga was another tell-tale sign that our holiday was jinxed.

We caught a taxi to the Hard Rock Hotel. It was about 3 p.m. Hughesy was already there. He'd flown in from Perth earlier in the day. So, after checking in and dropping our bags in our room, we went down to the pool bar to meet him. In that watery heaven, we also caught up with Steve Armstrong and Vards. We chatted, had a splash and downed a few Bintang beers over a couple of hours. If there are many better luxuries in life, I haven't experienced them.

Two of Hughesy's mates were scheduled to arrive in Denpasar, so he went to the airport to meet them. Mick and I told Stevie and Vards that we'd probably see them later on at the Sari Club and headed upstairs. We showered and lay down on our beds, relaxed and refreshed. I rang Nerissa to let her know we had arrived and all was well. Mick rang Leah and expressed similar sentiments. Little did we know that the next time we spoke to our partners all would not be well. Very far from it in fact.

It wasn't until about 10 p.m. that we went into Kuta to the Macaroni Club, a restaurant and cocktail bar, where we had arranged to have dinner with Hughesy and his two mates. When we got there, Hughesy had only one of his mates with him, Gary Nash.

The story of what happened to Hughesy's other mate is remarkable in itself. The bloke was expected to fly into Bali from Perth on his own. When the plane landed, the bloke was a no-show. Hughesy and Nashy were concerned. What had happened? They hadn't heard from him — no phone call, no message, nothing.

Hughesy knew his mate would have a good excuse. Maybe he had an emergency or a death in the family. Maybe he was crook. Hughesy made a phone call from the airport to discover the answer. As it turned out, his mate had never flown overseas before. He took his seat on the plane — so far, so good — and, as the rest of the passengers were boarding, the poor bloke had a panic attack and freaked out. He got off the plane and didn't go. While we joked about it at the time, that decision may well have saved his life.

PETER HUGHES: He had a fear of flying and decided that the plane was too small and that it wasn't going to get him over water to Bali. He just said no, he wasn't going. While we were in comas, he had this guilt for a couple of weeks. He had to carry that for a while until we actually sat down and talked about it.

He suffered. He just felt that maybe if he was there he could've made a difference. Maybe we wouldn't have gone out. It was all these little decisions that became so important. When the bomb went off, he might've helped us or vice versa. We might've been in the Sari and we might've all been killed. Sometimes it only takes one person to change something.

But it saved his life and we're all glad for that.

I must admit though, when we were at the Macaroni Club we gave it to him big-time. Jase and Mick hadn't met him before, so it was basically, 'What's wrong with the bloke?'

I think we all felt for him too, even though the other boys didn't know him. It's a good-luck story really when someone makes a decision like that. It's like someone missing a plane and it crashes. If he had turned up, I'm sure he would've died.

When we got to the Macaroni Club, Hughesy and Nashy were finishing their meals. Mick and I had a feed and the four of us had a few drinks. We were just starting to liven up a little. I had shaken my lethargy.

MICK MARTYN: We'd had four or five beers and were taking it nice and easy. We were sharing a few laughs. It was all pretty casual, hanging it on each other as blokes do. It was shaping up as a pretty good night.

We left the Macaroni Club just before 11 p.m. It's on the same side of Legian Road as our traditional haunt, the Sari Club. I thought it was too early to go to the Sari Club because the atmosphere there is usually at its peak around midnight, and I wanted to get a few more drinks into me before we entered that crowded environment. I also didn't want to be at one place all night. Besides, we generally went somewhere else first anyway.

Almost by habit, I started crossing the road to Paddy's Bar. Mick and Hughesy said, 'What are you doing?'

'Going across here,' I replied, pointing to Paddy's Bar.

'Oh yeah, all right,' they nodded and followed.

Although we hadn't been there for a year, we sauntered into Paddy's Bar as though it was our local pub. And just like our local, we were bound to see some familiar faces.

Paddy's was a modern, double-storey building. It was in complete contrast to the Sari Club, which was like a big hut made of straw and sticks. On the ground floor of Paddy's, there was a long, oval bar, another bar along one side and the DJ's booth and dance floor at the far end. You could go upstairs where there was a bigger dance floor with bars on either side.

It was an Irish-themed bar, but unlike the Irish pubs back home, where bands play traditional Irish songs like 'Whiskey in the Jar', Paddy's pounded out pop and dance music. We didn't care what music they played, or if they played any at all. We were just happy to be in each other's company again, catching up on the developments in our respective lives and looking forward to a week together.

As a rule, there aren't many dance moves between Mick, Hughesy, Nashy and me anyway, so to avoid embarrassing ourselves, we were strategically positioned at the end of the bar. We rested our drinks on a skinny table and stood talking, laughing, joking. Typical blokey stuff.

When we arrived, I wasn't sure how many people were upstairs but there weren't many downstairs. The place gradually filled.

I started on my first Balinese cocktail, the ominously named 'Arak Attack'. It's my favourite among the local 'jungle juices' and consists of Arak, a white spirit, mixed with a few others and your choice of lemon or orange juice, and honey, presented to you in a cocktail shaker.

I'd only had a few sips when Leanne and Samantha Woodgate and their girlfriend Rachael rocked up. Mick and I knew Leanne well. She was a masseur at Carlton Football Club and, along with a few of our teammates, we had also seen her as a private masseur to aid our recovery between games and training sessions. Masseurs are like doctors and hairdressers — when you find a good one like Leanne, it's a good idea to stick with them.

I had seen Leanne a couple of weeks before, so I knew that she and her sister Samantha were planning to go to Bali. They'd arrived about a week before we got there. I was surprised to see Rachael, though, because in my last conversation with Leanne, she'd said that Rachael had told her she wasn't going. But in the end she'd got her act together at the last minute. They are all good-natured and easy to talk to — no airs or graces — and it was good to catch up with them. As it turned out, the reunion wasn't to be long enough for any of us.

LEANNE WOODGATE (MASSEUR, CARLTON FOOTBALL CLUB, YOUNGER SISTER OF SAMANTHA WOODGATE): We were doing what we normally did — first go to Paddy's for a while and then go to the Sari. We didn't know Jason and Mick would be there — we just turned up and they were there …

I walked away from the end of the table and spoke to Leanne briefly. We were slightly under the staircase, only about three metres away from where Mick, Hughesy and Nashy were talking to Samantha and Rachael.

NERISSA: We were in the middle of a big girls' weekend. There were 12 of us. We'd been out on the Friday night and stayed together, then we all went out Saturday night. We kept drinking the whole time.

We got back to Corey (McKernan) and Robyn's place. Robyn and two other friends, Ally and Cee, and I sat up talking. It was about 3 a.m. and I started carrying on like a pork chop, saying things like, 'You've heard from Jason, haven't you, Robyn?'

She said, 'No.'

But I kept going, 'You have. Something's happened. He's done something, hasn't he?'

She was adamant. 'No.'

I said, 'Well, something's not right,' and started crying. I said to Ally and Cee, 'How come you're just sitting there? You know something, don't you?'

It was really bizarre because I was paranoid about something and it was making me really upset. But I didn't know what it was. I had a bad feeling and I related it to Jason.

The worst thing you think can happen to your relationship is betrayal. That's the only thing I could think of. I said to Robyn, 'Maybe he's been unfaithful.'

Robyn said, 'Don't be silly, Nerissa. Just go to bed. You need to get some sleep. You haven't slept all weekend. Sleep it off and Jason will ring you later. You'll be fine.'

I said, 'No, I'm not going to sleep. I'm sitting here.'

They were having something to eat, so I sat with them. A bit later, I said, 'Girls, I'm sorry. I don't know what I'm crapping on about. But something just doesn't feel right.'

ROBYN WOODLEY (COREY MCKERNAN'S PARTNER): All of a sudden, Nerissa just clicked. It was really bizarre. It would've been about the same time that the bombs went off in Bali. Looking back on it now, it was freaky. I don't know if it was coincidence or what.

She said, 'Something's wrong.'

We said, 'What?'

She said, 'You girls know something. Something's going on with Jason.'

We said, 'What are you talking about?'

Nerissa said, 'I just think you guys know something. What is it?'

We said, 'No, Nerissa, we're not hiding anything,' because Jason couldn't love her any more than he did already. We said, 'Where have you got this from?'

She started crying and getting really emotional. We tried to calm her down.

I initially put it down to Nerissa having pre-wedding jitters because everything had happened so quickly in their relationship and it had really been a whirlwind romance. I remember Nerissa saying to us a few times that night, 'You girls think I'm doing the right thing, don't you?'

We said, 'Of course, you guys are a great couple and you'll be perfect together.'

Because none of us had had any sleep and we'd all been drinking, it wasn't like it couldn't all be explained away.

There was a group of guys behind us, right near the dance floor. They were obviously on some sort of group trip or fancy dress night. They all wore floral shirts and carried ironing boards so they could pretend they were surfing. While the rest of us were still settling in, these guys were having a wow of a time. It's refreshing to see carefree people like them. Nothing matters. It was as much for the entertainment of others as for self-amusement. Show-offs? Maybe. Love life? Certainly. I cast a curious eye over these shenanigans and imagined Mick as one of them. That was probably the funniest part of the whole thing.

I swapped positions with Mick so that he could talk to Leanne, and I joined the others. I turned to Rachael and said, 'What are you doing here? I didn't think you were coming?'

I mightn't have even spat that out — they'd only been there a few minutes — when our conversation was abruptly cut short by an almighty explosion.

It was an ear-bursting, almost sonic boom. It reminded me of New Year's Eve fireworks over Albert Park Lake, except it was right in our faces. It was as though dynamite had gone off in my ears. It was deafening. People heard the bang from miles away. It actually registered 0.2 on the Richter scale. That's some bang.

There was a flash of orange flame, which fizzed and sizzled. My natural reflex was to turn my back on it to shield my face. But that didn't stop me from being hit, and hit hard. Harder than I'd ever been hit on the football field. I crashed to the deck with a thud. But I took the same attitude as I would in a game of football; Dad taught me from a young age, 'No matter how hard you get hit, son, just get straight back up again.' It took a bit of strength — perhaps more mental than physical — but I stumbled to my feet.

I tried to open my eyes, but my eyelids were stuck shut, like they'd been nailed down. The flash of light had blinded me.

'I'm blind!' my brain screamed.

In the madness of the moment, my mind raced. Even now, it's hard to imagine the mind-space that I had entered.

'What am I going to do? I'm never going to see again!'

I was petrified. I tried and tried to force my eyes to open. Thankfully they did. My temporary blindness lasted all of about three seconds. In reality, that's gone in a snap of your fingers, but it seemed like a mini-eternity.

I couldn't have opened my eyes to a worse sight. I had entered a living nightmare.

There was silence. It was scary and foreboding. The world had become a black hole.

Everything was in slow motion. But my mind sprinted in many different directions at the same time.

I had been hit with such force that I thought, 'I've been shot. Nah, it must have been fireworks gone wrong.' That made sense because I'd seen fireworks in Bali before. I thought, 'Maybe those hoons with the surfboards had accidentally set one off. Or it might have been a gas explosion.'

It had to be some kind of accident.

MICK MARTYN: I thought someone had hit me with a petrol bomb or a flare. There was a lot of electricity buzzing around, as well as flames. The blast hit us full-on. It went off right near us, about 7 to 10 metres away.

It was dark, apart from a few spot-fires. I could see where the entrance was.

There are a lot of grey areas — I didn't know if I was momentarily knocked out or if I lost any seconds.

I crawled a bit and then got up. I had feeling in all of my limbs, so that was the main thing. If you couldn't move, even if someone had pulled you out, or you lost an arm or a leg, which a lot of people had, there was a good chance you would have died.

Whatever had happened, it had caused enormous damage. For the first time in my life, survival — in its most basic form — became my number one priority.

I saw Leanne standing near me. She was stunned and in a state of shock.

LEANNE WOODGATE: I remember catching on fire and picking myself up off the ground. I looked at Mick and said, 'What the hell's going on?'

People's jaws had dropped in disbelief, as if to say, 'What the hell happened?' But there wasn't any time to waste analysing it. We had to get out of there. Be quick or be dead. Self-preservation was the key.

Until that point, I wasn't aware that I'd been burnt or injured in any way. But as I looked over my left shoulder, I could see flames roaring up my neck. My hair was on fire too.

Instinctively, I ripped my T-shirt off over my head in a flash. That extinguished the fire on my hair and neck. Thank goodness for that. Strangely, I couldn't feel any pain, although it makes me cringe even now at the thought that flame of any sort had been in contact with my neck and hair.

I still didn't feel hurt in any way, so I naturally figured that I must have been OK.

MICK MARTYN: Although we'd all been within about a 2-metre radius of each other, we lost contact in the rubble and darkness. But I heard Jason calling out a few things like, 'I can't see — I'm blind,' 'I'm on fire.'

Suddenly, everything went dark. Pitch black. People screamed — some shrill, some guttural like their voices were breaking. Smoke quickly engulfed the place. I grabbed whoever was next to me. (Even then, mateship was a priority — probably more so than ever before.) I felt an arm. I knew it wasn't Mick because it wasn't hairy enough. It was a woman — Samantha. I can't even remember if she was standing up or lying down. In any case, she was severely burnt. I grabbed her by the hand because it was so dark that you couldn't see anything and I wouldn't lose her if I had hold of her. We had to get out of there, get to the street.

The small bar that we'd been leaning on only moments earlier had disappeared. I did a double take. I thought, 'Hang on, that's not there any more; what's happened to it?' The bar had obviously been blown to pieces.

I can't remember saying anything — it wouldn't have mattered anyway because neither of us could hear anything.

I took five or six steps in the direction of the front door — or at least where I knew the front door had been — and fell over again, knocking Samantha to the ground in the process. I thought, 'Bloody clumsy bugger.'

I later found out that I had been knocked off my feet by the force of a car-bomb that had exploded out the front of the Sari Club. Although the blast took place across the road and a little further down, it was so big that it had shaken everything in the vicinity. Like an earthquake tremor.

SAMANTHA WOODGATE (ELDER SISTER OF LEANNE WOODGATE): I don't remember which direction I was thrown in the first blast because it was too dark in there. I picked myself up off the floor and started heading toward the exit. I stumbled a bit and somebody grabbed my arm. It was Jason. We'd staggered into each other, tried to hold each other up and we knew we had to get out to safety as quickly as we could.

I didn't hear the second bomb because my ears were still ringing from the first explosion. I found out later that, along with most other survivors of the blasts, I had perforated eardrums.

In some ways, it was like the opening scenes of *Saving Private Ryan*, where Tom Hanks's character has lost his hearing and it's just pandemonium and carnage all around him. It was also like being under water and trying to hear people talking above me.

Because of the darkness and the smoke, I couldn't see the carnage — the bodies, the rubble — that I now know must have surrounded me and been under my feet. I couldn't see anything. There was also a constant, dull ringing in my ears.

MICK MARTYN: It was like an old war movie in slow motion. I'd read about World War I and II but this was a real-life experience of what might have happened in the wars. You can understand how soldiers still have mental problems 20 or 30 years after the event. It's just so graphic. I didn't know if I was dead or alive. When I saw things around me, like bodies lying on the ground, I was thinking, 'Are they really there or not?' But I knew they were.

Everything was a blur. Perhaps that explains a significant gap in my memory. I cannot, for the life of me, remember what happened between the time Samantha and I picked ourselves up off the ground after the second blast, to when we were in the street. It's a gap of 15 to 20 metres — less than that in seconds — which I can't account for.

The next thing I knew, we were out the front. Smoke everywhere, and so strong in the air. No matter how hard you tried, you couldn't help but inhale it — and cough uncontrollably.

SAMANTHA WOODGATE: When we walked out, that's where I found Leanne, and Mick walked out with Rachael. Jason was a bit singed, a bit black. None of us knew the degree of any of our injuries. We were all deaf.

We got separated, we lost Jason, and we went back to our hotel.

I was about 25 per cent burnt, mainly to my upper body, my right arm, shrapnel wounds and holes in my legs. A lot of superficial wounds from head to toe. I was quite lucky.

I looked at my arms. They were black, like they were covered in soot. But I didn't look too closely at my body because of the commotion around me. There were other people to worry about. As I looked at what remained of Paddy's Bar I thought, 'Where are my friends? Please don't tell me they're underneath all that.' Even though people were all around, I felt so lonely, so isolated.

LEANNE WOODGATE: When I got out the front, I stood there, not knowing what had just happened. I turned around, did a few circles, and luckily I saw Sam and Jason coming out, and then Mick and Rachael.

Everyone looked as though they had been singed. They had soot on their faces and they were bleeding a bit. Jason had some blood on his face but I never thought he would have been as burnt as he was.

About 15 per cent of my body had burns, mainly my upper body, and I had holes in the soles of my feet and my thumb. But I couldn't feel anything. It was just shock kicking in. My thumb was hurting, but that was because I was worried about my hands because I'm a masseur.

Thankfully, only about a minute later — another mini-eternity — a familiar, hulking figure emerged from the smoke and made its way towards me, like a gorilla out of the mist. It was Mick. Phew! He might not be the most glamorous looking man in the world — even Mick would admit that — but even if it had been Nerissa, I couldn't have been happier.

It was a huge relief to see him. We didn't hug or shake hands like we might have because we were burnt and sore.

Mick had helped Rachael to get out of the bar. She was pretty badly hurt as well. I didn't see the girls but Mick assured me that they had gone back to where they were staying at the Bounty Hotel, which was about 500 metres up Poppies Lane, almost directly opposite Paddy's Bar.

MICK MARTYN: Jase was standing by himself, stunned and shocked. He held his hands out because they were burnt. He was able to stand and walk and talk, so I thought, 'He mustn't be too bad.' As I've learnt since, it's the day or two after you get burnt, when your body swells and bloats, that you feel the effects.

I could hardly hear anything. I couldn't understand what Jase was saying, even though he was shouting at the top of his lungs. I had to try and lip-read.

It was pretty clear that Jason was in worse condition than I was. He started saying things like, 'Help me, save me,' 'I'm gonna die,' and 'Tell Nerissa I love her.' That's when I knew that he wasn't in the best shape. He was walking and talking, so he wasn't dead. If he had been lying on the ground and not moving, it would have been a different scenario. But I did realise he needed medical attention. I know now that he could have died.

I just kept saying to him, 'You'll be right, mate.'

We didn't know if acid or chemicals had been involved, either. With Jason's skin peeling away from his hands, we didn't know if something was eating into his flesh. I thought, 'Bloody hell, we could be maimed here.'

And there was this really foul smell. I'll never forget it. It was all over us. Burning flesh.

3

Good decision

Mick and I were so naive when it came to our injuries, particularly mine. We tried to talk to each other, but neither of us could hear very well. I became self-conscious. I started yelling, 'How do I look? How do I look?'

Things like that don't normally concern me, but I was, after all, due to get married in two months.

Mick looked me up and down and, in his typical stammering and mumbling manner, quickly summed up: 'There's a bit of blood, but you don't look too bad. You're covered in char.'

I returned the favour by giving him a quick once-over. 'You're not too bad,' I assured Mick, 'but then you're not that good at the best of times.'

It's terrible, I know, but I had to chuckle. Picture this: Mick had a couple of minor cuts dripping off his bald head and he had been wearing a button-up shirt, the buttons of which had blown off, revealing his hairy chest — his 'love rug' — with one side singed and the other side untouched.

I find it amazing that, despite the chaos, we were still able to find humour in our predicament. Admittedly, we didn't realise the seriousness of my injuries, but looking at the positive side of things is a very Australian trait. You either had to laugh or cry, and I'm glad we laughed because it was a welcome distraction in the circumstances. Besides, there would be plenty of time for crying later on.

The ribbing between us had started when we were getting ready to go out that night. I was wearing a pair of grey Oakley sandals and Mick was wearing a pair the same, except in a not-so-cool red — as far as I'm concerned, that colour should be confined to footballs and fast cars. They didn't look the part at all. So Mick changed into a pair of runners. I asked, 'Are you gonna wear runners?'

He said, 'Yeah. I'll look like a goose if I wear red thongs with bone cargo pants.'

I giggled, amused that Mick had finally conceded that buying red sandals had been a bad move. He was clearly worried about being caught by the fashion police.

MICK MARTYN: What we wore that night was crucial. Normally you'd go out wearing shorts, a T-shirt and thongs. This particular night I wore cargo pants and a collared shirt, which were thicker and less flammable. I'd never really worn runners when we'd been out because they're really hot on your feet and can be uncomfortable. With the runners on, I didn't think I scrubbed up too bad. Luckily, Jason changed his mind too and put his runners on.

I'm glad we took Mick's suggestion on board. If we'd worn sandals or thongs instead of runners, we would have done untold damage to our feet, as we had to walk through glass, iron and hot rubble — none of which we could see. Our feet would have been mincemeat.

But even if that had happened and I couldn't walk again, at least I had my life.

At that point, all I could think was, 'Where are Hughesy and Nashy?' They're blokes who would gladly choose life in a wheelchair over death. They love life. But the more I thought about what had just happened the more I worried for their well-being. Were they alive? Were they dead? Were they somewhere in between life and death, trapped underneath the wreckage? Did they need help?

Smoke billowed out of Paddy's. There was no way anyone could go back in there. It was far too dangerous. You'd probably collapse from smoke inhalation. My prediction about the fate of Hughesy and Nashy grew darker by the minute.

PETER HUGHES: I was at the bar when the bomb went off and I actually saw the bomber. He was sort of standing there, with his backpack on the ground. It seemed a bit unusual, but nothing too out of the ordinary. I turned around to give the boys their drinks. Jason was on the jungle juice, which comes in big bottles with a straw hanging out of them. He used to throw the straw away and drink it straight from the neck. Mick wanted a Canadian Club, a whisky that Mick called 'CC'. I kept saying to Mick, 'CC? What? A bourbon and coke?'

He goes, 'CC.'

I'm going, 'What's a bloody CC?' I remember that as clear as day.

Nashy wanted a Bintang, so I ordered two, one for him and one for me. I didn't know Leanne and Samantha, so I didn't buy them a drink.

When I came back to get my beer, the bomber actually walked away to my left. The bomb went off as I reached for my beer. I didn't even get a sip out of it.

I also remember the song that was playing at the time. It was Eminem's 'Slim Shady'.

Ironically — prophetically — Eminem calls for everyone's attention and announces that there's going to be a problem.

PETER HUGHES: It was nine months until I heard that song again. I heard it twice in one day. I walked into a pub and someone was singing it karaoke. I had been trying to remember what song was playing in Paddy's Bar but I hadn't been able to. As soon as I heard it, it scared the hell out of me. I thought, 'That's that bloody song.' It actually took me back to the moment the bomb went off.

The blast lifted me diagonally. I was aware of what was happening the whole time; I wasn't knocked out. A young lady landed in my arms. I wasn't in a panic. I'm in the building trade and through my experience, I thought a gas bottle had exploded. I knew we had to get out fairly quickly.

My first thoughts turned to my son, Leigh. My second thought was, 'Where's Jason and Mick? Where's everyone gone?' I couldn't see anyone. I just sort of felt, 'Well, we've got a problem here.'

When I walked the young lady to the front, the car bomb went off. That was within 30 or 40 seconds. I got blown straight back into Paddy's Bar, about 5 or 6 metres, to where I'd walked from. So it began all over again.

I started to become concerned about where Jason and Mick had gone and why they'd left me. I kept saying to everyone I ran into, 'We need to find Jason and Mick.'

They couldn't find them, so I was left in the dark thinking that no news was good news.

I helped a couple of girls after that and hung around just to see what the hell was going on, and to try and help out because I didn't know I was hurt.

While I was alive and breathing, I was OK. There were just too many tragic sights. I saw people dying around me.

GARY NASH (FRIEND OF JASON'S CLOSE MATE PETER HUGHES): When the bomb went off, I saw a huge wave of heat coming. I knew it was a bomb. I knew it was more than just a gas cylinder. You could see the shimmer of the heat, and the glint of the shrapnel coming out of it.

A woman came flying across the floor and hit me with her back to my front and knocked me over ... After I'd regained consciousness, she was still lying on top of me.

My ears were ringing — they still are — and my ankle was giving me a bit of grief. Only a year before, I'd had a hip-replacement operation. I thought, 'If my hip has gone, I'm going to have to crawl out of here, and there's no way I'm going to be able to crawl out of here. I'm going to die here.' The flames were getting bigger and bigger and the heat was getting worse.

I said to this lady, 'Love, you've got to get off; I've got to get out.' I said that to her twice, but got no response, so I made my way out from underneath her and got up. In the glimmer of the light, I could see that she was shredded, unrecognisable. There was no chance that she was alive. I was pretty upset when I saw that.

I stood up and took a couple of steps — my hip was all right. I looked around and could see a small opening, which I believed was a door, at the back of the club. I made my way towards it, surrounded by other people who were screaming and on fire. We were stepping over dead people on the floor. I tripped over a couple of times and managed to get myself out.

I looked around at the carnage and the mayhem — people running everywhere and screaming, people on fire — and I said to myself, 'Jeez, I've survived this.'

I sat on a little brick wall to the left of what had been the front of Paddy's Bar. I took stock of myself and looked down at my arms and legs and knew I was in a pretty bad way because all the skin was just hanging off. I thought, 'I'm not as good as I thought I was.'

At that stage, I didn't know that I had a 14-inch (35-centimetre) gash across my stomach — right across, below the navel to the right-hand side. I thought something must have fallen on my ankle, but I didn't know that shrapnel had hit it and ripped a great hunk out of it.

I hobbled over to where we'd had dinner at the Macaroni Club because there were a couple of chairs out the front. I sat myself down and took a few deep breaths. Once again, I took in what was happening around me: people on fire, people trying to put it out with bottles of water.

A guy ran past carrying one of his arms. I yelled at him to stop because you could see the blood just spurting out, but he just kept running. It was the shock and adrenaline keeping him going. He would've got probably 20 or 30 metres up the road — who knows? — and he would have just fallen over. That would have been the finish of him.

The fire started to spread up the street. A couple of young Aussie guys came along and said, 'Look mate, we've got to move you from here because this fire's coming up pretty fast.'

They wrapped a couple of towels around the front and back of the chair and carried me up the road and put me on the back of a ute. Lying beside me was a young bloke who was in a very bad way. Across the front was a young girl, and I was sitting up beside them.

It was a very slow journey — the streets were blocked. I was talking to the young bloke next to me, trying to keep him going. About five or ten minutes from the hospital, he gave one last, big gasp of air and then he died …

I'm a former Navy man and was on the HMAS *Melbourne* when it collided with the HMAS *Voyager* in 1964 and lost eighty-odd guys. That was a pretty traumatic experience. During my time, I was also a volunteer ambulance driver, so I'd seen a fair bit of carnage. But no matter how much you've seen before, you never become immune to it.

There was so much smoke outside that I didn't know about the blast at the Sari Club. If I had turned my head 5 or 10 degrees to the right, I would have seen cars on fire and people running, screaming, charred and bleeding. And who knows what else. But to this day, I'm thankful that I didn't see it — thankful that an invisible hand guided my face away from that horror. It certainly saved me a lot of psychological scarring.

I saw injured people, but I didn't see any dead bodies. Survivors and passers-by endured far more gruesome sights and, understandably, many struggled to come to terms with what they saw. Unfortunately, many are still haunted by those visions.

I didn't know it at the time, but Melbourne footy boys Steve Armstrong, David Robbins, Steven Febey and his best mate Mark Andrews had been standing between Paddy's Bar and the Sari Club and were blown across the street and separated.

STEVEN FEBEY (FORMER AFL FOOTBALLER WITH MELBOURNE): I knew very quickly that something terrible had happened. The first person I saw was a gentleman lying on the road. He put his hand up to me and said, 'Can you help me?'

I looked at his face. He had fear in his eyes. Then I looked down and saw that both of his legs had been completely blown off. He was lying pretty close to where I was. I didn't say it but I thought, 'I can't help you.' I couldn't physically help him; there was nothing I could do for him. Fortunately, a lady beside me covered his legs with a T-shirt and comforted him.

My main focus was then to move on, help people if I could, and find my mates. I helped a couple of people out of the Sari Club.

I saw a big bloke with his leg hanging off. His ankle was just hanging there. I thought it was (Geelong star) Steven King because we'd had a drink with him the night before. I sat him down and thought, 'He won't be able to play footy.'

I kept looking through the rubble and lifting corrugated iron, trying to find my three mates. I'd never seen a dead body before, but now I saw numerous dead bodies, limbs and parts of bodies.

When the fire took hold, I could hear people screaming from inside the Sari Club. I could hear and almost see people trying to get out but you couldn't go in and help because it was just so hot. You couldn't even move a centimetre forward.

Your senses were being bombarded with stuff that you would only ever see, dare I say it, at war. The horrible sights, the terrible screams, the heat, and the distinctive smell of burning flesh. I'd never smelt it before, and I never want to smell it again. It was such a vulgar, vulgar smell.

Those things still appear in my dreams and in my quieter moments.

As footballers, we'd seen some terrible injuries on the field — concussions, split heads, broken limbs, sickening knee injuries — but nothing prepared us for what we confronted in Bali.

People screamed — in agony, in fear. Men sounded like young boys; women sounded like young girls. Sheer hysteria. The kind of scenario that has always been so far removed from Australia, and Australians — or even Bali.

People had ash and dirt all over them, blood on their faces and clothes. I didn't see anyone missing limbs. Thank Christ for that.

Unfortunately, Mick and Hughesy weren't spared some gut-churning sights.

MICK MARTYN: You couldn't go back in to Paddy's and help anyone; you couldn't get near the Sari Club either because it was just a ball of fire. The whole place was burning. Cars were on fire, people lying and slumped over on the ground, obviously hurt, some with missing body parts. It sort of registered in your mind but you really couldn't help them. Some were dead anyway, so they were beyond help.

It was like it had been hit by a bomb that had been dropped out of the sky. For all we knew, there could have been more explosions.

I looked around and saw all that, but Jason was in shock; he didn't know what to do. He's one of my best mates, so I focused on helping him in any way I could. The first thing we had to do was get the hell out of there.

PETER HUGHES: People were basically dismembered — no legs, arms, a lot of skin hanging off, a lot of blood. There were people with no clothes on because they had been blown off in the blast; people had burnt hair and cuts all over their faces.

Strange as it sounds, it all seemed quite normal to me because I was looking at myself thinking, 'Well, I'm not too different.' But I did have my limbs.

It was as real as you get. We knew that we were in a bit of trouble and the worst place to be was where we were.

We were all hanging on. It was very graphic, very traumatic. But we really had to fend for ourselves because there wasn't anyone else there to help us. We were lucky to be alive.

We were lucky we were in the first explosion and got outside reasonably quickly. Others must have been stuck inside. I hoped — prayed — that Hughesy and Nashy had already made their way out and got to safety.

Although Mick's hearing was gone, he knew he had only minor burns and that everything was intact. He kept his composure when a lot of people would have panicked or completely flipped out.

In his wisdom, Mick, the master of understatement, shouted to me, 'We don't know what's happened. There could be more trouble. We've got to get out of here. Back to the Hard Rock. The doctor there speaks English.'

I thought, 'Well, that's a start. At least he'll be able to understand what the hell we're saying.'

MICK MARTYN: I'd been to the Hard Rock Hotel before and received medical treatment there. I knew they had a good doctor. A couple of years before that, I had split my eye when I bumped into a wall and they gave me a couple of stitches and everything was fine. In all the confusion, that seemed like the best place to go. But we had to get a lift there, either on a motorbike, or 'mo-ped' as they call them, or in a mini-van. That was going to be the tough part.

We ran — OK, it was more like a shuffle; certainly not at pre-season time-trial speed — up the middle of the road, with Mick leading the way. As I set off, I felt a sharp pain in my left calf. I thought I'd strained it, which made sense because we'd played our last game of footy a few weeks before and hadn't exercised much since. I'd done a calf before so I knew how it felt.

Little did I know that during the blast I'd been hit with shrapnel in the lower left leg. (At least it wasn't my natural kicking leg!) It had blown a hole the size of a golf ball in my calf muscle. I didn't even look at it because I was satisfied with my initial self-diagnosis. There wasn't much good looking at it anyway, because a calf strain is an internal injury. It was best that I didn't look because it might have slowed our progress even more and caused me to panic. It's like the old saying, 'What you don't know won't hurt you.' I struggled to run, and started dragging my leg. There was blood in that general area but I didn't think it was related. It was like I had been shot in the calf and someone was aggravating it further by stabbing the wound with every step I took.

Mick was about 5 or 10 metres in front of me and saw that I was doing it tough, so he encouraged me along — 'Keep going, mate; keep pushing' — and tried to clear the way for me. It was one of the few times that Mick has ever outrun me — usually I was the one clearing a path for him to charge through centre half-back.

Mick screamed at a group of locals to give us a lift back to the Hard Rock, but they didn't want to know us. They said, 'No,' shook their heads and gestured with their hands for us to go away. There was no way they were going to have two strapping 190-centimetre foreigners, with burns, blood all over them and ripped clothes, no matter how badly injured they were, clinging to them on the back of their bikes for a 2-kilometre journey. As far as they were concerned, we were mobile — at least Mick was — so we were OK. They weren't injured themselves, but they were definitely in shock. While we were frustrated with their attitude at the time, I can understand why they reacted like that. They were scared. It was a hostile situation. Like a war zone.

Mick, as loyal to his mates and big-hearted as ever, hailed a passing Balinese motorcyclist. He slung the rider about 50,000 rupiah (about $A9) and shouted to me, 'Get on the bike and get back to the hotel. I'll meet you there.'

I looked at my hands and was distraught to see the skin melting away from the bones on my fingers. It was like hot wax dripping from a candle.

As I got on the back of the motorbike, all I could think about was my wedding two months away — the biggest day of my life. I pleaded with Mick, 'Mate, I love this place, but don't let me die over here. Just get me home. Get me out of here.'

Mick nodded and repeated that he'd see me back at the Hard Rock. By the intense, almost pained expression on Mick's face, I could tell he had begun to understand the seriousness of the situation, and the need for me to get medical attention.

People marvel at the fact that I had burns to 50 per cent of my body, my leg had a hole in it and skin was melting off my fingers, yet I was still able to get on the back of a motorbike and weave through heavy traffic. A ride like that can be uncomfortable at the best of times.

People have asked me since, 'I burnt my finger on a stove once and it hurt so much. How did you handle the pain?'

The truth is I was in excruciating pain for some time, and I thought I might have been a goner. It was a level of pain that I'd never experienced before. I can't even equate it to a footy injury because I was relatively injury-free throughout my career. I'd had minor injuries like hamstrings, calf strains and a bout of osteitis pubis, but I hadn't had an operation in 12 years of AFL football. It was more luck than anything, but few players could boast the same thing. The only time I'd gone under the surgeon's knife was when I had my appendix removed when I was in primary school. The only other thing I had as a kid was German measles.

Gradually and, in hindsight ominously, the pain disappeared. I didn't know it at the time, but I was so badly burnt that I'd gone through the pain barrier. I'd gone to the next stage — shock. The human body is an amazing thing. It didn't take long before my body went into pain shutdown mode.

I was numb. I shook like a leaf. Although I welcomed the fact that I wasn't in agony any longer, I knew I was in some kind of trouble. I just didn't know how much.

We knew nothing about burns. How do you treat them? We didn't have the slightest idea. The dos and don'ts were a mystery to us. The only experience I'd had with burns was back when I was about 13 or 14. A mate's ute was bogged on the side of the road at his farm. I was pushing the ute, rocking back and forward, and just as he was coming out of the bog, I slipped on the edge of the road and fell under the back of the vehicle. My mate thought he was bogged again so he spun the wheels, causing a painful friction burn on my right calf. When we got to the Nhill Hospital, the doctors thought I might need a skin graft, but thankfully I didn't. Six weeks of dressings and bathing it in antiseptic healed it just fine. Ironically, the scar had almost faded away when I was burnt again in the same area, except this time it covered a much bigger surface area and was only part of my overall injury list, which was bigger than those listed by some football clubs.

In a medical sense, first instincts are often harmful. The very thing that you want to do could put you in danger. Like when you get knocked out in a football match, all you want to do is have a couple of Panadeine Forte tablets, curl up and go to sleep. The reality is that sleeping with a bruised brain could cause you to slip into a coma. Nasty stuff. Burns are no different. All you want to do is go to the beach and lie in the water. But this would certainly result in infection.

And I couldn't move very well; at least, not without difficulty. I dreaded the next few days, as I knew I'd be very sore. Sorer than after any football match I'd ever played.

Mick's decision to hail a motorcyclist was a masterstroke, and perhaps helped save my life. The roads were a bumper-to-bumper bedlam — traffic everywhere, banked up, hardly moving. Snail pace. Imagine Bourke Street, Melbourne, in peak hour and you're not even close.

The roads — they are more like glorified laneways — are usually of the one-lane, one-way variety. No room to move. Nowhere to escape the congestion. That is, if you're in a four-wheeler.

It was actually a blessing in disguise that the group of local guys had knocked us back for a lift earlier. If we had gone with them, I would have been able to lie down in some semblance of comfort, but we would have been stuck in the traffic jam. It would have been unbearable. Helpless. Hopeless. Time ticking away. Energy, indeed life, being slowly sapped. A kind of passive desperation. It might have been my funeral procession.

But my cyclist — my saviour on two wheels — was quite skilful, and made use of every millimetre available to him as we scooted and manoeuvred in and out of the traffic. I was ultra-conscious of not brushing up against anything, whether it be a car, a kerb or another cyclist. I didn't want anything to touch me. Except for a doctor. Or, impossibly, Nerissa.

I was frantic about any implications my injuries would have on the wedding, which was set for 14 December, just two months later. Was I going to be right for it? I wished that I was home with Nerissa right there and then. Far, far away from this holiday hell. I love her so much. Like nothing else. I want to be with her for the rest of my life.

My little chauffeur snapped me out of my emotional delirium. 'I'm sorry, I'm sorry,' he repeated over and over.

I shook my head and reassured him. 'Mate, it's not your fault, it's not your fault,' I insisted again and again as I held onto him. He had nothing to be sorry about. He wasn't responsible.

But he, like many of the locals, realised that something terrible had happened. Perhaps he had already worked out that it could spell even harder times for him, his people and the island. Their lifeblood — overseas tourists — were certain to punish them for what had happened by abandoning Bali as a holiday destination.

It took less than five minutes to get to the Hard Rock. It seemed longer, and shorter. Shock does that to you.

As I got off the motorbike, I looked at my hands again. They were a mess, covered in ash and blood. It was going to take a while for them to heal and be fully functional again. Would I be able to grab a footy? Open a door? Shave? Hold Nerissa's hand? Would I retain my sense of touch?

But with all of those questions crossing my brain like a series of newsflashes, I still held onto hope. I hoped — fantasised — that the doctor at the Hard Rock would simply wipe me down with a wet cloth, bathe me, dress my wounds and I'd be able to continue my holiday as though nothing had happened.

In my delusional state, I really needed Michael Caton's character from that great Aussie movie *The Castle* to tell me I was dreamin'.

Mick, reliable to the core, had caught the next available motorbike — he probably would have thrown the rider off if he had to — and was right behind me.

We walked into the foyer of the hotel, which, I was told, Aussie legend Jimmy Barnes had rocked the previous night. There was another great band playing on the stage at the time. Earlier in the night, we'd had a couple of Bintangs and watched them before we went out for dinner.

But as soon as we walked in, the focus shifted from the band to us — in particular, me. Talk about a party-pooper. It was as though a scantily clad Frankenstein had entered the building. Revellers looked at me: bloodied, covered in ash, bare-chested, wearing only a pair of barely there shorts that would have looked at home on Tarzan, and torn shoes that somehow clung to my feet.

For the first time in our lives, Mick was a more attractive proposition than I was.

Perhaps the most disturbing thing to those near me, though, was the smell that followed me. When I first noticed it, I screwed my face up and thought, 'What is that?' It wasn't ash or blood, or even a mixture of the two. It was an uncomfortable odour. A distinctively strong stench. Unlike anything that I had ever experienced.

It wasn't long before I worked out what it was. Burning flesh. Mine! It stuck with me for a couple of weeks. Although it didn't actually smell like pork, it wasn't too dissimilar. I later found out that the smell came from the fact that my body was so badly burnt that it was cooking from the inside out. Like in a microwave oven.

The party of about 40 people at the Hard Rock was clearly repulsed by the sight of my battered and bloodied figure. They narrowed their stares, contorted their faces, gasped in horror and tapped their friends on the shoulder and pointed at me.

The entire place erupted in screams. I now know exactly how the Elephant Man felt.

MICK MARTYN: You can understand why people were so shocked at what they saw. You don't see that kind of thing every day — two big blokes walking in, bloody, burnt, clothes ripped. I don't know if they thought we'd been involved in an accident or a fire or something, but they were horrified.

Hotel staff tried to quell the commotion by announcing that everything was OK. After that, the band started playing again. That didn't bother me. It was probably best to keep people occupied. It reminds me of a scene from Titanic, where the band plays to cheer up the passengers as the ship goes down. Nothing could cheer me up though.

And things were to get a lot worse before they got better.

We were ushered into a small, quiet room to wait for the hotel doctor. The more I waited, the more I shook — a symptom of shock.

Steven Febey walked in. I thought he'd also hitched a ride on a motorbike but I later found out that he had sprinted the 2 kilometres or so from the Sari Club. 'Febes' wasn't hurt, but he was frantic. His three mates were missing and he feared the worst.

Febes had already sent a text message to his twin brother, Matthew, also a former Melbourne player. Matthew was supplying audio and communications on the Australian football team's International Rules tour of Ireland.

MATTHEW FEBEY (FORMER AFL FOOTBALLER WITH MELBOURNE AND TWIN BROTHER OF STEVEN FEBEY): It was about 5 p.m. Dublin time. We were playing golf at the European Golf Club. I was with the Brisbane boys Chris Johnson and Brad Scott, and Geoff Slattery of AFL Publishing. It was freezing cold — another world away from Bali.

Just when we'd finished our round of golf, I received a text message from my brother which said, 'I'm alive, call me, there's been a bomb.'

It didn't make much sense, so I rang him straight away. He was hysterical. I'd never heard him like that before.

He said, 'I can't find my mates. I think I've killed my best mate.' He was holding himself responsible because he'd organised the footy trip. He was talking to me but he was also preoccupied with trying to find his mates.

I told Chris, Brad and Geoff and they couldn't believe it. One of the guys my brother was looking for, David Robbins, was a good mate of Brad Scott's, so Brad was shocked and got quite upset.

I also got a phone call from an ex-girlfriend, Rachael, who had been in a group with the Woodgate girls, Jason McCartney and Mick Martyn when the bomb went off. She was hysterical too. She said she was in the 'Shiralee' hospital when it was actually Sanglah. She was screaming for help and trying to get some of the Melbourne footy guys to the hospital.

The girls knew quite a few of the players but the boys had left that night.

Then the phone cut out and Rachael was gone. I didn't know how badly hurt she was, but I knew she must have been pretty ordinary because she was hysterical. But at least I knew she was in hospital.

On our way back to Dublin, it started to sink in that something terrible had happened. I was fairly clear-headed about it all. I passed on the information to the guys at the hotel and we started watching CNN on TV.

They were having their team dinner because they were playing the First Test the next day. A couple of the North Melbourne guys knew a couple of their teammates were there. Adam Simpson was pretty upset by it all.

ADAM SIMPSON (KANGAROOS TEAMMATE): I actually got told that Jase and Mick were badly burned and they weren't going to make it. I didn't know what to think to start with. They had an Internet connection in the hotel where we were staying, but the computer looked like it was made in 1982. I was trying to log on to get on to the AFL website or the *Herald Sun*'s.

I thought, 'Well that's it then, they're gone.' So I tried to ring back home but no one knew anything. It was two o'clock in the morning.

MATTHEW FEBEY: A few of us Melbourne guys were in the same room — Garry Lyon, Jimmy Stynes, David Neitz, Adem Yze, Cameron Bruce and myself — and we were watching CNN and waiting on phone calls.

The death toll climbed from four to twenty, then eighty … Brad Scott was pretty cut up and so was Adam Simpson. We got a call from Steven to say he'd found his mates and they were all OK. That was at about midnight or 1 a.m. These guys had to play the First Test the next day. It was very emotionally draining on everyone. I struggled to sleep. I rang Rachael's parents and told them what had happened.

The next day it was a very cold, rainy day in Dublin.

ADAM SIMPSON: I went into the game thinking pretty much that Jase and Mick and all those Australians were in a bit of trouble. They played the national anthem before the game and I shed a tear for Jase and Mick. It was very emotional. I was really shaken up for a while. Back in Melbourne, not many people would have been watching our game, but I wanted to really win for those blokes.

MATTHEW FEBEY: In the first quarter, the boys were all over the top because they were emotionally all over the place. They played poorly but they got it together and won the game. There was the loudest singing of the team song imaginable. Everyone was involved. There were a few tears and a lot of phone calls.

Febes felt helpless. He wished me the best of luck and took off to look for his mates. Steve Armstrong and David Robbins turned up at the Hard Rock later, while Febes found his best mate in hospital. All were injured but at least they were alive.

The Balinese doctor, Dr Bayupasti, arrived after five or ten agonising minutes. He was on call for the Hard Rock and was on duty that night at the Kuta medical clinic. Sure enough, as Mick had said, he spoke English. I was surprised when he simply gave Mick and me some damp cloths, like face-washers, to soothe our heads and necks. There certainly wasn't any science about his methods. I don't know what I expected him to do exactly, but certainly something more medically astute than give us a couple of wet cloths. That's the very thing we wanted to do most, but remember, our instincts are often wrong.

DR BAYUPASTI (BALINESE DOCTOR WHO FIRST ATTENDED JASON): I couldn't treat Jason at the hotel. We had to get him to the hospital quickly. I knew his condition was serious, but I knew he would get worse.

To be fair, the doctor had only examined me for about two minutes when we heard the siren of an ambulance that had arrived to take us to hospital. He came with us and, for a time, became a pivotal person in my existence.

I hobbled to the ambulance as quickly as I could. It was a beat-up old panel van like one we could have had in the country while I was growing up. The red and blue paint had faded. So did my hopes of survival.

Such a vehicle hardly inspires confidence, but in my sick and sorry state, I would have gone to hospital on the back of a donkey if I had to. I lay down on a stretcher in the back, which had no medical cabinets, first-aid kits or any form of medical equipment.

Mick, bold as ever, leapt straight into the front passenger seat. He was going to attack this thing head-on.

A girl came with us — I think she was European — and sat at the end of my stretcher. She might have been seriously burnt but I couldn't tell because she didn't say a word. I don't think she could speak English anyway. Obviously traumatised, she sat motionless, staring out the window. Nothing seemed to register. The lights were on but no one was home. She was another reminder of the circumstances in which we found ourselves.

From the moment we sped down the road, I knew I was in for a painful ride. I wasn't strapped in, so each time we swung around a corner, I slid about, scraping my burns and generally getting more aggravated and agitated. I felt every bump in the road.

MICK MARTYN: Jase started to shake. He was going into shock. At that stage, I thought, 'He's not looking good.' I just tried to calm him down. I said to him, 'There are other people that are much worse off — they're pretty bad.' I didn't want him going into a complete state of shock like in the movies, where people go into shock and pass away. But I thought, 'Once we get to the hospital, he'll be all right.'

The traffic was still mayhem, so for most of the time we made slow progress. I tried to grit my teeth and take whatever pain was thrown at me. Football had taught me to be tough and not complain — just grin and bear it. That's fine in theory but impossible to follow in reality. I was all screams and moans.

'How far have we got to go now? How long?'

It was like the clichéd line that kids torture their parents with — 'Are we there yet?' — but with considerably more desperation and expletives, and a lot more at stake.

DR BAYUPASTI: Jason was saying, 'Please, God, help me!', 'Please, doc, help me!' and, 'I'm going to die!' I said to him, 'No, you're not going to die. You will be all right. You're just feeling the pain from the burns.' I tried my best to keep him relaxed.

It took about half an hour to get to Sanglah General Hospital in Denpasar. Like most parts of this saga, the trip seemed longer because of the pain.

Strangely, despite all my trips to Bali, I didn't even know where a hospital or a proper medical centre was. But I certainly wouldn't have been on my own in that regard. If you conducted a survey of people who had been there, I'm sure most people would share my ignorance of the local medical services.

I was just so lucky that Mick had taken control and got us back to our hotel. If I had been on my own, I might not have taken the same decisive course of action. Most likely, I would have muddled my way through it and wasted valuable time and energy. The delay and physical exertion could have even cost me my life.

I'd only ever spent one night at the Hard Rock before, so I reckon I would have followed a lot of other injured people to the Bounty Hotel, about 500 metres down Old Poppies Lane. It was the closest big hotel that I was aware of and was the logical choice for a person in an illogical frame of mind. I'd never stayed at the Bounty before but it was situated in an area that I knew well.

But now I was in unfamiliar territory. I was scared and didn't know what to expect.

4

The hospital

When we arrived at the hospital, I was still under the impression that there had only been one blast. I didn't have a clue about the full extent of the devastation. I thought, 'Oh, there could be 20 or 30 people hurt and needing attention.' We were in the first bunch, and there were probably 15 or 20 bomb blast victims there. I figured that would be the extent of the casualties.

Tragically, I was wrong.

Within 15 minutes, there were about 100 people, including me, lying in the emergency entrance of the hospital.

I thought, 'Bloody hell, this is bigger than a gas explosion.'

It certainly was a state of emergency, panic and confusion. People were screaming hysterically: 'Help me, please!' 'Doctor!' 'Water!'

MICK MARTYN: It was mayhem.

People everywhere, bleeding, burnt. Chaos.

The hospital wasn't prepared for anything like that. It's not their fault — there were just so many injured people, many of them in serious and critical conditions, coming in one after the other.

Everyone was different. Some were in extreme pain and screaming because they were burnt to a crisp, others were in shock and hardly making a sound. Some had glass and shrapnel wounds. There was constant screaming and shouting. People came in carrying body parts.

There was blood all over the floor, like a red sea.

Nothing can prepare you for a situation like that. Mick was by my side, trying to comfort me in any way he could. Just having someone familiar around in an utterly unfamiliar environment helped immensely. It was something positive to cling to.

I was a bit selfish, too, in that I hounded the doctor who had accompanied us from the Hard Rock Hotel. I tagged him closer than Tony Liberatore ever tagged anyone. I didn't let him go because he could speak English and I was terrified of what might happen to me if he left.

Dr Bayupasti: I gave Jason an injection of tramadol to ease the pain. Burns cause dehydration, so I put him on an intravenous drip to put liquid back in his body. This seemed to relax him a little bit.

I had no idea about the standard procedure for burns victims — the one-percenters, the little things, that could be the difference between life and death. Every moment was a revelation. On a bigger scale, I also didn't have any idea about how the clearly under-staffed and under-resourced local medicos were going to properly examine and accommodate everyone.

I was very aware of my mortality. I knew there was a possibility that I could die there. It was sheer panic.

'How are we going to get home?' I asked Mick. 'We've got to get out of here.'

I became irrational, understandably so. 'I'm never coming back to this joint again,' I declared. Mick didn't argue with me. It was the last place on earth either of us wanted to be. It could have been the last place on earth that I ever saw.

As it turns out, I've been back to Bali three times since — to face my fears in the following March; to attend the trial of the terrorists in June; and for the anniversary, or 'remembrance' as the locals call it, of the bombings on 12 October 2003 — but at that moment I decided that 11 trips was enough.

Yet I was lucky. Lucky to be alive, to be mobile, to have Mick with me, to have been able to get an ambulance. I don't think many people had that luxury because there simply weren't enough ambulances to go round. I've heard stories since of injured people, such as Nashy, riding on the back of utes to medical centres and hospitals around the place.

To get away from the bomb site quickly was one thing, but to get an ambulance to the main hospital on the island was something else entirely. It was a godsend.

People have told me that some of the smaller medical centres along the street struggled to cope with the volume of people requiring attention. They were overflowing. There was slow progress, if any at all. People were sort of getting looked after, but sort of not, and it was a long time before they got to a major hospital for anything that resembled half-decent medical treatment.

It sounds selfish but, in my frail state, all I could think about was the well-being of one person — me. That's what I had to do to get through it and survive.

As I lay on my stretcher in emergency, my legs shook furiously. I had a chill. But more disturbingly, when my legs were straight and outstretched, my feet constantly rose about 15 centimetres off the stretcher. It was like the effect you get when a doctor tests your reflexes by hitting you just below the knee with a little hammer, except it was as if he was doing it at split-second intervals.

I was desperate to know what was going to happen to us. Would they operate? Would they patch us up as an interim measure before they flew us home for proper treatment? So many questions, but no answers. I couldn't understand what the Balinese doctors and nurses were saying, which was incredibly frustrating. I continually asked Dr Bayupasti (whose name I quickly abbreviated to Dr Bayu) to interpret for me.

DR BAYUPASTI: Jason is very, very strong and he was conscious. He kept asking questions like, 'What is going to happen now?' I tried to keep him calm and find out when he would be operated on. I consulted the surgeon about cutting off the skin that was already burned in the bomb blast.

I continued to shake uncontrollably. But I started to think, 'Maybe I'm not too bad because, although the pain's terrible, they seem to be treating others before me. They must be more seriously hurt; I must be a lower priority.'

That was wishful thinking. There was no prioritising with patients. It was simply a case of first in, first served. They were just doing the best they could to cope with the seemingly endless stream of casualties who flooded into the hospital.

They say you should try to stay calm in a crisis. Take it from me, it's easier said than done. I panicked. As feverishly as they worked and as much as they tried to maintain their composure, the medicos also panicked. Everyone panicked.

My mind raced like a computer. I thought, 'Are the girls all right? What's happened to them? Where's Hughesy?'

It's strange what goes through your mind when there is chaos all around. Just before I went to Bali, I had a bungle with a credit card and went through the process of getting a new one. (We all know what a pain in the neck that is.) On that first night in Bali, I wanted to travel light — who likes having an uncomfortable wallet in their shorts? — so I wrapped some Australian and Balinese notes around my new credit card and put it in my right pocket. God only knows why, but, while I lay on a stretcher — burnt, bleeding, shaking — I thought, 'My money! My card!'

I said to Mick, 'Check my pants, will ya?'

He said, 'What for?'

'See if my money's there.'

Mick ducked into my right pocket (luckily that side of my shorts was still intact). The money and credit card were still there — about $A200 and 550,000 rupiahs (around $A100). Phew!

'It's all right, it's all right,' I sighed. I told Mick to hold onto it for safe keeping.

Money was such a trivial matter at the time, I don't know why I was so concerned about it. Hell, I was alive. That was the main thing.

Hughesy's mate Nashy came in. Mick went to see how he was.

'Thank Christ!' I thought. 'That's one piece of the jigsaw. Hughesy can't be too far away then.'

It's amazing how close you can feel to people in desperate times. We'd only known Nashy for two hours. It was a turbulent way to start a friendship, but in that short time he impressed me as a genuine, relaxed, knockabout bloke. He was a bit rough around the edges though, having been in the navy as a youngster, and he had self-drawn tatts. If we'd stayed for the week, I'd hate to see what would've become of Mick and me with Nashy to push us along in the drinking stakes. Hughesy had told me that the big fella could drink like a very large fish and he had certainly impressed us with his beer-swilling abilities in the short time we'd known him.

MICK MARTYN: When Gary Nash came in, I wasn't too sure if it was him or not. Gary's a big bloke, 50-odd years of age and he'd been drinking, so he wasn't in the best shape.

A doctor also gave Mick wallets and jewellery that belonged to complete strangers. The poor old doctor must have been confused and thought that Mick knew everyone and was some sort of guardian of the group. I suppose Mick just has that solid, reliable look about him.

MICK MARTYN: I said, 'Look, I don't even know these people. You're best off leaving them on people's bodies.'

Unfortunately, with such confusion and vulnerability comes the opportunity for looting. As much as it pains me to say it, I'm certain some of that went on. The medicos were taking chains off people's necks, bracelets off wrists and rings off fingers to enable them to treat people. They were just putting jewellery on the chests and stomachs of the injured. I'm sure many of these items were quite expensive and held enormous sentimental value. A thief — of the worst kind — could easily have walked away with thousands of dollars worth of jewellery and cash if they wanted to. It wasn't like any of us would have been able to jump off our stretchers and chase the bludgers down.

A photographer from the *Bali Post* newspaper also took the opportunity to snap a photo of us: Mick standing over me and Dr Bayupasti with his back to the camera. My face is blackened and bleeding in parts, while Mick has sponges to soothe the welts on his head. You can see the total fear in our eyes.

MICK MARTYN: The doc stayed with us as long as he could but there were massive problems elsewhere. Once Jason started to feel a bit better, the doc went to help other people who were dying or half-alive. You'd see him going from one person to the next.

It would have been an enormous job for the doctors and nurses. When you get burns to 50 per cent of your body, like Jason, you're in a pretty bad way; but there were also people who were bleeding to death from open wounds. They had to be cared for first. It's weird, because compared to a lot of people at the hospital, Jason was all right. But later on it was life or death. It makes you think how much pain these people were really in.

I was one of the lucky ones. I later found out that I had burns to 10 per cent of my body — my right hand and arm, my face, scalp and chest. I was fine from the waist down.

Like most people, I've had bad sunburn before, but this was a really intense heat. It was magnified in the areas that I'd been burnt, and I couldn't get rid of it.

But that was nothing compared to the injuries of others.

A young woman was brought in next to me on a stretcher. She was badly burnt all over her chest. The medicos ripped off her bikini top. She screamed in excruciating pain. A bloke was with her, comforting her. I don't know if he was her husband, boyfriend or just a friend. It made me think of Nerissa. She'd never been far from my thoughts anyway. 'Thank God she's not here,' I thought.

When I'd taken Nerissa on her first trip to Bali the year before, in October 2001, we hung out at the regular hotspots, including Paddy's Bar and the Sari Club. It's only luck that the terrorists weren't ready to go into action 12 months earlier. The situation was bad enough already; I wouldn't have been able to handle it if any harm had come to Nerissa.

'I don't care how bad I am,' I thought. 'I'm just glad Nerissa's all right.'

MICK MARTYN: There was another bloke who was particularly in pain. All they could do was pour cold water over him. They tried to throw wet towels over him but he was just writhing around. He was very badly burnt. I don't know if he lived or not.

About 12.30 a.m., I was moved to another part of the hospital. Mick, as loyal as a bull terrier, stuck to my side. It felt like I was wheeled hundreds of metres before we came to a stop. I thought we were outside the hospital because it was dark. I didn't know it at the time but, having been back to the hospital since, I've found out that the entire building is 'outside.' It's all linked by verandahs. There aren't any visiting rooms there either, so people just sat outside and waited around for their loved ones.

People, mainly Balinese, stood up on their toes to peer at you. They weren't being ghoulish — they were just checking to see if you were someone they knew. Still, it did feel like an invasion of privacy.

I was caught in a logjam of stretchers outside a tiny room. I was stationary for about 20 minutes.

A bloke started carrying on right next to me. It was his first trip to Bali and he was screaming out things like, 'I'm never coming back to this place!'

He didn't look too badly burnt, but like me he could've been a lot worse than he appeared. He was obviously in a lot of pain. A couple of his front teeth had been knocked out — perhaps by the force of the bomb or maybe he smashed his face on something when he landed. I can understand him venting his anger and frustration — I felt like doing it too — but his outbursts made everyone else uneasy, frightened even.

He kept going on and on. Mick wanted to belt the bloke to give him something else to squeal about. I was the pacifier. 'Just settle down, mate,' I told him. 'Settle down.'

That quietened him down — for a little while.

Just as I was to be moved into the little medical room, they told Mick, 'That's it for you. You can't go any further.'

Although neither of us could mask our disappointment, Mick said, 'You'll be right, mate. I'll see you soon.'

I was shattered. Scared too. Mick, my saviour, was gone. I had to face this thing on my own. The stark reality and the terrible uncertainty of it all hit me.

'Here I am,' I thought, 'in a Third World country, in a hospital waiting to get operated on, and I'm on my own.'

MICK MARTYN: After they said I couldn't go any further, I went to another waiting area. I thought Jason would be all right. I thought they'd clean him up and give him the proper treatment for his burns. I waited for about an hour and a half — not many people were coming out. I thought they must be holding him overnight, and since it was hard to communicate with the hospital staff, I went back to the Hard Rock Hotel.

I called my wife, Leah, because I knew a fair few people had died and there were a lot of casualties. I told Leah that Jason had been hurt but that he was being looked after.

5

The news gets home

It had been a running joke during previous trips that you should avoid hospitals in Bali because you'll never come out. We always got a laugh out of it because there was always that stigma about the place. But this was no laughing matter.

It was a living nightmare. We all knew that. But you've gotta be positive, composed.

I was wheeled into a little room that could only be described as a holding pen. There were 20 or 30 injured people waiting on beds outside, with four at a time moving into this poor excuse for a waiting room. One by one we were taken through to the operating theatre.

The other three people with me were the guy who had been carrying on earlier, a Balinese lady and an old man. The local lady just sat there in complete shock, silent and covered in blood. Blood all over her. The old man — I thought he must have been around 60 or 70 — was just moaning, 'Water, water' in a gravelly, old-timer's voice. I got a shock when I looked at him and saw that he was actually a young bloke in his twenties. It was a sobering realisation. Things weren't as they seemed.

My football upbringing emerged and kept me sane. I'd never been in a life-or-death situation. The closest thing I could relate it to was a tight contest in an important game of footy. But while coaches pump football up as a matter of life and death, it's not. This was a matter of life and death. This was the real deal. But that didn't stop me from drawing on my football experiences to stay calm.

During my footy career, I tended to worry too much about myself, especially if I'd made a couple of mistakes. My long-time coach at the Kangaroos, Denis Pagan, really helped me turn that attitude around. One of his favourite sayings was, 'Only worry about what you can control.' In footy, that meant, 'Focus on the next contest.' In hospital in Bali, it meant, 'Grit your teeth, get through the operations and do whatever you can to get yourself right. And get home.'

We lay there for the next half-hour. It was an agonising wait, almost like being on death row, except I couldn't wait to get there — the operating room, that is. I just wanted something to happen. But I was afraid of the unknown.

I pride myself on never taking anything lying down, and being proactive, but I had no choice. All I could do was lie there and wait — and think. Composure was fleeting. I wished I could just flick a switch to stop my brain from functioning, but — damn it — I couldn't stop it from running through the possibilities. 'If they operate, will I wake up? I hope it doesn't end like this. What I'd do just to see Nerissa again.'

NERISSA: An hour after I apologised to the girls for carrying on, the phone rang. It was Mick's wife, Leah. She said to me, 'Where are you?'

I said, 'I'm with Robyn at her place.'

She said, 'OK, can you sit down?'

I had calmed down by this stage. I said, 'Yeah, why?'

Leah said, 'Well, something really bad has happened.'

'What?'

She said, 'There's been an explosion or something. Something's happened in Bali. There's been an explosion and Mick and Jason have been hurt.'

I said, 'What do you mean hurt?'

She said, 'Well, I'm not sure, but I think they're a bit burnt.'

When you don't have any understanding of burns, you think, 'Oh, just burnt a bit. They'll be all right.'

I think perhaps I went into shock, because I didn't get hysterical and I didn't carry on. I sort of just stood there and Leah said, 'But they're OK, they're OK. Jason's a bit more burnt than Mick, but he's OK, he's fine.'

I thought, 'That's OK then. He's all right.' I hung up but then I thought to myself, 'No, hang on, that's pretty bad to be hurt in Bali.'

Robyn saw the look on my face and said, 'What's wrong?'

I started crying. 'Something's happened in Bali. There's been an explosion and Jason ...'

Robyn turned the TV on and I remember seeing fire everywhere. She turned it off and said, 'We won't watch telly. Let's do something else.'

Someone said, 'Let's turn the radio on,' so the girls ran around turning the news on and then off because they didn't want to throw me into even more of a panic.

Robyn grabbed me and said, 'Come with me. Let's get on to the Australian consulate in Bali.'

She was great. She was on the phone and looking for information on the Internet. She even rang people who she thought might have contacts.

All I remember is everyone running around me. It was a blur. I was in shock and I just didn't know what to do. I was thinking of Jason the whole time, just worrying about him — what he would be going through, and the feelings he'd be having.

The girls sat me down and that's when my phone started going crazy. Then I thought, 'I have to ring his parents.'

I rang Jason's father, Ian, and I said, 'Is Jan there?'

He said, 'No, she's staying with your mum in Millicent (in South Australia).'

I said, 'Well, Ian, I have to tell you something. Something's happened to … ' That was all I could blurt out before I started crying. 'Something's happened to Jason.'

I just couldn't bring myself to tell him, so I threw the phone to Robyn. She said, 'Hi, it's Robyn here, Corey's partner. Look, there's been an explosion in Bali.'

She explained it to him and I stood there howling. I got back on the phone and Ian said, 'Are you all right?'

I said, 'I'll ring Jan', and he said, 'OK.'

IAN MCCARTNEY (JASON'S FATHER): When Nerissa called me, she was bawling. I thought, 'What the bloody hell's going on here? Oh, they've had a blue.' But then I thought, 'That can't be the case because Jason's not home — he's in Bali.' I was fairly curious at this point.

Corey's partner got on the phone and told me what was going on, but the phone cut out before we'd finished.

I didn't know what to do. I had no phone numbers to ring anyone who knew what was going on. Of course, Jan wasn't home. I was a mess.

I rang Brenden — he lives just across the road.

BRENDEN MCCARTNEY (JASON'S BROTHER, 11 MONTHS HIS JUNIOR): I was sound asleep in bed when the phone rang at about 6.30 a.m. My wife Ange answered it and she said, 'Oh, it's your dad. He sounds upset.'

I got on the phone and all I could get out of him was, 'There's been an explosion.'

I thought, 'Oh, Jesus.' I didn't even know Jason was in Bali. I thought he was still in America on the footy trip.

I got dressed straight away and went over to Dad's place. He was waiting for me. I thought, 'Jason's been killed.'

I'd never seen Dad in a state like that before. I remember when Grandpa died — Dad's dad. At the funeral in the church, Dad had a few tears rolling down his cheeks and then, on the way to the cemetery in the car more tears were rolling down his cheeks and I was in the back crying because I'd never seen Dad like that before. You get a crook feeling in your guts when you see your old man like that. He said he'd called the Kangaroos to see what they could do, even though he was shaking and couldn't really read the phone numbers.

I said, 'Righto, what are we going to do?'

He shrugged his shoulders. I thought, 'Oh, jeez, this is not Dad. He's not himself. I've got to put emotions aside here and grab hold of the situation.' Mum was with Nerissa's mum, so she wasn't there for him.

I rang Leah Martyn but she wasn't fully aware of what had happened. She gave me Mick's room number at the Hard Rock, so I eventually got through to him. Mick had seen what had happened but he wasn't really in a mood to talk. I just said to Mick, 'Look, mate, I don't want to keep you, I've roughly heard what's happened. I just want to know what's going on with Jason.'

Mick said, 'There's been an explosion and he's got a few burns but he's all right. He's in hospital.'

The way Mick described it, it sounded like Jason had just burnt his mouth on a hot pie. I thought, 'That doesn't sound too bad.'

IAN McCARTNEY: We turned the telly on and it was probably the worst thing we could have done. We saw the carnage and thought, 'Holy hell!'

We first heard that eight had been killed, then we heard 40, and it kept climbing after that.

STEVEN McCARTNEY (JASON'S YOUNGEST BROTHER, FIVE YEARS HIS JUNIOR): I was lying in bed when I heard Dad come flying up the driveway in his ute, tooting the horn and banging on the front door. He said, 'A bomb's gone off in Bali and Jason was involved in it.' It wasn't the type of thing you expect to hear first thing on a Sunday morning.

Dad wasn't looking real well. He took off again.

News of the bombings was all over the TV. I thought, 'I'd better get around to Mum and Dad's place.'

I'd been to Bali once before with Jason, so I was trying to picture it in my head. I couldn't picture any hospitals or anything like that because I never saw one.

NERISSA: I rang Mum's place straight away to speak to Jan. I was glad that my mum (Marleen) and Jason's mum were together because Jan would need a girl around.

Mum answered the phone. I said, 'Hi, Mum. I need to talk to Jan.'

Because I was ringing at a ridiculous hour, Mum said, 'She's asleep, dear.'

I said, 'Mum, I really need to talk to her.'

Mum said, 'What's wrong? Tell me.'

I said, 'I just need to talk to her first. I have to tell her first.'

My mum started panicking but she got Jan on the phone.

I said, 'Jan, something's happened to Jason.'

I became hysterical so I gave the phone to Robyn and she explained who she was and told Jan what we knew.

Then they said, 'Right, we're coming to Melbourne. We're coming straight there to be with you.'

In the meantime, the girls and I sat outside Robyn and Corey's place and Robyn kept feeding me wine. She said, 'You need to calm down.'

JAN McCARTNEY (JASON'S MOTHER): Nerissa couldn't talk, she was too upset, so she put Corey McKernan's fiancée Robyn on. I didn't know what to think. But I thought, 'It must be something to do with Jason.'

When Robyn gave me the news, I collapsed on the bathroom floor. I froze. I was so cold. It didn't matter how much people got around and hugged me, I was freezing.

All hell broke loose. I was ringing Ian to see what was happening. Brenden had been on the phone ringing everyone.

I rang Leah Martyn to see exactly what the story was. It was the same thing Robyn had told me. There had been an explosion, Jason had been hurt but he was being looked after.

It was every parent's worst nightmare.

Just as my emotions started to get the better of me, doctors and nurses emerged from the makeshift operating theatre. They had finished with the previous patient, who was still unconscious after being anaesthetised. At least, I hope the person was unconscious.

The medicos then focused their attention on me and, without a second's delay, wheeled me into the operating room. I was relieved that I would be seen by the surgeon. Finally. But relief was quickly overwhelmed by fear, a fear that made running with the flight of the ball to cut off a Tony Lockett lead look like a soft option.

Survival instincts took over. I looked up at the four Balinese doctors who were examining me. They looked confident after treating a lot of injured people already. But they still had a lot to do. Their time was precious, but I wanted to make sure that they didn't take any shortcuts in treating me. After all, my fate was in their hands.

As if they couldn't already see the desperation in my eyes, I looked into theirs and pleaded, indeed prayed, 'You blokes, please, please look after me. Don't let me die. Please don't let me die.'

The doctors spoke poor English but they tried to reassure me. 'Everything will be all right,' they said. But, in the circumstances, their words were cold comfort.

I was given a very strong anaesthetic. Apparently, it's cheap, unavailable in Australia and the western world, but very effective. The fact that I mightn't wake up from it didn't even cross my mind. In a sense, I didn't care either. I was in a world of pain and I needed an escape route. The drug charged into my veins like the cavalry.

But there are still images, vague recollections, in my mind about the operation. I'm not sure if the anaesthetic started wearing off, or if I dreamt it, but I have images of the doctors peeling charred, dead, skin from my body and throwing it to the side. It seemed more like a farmyard procedure. Scrape. Cut.

Hack. Rip. I felt like a rabbit being skinned.

If I was actually conscious while this was going on, the doctors must have whacked more sleep-juice straight back into me because it didn't last long. But it was certainly long enough to give me a lasting memory of that part of the ordeal. I can still picture it now.

When I woke up, I felt like I was in a horror movie. I was very drowsy from the effects of the anaesthetic. I tried to lift my head but it fell back down again. I felt like I was tumbling, rolling forward. Everything was in slow motion. I felt ill, like seasickness, only umpteen times worse. Surely I was having a bad dream, but it was a bad dream that I couldn't wake from. It was hard to think. Hard to exist.

Then I had a sudden, sickening realisation. I seriously wondered, 'Am I alive or dead?'

I had never contemplated anything like it before — and it scared the hell out of me! All I could think about was Nerissa. 'If I'm dead, I'll never see her again,' I thought. It was simplistic, I know, but so was my existence, or lack of it, at that point. It was all too much for me.

'Nerissa!' I screamed at the top of my voice. 'Nerissa! Nerissa!'

Tears ran down my face.

NERISSA: I was numb. Another terrible thing had happened to one of my closest friends here in Melbourne, Peta. Her dad had died on the Friday after battling cancer. We work together at St Joseph's Catholic School. I said to her, 'Don't you come to school. I'll do everything for you.'

I had planned to support her through that terrible time, and then Bali happened on the Saturday night. So I wanted to be there for her, and she wanted to be there for me, but we couldn't — not in person anyway. We spoke over the phone but we didn't speak to each other for a little while because we had our own situations to deal with.

So Jeremy, another friend from work, came over with flowers and a box of chocolates. He didn't know Cee or Ally or Robyn but he spoke to them because I wasn't talking. I just sat there.

My mobile phone was running hot and sometimes I slid it across the table to Robyn and said, 'Can you answer that? I don't want to talk.'

I felt helpless. I had a pain in my chest — like my heart was hurting. If I'd had to describe at the time how I was feeling, I would have gone crazy. I kept it all inside. It was so hard to deal with. My mind was racing, I was crying on the inside, aching. 'Jason … Jason.' He was my every thought.

ROBYN WOODLEY: After a while, I thought, 'Let's go down to a local hotel and have a few glasses of wine. It's better to be out than sitting around waiting for bad news.'

It was probably four or five hours before we heard anything.

Someone who'd heard about Bali saw Nerissa and said, 'Have you heard anything? Is

Jason OK?' It put the worst fears into Nerissa's mind. I just wanted to get that element away from her. I snapped at them, 'She doesn't need this right now! We don't know what's happening!' The person walked off.

Nerissa started getting teary again and I think I even snapped at her, 'Just calm down. He's probably fine. You're not going to help him by getting upset.'

We were all emotional and tense.

NERISSA: We sat around waiting for Mum and Jan to arrive. The girls wouldn't let me watch any TV or listen to the radio. I don't know whether it was a good thing or a bad thing. Maybe it was a good thing because I would've been absolutely hysterical if I had seen the full devastation of the bombs. I would've wanted to get on a flight and go to Bali straight away — by myself if I had to.

A voice responded to my wailing for Nerissa. It was Hughesy's mate Nashy. Big, solid, man's man Nashy. 'Jase, Jase, you've got to relax.' he said. 'It's OK, it's OK.'

I tried to talk to him, but it was too difficult. Too much of an effort just to stay awake, let alone concentrate and have a coherent conversation. Again I tried to lift my head, again it thudded back to the stretcher.

GARY NASH: Jase was a little bit upset, like all of us. He was a bit worried he wasn't going to make it home and he wanted to 'make the noise stop.' I tried to talk to him and calm him down, and told him everything was going to be all right. Then they wheeled him away, and I assumed he was going in for more surgery. That was the last I saw of him in Bali.

I must have dozed off to sleep because the next thing I remember is waking up a few hours later. It was Sunday morning. I felt like I could have slept for a week. I certainly needed the beauty sleep. I must have looked a treat.

Five Balinese nurses fussed over me. Although I was still affected by the drugs, reality hit me with the force of a Glenn Archer shirt front. 'Jeez,' I thought, 'this really is happening.'

It was surreal. Sometimes, usually when I wake from sleep, I still have to remind myself that it happened. One minute you're having a few quiet drinks with your mates in a place that you love; the next, your life is on the line. It was almost like an out-of-body experience. An out-of-body experience, that is, with all the pain.

I knew it would be days, weeks, months, even years, before I would recover — if, in fact, I ever did recover. In any case, it would be a long road back to full health. I hoped Nerissa would stay with me for the journey.

NERISSA: At times, I didn't feel anything. It's a big blur. The fact that we hadn't had much sleep because we'd been out didn't help. It can be hard to recall those really stressful moments, probably because your mind just blocks out that kind of trauma. When I look back now, all I see is myself sitting there in shock, not knowing what to do and wondering, 'Will I ever see Jason again?'

It was very lucky that I was with the girls because if I'd received news at home by myself, I don't know how I would've reacted. I would've watched the telly and been a lot worse. I would've rung someone. I think it was a blessing in disguise that I was actually with my girlfriends when I received the news.

Brenden kept calling to update me and say, 'Look, I've done this and that.' Every time I received an update, I'd realise how serious it all was. I still hadn't watched the news or anything — the girls never allowed me to sit in front of the television.

It was like I was in a trance.

I was a mess. I felt helpless.

I just needed to hear Jason's voice.

I didn't know it at the time, but Mick, the consummate team man and staunch friend, came looking for me at the hospital that next morning.

MICK MARTYN: I tried to contact the doctor who had taken us to the hospital but he was understandably busy. I called the hospital and I think they got some of their records mixed up because they said they didn't have anyone by the name of Jason McCartney.

I went back to the hospital and went through the wards and saw many of the people who had been among the initial group of injured people to arrive at the hospital. I tried to find out where Jason was and they said that he'd been transferred and was going to fly out on one of the Hercules flights. I thought, 'He must be all right.' I was pretty relieved.

I just knew that if something had happened — if he'd gotten worse or died — I would've known there and then. They would have said that he might not make it.

Two days after the bombing, I was leaving the Hard Rock Hotel, carrying Jason's bags, when I ran into a couple. They were leaving as well. The father (John) said to me, 'Did you lose someone?'

I said, 'No, he's already gone back to Australia to get urgent attention.'

They said, 'You're lucky, because we just lost our daughter.'

Their daughter, Angela Golotta was one of the first bomb victims identified as being dead. She was only 19.

Angela's mother Tracey was in a daze, like she was crying out for someone to comfort her. All I could do was give her a hug. She didn't want to let go. She held and held and held me.

I'd asked a lot of people, 'Where's Hughesy, where's Hughesy?'

A Balinese man called Leo came in and told me, 'Pete's burnt but he's here. He's in hospital. He's in safe hands.'

I hoped to God I was too.

Fluid levels are integral to the survival of burns patients. Nurses constantly monitored how much fluid went in and how much went out.

Nature dictated that I needed to urinate a couple of times. As I was immobile and confined to a stretcher, nurses gave me a bottle to relieve myself into. It was a simple matter — well, OK, a not-so-simple matter — of leaning on one side and doing my business. Not so simple because I couldn't make any movement without discomfort. Sometimes it hurt just lying still. But I accepted it as something that could not be avoided. It was beyond my control.

I tried to take control when an official-looking American guy — I think he had been in contact with the Australian consulate — came by with a mobile phone. I begged him to let me call home. 'I won't take long, I promise,' I said.

He looked at me with sympathetic eyes and kindly handed me his phone. The pocket-sized gadget was such a precious commodity to me that it may as well have been made of gold.

I didn't have my mobile phone with me because I didn't have it on global roaming. Chances are that if the phone had been in my pocket, it might have jarred free and melted at Paddy's Bar anyway.

I immediately rang Nerissa. I tried to be strong, brave and bottle up my emotions. I failed miserably.

'Honey, there's been a bomb, I'm in hospital, but everything's all right,' I blurted out, my voice quivering a little at the end.

I was then engulfed by a tidal wave of emotion that crushed my plans to keep it together. The floodgates opened. I cried and cried, bawling my eyes out like a little kid.

'I love you so much,' I told Nerissa, over and over.

Not the most masculine reaction from a supposedly big and strong footballer, but I couldn't help it. I didn't care what anyone thought. It was just so good to hear Nerissa's voice, particularly after doubting whether I would ever hear it again. Eventually I gathered myself and told her that I would keep in contact. We signed off with a reciprocal, 'I love you.' There was hope amid the horror.

NERISSA: It was about 1 p.m. when my mobile phone rang. A strange number was on my screen. I didn't think it would be Jason, but I answered it anyway and then when it was him, I started crying.

I could tell in his voice that he wasn't the good old Jase that I knew. He sounded scared, a bit unsure, like he was thinking, 'What's going to happen to me?' He didn't sound like the

Jason I had spoken to the day before and it really scared me. The pain inside was ten times as bad then. I wished I could dive through the phone and hold him.

I ran from where we were all sitting into the bedroom, tears streaming down my face. All I could say was, 'I love you, I love you' — I even screamed it down the phone a few times — and he was saying, 'I love you too.'

He got upset and started crying too.

I said, 'Are you all right?'

He reassured me. He said, 'I'm fine. I'll be all right. I love you. I can't talk long, I'm on someone else's phone. They're looking after me and they said I could ring you. I'll try and call again later.'

I think someone looking after him got on the phone after that and I said, 'Thank you so much.'

He said, 'Yeah, look, he's all right. We're doing the best we can.'

Although we only spoke to each other for about five minutes, it was amazing. It snapped me out of that numbness that I was feeling, that shock. I became more alert and with it. When I walked out of the bedroom and back to the others, I said, 'That was Jason.' I was crying. Hearing his voice was the most important thing.

It was a huge relief. I felt overwhelming happiness, because it proved to me he was alive. I had been panicking, so that was one of the best things that could've happened. It made me feel better to know he was OK and he was being looked after. He wasn't well, but knowing he was alive meant the world to me.

I felt Nerissa's sense of hopelessness. It would have been indescribably tough for people like her whose loved ones were injured, missing and dead in Bali. They're in Australia, the bomb blasts and the rising death toll have blanket coverage on the major news services, and the only point of contact is the telephone. The fact that I had to beg to borrow someone's mobile phone only amplified that sense of helplessness and isolation.

In a perfect world, I would have spoken to Nerissa until I either slipped off to sleep or the mobile phone battery went dead. But I was using someone else's phone, so I had to keep it short and sweet. Well, it was short anyway.

Soon, there was another reason to be concerned. Two ladies from the Australian consulate told us that all of the injured Australians and New Zealanders would be moved to another area. I didn't know it at the time but they were worried that there might be further terrorist attacks on the hospital. Just to finish us off. As if those inhumane bastards hadn't caused enough death and destruction already.

6

Helping hands

There is a gap in my memory where I must have drifted in and out of consciousness because the next thing I knew we were in some offices at the hospital. I can't remember being wheeled there, or how long it took to relocate us. The offices had been cleared out and there were two or three injured people to each room.

About that time we found out that all of the human carnage had been the result of a terrorist attack. It made me feel even worse. I could handle it if it was an accident. But hearing that it was a deliberate act, obviously planned and carried out with precision, made my skin crawl.

It was going to take a lot to restore my faith in the world.

You'd think that being a victim of a terrorist attack would make you immune to surprises. Not so. I was pleasantly surprised, shocked even, when sisters of my former captain Wayne Carey, Karen and Sharon, walked in. Mick and I didn't know they were in Bali. They were actually holidaying with their mum. They'd seen a news report that said there was an urgent call for a rare blood type (RH–), which Karen had. They also knew Mick and I were there, so they came looking for us.

I was so relieved to see someone that I knew.

The Carey sisters are both trained nurses, so they helped care for me for five hours. They even took turns fanning me because it was so hot and there was no air-conditioning. They generally made me as comfortable as I could have been given the circumstances.

Although I'd spoken to the girls a few times at the footy club when they would come down to support Wayne, I didn't know them all that well. But they were related to someone I knew well, so I latched onto them and lapped up their company. For a while there in hospital, Shazza and Kazza became my two closest friends.

KAREN CAREY (SISTER OF JASON'S FORMER TEAMMATE WAYNE CAREY): There was just so much confusion. Initially, they had Mick Martyn listed as missing. I can't tell you what I felt then. I thought I was going to faint.

We walked through a ward looking for Jason, but he wasn't there, so they pointed us to another ward. Then we ran into an Australian social worker who had been living in Bali for 12 years and she said, 'I know where he is. He's in the operating room.'

They started to lead us into the operating room and I was saying, 'Hey, no, you don't go into an operating room.'

The operating room was actually a sleep-out, a veranda-type thing with louvres.

They pointed straight at Jason, but it took me a couple of seconds to say, 'Yes, that is him.' Initially I didn't really recognise him.

His face was so swollen and he held his hands up in the air — they were dripping serious fluid. As soon as he saw my sister and me, you could just see the excitement in his face. It was like, 'I know you,' because he was surrounded by people that he didn't know.

One of the first questions I asked Jason was, 'Where's Mick?'

He laughed and said, 'Karen, you wouldn't believe it, but in the thick of all of this, Mick's head is burnt.'

I started laughing too — that Mick's head was burnt and that he was OK. I said, 'Well, where is he?'

Jason said Mick was back at the hotel.

Then he started talking about Nerissa and he said, 'I'm getting married in a couple of months. I'm never leaving the country again.'

We talked about so many things. What astounded me was how alert he was. A couple of times I said, 'If you want to rest, I'm here, I'm watching,' but I don't think he could.

I noticed that he had a number written on him. I found that a bit distressing. It was like they were cattle, not people. I wanted to wipe it off. People were coming in and they were just numbering them.

I fanned him to keep him cool but I knew that wasn't the right thing to do. When you fan someone when they've got that many burns, you're taking fluid out of the body. But it was what Jason wanted.

Only one bag of fluid had gone through Jason in the whole five hours, and there was no fluid balance chart, so nobody knew what he was taking in, and nobody knew his output.

At one stage I had to leave him. There was a girl next to him, who later died in Perth, and the girl's veins were closing down. An anaesthetist from Perth actually abused a Balinese doctor, saying, 'If you do that, you'll kill her now.' He was trying to get a line in to the girl's neck to inject fluid into her. At one stage they were losing her and calling her name, because she had fallen unconscious. I had to leave Jason and squeeze fluid into this girl. The space was so confined that whenever the doctor walked up to work on her, he'd accidentally knock Jason's hands. It hurt Jason each time — you could see it on his face.

That really stressed Jason — me leaving him. He was really agitated. When I got back, there was so much relief on his face. I was standing over him, crying my eyes out. My sister was actually standing outside because it was so cramped in there. I looked at her through the window and she said to me, 'Don't look,' meaning don't look at the girl. But you couldn't not look.

There was lots going on, lots of confusion, lots of voices. A lady beside the girl was being operated on while we were there.

Unfortunately, Jason had to listen to all of that. He was very aware of all that. It was absolutely horrific, doctors working on these people right next to him.

At one stage I turned around and looked outside and saw Sharon being led away by uniformed guys with machine guns. Everyone was getting pushed away from the building. The guys with guns were saying, 'My prime minister's coming.' But of course, those of us inside didn't know that. It was pretty scary. The Indonesian Prime Minister, Megawati Sukarnoputri, actually did a press conference just outside the window, less than five metres from us.

BRENDEN MCCARTNEY: I finally got through to the hospital and spoke to a lady called Kay. I'm not sure if she was a nurse or just working at reception. I said, 'I've heard that my brother's there and I just want to know how he is.'

She said, 'He's got severe burns but he's in good spirits and doing fine ... Do you want to talk to him?' I nearly fell over.

She said, 'You might only have a minute or so because the phones are going mad,' but I didn't care — I just wanted to hear his voice.

She put him on and I said, 'How are you going, mate?'

He broke down as he said, 'I'm all right. I just got out. I was on fire. I looked up and the roof fell down. But I've lost Hughesy.'

I said, 'Well, where was Hughesy?'

He said, 'He was further in (Paddy's Bar).'

He broke down again. I thought, 'Oh, jeez.'

I'd never heard Jase like that before. I could tell he was hurt and worried about what was going to happen. I thought, 'This is just getting worse and worse.'

He was crying. He said to me: 'Just find Hughesy for me. Find Hughesy, please.'

I didn't know Hughesy's numbers.

I said to Dad, 'If Jason just got out and the roof fell down and Hughesy was further in, you don't have to be too smart to work out where Hughesy is.'

KAREN CAREY: I got a bit concerned when Jason spoke to his brother on the phone because Jason kept telling him he was fine. 'I'm OK, don't worry.'

I just wanted to get hold of the phone and set his brother straight and say, 'Mate, he's not OK. Be prepared for what you're going to see, because it's certainly not good at all.'

Another emotional tidal wave came crashing down on me when I talked to Brenden. 'If I don't make it,' I thought, 'I might never see my family again.' It was a feeling that consumed me. And I was desperate to tell the people who I cared about the most how I truly felt about them. Although I love my family and we're very close-knit, I hadn't opened up like that very often.

BRENDEN MCCARTNEY: Kay got back on the phone. 'Time's up, Brenden. Ring this number back in two hours.'

I said, 'Just bloody look after my brother for me.'

I rang around to try and find Hughesy. I rang Mick to see if he knew anything. He said, 'No, look ...' and nearly broke down. He said he thought the worst.

I rang Tim Harrington (the Kangaroos football manager) and said, 'He's not good and he's lost Hughesy. He won't leave without him; I know what he's like.'

Tim and I decided that we'd go to Bali, but Tim found out that flights to Bali had been cancelled. But it wasn't long before we found out that the RAAF were going to fly them out.

The doctors said they wanted to make it easier for me to urinate by inserting a catheter — a flexible, hollow tube that helps to drain the bladder. It sounded like something a mechanic would put in a car. A muffler, a carburettor, a catheter — they all sound related. Anyway, aren't catheters for old blokes with prostate problems? In any case, my response left them in no doubt about what I thought about the proposal.

'There's no way known that you're touching me down there!' I roared. 'Leave me alone!'

KAREN CAREY: I said, 'Jase, you've got fluid going into your kidneys. You have to pass urine. You have to do it or a catheter's going in.'

He said, 'Get me the bottle. I'm not having that thing in here.'

He was adamant it was not happening. So he got a bottle and he passed urine straight away.

Despite my strongest protests, the doctors eventually — I don't know exactly when — got their wish and a catheter was inserted. I didn't know much about how catheters worked. I assume that few young blokes would. But I did know that it wasn't a very nice, or natural, thing.

In my naivete, I tried to pull the catheter out, but it wouldn't budge because there was a catch on the end of it that guarded against such acts. I didn't feel much, if any, pain because I was juiced up to my eyeballs on painkilling drugs. Without them, I reckon the pain would have been so all-consuming that Nerissa would have heard my screams. Even now, I cringe and clutch at my groin when I think about it.

After much debate, I convinced the doctor to take the catheter out. I didn't need it; I was functioning just fine. I celebrated by leaning on my side and having a leak into a bottle.

By then I had been assigned a former New Zealand nurse-cum-police officer named Fiona McPhail. She was in the middle of a two-week holiday with her husband Phil and two friends, one of whom was playing in the Rugby Tens tournament. They had been at the Sari Club exactly 24 hours before the blasts and might have been there the following night if Fiona hadn't gone to bed early after catching a cold at the rugby.

Like many other good Samaritans, Fiona, Phil and their friends rushed to the hospital to offer help as soon as they heard about the blast.

Fiona found herself with the (unenviable) job of looking after me. I was so relieved when I first laid eyes on her.

The Balinese nurses were doing a great job, but the language barrier was sometimes a problem. You could waste a lot of energy and become frustrated just trying to understand what they were talking about. After all my trips to Bali I'd picked up the odd Balinese word or phrase, but 99 per cent of it was mumbo-jumbo to me.

It was much more comforting to have someone like Fiona with you who could speak English. I could just relax and concentrate on what was important — my survival. And I could do it stress-free.

Fiona was virtually my carer and not just for an hour or two either. She spent 14 hours by my side. What a selfless person. I didn't find that out until later because I wasn't awake very often. She may as well have been there for 14 days. I don't know whether I'd still be here if it wasn't for her.

FIONA MCPHAIL (VOLUNTEER NURSE FROM NEW ZEALAND): I was asleep at the hotel when I was woken up by a noise similar to when you hear an earthquake coming, but louder. There was then a huge crashing sound; you could feel it too.

I thought we had an intruder in the room and that they had smashed the mirror in the bathroom. Phil said he thought someone was trying to kick the door in because he saw it move. He looked outside and then we heard a lot of movement above us, so we thought it must have been something they did.

We didn't know what it was until family started ringing at about 4 a.m. to see if we were OK. The BBC (TV channel) wasn't connected in our hotel for some reason, so the information we got was from other guests and ex-pats. It was a big shock to find out that a bomb had exploded at the Sari Club.

Phil and I went to an ex-pat's house where we saw on the BBC that Denpasar Hospital was short of medical staff and blood. I used to be a registered nurse, so we both decided to go and help. I had worked as a general surgical nurse for five years — in the United States for 18 months, and then at Lower Hutt Hospital in Wellington — but had been in the police force for the previous eight years.

I collected medical supplies from the International Schools Clinic and then went with Australian consulate staff to the hospital.

What we walked into was pretty mind-blowing. Chaos is the only way to describe it. I'd seen it on TV in other countries, where something awful happens and you have what seems like hundreds of people all crammed in, yelling and just bedlam. Well, we experienced it.

I worked in the Melati ward. The consulate was trying to coordinate all westerners to come to this ward from outlying areas to identify the injured and dead, and to make sure no one got left behind when the evacuations got going.

Conditions in the hospital were absolutely horrific. It was hot — no air-conditioning. There was no security on the door, so you could hardly move, the ward was so packed. When I arrived, there was still little coordination or western staff. A lot of volunteers were turning up. Medical staff like myself and people like my husband and friends, who ended up sitting with the injured to be there for them. Local people who spoke English came to help with translating between the westerners and the Indonesian staff. Then there were the people who were life-savers for me — the ones who took it upon themselves to look after the people who were looking after the people. They made us drink, eat, wiped our brows, etc. because you were so focused you would forget about yourself.

I started working in a small room separate from the main ward. This seemed to be for people who still needed a lot of care and work to be done on them. The smell was awful, as burns victims lose a lot of fluid, so there was this kind of sweet smell. I'd never smelt it before. The floor was sticky and covered in God knows what. I was in jandals (thongs) so it was very unpleasant. The only toilets were the open 'long drop' type — you just pour water in to dilute the waste. Having to go in there to empty bedpans was horrible.

Injuries included fractures, loss of limbs, shrapnel injuries and internal injuries. But the thing that immediately struck me was the number of severely burnt people, ranging from first-degree, less severe to people with 70 per cent, third-degree burns requiring fasciotomies — cutting the skin to stop it splitting.

I had seen burns victims before, but nothing of that scale or severity.

The strange thing I noticed was that while most people had badly burnt faces, their hair was only singed, not burnt off. All the burns victims looked the same — their faces were swollen and eyes swollen shut.

The ward itself held about 80 or 90 beds, most for burns victims. As soon as people were evacuated, the beds were refilled.

Just next to the Melati ward was a courtyard area where they put the bodies from the site — most were unidentifiable because they were so badly burnt.

At one stage I went to the intensive care unit. That was completely different — modern and quite up to date. But, of course, it only had about ten beds.

I had been in the ward for about an hour when Jason arrived in the room. I was working with a doctor in between Jason and a young woman who was critical. Jason had been to theatre to have the excess burnt skin scraped off, but he had no dressings yet.

KAREN CAREY: I really feared for Jason's well-being but I told him a lot of lies to reassure him. I was really concerned because he was in quite a lot of pain. I must say in the whole time that I was there I didn't see a fluid balance chart and I didn't see him have any pain medication whatsoever. He was in a lot of pain while the dressings were being done and I was saying to him, 'Jase, that's a good sign, mate. I know it hurts, but it means that the burns are superficial, which is a good thing. If the burns were deeper, you wouldn't feel it.'

BRENDEN MCCARTNEY: I asked Kay whether he could fly unassisted or needed medical supervision. She said, 'No, he's needs medical supervision.' I thought, 'What exactly is wrong with him? He's saying he's all right but he can't fly unattended. This isn't good.'

Then a lady from the RAAF gave me the rundown on what was going on. She explained that they had to get everyone out because infection was such a problem.

She said, 'Your brother and everyone else will be flown to Darwin and when they all get there they'll be processed and distributed to Brisbane, Perth, Adelaide and Melbourne.'

They were pretty concerned about him. She said, 'He's got to go out on the first flight.'

We decided that Dad and Steven would go to meet him in Darwin.

FIONA MCPHAIL: I began doing Jason's burns' dressings. Conditions were very bad. I was constantly aware that keeping everything sterile for burns victims is paramount. This was impossible in the conditions but you could only do the best you could.

KAREN CAREY: You wouldn't put your dog on the mattress Jason was lying on. It was atrocious. I said at one point, 'Can we get him off these sheets? Someone please find us some sheets to get him on. Something clean.'

FIONA MCPHAIL: The supplies I got from the clinic were invaluable because I had everything I needed at that stage, and for others in the room to use too. The supplies were limited when I first got there. That improved after a while, with supplies coming from the Australian air force.

KAREN CAREY: There were lots of discussions about running out of pain medication. At one stage, there was a discussion about money, because painkillers were already being sold on the black market right outside the hospital. There were people outside selling painkillers. My sister came in at one stage and said, 'Have we got any money?'

FIONA MCPHAIL: Jason was about 50 per cent burnt with what appeared to be second-degree burns. I knew he was badly burnt. I also knew that although a lot of burns victims survive the first days, a lot succumb to infection later on. This was a big worry for me.

Jason was quite uncomfortable on arrival as he had no dressings. It took me about two hours to do his dressings with help from some Indonesian nurses. It was hard going for both of us. I was using betadine, which is very important to clean and sterilise wounds, but it stings, so Jason found this quite hard. Due to the filthy conditions, it really needed to be done.

The beds were low, so my back was killing me. I was dripping with perspiration, but the Indonesian nurses didn't even break a sweat! Things got better slowly as his burns got covered up. I continued monitoring Jason's IV fluids, output, dressing leakage and pain relief. I also kept assisting with other people who came into the room.

It was a very hard room to be in. There were three beds in it, only about a metre apart. No curtains, no privacy, with every man and his dog still wandering through to have a look.

The noise was still incredible — hundreds of voices.

Due to the amount of drugs that had been pumped into my system, the edge was taken off any pain I felt. It also took the edge off my ability to think clearly at times. But without these substances, I would have been screaming and writhing in agony like some of the other poor souls on stretchers around me. That was something to be thankful for. I knew that eventually the pain would come, and perhaps be overwhelming, but for the moment I was happy enough to live in the world of artificial well-being.

Although I didn't realise it at the time, I was, in fact, fighting for my life. The longer I spent in Bali without specialist treatment, the higher the stakes.

But amid the confusion and chaos, I felt honoured to witness and benefit from some selfless acts. Many Australians who weren't seriously hurt or who hadn't even been in the direct vicinity of the blasts were either in there looking for friends or family, or offering their services. Plenty of New Zealanders did the same. They were bending over backwards to help. It was a special thing to see.

Like most Australians, I'd heard and read about the so-called Aussie spirit and how we're supposed to be a resilient and intensely loyal bunch who stick up for each other in times of hardship. Growing up in the country, I'd seen it on a smaller scale. Out there, helping people out is just the done thing. Everyone says g'day to each other and it's a very friendly, caring environment, whereas in the city, sometimes people struggle to help their next-door neighbour. A lot of city people don't even know what their neighbours look like.

They say that spirit, the Anzac spirit, was born on the shores of Gallipoli in World War I. I'm sure some of the sights and sounds in the hospital in Bali would have been similar to that famous battleground.

In my previous experience, when you meet up with other Aussies overseas you tend to stick together and look out for each other. The efforts of those who volunteered their services and went out of their way to help people in need just reinforced in my mind the legend that had been created by Australians at war.

There's something pretty special about the Aussie, the 'old digger', and it came out in a lot of people in times of dire need in Bali. It was heart-warming, faith-restoring stuff.

I needed all the faith I could muster. I could barely speak and was struggling just to stay awake, let alone make any sense. But, as quick as a flash, I replied, 'Well, don't say anything bad about Wayne Carey because they're his sisters.'

I could tell that some of the people coming in knew who I was because they looked at me in a familiar way. One was a bloke who was with the RAAF or the army — one of the armed forces anyway. (You'll have to excuse my occasionally hazy recollection, as I was higher on drugs than Joe Cocker in his prime!) With a mixture of anger, frustration and sympathy in his eyes, the serviceman leant over me and said, 'Mate, I'm going to fly you the hell out of here and then I'm gonna come back and blow the hell out of this place!'

He meant well and thought he'd make me feel better by giving me the 'we'll get these bastards for what they've done' type of talk. I'm sure that's exactly what he wanted to do, but it was misguided. Knee-jerk anger is rarely a good idea. It was the furthest thing from my mind. My number one priority was survival.

Little did I know that my hopes of survival hinged on getting home — pronto. When word swept through the hospital that we were to be evacuated to Darwin I thought, 'Finally, I'm going home.' Nerissa, Dad and my brother Steven had arranged to fly to Darwin to be there when I arrived. I had never been so desperate to see them.

NERISSA: I sat with the girls until Mum and Jason's mum Jan picked me up from Robyn's. They gave Robyn a big hug and said, 'Thank you for looking after her. We're so glad she was with you when she got the news.'

Mum and Jan took me home. They'd been watching the news and they told me a few things but I don't remember exactly what. It was like I was on auto-pilot. I still didn't understand the enormity of it all or the devastation that had taken place. All I cared about was Jason.

Brenden rang and said, 'Look, they're not telling us where they're going to take him; they'll just take him anywhere in Australia to a hospital. But I'm going to try and get you to fly to wherever they take him.'

I really appreciated Brenden's efforts, but it was a bit of a panic too because I just thought, 'No, no, I want him home, not interstate somewhere.'

Then Brenden rang again: 'I've made them promise me that they'll take him to Darwin, nowhere else. That's the first port of call. They're going to take him to Darwin, and you can go there with Dad and Steven.'

I said, 'But don't you want to go?'

He said, 'No, no, it's really important that you go. Jason wants you and Dad there.'

So I said, 'OK.'

It meant so much to me to know that Jason wanted me there. It meant the world to me that he wanted me to be in Darwin when he got there.

When he finally arrived in Australia, I wanted to be the first person he saw, because I wanted to let him know that no matter how bad things were, or how bad they got, I was going to be there. That was really important to me. But then I also thought, 'His family's important too, so if I don't get to see him first and his family does, that's OK.'

KAREN CAREY: Jason was due to fly to Darwin. The first flight was there and the second flight had landed and he was going on the next flight. They'd teamed him up with a nurse, because they'd buddied everyone up. I thought that all the extra people hanging around were going to create more confusion, so we left, confident that Jason was in safe hands.

My understanding was that I would be on the first plane out of Bali. In my mind, it couldn't happen soon enough. I was anxious — what an understatement. I interrogated the nurses — and anyone else in the vicinity for that matter.

'When am I going?' I asked several times.

The answer was always a measured and non-committal, 'Soon. We'll find out soon.'

I was getting more than anxious. Finally an official of some sort came in to break it to me that I had been downgraded and that I would be on the second plane.

I was disappointed.

I wanted to be back in Australia, but I wasn't overly concerned because the flights would only be a couple of hours apart. It wasn't like there was only one plane making return flights. It was just a temporary inconvenience. 'I'll definitely be on the second flight,' I thought.

I wasn't. Then I became really anxious.

7

An anxious wait

The human spirit can be such a beautiful thing, especially in trying circumstances. The hospital must have been revolting, but it didn't seem to matter. We needed help, and help was offered so freely by so many. The way people gave of themselves was overwhelming.

Enter Sydney couple Tim McGill and Zoey Keir — two complete strangers to me at that point. Tim and Zoey were living and working in Singapore. They were in Bali representing a Singaporean team in the inaugural Rugby Tens carnival, which also attracted teams from places like Hong Kong, Jakarta and, of course, Bali. Along with their teammates and another Singaporean team, Tim and Zoey had planned to go to Paddy's Bar or the Sari Club after they ate at the classy Ku de Ta restaurant — one of my favourite eating places on the island. It was a busy night, though, and their meals were late. The delay almost certainly saved some — if not all — of their lives. Eight players from another team were killed in the bombings.

Like the Carey sisters, Tim and Zoey went to the hospital to donate blood and stayed to help out in any way they could. I'm eternally grateful that they did.

I had been frantically searching for positives. I needed something to cling to — not physically, but emotionally. At times, it had been like trying to find a needle in a haystack. I was alive, which considering the circumstances was the biggest plus, but there wasn't much else to be happy about.

At that point, Tim, Zoey and Fiona were my world. I am so grateful that they dared to enter it. I'm sure it would have been easier for them to tip-toe away from a big bloke with severe burns and a worse temper.

Tim and Zoey sat by my stretcher and kept me company. We talked, found out snippets about each other's lives and generally passed the time away. Rarely have I ever been so thankful for simple conversation. I'm sure they didn't realise just how much it meant to me. Even if they did, they're the type of self-effacing people who would blow it off as nothing.

It didn't take long for me to notice an uncanny resemblance, both physically and in terms of personality, between Tim and my Kangaroos captain Anthony Stevens. Stevo is a real man's man, a knockabout bloke who keeps things simple, and he'll be there for his mates through good times and bad. Especially bad times — that's when he's at his irrepressible best. Tim was in the same mould — genuine, sincere, no fuss, straight-down-the-line.

Zoey seemed his perfect match — kind, considerate and, if I may say so, strikingly attractive. Tim was a lucky bloke. But with both of them, along with Fiona, at my side, I felt luckiest of all. Without them, I think I might have broken down. Reality seemed so far away.

ZOEY KEIR (AUSTRALIAN VOLUNTEER HELPER AND PARTNER OF TIM MCGILL): We walked into the Melati ward, where the victims had been treated as much as they could be and were waiting to get on planes. We were told these people didn't have any family or friends with them, so they just needed people to talk to and comfort them.

There was this overwhelming smell. It was burnt flesh.

Off to both the left and the right were just rows of hospital beds and all these bodies lying there. Alive and barely alive people.

I was like a zombie, looking around thinking, 'Oh, my God.' I felt like I was going to vomit. I had to get out of there. I stood outside for about ten minutes. They had people there with food packages and, because the Balinese water's no good, they had little drinks with straws. Someone gave me a drink of water and I just stood there sweating.

Finally I felt OK and I went back in.

I knew one guy's face from Singapore. He was pretty badly burned and I talked to him for a long while. I fanned him and sprayed him with antiseptic spray as well.

There weren't very many staff there and the ones who were there didn't speak English very well and they didn't seem to know what to do.

We started fanning people and giving them drinks of water, and we also used the antiseptic spray.

People needed to go to the toilet, so you had to help them urinate into a container, which you had to hold. The container was disgusting — supposed to be yellow plastic, but the actual tone was different because it had mould on it. And it smelled too. I thought, 'I don't even want to touch it with my hand, let alone put any of my other parts near it.' We were busting to go to the toilet ourselves, but I would rather have gone outside on the ground.

TIM MCGILL (AUSTRALIAN VOLUNTEER HELPER AND PARTNER OF ZOEY KEIR): People were basically packed into this ward like sardines. Most of them were covered up with bandages, so we didn't really see the extent of their injuries, but we could see lots of blisters and black skin.

And then there was a repulsive smell. It hit you right in the face. It smelt like pus and blood.

Zoey got talking to some people so I went into this small room near the entrance. Jason was in there. There was another guy in there with him who was in all sorts of trouble — he'd lost a lot of blood and he had severe internal injuries.

I started talking to Jason. I thought it would be really difficult but he was just so easy to talk to. He was just a really good bloke. It was as though I was just at the pub with a guy and we were just talking about life. It was completely normal and I was so comfortable with the whole thing, which was amazing considering it was a very uncomfortable situation.

There was also a nurse there looking after him. She was great and really did make a lot of difference. I was basically there as a mate.

I gave him water, fanned him and tried to keep him cool.

But he looked horrible. Obviously, I didn't know what he really looked like until I saw a picture of him on the Internet when I got home.

He was busted up. His face was completely swollen and all his eyebrows and hair were singed. His arms and legs were basically all bandaged up and he had a bed sheet covering the rest. His clothes must have been burnt off. He was in pretty bad shape.

But his attitude was terrific. We talked about the blast and I couldn't believe that he didn't know anyone had died. He had no idea about the extent of the situation. He thought that he was one of only a few victims. I didn't know much about the seriousness of it either, so I didn't elaborate. I just told him that there were people missing.

Surprisingly, he was very calm.

He talked about his fiancée a lot. We talked about how they met, about their upcoming wedding, their plans and their honeymoon.

ZOEY KEIR: Tim introduced me to Jason and told me he played AFL for the North Melbourne Kangaroos, which didn't meant much to us because we're big rugby fans. We knew that he must have been a pretty good footballer though.

But it was interesting that he didn't mention much about his football, at least not to me. He was really excited about his wedding and he was adamant it was going ahead. Footy didn't seem to even cross his mind. He didn't say, 'I'll be fine to play' or anything like that. The wedding was the number one thing on his mind and that was the main thing he wanted to talk about.

He seemed really full of life and, by the way he was acting, there didn't seem to be a lot wrong with him. He just wanted to talk. He told us how it all happened. I think he was quite blurred; he couldn't remember a lot. Then he asked me, 'Did anyone die?'

I couldn't believe it. I didn't want to tell him, but I said, 'Yes,' and it went silent. This was about 24 hours after the blasts.

FIONA McPHAIL: Later on, Jason asked me how many were killed. By that time, we had heard the death toll was in excess of 180. That seemed to hit him really hard. But he still stayed quiet and uncomplaining.

ZOEY KEIR: He started saying that he wasn't too bad and, quite honestly, looking at some of the people in there, I didn't think he was that bad. He was burned but he didn't look horrific. He looked very different from what he really looks like. His face was a lot fatter, very puffed and swollen, and it was burnt. But the burns on his face were quite superficial; they weren't severe.

He told us how he'd got his mate Mick to book some Qantas flights and how he was going to get on the flight. We started laughing because, while he didn't seem that bad, we were like, 'Yeah? And how do you plan on doing that?'

He's like, 'No, no, I've got two seats. I'll be all right.'

We were like, 'OK, sure.'

He seemed worse off to us than he did to himself. But there was no reason to think that he could possibly die.

I was exhausted. My brain was tired after analysing all that I had seen; my body was, to put it bluntly, knackered. I could hardly raise a limb. I constantly thought of Nerissa and how she might be feeling. Visions of her filled my head. Although she was thousands of miles away, I could smell her perfume and feel her soft hair. It killed to know that she would be doing it hard, and that I couldn't wrap my arms around her and tell her everything would be OK. Even if she somehow, magically, appeared in front of me, I wouldn't have been able to truthfully reassure her like that, as I didn't know if everything would, in fact, be OK.

ZOEY KEIR: Jason started telling me how he was going to get home and start reorganising his life. He said, 'Well, first thing I'm going to do when I get back is cancel my honeymoon to Thailand.'

He knew the travel agent and he was very worried about whether he was going to get his money back. He wanted to get hold of Nerissa so she could get in touch with the travel agent. It sounds ridiculous when you consider the circumstances, but Jason obviously wasn't himself.

I said, 'Do you want to make a call?'

Did I ever. 'Oh, that'd be great,' I gushed. 'Would you mind?'

'Not at all,' Zoey insisted.

My attitude lifted immediately. It was my link to the outside world, to Nerissa and my family.

I wanted to speak to Nerissa. I couldn't dial the numbers fast enough; in fact, I didn't dial the numbers at all because of the state of my fingers, so Zoey obliged.

ZOEY KEIR: It must've been after midnight Australian time when I called Nerissa. I think Nerissa's mum answered. I told her who I was and that Jason wanted to talk to Nerissa. When Nerissa picked up the phone, she thought it was him, so she was really excited and said, 'Hi, honey.'

I was like, 'Hang on, hang on.' I had to hold the phone near Jason's ear, but I couldn't hold it too close because his ear was all burned. The first thing he said was, 'Hi, honey.'

Their first words to each other were exactly the same thing, so that was really cute.

I was bursting to hear Nerissa's voice again. I told her what was happening — or, more to the point, what wasn't happening — before blurting out that I loved her and how much I was looking forward to seeing her.

TIM MCGILL: He was really strong; he didn't cry or anything. He said, 'I'm OK, I'll be home soon, I can't wait to see you, I love you,' and all that sort of thing. All he wanted to do was see the people that he loved and cared about — that's all that mattered to him. He didn't really talk about himself or his injuries. In fact, he seemed unaware of how serious his condition was. He was worried about everyone else worrying about him. He didn't care about himself; he just wanted to make sure that everyone else was OK.

I was desperate to see Nerissa. Just to look into her eyes and see that exquisite smile. 'I'm gonna marry that girl,' I thought, 'even if it kills me.' That thought was the very thing that kept me sane and, more importantly, alive.

NERISSA: I was so tired that I slept through the phone ringing. My mum answered it and she woke me up and said, 'It's Jason.' I was so excited that I woke up straight away.

I said, 'Hi, honey. Hi, honey.'

He was saying, 'I'm going to Darwin.'

I said, 'OK, good. Brenden's been great. He's organising a flight and I'll be there. I can't wait to see you.'

He said, 'You might need to pack a bag for me because I don't have any clothes.'

I said, 'I'll pack some for you.'

Although we were both very emotional, it was a very exciting conversation, full of anticipation.

Although Brenden had been calling for regular updates, I rang my family as well. They had heard that I missed out on the first two flights and were as disappointed as I was. They were trying to work out when they needed to get to Darwin to meet me. I was sure I'd be on the next flight, the third one.

BRENDEN MCCARTNEY: When I spoke to him, I held the phone out so that Mum and Dad could hear his voice. He said, 'I'm going all right.'

But I could tell in his voice that something wasn't right. It sounded like he was shivering.

I said, 'Sorry, I've tried but I can't find Hughesy.'

He said, 'No, it's all right, I've just been talking to the bloke who's been treating him and he's OK.'

That seemed to lift his spirits a bit.

JAN MCCARTNEY: We got back to Nhill and the house was full. Mum and Dad were there, Ian's mum — all Jason's aunties and uncles had been.

The phone rang and it was Jason on someone's mobile phone. He was still in Bali. He said, 'I'm a bit singed, but I'm all right. I'm one of the lucky ones.'

He was crying. He didn't sound like normal Jason.

When I found out that they were flying Jason out on the Hercules and Mick wouldn't be on it, I was thinking, 'This so-called singe isn't just a singe. It's a lot more serious than that.'

I was trying to prepare the others for what we might confront when he got home. I was saying, 'He's not good.'

The only reason I could then get in the car and drive to Melbourne to be with Nerissa was because I'd heard his voice.

IAN MCCARTNEY: When Jason called, at least we knew where he was. Up until that stage, we didn't have a clue where he was, whether he'd got to the hospital or what. When Brenden had a yarn with him, it settled us down a bit for a while.

ZOEY KEIR: I realised that a lot of people hadn't talked to their families as Jason had, to let them know that they were alive and in hospital. I went and asked in the office whether they had international dialling and whether people could call their families. They didn't. We could only dial within the hospital.

I thought, 'God, this is going to cost me a fortune.'

But I went around to everybody and just said, 'Have you talked to your family? What's the number?'

My mobile phone eventually went flat, so I found someone else's and stuck my SIM card in there.

I can imagine how I'd feel if it was my family worrying about me at home.

When the time came to leave for the airport, much of my anxiety had dissipated. I was completely at ease in Tim and Zoey's company and felt in better physical shape. It's funny how you can ignore many of your aches and pains — even when you've got burns to 50 per cent of your body and other shrapnel wounds — when your emotions are under control and you are surrounded by good people. Basically, in order to recover, you need to relax. I was lucky enough to be able to do just that … for a while.

ZOEY KEIR: I started talking to Fiona, the nurse. I'd said hello to her and she'd given me a fan to use on Jason when he wanted it, but we hadn't really talked to her because she had been so busy.

Jason's legs were all bandaged and stuff was oozing out of them. Fiona drew black circles on his legs with a marker. I thought, 'Isn't that going to get infected?' I asked why she was doing it and she said she was putting circles around the edge of seeping areas, so she could tell how much was seeping. She was taking notes on it.

There weren't any other real medical people in the ward — they were more like assistants — so Jason was very lucky he had her to look after him.

In my improved condition, I started to think less of my welfare and more about other people. I recalled Mick's words from the previous night: 'Jase, don't worry, mate. You're a bit burnt but you don't look too bad. There are people coming in here who haven't got arms and legs. You'll be all right. You'll be all right.'

Some of the other injured people around me seemed anything but 'all right', especially the poor bloke in the room with me. Some moaned in pain. No matter how much you hear that droning, depressing din, I don't think you could ever get used to it. I wished I was immune to it because the moaning was breaking my heart. The worst thing was, there was nothing I could do about it. For starters, I didn't know how to help them. Secondly, I was in no state to offer help. I was consigned to a stretcher, immobile. By then, with my body stiffening and seizing up, it was physically impossible for me to put my feet on the ground, much less walk.

ZOEY KEIR: The guy next to Jason wasn't speaking. He was lying there and there were people around him, like medical people, but I don't really know what they were doing. They weren't dressed like medical people, they weren't his friends, they weren't talking to him; they were just looking — at something.

Then a doctor came in — she wasn't dressed like a doctor — who must have been an Australian doctor on holiday.

A piece of shrapnel had severed the main artery in this guy's arm and he was losing loads and loads of blood. They couldn't even give him anything for the pain because the situation was pretty desperate. But he wasn't in a conscious state anyway.

They gave the guy a blood transfusion in his neck. My natural reaction was to grab his hand because it looked like such a painful thing to go through.

The other two people standing next to him said, 'Do you know Paul?'

They'd obviously been trying to find somebody who knew this guy. All they knew was that his first name was Paul.

I said, 'No,' and I felt really stupid. I thought, 'Why did I push myself in there?' But he just looked like he needed somebody.

I don't know what happened to him. I think he left on the flight that Jase was meant to go on. I wasn't in the room when they took him.

FIONA MCPHAIL: Jodie, the young woman next to us, almost died. We had about eight people furiously working on her trying to bring her back. I remember a young guy standing near her head just yelling over and over, 'Jodie, come back to us! Come on, Jodie!'

It was really hard being in the room during that. They got her back, but I learnt once I got back home that she died on the flight back home.

All I could do was lie there, breathe and talk. It was hard work because being passive just isn't in my nature. I had always been taught to use initiative and be proactive. If there is a problem, fix it; if someone needs help, give it to them. Keep yourself occupied, find something to do. Don't sit idle if you can help it. In these circumstances, I couldn't help it.

However, I tried to put things into perspective. Here I was, not in too much pain, fairly coherent and comfortable, and I was about to be flown back home for treatment. Meanwhile, people were in obvious agony around me. 'Surely they must be worse off than me,' I thought. 'They've already downgraded me twice, so maybe I can wait for the next plane. It's only another couple of hours. Besides, how would I be able to sleep at night knowing that I'd put my own needs before those of people who needed medical attention more urgently than I did?'

That was it. There was nothing else to consider. I gave up my spot on the third flight. It was the right thing to do. I'd stick it out. I desperately wanted to get home to see Nerissa and my family and get treatment to start the recovery process, but I didn't want to do it to the detriment of someone else. I didn't want that on my conscience.

People call that brave, gutsy and heroic; I call it being courteous and using common sense. I'd expect someone else to do the same for me if the roles were reversed.

TIM MCGILL: Jase was really strong about it. He said, 'Look, I'm probably not as bad as him. Let him go instead of me.'

I sort of wasn't happy about that because I knew he was pretty keen to get on the plane. They kept coming in and telling him that he was going to have to miss this one and wait for the next one. He wasn't angry; he was just a bit frustrated. He wanted to get on the plane desperately but in no way was he abusing people or anything. He took it on the chin.

FIONA MCPHAIL: It became a really frustrating time. Every time we heard another flight was due, I would go and hunt down the guy with the 'list' to ensure that Jason would be on it. Each time we were told, 'Yes.' In the meantime, the medical team would do the rounds and prioritise patients. Each time I would have to go back and tell Jason that he was going on the next flight.

He was amazingly stoic and uncomplaining. He did better than me.

By the time the third flight came, I had gone away to hunt down the guy with the list. I was told, 'Yep, he's on this flight.'

I got back to the room and the doctors had been. There was an air force guy in the room who appeared to be in charge of things. I heard them saying that a guy who had arrived in the room earlier was going but Jason wasn't. Well, I pretty much lost it then, out of frustration and exhaustion. I yelled at the major, or whatever rank he was, about Jason not going. Poor guy. I then got it together and said to him and the doctor, 'Is this based on medical reasons?'

They said, 'Yes,' so I couldn't argue with that really. But I felt I had to stick up for Jason because he was lying there quietly putting up with everything. So I went and told Jason the decision.

I saw the air force guy later and apologised, saying, 'I'm sorry. I'm absolutely exhausted and stressed.' He was really good and said, 'No problem, I think we all are.'

I've since learnt that while I was away looking for the list guy, and the doctors did their rounds, Jason had said to them, 'Look, I'll go on the next one. There are people worse off than me.'

What an amazing thing to do, considering how awful it was being there.

So it continued.

People would come into the room where we were, and they would be evacuated out. And Jason would still be there. He asked at one stage to go out into the main ward. I think he was going stir-crazy in that small room. I looked into it for him, but one of the other nurses said the heat and smell and noise was even worse out there and recommended it would be better for him to stay.

ZOEY KEIR: I went off to find out which flight Jason would be on. It was like everybody needed somebody pushing their name forward for them because there were so many people.

The person I was asking was just another me who happened to get the job of writing down everybody's names and when they were going. It wasn't anybody of authority. But I didn't realise that at the time. I just said, 'OK, can you tell me what's happening?'

You couldn't really say anyone was worse than anybody else because everyone in there was in a pretty horrible state and in enormous pain.

I kept running back and forth because nobody really knew what was going on. The order of patients was changing all the time.

It was so disorganised that Tim picked up a clipboard one time to make sure Jason was listed on there and all of a sudden everyone thought he was in charge. I'm not kidding — everyone started asking him for directions: 'Where does this person go? Where does that person go?'

FIONA MCPHAIL: I was pretty much a zombie by then.

At least it was quieter though and not as chaotic. My husband and our friends wanted to return to the resort (Hotel Santika Beach).

I was torn between absolute exhaustion and wanting to see that Jason was safely evacuated. We had arrived by scooter too and it would have been very difficult to get back to the resort by myself, so I decided to go.

I asked Tim and Zoey if they were going to be staying and they said yes, so that eased my mind a bit.

ZOEY KEIR: Fiona was obviously pretty exhausted. She said she really needed to get some rest and she wanted to go, but she was only going to go if we would stay until Jason got on the plane. She wasn't going to leave if we had any intention of leaving ourselves.

I started thinking, 'She's either very concerned because she's been with him so long or something's not quite right.' I wasn't sure which.

There were other people around that were in a really bad way visually and she wasn't attending to them. Maybe she's thought, 'If I try to do 50 things at once, I'm not going to make a difference to anybody. If I focus on one person, I can make a difference.'

Or maybe Jason was in a worse state than I could see.

We told Fiona, 'Yeah, sure, we'll stay.'

She had been filling in a file on Jason and she said, 'Make sure that goes with him on the plane.'

FIONA MCPHAIL: There was also an amazing Australian nurse who lived in Bali. I had been working with her all evening. I handed over to her with the promise she wouldn't leave Jason forgotten in the room.

I said my goodbyes to Jason and we went back to the resort. I don't even know how I held on to Phil on the back of the scooter on the way back.

Even after a shower, you could still smell that smell; it felt horrid. I think I chucked my jandals out.

During the following days, we travelled down the interconnecting alleyways that run between the main streets. You could see how the blasts' waves had travelled down the alleyways, punching in corrugated iron roller doors, blowing off roof tiles and smashing windows as they hit a corner and then carried on.

The actual bombsite was an incredible and awful sight. When you saw the damage, it really hit home how big the bombs must have been. The concrete and stone in Bali is softer than it is at home in New Zealand, so even concrete buildings were destroyed. Because of the humid weather over there, most restaurants and bars are open plan, so they didn't offer much protection from the blasts.

During the daytime, you could not get to the bombsite, but the security at night was lax. We were able to walk right up to the site. We didn't go up to the tent that was covering the crater left by the car bomb but I did see a television camera crew go right up to it. This was on the Tuesday night.

There were a lot of people there, ranging from tourists, survivors and lots of Indonesians in their religious clothing. The security staff were all Indonesian.

It was very moving to see where we had been sitting on the Friday night at the Sari Club. There were huge monuments of flowers and candles. It was good to spend time just sitting there and crying.

We stayed the following week as planned. We decided the last place we wanted to be was at the airport with hundreds of other tourists trying to get out. It was very healing too, because we got to spend a lot of time with other ex-pats who had been through similar experiences, and a lot worse. It was also good to spend time with the local Balinese, who were just as horrified as us. I don't know how many times they apologised to us.

It was very sad to see all westerners disappear over the next week. The following Friday when we went into Kuta for dinner I think we counted 14 westerners, including ourselves, on the way. A dramatic change from the week before.

While we were still in Bali, I read an article in a newspaper about Jason. It said he was in the intensive care unit at the Alfred Hospital in Melbourne and had deteriorated.

It only really hit myself and my husband when we returned home. While it was wonderful seeing our family and our daughter, we had to deal with getting back to our comfortable lives. But the world was a very different place to the one it had been when we left home.

I was now getting really anxious. Not only was the hospital short of blood, but it was also running out of painkilling drugs, oxygen (which was only administered in the gravest cases) and intravenous fluids (which were rationed).

I had to get out of Bali.

ZOEY KEIR: We fed Jason water the whole time. He also had a piece of banana one time and then he lost his chirpiness and started to feel sick. He just needed something. He got more morphine. He seemed to go a bit downhill. He wanted to sleep but he couldn't because he was too uncomfortable. He was like, 'Just hurry up and get me out of here. I've had enough of lying here. I want to go home. I just want to be fixed.' He wasn't chatty any more.

Tim mentioned that I also had the option to catch a flight to Singapore, where some of the injured were being sent for treatment.

TIM MCGILL: They were flying loads of people out. We thought we'd try to get him to Singapore if we couldn't get him to Darwin. We inquired about it but we just kept being told, 'No, we'll get him to Darwin. That's the best option.'

The only guys that were going to Singapore, I think, were the guys who were from Singapore and I think they were flying SOS.

It was just another option.

I considered, then rejected Tim's proposal to fly to Singapore. I've got nothing against the Asian countries but I would just be further away from home. And Nerissa and my family, my support network, wouldn't be there. Then, after receiving treatment, I'd face an even longer flight back to Australia. Darwin was the place to be. It's not that far from Bali — only three hours by plane (five hours in a Hercules).

NERISSA: At about 7 p.m., Brenden rang with some great news. He said, 'I've booked a flight for you to Darwin.'

I was like, 'Oh my God, thank you, thank you, Brenden. That means the world to me. When do I go?'

JAN MCCARTNEY: Ian, Steven and Brendon told Nerissa, 'Take some clothes for him because he might be able to fly home with you.' I was sitting in the background, thinking, 'There's no way that'll happen.' But I didn't say too much because I thought I might be wrong.

I hoped I would be wrong.

NERISSA: I said to Mum and Jan, 'We have to take Jason some clothes; he's going to need clothes.'

So we got the big suitcase out and I packed a week's worth for me and a week's worth for him because Mum and Jan and I were thinking, 'Well, he'll probably stay in that hospital a little while, just 'til he's well enough to come home.' We decided I should take shorts and things. Maybe he'd just need some clothes to lie in bed while he was in the hospital.

I packed all his stuff really happy to know I was going to see him.

BRENDEN MCCARTNEY: I drove Dad and Steven in the truck to Adelaide airport and we arranged for Nerissa to meet them in Darwin. I said to Dad, 'Ring me when you get there and I'll tell you exactly where he is — what ward he's in and everything.'

During the four hours they were on the plane, I rang Darwin to find out where he was. They said, 'No, we're sorry but there's no Mr McCartney here. Have you tried Perth?'

I was getting pretty wild by this stage. I said, 'I was assured by the RAAF people that he was going to Darwin.'

'Well, he's not here, sir. We're still processing them but we're fairly sure he's not here. He may have gone to Brisbane.'

I said, 'Oh Jesus! What sort of a circus is this?'

I regret saying that because they were doing their absolute best. But it was just raw emotion coming out because I couldn't find Jason. It's a shocking feeling when your brother is hurt badly and you don't know where he is.

I rang Perth Hospital and it was the same: 'No McCartney here.'

I didn't realise at the time that the injured people had no passports, no luggage, no wallets, no nothing. Nobody knew who was who, especially when someone was unconscious.

When Dad touched down in Darwin, he rang me and said, 'Where is he?'

I said, 'We don't know if he's even there.'

He said, 'What's going on?'

I said, 'Well, I don't know. I can't find him.'

I teed up an old friend from Jason's schoolboys' footy days to pick up Dad, Steven and Nerissa. He's a prison warden up there and actually knew someone very high up in the hospital.

IAN MCCARTNEY: When we got to Darwin, a mate, Barry Mealey, picked us up — we met him when Jason played in a Victorian schoolboys' footy side up there in 1989. We were going to stay at his place because we didn't know how long Jason was going to be in hospital up there. My mate had already been to the hospital but Jason wasn't there.

He drove us to the hospital and said, 'I'll go and see if I can find Jason.'

We sat there and had a cuppa. No one could tell us what was going on.

NERISSA: We got up early the next morning and went out to Melbourne airport.

We were all so stressed and panicky. We weren't exactly sure of the time but we arrived around the time that Brenden had told us to be there. When we got there, we were confused because we thought it was a domestic flight straight to Darwin, when it was actually an international flight. We were supposed to be there two hours before the flight. One of the ladies working there said, 'You can't go on that flight; they're boarding now.'

The three of us just started crying. This was the last thing we needed.

I said, 'I have to be on that flight! Look, I just have to be on that flight. My fiancé was hurt in Bali and I have to get to Darwin.'

She said, 'OK, look, I'll get you on the next flight,' which was leaving in half an hour. But then she said, 'You can't take your luggage.'

I said, almost through gritted teeth, 'I have to take this luggage; he's got no clothes.'

If I knew what the situation was, I would've just got on the flight without the luggage because Jason wasn't going to need any clothes. But I thought that was something I was doing for him. I felt useful.

The other really upsetting thing was that I was flying on my own without Ian and Steven. It was really hard. Nerve-racking.

When I arrived, I was in for a rude shock. I was obviously very tense about the whole situation and wondering what I'd do next and how I would find Jason. When I got off the plane, I saw a man holding up a sign with what was meant to be my name on it. It was spelt incorrectly but it had the key letters. I thought, 'Great, Ian's organised a direct ride for me.'

I walked over to the guy and he said, 'Nerissa?'

I said, 'Yes,' with a huge sigh of relief.

Then a camera and a microphone came out, and they started asking all these questions. I didn't say anything — I was taken aback and scared. I just stood there and cried. That didn't bother them though — they kept firing questions at me about Jason.

Then Ian came running over, gave me a big hug and said to them, 'Just leave her alone!'

They kept asking, 'How's Jason?'

Ian said, 'Look, we haven't even seen him yet!'

Then Ian whisked me away.

I felt totally invaded. Like I was being attacked. It was totally the wrong thing to do — so insensitive. I had no idea how Jason was; I'd only spoken to him twice.

I thought, 'How dare you?' It felt like I'd been tricked. I was thinking, 'This guy is holding a sign because he doesn't know what I look like, but he looks legit — someone I can lean on at the moment.'

I needed all the support I could get because I felt so helpless. I was amazed by the lengths that some people go to. I just couldn't get over it.

If I had my wits about me, I would've screamed at him, 'You bastard!'

Ian rang the Kangaroos football club and said, 'What they did to her was just disgraceful.'

That was my first experience with the media.

IAN MCCARTNEY: I saw the sign with what was supposed to be 'Nerissa' written on it. I thought, 'There must be someone else flying in with the name Nerissa.'

We were standing back and she was the last one to come through.

When she walked over to this bloke with the sign, I walked straight to her. He was starting to fire questions at her and I said, 'Come on, give us a go. We haven't even seen the poor bugger yet. We just got here.'

We'd been up there on a fishing trip a fortnight before and this guy said he was at one of the footy clinics that Jason took while we were there.

It was no big deal, but it was an eye-opener to see that's how they operate. I called the club to tell them what had happened, just so that we could try and control it somehow.

Di Lloyd (Kangaroos communications manager): I contacted the newspaper to voice our displeasure. It just wasn't on. Ironically, it was actually a newspaper where I had worked four years previously as deputy sports editor for six months. The person who put up the sign was actually one of my former colleagues.

Nerissa: We went straight to the hospital. We had to wait for so long to get to see Jason. They kept saying, 'He hasn't arrived yet, and maybe he's not going to arrive. You might have to go to another hospital.'

Little did we know that Jason had been saying, 'Other people need to go ahead of me.'

During a conversation with Karen Carey a few months later, I was reminded about the constant delays and upheavals in Bali. I asked Karen, 'What time did you leave the hospital?'

'When you left on the first plane,' Karen replied.

I shook my head. 'I didn't leave on the first plane. I actually went on the fourth one, at about six o' clock Monday morning,' I said.

Karen's jaw dropped. 'Oh my god, I didn't know that,' she said.

Karen Carey: I couldn't believe it. Then I understood why he went into such a decline when he got back to Australia — because of the fact he was stuck in such dreadful conditions for such a long time.

I understood the way she felt. She and Sharon had tried to be there for me as much as humanly possible and understandably assumed that I was to be on the first flight. But, due to unforeseen dramas, they had left hours before they might have otherwise. In reality though, they had done more than I could have ever expected.

When it finally was my turn to fly home, I asked, without any sarcasm, 'Are you sure this time? 100 per cent sure?' They assured me that the time I had been waiting for had come. 'Thank God,' I thought. 'I can't stand being here a second longer.'

It had almost been like sitting on the interchange bench in a football match, with the side losing and you're just itching to get into the action and have an impact. I had a keen sense of that frustration and anxiety. Except, in my current scenario, the stakes were much higher and there was no chance of the status quo being improved in the space of a couple of hours.

ZOEY KEIR: When it was time for patients to go on planes, they basically lifted them off their beds and put them on stretchers with wheels. The little Balinese were trying to lift people up and they just couldn't, so we were there trying to help. I'm sure I could've lifted them if I'd wanted to, but you had to be really careful to just touch a bit of the sheet and pull as hard as you could because if they moved, they screamed. It was horrible. They were so burned and hurt, so you were just trying to lift them from one place to the other by the end of their sheet and not hurt them. It was difficult.

When they lifted up the sheet, the gross, spongy mattress underneath would be covered in pus and blood. They would just get another sheet and stick it over the top and then lie somebody else down there. I don't know what else they could've done. I couldn't think of a solution.

I was just thinking about AIDS and other terrible, incurable diseases that these poor people might contract. As if they weren't badly enough off already. It was probably the last thing on their minds but, at the same time, you never ever know who's got what. It's no wonder people got infections, with wounds weeping and seeping through.

We helped to wheel some of the victims down the corridors and onto the plane.

It almost seemed like they kept the more severe patients back — not in the Melati ward, but maybe in this other ward where they were doing the surgery. I mightn't be right in saying that, but it just seemed that a lot of fairly critical people came through for the last plane.

I don't know why Jase seemed to get pushed back in the line. I don't know whether it was because he was in good spirits or because he was in that separate room and they didn't actually see him or forgot he was there, or because we were with him and he was getting attention.

They started bringing a few Balinese people into the ward. They weren't going on the plane. They'd obviously been brought in once all the Australians were evacuated. They were in just as bad a state as the Aussies and they had to stay there ...

Eventually there were about 30 people to get out of there and only six or eight of us to lift them onto the stretchers. Two people would wheel them down to ambulances to get to the plane, then you'd come back for more people. It was a very hurried process to get everybody out of there.

After being wheeled through the hospital's vast network of corridors and verandahs, I was driven to the airport. It was such a relief that something positive was happening. I could see a flicker of light at the end of the tunnel, and I was willing to stick it out until I got there. I really had no other choice.

I was taken to the hangar where the RAAF C130 Hercules planes — which were later involved in the war on Iraq — had been housed in between flights to and from Darwin. It was an awesome feeling. I knew the RAAF would perform its side of the deal with military precision. The force was with us.

I was on a stretcher — the same one that I'd been on for about 30 hours. I didn't know who or what was around me, but I knew I was first in line to board the plane.

ZOEY KEIR: After we'd wheeled Jason and everybody away, we folded and packed away all the stretchers, which was horrible. I basically kicked these things because I didn't want to touch them. After that, the ward was empty. I actually felt empty too. We were so glad they had all gone to get proper treatment, but we were still so pumped because we'd been in this surreal situation. Suddenly there was nothing left to do, when not long before it was so busy. It was 5 a.m. but we weren't ready to go home to bed.

I called Nerissa once Jason had left and I got the answering machine. I just left a message to say he was gone and if she wanted anything, not to hesitate to call me.

It was 6 a.m. and dark — just before sunrise — but it wasn't cold. Just comfortable, temperature-wise anyway. I must have lain there for an hour as they gathered all of the other injured passengers and arranged them in some sort of order.

Although a man-made disaster had put me in this situation, a natural wonder made me forget about it for a few fleeting minutes. I saw the sun rise. It was beautiful. When you see such things, you feel like jumping up and screaming, 'It's great to be alive.' I couldn't jump, but it was, indeed, great to be alive. I couldn't see any of my fellow passengers — after all, I was first in line and could barely move — but I could sense they felt the same way.

LIBBY SWINDEN-MCCONVILL (NURSE, ROYAL AUSTRALIAN AIR FORCE): I'm an AFL supporter, so I certainly did know who Jason McCartney was, but I didn't recognise Jason when I first saw him. Although he was clearly very burnt and suffering from a fair bit of oedema (swelling), he was a very, very selfless person who didn't ask for any attention. He didn't ask for a thing. He didn't want to trouble anybody.

We were giving everyone morphine, but each time I approached him and asked, 'How about some morphine?' he'd say, 'Look after the others. Look after the others.'

We persisted and said, 'No, you're going to have to have it.'

He said, 'Well, if that's what you reckon,' and reluctantly took some morphine. He was a very brave man. He was quiet, and said hardly a word. Although he was conscious and able to talk, he was probably one of the more seriously injured people there. I expected him to be quite ill for some time to come.

If it wasn't for the fact that he was so healthy and so fit, he wouldn't have survived.

I didn't waste any energy on negative thoughts like, 'Why me?' Positive thoughts breed positive results. I tried to channel what little energy I had into positivity, whether it be in words or actions. It wasn't going to serve any purpose to dwell on things and wonder, 'What if?' No matter how much you think about it, you can't jump into a time-machine and stop what took place. Yes, it was unlucky. Yes, it was a terrible thing. But the simple fact is that it happened. You can't do anything about that now. Just deal with it.

I didn't feel unlucky to have been hurt. (OK, maybe just a little.) Truth is, I'd been to Bali a lot;an unusually high number of times. It was my eleventh trip, and I'd spent a week there every time. That's 60 or 70 nights in those bars on previous trips. That's enough to know that it wasn't just pot luck. If it had been my first trip there, I might think differently.

I don't know exactly how many injured people were on the Hercules that I boarded, but we were stacked three high and three deep, so I figured that maybe 30 or 40 made the trip.

Lying on my stretcher on the tarmac, I decided it was 'me time'. I had to focus on myself — relax, take deep breaths. Just chill the hell out. Don't analyse or interpret. Don't think about what's happened or what you think is going to happen. Don't remember anything except good things, like Nerissa and the family. The past and the future don't exist. There is only the present — the now.

8

To Darwin

I was mightily relieved when the RAAF guys – our saviours – started loading us onto a Hercules aircraft.

PETER KENNEDY (FLIGHT SERGEANT, ROYAL AUSTRALIAN AIR FORCE): When we got to Bali, it was pretty devastating. It was like a scene out of M.A.S.H. We tried to remove ourselves from it emotionally, because we knew we had a job to do — get them on board, fly the plane, get them back to medical attention. There was a big fella lying there on a bed. We went to pick him up and I said, 'Jeez, mate, you're a big bastard. You're not a footballer by any chance?' because we'd heard a few footballers had been injured from different teams. I didn't even know who Jason McCartney was — I'm a rugby league supporter.

He said, 'Yeah, mate, I am actually.'

I said, 'Jeez, mate, you've had a big off-season,' making out that he was heavy. So my mate Warrant Officer Graeme Clark and myself put him down and had a bit of a rest.

Jason said, 'What are you doing, fellas?'

'Mate, you're too heavy. We can't bloody carry you. We've got bloody crook backs.'

He said something along the lines of, 'Jeez, that would be my luck. I've been in a bomb blast and now you bloody RAAFies are going to drop me.'

So we turned around and said, 'Fair enough, mate. No worries,' and walked away.

He gave us a look. 'Where are you blokes going?'

We said, 'We're only joking, bud.'

We took him on the plane and had a bit of a laugh. He was in a fair bit of strife, so we used some black Aussie humour. It cheered him up. To us, it probably made it more important that he wasn't trying to ask for special treatment for who he was. He was just another bloke and a decent bloke. We said, 'Let's have a yarn about football, mate,' just to take his mind off the job. He probably doesn't even remember. He was drugged to the eyeballs.

We said to him, 'Don't worry, mate. It's going to be all right. We're taking you back home to your family in Australia. You're going to be in better hands than in this sort of joint.' He just gave us a wink and said, 'Thanks, guys.'

It was only something little, but it meant a lot to him that he knew that he would be in better hands than where he had been.

We left Bali at about 7.30 a.m. It felt like we were travelling in a rocket. It was an awkward five-hour flight to Darwin. I was uncomfortable throughout, mainly because of my injuries, but partly because of my stretcher. We've all slept in a bed that has been uncomfortable in some way — whether it's too hard, too soft or the pillow isn't quite to your liking — but that's nothing when you consider I'm a bit bigger and broader across the shoulders than the average bloke, and I was hanging over the side. It seemed like my stretcher had been made to the dimensions f the smaller, lighter Balinese variety of patient.

The RAAF nurses did their best to ease our discomfort. They dutifully, sincerely, answered our every whim.

When we finally touched down in Darwin, I was so relieved to get there that I would have kissed the tarmac if I was able. But the truth was I could barely kiss my pillow. We were rushed to the emergency area of Royal Darwin Hospital. The doctors and nurses had been under enormous pressure there because that was the first port of call for most of the Australian bomb victims. It seemed like the entire Darwin medical fraternity cast its collective eyes over me — and gave different prognoses. It was daunting. I didn't know exactly how serious my condition was, and I'm sure many of the trained eyes that caught a glimpse of me were nonplussed.

The nurses painstakingly unravelled my bandages, but try as they might to inflict as little suffering as possible, pain was inevitable. The problem was that the bandages had stuck to my skin in certain areas and, along with direct contact with the burns, it stung like hell — virtually all over my body. Never again would I complain about having to rip off a band-aid.

They also wiped off the special cream that had been applied to my burns in Bali. Again, the direct contact with the burns intensified the pain and made it hard for me to ignore. But there was nothing I could do. Absolutely nothing. It was beyond my control. I just had to lie there and cop it. The only small consolation was that it was actually for my own good.

To my surprise, they wrapped me in gladwrap. It was to try and keep me free from infection. Strangely, it made me think of a weird Aussie movie called *Bad Boy Bubby*, whose warped main character became known as the clingwrap killer.

I became impatient. I asked, over and over, 'Where's Dad? Where's Nerissa? They're supposed to meet me here.'

I must have sounded like a broken record, but if I annoyed the nurses they certainly didn't show it. Or, if they did, I didn't notice it. In such a traumatic predicament, it was hard to be tuned in to anything but my own emotions, needs and fears. And I was struggling just to do that, without worrying about making any astute observations about the people around me.

I didn't envy the nurses who tended to me. I don't think they envied me either.

EMMA BLOWES (NURSE, ROYAL DARWIN HOSPITAL): Jason was severely burnt and he was still in shock. But he was talking, and while you wouldn't say his mood was up, he was very brave about everything. He was clearly grateful to be in Australia.

The first thing he said to me was, 'Am I going to be all right to get married?' He was adamant that he wanted to marry Nerissa, which was really nice. Then he said, 'Will she still want to marry me?' I said, 'I'm sure she loves you and she'll marry you in the hospital bed if she has to.' When Nerissa saw him, she told him exactly the same thing.

Then he asked me, 'Do you think I'll be able to play football?' I said, 'I'm not sure, but if you're determined enough, maybe you might play again. We'll just have to wait and see.'

We gave him a lot of pain relief because he had extensive burns and because he was a big guy as well. They were all so brave because they didn't get the pain relief in Bali.

We washed all his burns and gave him clean dressings. In Bali, they must have given him just basic dressings to cover him up.

He was really thirsty and we had a tube in his nose that went down into his stomach. It was coming straight back out, but it made him feel better.

NERISSA: We waited for hours and hours. It was the longest wait in my life. We sat in a cafeteria, which wasn't much of a cafeteria — it was just a cold, empty room. Ian would wander around trying to find Jason, and I'd ring my mum or Jan and keep them up to date.

I felt so empty. I wanted Jason home. I just couldn't accept what was happening.

JAN MCCARTNEY: It was the worst day of my life.

We had a phone call from someone who was looking after him saying that he'd be in Darwin at six o'clock in the morning.

But Ian kept ringing and saying, 'He's not here, he's not here.'

It was horrible.

Then Ian said, 'There's another plane coming in now.'

I said, 'He better be on it. If he's not, I'm going to Bali. I'll go to the airport and get on the first plane. We know he's alive. But you ring me as soon as you find out.'

I was thinking, 'Oh, no, he's got lost, he's been sabotaged or something.' That's the worst thing, the uncertainty.

I remember very little about the ten hours I spent at Royal Darwin Hospital, but I do remember Dad and Nerissa finally finding me. I only have a hazy recollection of our emotional reunion because I was pretty drowsy and bordering on delirious.

EMMA BLOWES: Before Nerissa, Jason's dad and his brother went into the room, I said to them, 'He's extremely burnt and he doesn't look like he did when he left.'

IAN MCCARTNEY: I couldn't even recognise him. We walked into what was supposed to be his room and walked back out. I turned to Nerissa and said, 'He's not in here; not in this room.'

We'd been in a couple of other rooms. The doctor said, 'Who are you looking for?'

I said, 'Jason McCartney.'

He said, 'He's in here — the room you've just come out of.'

I said, 'He's not in that bloody room. He's not there.'

If he'd been in a line-up with no identification, I would have had to stand there for a while to figure out which one was him. The only thing I identified him from was a black toenail — from his footy boots. I looked at one of his big toes and, sure enough, he had a black toenail. Then I thought, 'Jesus Christ, it is him.'

His head was just about as wide as his shoulders. No one had told me what to expect. I never knew that their body swells up like that.

EMMA BLOWES: Jason's father was very shocked by what he saw. But Nerissa was fantastic. She was a tower of strength.

NERISSA: We walked into his room, said hello — actually I can't remember exactly what we said — and gave him a kiss on the forehead. His head was huge, all his hair was singed and he was just black. Even his ears were puffy.

We didn't want to show any emotion in front of Jason, so we walked straight out.

Ian and I were shocked, to say the least. We thought, 'Oh my God, what's happened to him?' We got really scared and started crying in the corridor. We cried flat-out for about 30 seconds. Then I just snapped out of it, like someone had clicked their fingers.

I grabbed Ian and said, 'What have we just done? What the hell are we doing? He needs us. We've got to be there for him. We can't do this to him; we can't leave him alone. We have to get back in there right now.'

I got so angry with myself for walking out. But when you're in shock, scared, and the one you love so much is hurt so badly, you can't think straight until you force yourself to.

I thought to myself, 'We cannot let him feel like he looks bad and we cannot let him feel like this is really serious.' At that stage, he hadn't even seen his own face.

I walked straight back in and just kept talking to Jason, making sure he was all right. We just tried to act as normal as we could so that he would be reassured that, 'Everything will be fine, you're safe now. We're here for you no matter what.'

I wanted him to feel as if everything was under control and that he didn't need to worry about anything. If we acted normal and controlled our emotions, that would keep him calm. The worst thing I could've done would be to stand there and be hysterical in front of him.

I kept thinking, 'I love you so much and I am going to support you through this every step of the way.'

About a month later, and still a few weeks before the wedding, I was sitting with Ian one night and crying when he said to me, 'Nerissa, you're an amazing person. I'll never ever forget what you did in Darwin.'

I said, 'What do you mean?'

He said, 'When we walked in and walked straight back out and we started crying, you just snapped out of it and said that we needed to get our act together.'

I said, 'Did I really do that?'

I had actually forgotten about many moments in Darwin, which upset me.

He said, 'Yeah, bloody oath. I'll never ever forget that. That's one thing I'll always remember.'

Not once did I think of the wedding or any of the possible repercussions. It didn't even enter my mind. All I cared about was Jason, nothing else. I was living moment to moment.

I wanted Jason to feel safe, to feel loved and to know that I would always be there. I didn't want to upset him; I didn't want him to panic or become scared. When someone's in that position, it's not good for them to feel those things while they're trying to cope, survive and fight the battles that they have to fight. I didn't want him to worry about anything.

IAN MCCARTNEY: Nerissa was somehow able to think in a rational way. She was right too.

We went back in and we were all right then. We had a yarn. He talked a bit. He said he was all right. He was in reasonable spirits. But he was all wrapped up and he had his hands in plastic bags and there was skin falling off them.

All I recall about the rest of my stay in Darwin is just lying there: doctors and nurses constantly assessing me; Nerissa, Dad and my youngest brother Steven lending their support and company. (Mum, of course, was with Nerissa's mum at my place, while Brenden was still manning the phones in his role as the McCartney Family's Minister for Information.)

Just having them there lifted my spirits. They didn't have to say or do anything. All they had to do was breathe and be themselves.

IAN MCCARTNEY: I'm a diabetic, and I left my bag with the tablets in it back at my mate's place. I hadn't had any all day. I nearly collapsed.

They took me away, fixed me up and got me going again.

One of the nurses said to me, 'We'll just go for a walk and a look around.'

They took me into one of the wards and it was the worst thing they could have done.

There were half a dozen people in there — victims of the bombings in Bali. They were just blown to pieces. Poor buggers. They were covered in black stuff.

To me, it looked like there was no hope for them. I don't know if any of them did pull through it or not. They were a lot worse than Jason.

One of them had half his face missing; another's legs were gone; another had one leg missing. Even now, sometimes I lie down at night time and before I go to sleep I can see them. I wish to God I'd never seen them.

When Nerissa and I were alone, my wife-to-be jokingly checked out the condition of my you-know-what. Well, maybe half-jokingly. Thankfully, all was well.

I was very vague around that time, and struggled to stay awake. It's little wonder either. I'd had little sleep, I'd been riding an emotional rollercoaster, and I'd been in pain for hours. I think I can be excused for being vague.

In a rare moment of clarity, I became very concerned about the welfare of my mate Hughesy. The last time I'd seen him, he'd handed me an Arak Attack. I could have done with some of that jungle juice right then. Anything to stay numb.

NERISSA: Jason was really worried about Hughesy. He started saying, 'Where's Hughesy? How bad is he hurt?'

Hughesy was the number one person he was worried about. He said to me, 'Can you see if Hughesy's here?'

I went running around the hospital trying to find Hughesy and I found out that he was in intensive care. I asked the nurse outside the intensive care ward, 'Is Peter Hughes in here?'

She said, 'I'm not really sure.'

I said, 'If possible, could you please find out because my fiancé is here as well and he's really badly hurt and worried about him. Just to put his mind at peace.'

She went in and came out and said, 'Yes, he's here, but he's not very well. He's in a serious condition.'

I said to her, 'Can I go in and see him?'

She said, 'No, you can't. Only family can see him.'

I said, 'But he has no family here. If he just sees a face that he knows, it might make him feel safe. Just let me see him for five minutes so I can tell him Jason's OK and that we're here for him.'

She was adamant. 'No, I'm sorry, you can't.'

I argued with her as long and hard as I could but she wouldn't budge. That was really disappointing. But I went back to Jason and said, 'Hughesy's here and he's OK.' I thought this type of feedback was best for Jason because he was in such a bad way that I didn't want him to worry. We later found out that Hughesy was taken to Adelaide.

IAN MCCARTNEY: Jason said, 'Dad, you might as well go home and do that bit of work that's got to be done to the unit because we'll have to sell it. I'm out of my contract and I won't get another one, so I've got no footy.' That was the first real time that football was mentioned and he didn't sound too positive about it.

DI LLOYD: The media in Melbourne inundated us with phone calls asking how Jason and Mick were and when they'd be flying home, but we were busy trying to establish that ourselves, especially in relation to Jason. I knew one of the guys in PR at Darwin hospital and he kept us updated, which was great. We pulled some fantastic moves with Qantas to fly Mick home to Melbourne without anyone knowing.

I'd read that Mick only had superficial burns, but when I saw the look in his eyes — he was quite blank — that's when I realised that they must have been through something more serious than we thought.

Along with other people injured in Bali, I was extremely grateful for the resilient and tireless work of the medical staff at Royal Darwin Hospital. Some of the doctors and nurses worked 35 hours straight. In the best of health, I couldn't stay awake for 35 hours, let alone work for that long saving and prolonging lives. Such efforts were phenomenal.

NERISSA: I kept a close eye on what the doctors and nurses were saying and doing, and tried to assess for myself what Jason's condition was. I felt scared the whole time. And scared for Jason. I watched his eyes and thought, 'What must be going through your mind?' That way, I was better able to understand what to do for him and how to act at certain times.

We were told that he needed a lot of fluid and they were basically prepping him for a move to a specialist burns ward in another city. They re-dressed his wounds and checked the treatment that had been given to him in Bali. There was a lot to take in.

It wasn't long before my condition started to deteriorate. It became apparent that I needed to fly to another city, another state, where my injuries could receive proper treatment.

I remember hearing Nerissa and my family asking, 'Where's he going to go now?'

Adelaide, Melbourne, Brisbane — they were all in the equation. My order of preference was Melbourne, Adelaide, Brisbane. There was talk that my last choice would win out. But, as they say, beggars can't be choosers. I was in no shape to argue.

At least I knew someone in Brisbane. Graeme 'Gubby' Allan, the football manager at Collingwood during my time at the club, now occupied the same position with the Brisbane Lions. I had lived with Gubby and his wife Anne in my first year at Collingwood. Anne had been on the phone to Mum and reassured her. 'Everything will be all right in Brisbane,' she said. 'You'll have a house, a car — you'll be fine.'

But the fact is I just wanted to be home. As much for the peace of mind as for the medical treatment. Mum and Dad were staying at mine and Nerissa's place in Albert Park, with the Alfred Hospital just around the corner. That would have been ideal.

Adelaide would have been OK because I've lived there, I've got a lot of friends there, and Nerissa's parents are from that way too.

It depended on whether they thought I would be able to handle flying to Melbourne or Adelaide. If they didn't think I could, Brisbane would be the best option. If flying at all was going to be a problem, I would have no choice but to stay and take my chances in Darwin

In the end they let me go to Melbourne. I was so glad.

NERISSA: We just wanted him home, so we tried to convince the doctors and nurses that home would be the perfect place for him, because we live not far from the Alfred Hospital. Everything would work well. It would create less stress for Jason because he would worry about his family and about me.

JAN MCCARTNEY: I was screaming down the phone at Ian, 'Get him to bloody Melbourne or Adelaide! It's closer for us!'

NERISSA: We weren't going to leave Darwin until we knew where they were flying him. It was a terrible waiting game. When they said he would be going to Melbourne, five minutes later they took Jason away to put him on the plane. It all happened so quickly. Like a snap of the fingers.

We had to book our flights immediately, which was difficult and stressful because we didn't want to miss a seat on the plane.

EMMA BLOWES: I knew Jason was at risk of deteriorating and because of the conditions in Bali, he was also at risk of contracting infection.

I knew it was going to be a long haul for Jason because he was so extensively burnt.

NERISSA: I wanted to be with Jason every step of the way. I wanted to be in Melbourne before he got there, which I would be because the Hercules was much slower. I just wanted everything to be perfect. I didn't want Jason to be upset in any way because I knew it wouldn't help him.

I never saw him upset or crying when we were in Darwin. He was so controlled. But when you look into someone's eyes, you can read a thousand words. That's something I always did; I would always look at his eyes and I could tell what was going through his mind. I could tell he was worried and scared but was putting on a brave face. I think he did that to help us cope. That's what he's like. He didn't want us to worry about him, so he'd put on this brave, controlled front.

It was really draining physically and mentally. I think we were in Darwin for 24 hours and we didn't sleep at all. I was very emotional, very vague, and wouldn't be able to really hold a conversation with anyone because I just had too many things on my mind. I was so worried about Jason and what was going to happen.

When we got on the plane, I sat down and fell asleep immediately. I woke up and said to Steven, 'Have we taken off yet?' He started laughing and said, 'You've been asleep for half an hour.'

When the plane took off, I didn't even sit back in my seat. I was still leaning forward with my head down because I was so exhausted.

When they gave us breakfast and we both saw it was Cornflakes, we both said, 'Oh great,' because we thought it would be the best breakfast ever. We hadn't eaten for ages, so we were easily pleased.

In as bad a shape as I was, I managed to jack myself up on my skinny stretcher by placing a couple of pillows under my upper-body to make myself more comfortable. It was going to be an eight-hour flight because we were stopping to drop a couple of people off in Adelaide, so comfort was my main priority.

When we were loaded back onto the Hercules, I felt a bit claustrophobic. They wanted to put me on the bottom bunk, where I would have to lie flat, but I wasn't having any of it. I hiked myself up even more with my pillows, so it was like I was lying on a banana lounge.

I got some much-needed sleep on the way to Adelaide. At one point, I woke up and one of the RAAF nurses said, 'We're only an hour out of Adelaide. Hang in there.'

I dozed off again.

After we landed in Adelaide, I awoke to sunlight filtering into the back of the plane, which had been opened so that several patients could be taken to Adelaide Hospital.

A few people have since told me that they think they were on the same flight, and were even right next to me. But I didn't pay much attention to people around me because it was hard enough focusing on myself.

While waiting to resume our flight to Melbourne, I focused on my surroundings. I gained strength from the fact that Adelaide is a very familiar place to me. I lived there for three years, went there a few times as a kid and had friends there. And, of course, we were only an hour away from home.

It was another small positive to latch onto, which, in isolation, doesn't appear much; but if you gather enough small positives, you've got a whole lot of positivity going on.

9

Back home

Finally, we were home. There had been times, especially lying in Sanglah Hospital, when I wasn't sure I'd make it. It was a small but significant step. I thought an ambulance would be waiting at the airport to take me to hospital. I got a surprise when I was loaded onto a helicopter. I was the only patient on it. There wasn't enough room for anyone else anyway.

DI LLOYD: When he was the only one airlifted to hospital, while the others were going in ambulances, I knew there must be a serious problem.

I wasn't expecting to see what I saw. He was covered in plastic — it almost looked like a body bag. I thought, 'Oh, my God,' because I'd heard stories that people had died during flights. But I saw his head move and I thought, 'No, we're OK, he's safe.'

I rang his family and said, 'He's landed. Are you at the hospital? Be careful, there's media everywhere.'

We would obviously get to the hospital much faster by air than by road. It was an indication that every minute counted. Such haste reinforced in my mind just how serious my condition was. I had hoped that airlifting me to hospital was just a precautionary measure but, deep down, I knew this was fair dinkum. I was in trouble, and I was going to need a combination of determination and luck to pull through. Well, handy doses of both of these elements had done the trick so far. I hoped that the trend would continue.

By this stage, I might have been told that I had burns to 50 per cent of my body, which doesn't really mean anything because it's the severity of the burns that are crucial, and I had second-degree burns. But the specifics of my condition certainly hadn't been fully explained to me. Even if they had, I don't think it would have registered with me because of my lack of knowledge about burns.

Flying in the helicopter was an unusual experience. Because of my height, they couldn't lay me across the back seat, so they placed me on an angle with my head in the front seat and my feet dangling across the back.

But I was home, and I had no doubt my family would be with me, by my side, all the way. Relief oozed from every pore.

When we landed on the helipad at the Alfred Hospital, I could barely lift my head because I was under the influence of some strong painkillers. Despite that, I did see the flash of cameras and I knew there were a lot of people there.

DI LLOYD: We'd worked so hard to keep him away from the cameras and get him into hospital without any vision or photographs taken. It was more for Jason and his family's privacy than anything else. But circumstances were against us. He landed on the helipad and there were journos there and they got vision and photos of him. I was pretty emotional because I thought we'd done everything possible to prevent that and I'm not quite sure what more I could have done.

It wasn't until weeks later that I saw the footage of me being wheeled off the helicopter. It was a real eye-opener. My initial reaction was to say, 'Did I look that bad?' I knew the answer: I looked terrible. I fully understood how Nerissa, Dad and Steven didn't recognise me at first in Darwin, and why Nerissa and Dad walked out of the room so fast when they first got to see me. It's not necessarily the burns themselves but the swelling that accompanies the burns that is just so disconcerting.

I've also seen the remarkable footage of Hughesy when he was interviewed by *60 Minutes* in the hospital at Denpasar. He was completely unrecognisable, but no one appeared too concerned about his condition, least of all himself. That says more about the type of person Hughesy is than anything else.

COREY MCKERNAN: I drove Nerissa and Jason's parents to the hospital and there were heaps of media waiting for us. I thought, 'Well, I can use my experience with the media a bit here.' I drove them right up to the door rather than parking out in the street.

Reporters started asking me questions, but what could I say? There was no use asking me. It was a bit of a circus at that stage.

When I got inside the hospital, I was greeted by Nerissa, Mum, Dad, Steven, Nerissa's mum Marleen and my mate Corey McKernan. When you are in unfamiliar surroundings, the familiar faces of loved ones can make it so much more bearable.

Corey had driven them there. Mates like him don't grow on trees.

COREY MCKERNAN: When Jason saw me, he said, 'Bull, how you goin'?' We call each other Bull. He said, 'As usual, Mick missed out; it didn't touch him.' I laughed.

I thought, 'He's not going to be too bad.' He was even asking me about the shoes for the wedding because a really good friend of ours worked at Aquila, the shoe company, so he was thinking ahead about things he had to do.

But I knew things weren't that good because he was on a respirator. And, of course, I couldn't see anything that was underneath all the bandages.

JAN MCCARTNEY: The Kangaroos club doctor, Con Mitropoulos, rang me and spoke to me for about an hour to prepare me for what I might see when I got to the hospital. He said that Jason wouldn't look good, that he'd be twice his normal size with swelling. He came to the hospital to be with us.

They said, 'You can only see him for a minute because we've got to take him to theatre.'

I walked in, put on a brave front and gave Jason a kiss. I got outside and broke down. I said to Dr Con, 'That didn't help.'

He said, 'I didn't think it would, but I had to try.'

The doctors also told me that if my flu got any worse, I wouldn't be able to see Jason. Dr Con put me on some antibiotics and that helped. God, how would I have been if I wasn't allowed to see Jason?

DR CON MITROPOULOS (KANGAROOS CLUB DOCTOR): There were a lot of tears and a lot of phone calls from Jan. She would want to know, 'What does this mean?' I'm sure the doctors really tried to put both case scenarios. He may not survive or he may survive, and if he does, there's no guarantee that he'll play footy. I don't think anybody expected that he'd come back and play any level of sport.

They're a good family, good country boys, his brothers. My role was very much to explain to them what was happening and what it meant and how long it would take.

Given the situation, all the intensive care unit doctors were really busy. It was very difficult to spend time with just one patient when they had several others all at the same time. The normal burns unit had other burns patients as well. So it was a really hectic time. The waiting rooms were full of people and the McCartney family was there 24 hours a day.

The burns unit staff were terrific and knew exactly what they were doing. It was almost predicted that Jason would crash, as far as lungs, kidneys and liver were concerned. Except, at that point he hadn't, and it was surprising to them that he'd done so well.

I didn't get the impression he was that sick. I knew he had a lot of burns, but I also knew he was a tough guy when it comes to putting up with pain.

I don't think Jason's family quite understood the severity of his injuries because, while he didn't look that good, he was awake and speaking to us. The talk at that point was about contracts, and whether the footy club would re-contract him because he was out of contract. I was liaising with the footy club and managers about contracts and what was going to happen, and really the big issue was that he could die.

DR HEATHER CLELAND (PLASTIC SURGEON AND DIRECTOR OF THE ALFRED HOSPITAL'S BURNS WARD): Jason was awake and alert to what was going on, so he was stable in that sense, as most burns patients are early on in their clinical course. It usually takes only a couple of days for things to go rapidly downhill. He had already started to get very full of fluid and swollen from the burns and the resuscitation.

About 50 per cent of his body's surface area was burnt, but a lot of it was not full-thickness — it was more the type of burn you get with a flash-burn rather than when you're actually on fire. And a lot of it was medium- to deep-thickness burns — the old second-degree type of burns. Initially, I thought that a fair bit of him would actually heal on its own without skin grafting. They weren't superficial burns; they were moderate in the overall scheme of things. He had some patches, especially his left arm, that were quite burnt to start with, but some of his burns on his legs were not as deep.

For any burns patient, the prognosis depends on the surface area that's burnt, and also how old the person is and how fit. In a Third World country with no sophisticated intensive care or surgical facilities, probably nobody with more than 60 per cent burns would survive, and you're really struggling over about 40 per cent. In a country like Australia, we would expect that a fit young bloke with 50 per cent burns, like Jason, would survive. Nonetheless, we do expect them to get very ill, and they require an awful lot of attention because if you don't look after them, they do die.

The plan was to assess Jason and the other burns patients and take them up to theatre for a change of dressing, an inspection of wounds, and the commencement of surgical excision of the burn wounds and grafting as soon as possible.

Our really sick patients, like Jason — the ones that need to be on a breathing machine and a ventilator and require specialised caring — are in intensive care.

A blast injury can cause damage to internal organs as well as external damage from shrapnel injuries and burns. From a burns point of view, you get a zone where all of the body's defence mechanisms start to come into play. The body is evolutionally designed to start the process of healing wounds. That's all very well if you've got a small arrow wound or something. If you've got anything more than 30 per cent body surface area burnt, this response just becomes a massive, overwhelming thing that affects all of the other body mechanisms. You get massive fluid loss — it just pours out of the burn wounds — and all of the fluid that's normally in your blood just pours out into your body tissues, where it's not meant to be. That causes swelling.

You become dehydrated and develop shock and renal (kidney) failure. Your lungs start to pack up, your heart doesn't pump as efficiently as it should and your immune system gets knocked for six. Your gut stops working. There's a major derangement of the mechanisms that keep you functioning. Basically, everything starts to go haywire.

In order to keep your blood pressure going and your vital organs defused, we have to keep on giving fluid. But while we're pouring fluid in, it's pouring out, and that goes on for a couple of days. If you lie a burns patient on a plastic sheet, they'll just be pouring fluid — like blister fluid, but there's no blister. There's just litres of the stuff, and they'll be lying in a puddle of their own tissue fluid.

MEL PACQUOLA (NURSE, INTENSIVE CARE UNIT, ALFRED HOSPITAL): I had no idea who Jason was when he first arrived at the hospital but I found out within hours because we started getting a heap of phone calls. There were a lot of cousins who came out of the woodwork — that's if you believe what the callers were saying. When I met his family, I said, 'We've been getting a lot of phone calls from cousins, can I put them through to you?'

They said, 'What cousins? It must be the media.'

I said, 'Why would the media be calling?'

They said, 'He's an AFL footballer.'

He looked quite bad but then he said he had no pain. He kept saying, 'I'm in Melbourne, I'm OK,' and all he wanted to do was see Nerissa and his family. He'd say, 'Can they come in? Can they come in?'

I'd say, 'Well, we've got a few things to do before that.'

It wasn't until we started unwrapping him that we got an idea of the extent of his injuries.

He said his face was sore and I said, 'I'm not surprised, it's pretty badly burnt and it's not covered.' When the wounds are uncovered, they cause much more pain.

But his pain tolerance was very high. He was quite stoic and we knew that when he said, 'It hurt,' it must have hurt really bad.

He was really positive right from the start. He didn't complain about anything.

When the anaesthetic wore off and I awoke, I was in the intensive care ward. I thought I was no longer a critical case. I was tended to by a nurse who looked after three or four patients. That signalled to me that I was on the mend. 'It should all be smooth sailing from here,' I thought. I couldn't have been further from the truth. My condition continued to go downhill. It couldn't afford to slide much further.

While it was apparent that there was major cause for concern, especially if worst-case scenarios were taken into account, the medical staff talked down my condition, which I now appreciate. If I had've known the truth, I might have panicked and become upset, which wouldn't have done anything for my health. In fact, it would have made it worse.

NERISSA: It's devastating when someone you love is in that situation. You're so scared of losing them, it's nearly heartbreaking. But your heart doesn't break. You survive it. You become stronger.

Because you love someone so much, it's like your mind is a computer: you can press the button that keeps you strong and stops you from crying.

The whole time I was just on this one-way street of strength. That was my sole focus. The thing that made me like that was when Jason arrived in Melbourne. He was awake and we were standing next to him, talking to him. I was so tired because I hadn't slept for days and I was really scared. My mum was there and when you have your mum there, that's when you get all soft. I just wanted to hug her. I started to feel weak and began to cry. I did it in front of Jason. I didn't mean to. I was so angry with myself, so I turned away.

Jason said, 'What's wrong? What's wrong?'

I said, 'Nothing.'

Mum said, 'It's OK, Jason, she hasn't slept much. She's trying to be strong.'

Then Jason said to me, 'I need you to be strong for me.'

From that day, especially in the dark days ahead, I just repeated those words in my mind the whole time.

BRENDEN MCCARTNEY: I got to the Alfred Hospital in the truck a few hours after Jason arrived there and we spent most of the day waiting around to see him. Mum, Dad and Steve had all been in to see him when he first arrived. When the time came, I thought, 'I've got to act like my normal self here. I don't want him to see that I'm down in the dumps.'

I walked in and said, 'Hey, how's it all going?'

I was probably a bit too loud really, especially for intensive care.

He said, 'Yeah, I'm all right.'

I nearly burst into tears as soon as he spoke.

They said, 'You'll have to go out now,' because they had to do some more stuff to him.

I said, 'All right, see you in an hour or two.'

As soon as I got out of there, I broke down. I howled. I thought, 'Bloody poor bastard.' But I didn't want to go back out to the waiting room and let my wife and Mum and Steven see that I was crying, so I just spent a bit of time there reading a notice on the notice board. Dad was standing there, about to break down again …

They took us into a room and told us what operations they were going to do. Of course, we didn't understand — or at least I didn't — so I stopped the main doctor and said, 'Look, I'm only a dumb-arsed truck driver, but is it OK if you talk our lingo so we really know what's going on?'

They were good. They got into the nitty-gritty and Con would just stop them and explain to us in a different way and make it a bit easier for us to understand, which helped us immensely.

They were really concerned about a few areas: behind his knee, his forearm, the shrapnel wounds. I thought, 'Bloody hell, he's done well to survive it.'

I thought it would be a hard road back but I wouldn't let myself think that he was going to die or anything. I thought, 'No, not Jason. He'll be right.'

A surprise visitor on that first day — within only a few hours of my arrival in fact — was one of my former coaches at Adelaide, Robert Shaw. A passionate Tasmanian, Shawy played 51 games for Essendon in the 1970s and early 1980s before coaching Fitzroy from 1991–94 and the Crows in my first two years at the club, 1995–96.

He and I hit it off really well, probably because I was a Victorian and he was never really accepted by success-hungry Adelaide fans. They even threw eggs at his house. When one of his former Fitzroy charges, Peter Caven, lobbed at Adelaide in 1996, Shawy, ever the larrikin, would often joke, 'These boys don't know how good they've got it with their state-of-the-art facilities, do they, Cavo? Remember when we were at Fitzroy and we had to train out at Bulleen? We would have killed for what these blokes have got.'

Shawy has been an assistant coach at Essendon since 1999, and, like many people you come across in footy clubs, it's hard keeping up with them when you're no longer at the same club. But that didn't stop Shawy from taking time to visit me at the Alfred.

Shawy had never met Nerissa, but he gave her a nice card and his most heartfelt sentiments. It was a nice touch.

ROBERT SHAW (FORMER ADELAIDE COACH AND NOW AN ASSISTANT COACH AT ESSENDON): We recruited Jason to Adelaide to get some strength of character into the club, which was a real priority at the time. He was a strong player, which was important because we needed a strong centre half-back.

I'm realistic enough to know that I didn't coach real well in Adelaide but people like Jason stand out to me because, under adversity at different times at Adelaide, on or off the field, he stood by me. I just knew that he was with me. Whether he liked the way I coached or he didn't was irrelevant. I was his coach and he gave me due respect. He did anything I asked him to do.

So when he was in hospital, I thought, 'He's stood by me, now what can I do for him?' I knew I had to stand by him as a token of his support for me. I went to the hospital because I appreciated what he'd done for me. It was the least I could do.

Unfortunately, I couldn't see him or speak to him because he was too ill. But I spoke to his fiancée. She was a remarkably strong young woman; remarkably strong. She was very optimistic.

10

Grave fears

I was struggling to breathe. I felt like a pillow had been placed over my face and I was being suffocated. My lungs must have looked like flat footballs. But I didn't let on that I was distressed, afraid even. Breathing is something we all take for granted until, for whatever reason, we find ourselves in such a situation. I fought it as long as I could.

It's that old footballer's mentality, mixed with a country upbringing, of not being a sook or a cry-baby. The never-complain-about-your-health-unless-you're-on-your-deathbed type of attitude. That's admirable, but it's not always the smartest approach. Little did I know that I was virtually on my deathbed. I was to come as close to it as you can get. My breathing was less than 60 per cent capacity. It was 2 a.m. and time to speak up.

I motioned for Nerissa, who was sitting in her usual spot beside my bed, to come closer. With every last breath of air I could muster, I whispered — gasped — in her ear, 'Honey, I'm really struggling to breathe.'

Nerissa looked into my eyes and could tell I was fair dinkum. She called the nurses in. They said, 'You've got to breathe more.'

I must have improved a little because the nurses thought my breathing was OK. They even told Nerissa to go home and get some well-deserved sleep. Poor thing. She was a real trouper, often spending 20 hours a day with me.

Despite being worried about my breathing, my biggest concern was Nerissa. I rose to the occasion to give her a part-lecture, part-plea. 'It's two o'clock in the morning,' I told her. 'Make sure you get security to walk you out to your car. I don't want anything to happen to you. You're too precious to me.'

She kissed me and, reluctantly, left.

NERISSA: He was really weak — he could hardly breathe or talk. I was really scared about leaving him. I kept saying to the nurse, 'Make sure you call if something happens. I don't care what time you call.'

She said, 'I will, I promise.'

My breathing didn't improve. I tried to take deep breaths, in through the nose, out through the mouth — like you're instructed to do when you're exercising. All I could manage were a series of short, shallow breaths.

A nurse suggested a remedy that I saw as a last resort. 'We might need to put the tubes in to help you breathe,' she said.

I shook my head and battled on. But I was fighting a losing battle.

'Time for the tubes?' the nurse asked.

'Yeah, OK,' I conceded.

The nurse allowed me to speak to Nerissa and Mum at home to tell them what was happening.

NERISSA: I'd only been home half an hour to an hour later when the nurse rang and said, 'Nerissa, we've actually decided to intubate Jason because he's not breathing well.'

I didn't realise that it would comatose him.

She put Jason on the phone and that was the most heartbreaking thing. He was talking so softly that I could barely hear him. He said, 'Everything's going to be OK, honey. I love you and I'll see you tomorrow.'

I broke down and thought, 'Oh, he's so bloody strong.' I had a strong intuition he was scared, that's why he was saying that to me.

He obviously didn't understand the extent of what was about to happen to him either.

I thought, 'Well, this won't be too bad. They'll bang a couple of tubes in and everything will be all right.'

I didn't know that the insertion of the tubes would mean I would be placed in a coma. I had absolutely no idea. But the fact was that it was 100 per cent necessary to my survival.

My body needed to rest fully and the only way to do that was to be completely motionless and free of stress. The only way to do that was to put me to sleep for a while in a drug-induced coma.

I can't remember anything after the phone call was made.

A few massive tubes, which were as thick as garden hoses, were inserted: one into each side of my chest to drain fluid from my lungs; the other in my mouth to help me breathe.

JAN MCCARTNEY: When they said they would intubate him, I thought that meant they would put a tube in his neck and he won't be able to talk to us for a little while, but he'd still be conscious and with it.

No one told me or Nerissa that it meant he would go into a coma. All they said was, 'We'll let him ring you before we do it.'

NERISSA: We walked in the next day and that's when they explained that because he was intubated, he had to be comatose.

DR CON MITROPOULOS: I spent most of my time trying to explain to Jason's family that it was not unusual for him to suffer a crash and, in fact, it was surprising he hadn't crashed already, given the trauma he'd been through.

For Nerissa, it brought some bad memories flooding back.

NERISSA: My dad, Ardri, got really sick on Father's Day in 1999. He'd always had problems with blood clots but this time he got really sick and they raced him to Adelaide.

My sister rang me with the news that night and I said, 'I'll go and see him after work tomorrow.'

I remember driving to school the next morning and I rang the hospital to pass on to Dad that I'd be there straight after school. They said, 'Are you a relative?'

I said, 'Yes, I'm his daughter.'

She said, 'Well, I must explain the circumstances to you. He is on a respirator.'

I said, 'Sorry? What?'

When I got to school, I was a mess. The school sent me home, so I went to the hospital. I remember clear as day walking into the ward they told me to go to. I didn't realise it was intensive care, and because it's it was my first experience of the whole intensive-care situation I found it very scary. I walked past this patient and thought, 'Oh, that poor guy,' and kept walking.

Then they said to me, 'This is your father.'

I just collapsed because he was hooked up to machines and he was asleep. I had to be lifted up again and I just ran out of the hospital. So, when they took me back in they apologised because they didn't realise that I hadn't been to an intensive care ward before. They explained everything to me and made me touch his hand because that was really scary, touching him. I didn't want to touch him at all.

Dad was in a coma for two weeks. I sat there every day by his side because I was his only child living in Adelaide. My brothers and sisters lived in Millicent and they came up for as long as they could.

I went through that experience and the rehab with him. He had to learn how to write again and how to walk and talk again because he had a tracheotomy. But he made a full recovery.

When Jason was in intensive care, it brought all those memories back. But I think it helped me be strong, I knew what the machines were doing, I knew what could happen and what couldn't happen. Having that experience with Dad, while you wouldn't wish it on your worst enemy, was a blessing in disguise really.

If I had to go through that with Jason for the first time, I don't think I would've coped as well. Because I'd been through that experience before, I understood the ins and outs of it all. But every situation is different and Jason had burns. It was just as hard and it was just as scary, but I could cope a little better.

Ironically, Dad came over from South Australia to spend a bit of time with me the day that Jason woke from the coma.

ARDRI VANDERHEYDEN (NERISSA'S FATHER, JASON'S FATHER-IN-LAW): I was really worried. I didn't want Nerissa to suffer again. I was there for ten days and helped the nurse undo Jason's bandages every day.

When I was in a coma, I was constantly dreaming. I dreamt about things that might happen in the future. I withdrew to a place deep inside myself. I was tired and I wanted to rest. It was time to do nothing. I was in regrouping mode. But sometimes I could hear certain things — voices and so forth. I was consciously unconscious.

I had an out-of-body experience where I was up in the top corner of the room watching over everyone crying and fussing over me.

I came close to dying four times. On three of those occasions, I saw a really bright light. The last time, I could see everything below me — mountains and hills. Then this really calm voice said, 'Look up higher, everything will be all right.'

The worst thing was that I could hear the nurses saying, 'He's not going to make it.' I felt totally on my own. I accepted that this would be it for me. They turned off the life-support. Then I woke up.

While I was comatose, doctors performed several operations on me. They cut and scraped infected areas and grafted skin from my stomach, back and legs onto my arms and legs. Even now, I shudder just thinking about it. Luckily I was blissfully unaware at the time.

BRENDEN MCCARTNEY: When they were going to do the skin grafts, they said Jason might not have enough good skin to graft onto different areas. I said to the doctor, 'Would mine and Steven's skin be any good to get the job going?'

He said, 'We'd rather not; we'd rather use his own skin.'

We said, 'Well, if it's going to help, we're up for it. We just want to get him better.'

STEVEN MCCARTNEY: The first time I saw Jason while he was in a coma, I was only in there for five minutes because my girlfriend Sheree burst into tears and took off, so I had to chase after her.

JAN MCCARTNEY: One day Corey came in with Nerissa, Marleen and I because he thought we might need a man for the day with Ian and the boys going back to Nhill to do a few things. We were sitting there waiting and finally they said, 'You can go in now.' We weren't prepared for what we saw.

Nerissa said, 'Oh, you go in, Jan. I can wait for a little while.'

Fair dinkum, I went in and I don't think the door shut and I was back out again in tears. Nerissa was saying, 'What's wrong? What's wrong?'

I couldn't tell her. I was distraught. So Nerissa and Corey went racing in and they were clipping my heels coming out too.

NERISSA: That was really hard because that was the first time that they had covered his face. It was as though he was fully mummified. We walked in and I just looked at Corey and he looked at me. All you could see were little gaps for Jason's eyes, mouth and nostrils, where the cords were going in. You could just see his eyelashes because his eyes were closed. There were thick bandages covering his whole head. That really devastated me because I couldn't see Jason at all. I just lost it. I looked at Corey and ran out. I cried and cried and cried. I was hysterical. Cried for ages. Corey broke down as well. The four of us were just sitting there holding one another — hysterical.

That was really scary. It was like Jason wasn't there. It was important to me that there was a part of his skin that I could touch and have that human contact, but to not have that was just heartbreaking. I thought it was just unfair.

JAN MCCARTNEY: After bawling our eyes out on poor Corey's shoulders for about an hour, we pulled ourselves together and the three of us went back in and stood there.

One of the staff explained it to us. I think one lot of staff thought that the other lot had told us what was happening, but no one had. It must have been lost in the crossover of shifts. But they explained that it was part and parcel of Jason's recovery. He had a litre of fluid in one lung and almost a litre in the other.

We resigned ourselves to the fact that, 'Well, this is it for a week.'

People have asked me, 'What's it like to be in a coma?' I wasn't in any pain; I wasn't suffering. It was just like I was in a deep sleep. You might be hooked up to machines and have tubes hanging out of you and be a physical wreck, but you don't feel a thing.

Another common question I get is, 'While you were in a coma, did you hear anything?' At one point, I felt like I was dreaming about Nerissa's sister Rachael running up the corridor outside the room and yelling out, 'Nerissa! Nerissa!' It must have been during one of the periods that my drug dosage was reduced. I might have been coming out of the coma, so I may well have heard something.

NERISSA: There is no evidence that a person in a coma can hear you or feel your presence, but some doctors and nurses believe they can. I spoke to many different nurses who looked after Jason. Some would say, 'Yes, I believe he can hear you and feel you.' Others would say, 'Well, I don't know, but ...'

It certainly can't hurt though. I just thought, 'I don't want him to feel alone. He's probably in his own world in the coma, in that deep sleep, but I just can't leave him.' When you love someone that much, you just can't leave them.

I was always scared that something would go wrong when I wasn't there. I was hoping that he would just open his eyes. I didn't want to miss that. I'd just sit there and hold — well, I couldn't really hold much because he was so bandaged up — but I would hold his arm with the bandages.

JAN MCCARTNEY: We'd just have normal conversations. That's all you could do. We didn't know if he could hear us or not. Ian would say how Leigh Colbert and some of his teammates had been trying to find out how he was going because they were overseas. We'd say things like, 'Nanna and Pa are coming down at the weekend but they won't come and see you until you're better.'

IAN MCCARTNEY: Sometimes I'd swear I saw him move. But the nurses would say, 'He can't hear you.'

But I'd say, 'I don't know about that.'

Brenden was in there one time and he was a bit emotional and he patted Jason on the shoulder I'm sure I saw Jason flinch. He must have had some sort of feeling.

NERISSA: I didn't talk to him a lot for the first few days because it was just too hard and too upsetting. Every time I went to say something to him, I'd cry. I'd just sit there and read a magazine or talk to the nurse.

I asked a lot of questions in the first few days. I asked what each monitor did, what each number meant, what they were doing. I wanted to know every single thing that was happening to him because that helped me cope better too. I could focus on something else and feel like I was in control of what was happening. I kept an eye on everything and when I understood and learned how everything worked, especially the drug that kept him in an induced coma, I would always check the readings of those drugs. I'd be excited if they had been reduced; if they had been increased, I would ask why. I'd walk in, say hi to everyone, walk into his room and check the monitors, his blood pressure, heart rate and so on.

Some of the doctors and nurses were quite amused. But some doctors were annoyed. I nearly had an argument with one doctor.

I was getting to a stage where I just wanted him to wake up — I was pining for it. I felt like I couldn't cope any more. I'd lost my patience. I just wanted to see Jason's eyes. I would always sit there and say, 'Just open your eyes.'

I'd wait for the doctors to come in on their rounds. I'd be given a time but they were never on time because they were so busy.

One day they all came in and the head doctor, the big boss of the intensive care unit, came in with them. Jason's brothers, Brenden and Steven, were in there with me. I said to one of the doctors, 'So, when are you going to wake him up? When are you going to start reducing the drugs?'

He said, 'Look, you have to understand that it's one day at a time.'

I snapped back really angrily, 'Yes, I know it's one day at a time!'

He said, 'This is the best way for him. His body is relaxed so it can fight the bacteria. It can try to heal itself without any other interruptions.'

I was on one side of Jason and he was on the other. I had my head down, with my hair covering my face because I was crying. He leant across, right into me, and said, 'Nerissa, you have to understand it's one day at a time. You have to understand that. That's the most important thing. We can't give you any information past this afternoon because we don't know what will happen. We don't know what will happen this afternoon. We have to wait. It's a momentary thing.'

I lifted my head and yelled at him, 'Fine, I understand!'

He was a bit taken aback when he realised I was crying and shaking. Stephen rubbed my back to calm me down and comfort me. I think I was starting to lose all my coping mechanisms because it was so hard waiting, hoping and trying to be strong hour by hour, day by day. But once again, there'd be that snap of the fingers and I'd say to myself, 'If you want him to survive, this is the best thing for him at the moment.'

I'd realise the facts and then cope better again.

STEVEN MCCARTNEY: I kept thinking, 'Gee, it's good to have him and he's still around,' but there were a few times there when I thought, 'What the hell is happening?' I'd be happy there for five minutes but then I'd get real low again. I was up and down like a yo-yo.

NERISSA: I wouldn't get home until two, three, four o'clock in the morning. I'd just lay in bed. We've got a big black and white photo of the two of us at the end of our bed on our chest of drawers. I'd just stare at that before I went to sleep and just think of him.

I'd get up at 6 o'clock and be there at 7 again. Three or four hours sleep was the most I got each night. It really took its toll at times.

ARDRI VANDERHEYDEN: Nerissa would be there all the time. She wouldn't go home. I'd say, 'Nerissa, I'll stay here with Jason, you go home and get yourself a good night's sleep.'

She'd say, 'No way.' She didn't want to miss anything. She wanted to be there if something happened.

I said, 'You've got to look after yourself if you're going to be there for him.'

If I could choose how I would die, I'd prefer to pass away while in a coma. It almost happened that way.

NERISSA: They had operated on him a few times, but this was one of the biggest operations he'd had. I think they fully grafted his legs. They would say, 'We can't give you an exact time, but this operation will probably go for about two to three hours.'

Well, the operation lasted about six hours. I sat in the waiting room thinking, 'What is going on?' I constantly asked the person at the reception desk to check for us. It became more and more stressful and tense.

We would always meet with the surgeons afterwards. Dr Heather Cleland and the other two burns specialists would explain things to us. Sometimes it would be frustrating because we wouldn't understand what it all meant. They would try to explain as much as they could and we would always ask questions. Then we'd say, 'When can we see him?'

They would say, 'Well, we're just prepping him again now, we're connecting him back up, so you can see him soon.'

Jan and Ian and I went in to see him and Corey turned up as well. The nurse suddenly became really busy. Because I was aware of all the machines, I was thinking, 'That doesn't look good. What's happening?'

The nurse said, 'He's just having a few reactions after the surgery. That happens sometimes.' Then she said, 'I'll call the doctors in.'

The doctors came in, then another doctor came in, and then another doctor came in. They were all talking in their doctor jargon and we were just standing there watching and starting to panic. It got worse and worse because you just think, 'This isn't good.'

Then they said, 'Can you leave the room for a moment? We just need to consult.'

We left. If you've ever been told by about three or four doctors that you have to leave, it's scary. We were thinking, 'What's going on? What's going on?'

COREY MCKERNAN: I thought, 'This is a bit sus, but I'll play it cool.'

NERISSA: As hard as it was, I'd always try to look on the positive side. I said, 'It's all right. They're just making sure he's OK. They're probably just going to maybe give him some more medicine.'

I would always try to grab every positive I could see.

I put on a bit of a front, especially for Jan. I pretended that everything was fine and that I was coping fine with it.

A really nice doctor came out to us. There was myself, Corey, Jan and Ian.

All of the consultation rooms where they take you to tell you bad or important news that no one else is allowed to hear except for the family were full, so the doctor took us into the corridor.

JAN McCARTNEY: It was the night of the shootings at Monash University (in which two students were killed and four students and a staff member were injured). The place was packed.

NERISSA: The doctor said, 'Jason hasn't reacted well to the surgery, his vitals aren't good. I don't know how to say this to you, but we just need to hope. We can all hang on to hope. We've given him every drug we can — he's on the highest level of drugs — and we can't give him anything else.'

We blurted out, 'So, what does that mean?'

The doctor said, 'This is the worst he's ever been. He has to fight it on his own. It's up to Jason to fight now.'

COREY McKERNAN: The crux of the conversation was that if Jason didn't get through the next half-hour, he could die. I didn't want to look at Jan or Ian or Nerissa. The enormity about what could happen, and was about to happen, really hit me. It was no longer, 'Jason's sick,' it was, 'He's either going to be here or he isn't.'

NERISSA: We were petrified. It felt like blood rushed from my head down to my toes in a split second. I thought I was going to either faint or scream. But I just stood there, like I was outside of myself.

I was thinking, 'No way, no way.'

Corey said, 'I'm going.'

I could tell he was in shock. He looked devastated. He walked out straight away.

COREY McKERNAN: I remember the day well for a number of reasons. Earlier that day, another mate of mine lost his wife after a long battle with illness.

I said to Nerissa, 'I'd better go.' Not only did I want to get out of there because I wanted to see my mate who'd lost his wife, but I thought, 'If I stay here, I'm going to lose it.' I didn't want to do it in front of them. As soon as I got out of there and into the hallway, I did lose it. The reality that he could actually die was hard to take.

DR CON MITROPOULOS: He had total body shutdown. That was a dangerous time for him. It really was touch-and-go. I actually didn't think he was going to survive.

NERISSA: Jan just lost it. She started crying and saying, 'I can't lose my son. I can't lose my son.'

JAN McCARTNEY: I lost the plot.

I'd been the one who'd been trying to prepare everyone for the worst. When the doctors told us after they got him to the Alfred that there was an 80 per cent chance that he'd be OK, but there was still a 20 per cent chance that we might lose him, I told the boys, Ian and

Nerissa not to get their hopes up too high, to remember that there was a 20 per cent chance that he might not make it.

Funnily enough, when the time came and the doctor told us that he could die within the next half-hour, I was the one who lost it.

I was crying and shaking. I told the doctor, 'Don't you bloody go home. You're not leaving him.' The poor doctor was supposed to knock off at 7.30 p.m. and this all happened at about 9.30 p.m.

NERISSA: Ian was just sitting there and I was on my knees to Jan, saying, 'We can't give up hope. We have to send him all our positive energy now. He's not going to die. There's no way. I can't imagine it.'

I said to her, 'Don't give up, Jan. Like the doctor said, all we have is hope now. He has to fight now, and we'll fight with him. Jason's strong and he's fit and he'll fight. We can't give up on him. I'm not going to let you give up on him.'

I kept myself sane by thinking and believing that he would make it and he would get through it. I was thinking, 'Come on, Jason. Come on Jason. You can get through this.'

Because Jan had broken down, that gave me something to focus on. I was trying to convince Jan not to let herself think bad thoughts. I never, ever let myself think that he would leave us. Never.

JAN McCARTNEY: The doctor would be talking to us, then he'd run off and came back to us and he'd say, 'Look, it's come up a little bit. He's improving.'

IAN McCARTNEY: I walked down the front of the hospital. One of my nephews was there, so he stayed with Jan.

I walked away thinking, 'No, this won't happen, Jason. It can't happen. Not you.'

NERISSA: It was said later in the media that Jason was given his last rites. That's not true. We never even asked for a priest. My goodness, if that had been the case, I certainly would've been hysterical.

I'm Catholic, so I do say prayers sometimes. I didn't pray a lot, though because I was too focused on staying positive. I didn't rely on prayers too much; I relied on my own belief that he would live.

I also thought, 'How can you fall in love with someone so quickly and be so in sync with one another, and be so happy in your life and everything be so right, and have it end so suddenly?' That made me realise that we've got too much to look forward to. I thought, 'We've only known each other for a year and a half. We fell in love straight away, we're engaged, we're going to get married and have a family. There's too much to look forward to, and there's so much we haven't done together for things to end now.'

BRENDEN MCCARTNEY: The phone rang and Ange answered it. She said, 'It's your dad.'

I said, 'I can't talk to him. This is not going to be good.'

She said, 'Ian, he can't talk to you.'

Dad said, 'You better put him on.'

Dad wasn't himself. He said, 'He's not expected to make it through the night.'

It was about 9 p.m. I said, 'Right, I'll get dressed. I'm coming down.'

Dad said, 'No, stay there. There's nothing you can do apart from hope and pray that everything's going to be all right. Just come down in the morning. Don't overdo it through the night. You'll end up having a bingle yourself. If there's any news, I'll let you know straight away.'

Poor Ange didn't know what to say to me.

TONY 'OOGY' AUSTIN (CLOSE MATE): A mate of mine got a friend, Alan, to paint my new house. He came out and said, 'I just heard that Jason McCartney is critical.' Alan knew that I knew him but he didn't know that we were really good mates. That really sat me down on my bum. I bawled. I thought, 'Jeez, there's a fair chance that I might lose one of my mates.' I'd never lost anyone before. It was the lowest point of my life.

My wife, Tanya, is a paramedic, so she sat me down and went through all the body's reactions to burns and the short-term and long-term effects. She said, 'There's a chance he might not get through this.' You don't want to hear that. But that was the harsh reality of it all.

I had to accept the fact that while Jase is tough and strong, this could be it. The closest person that I've lost was my grandfather, and I said to Pa, 'Come on, I need a bit of a hand here. I can't afford to lose such a good mate.'

More than once, I thought about what I'd say at Jason's funeral. I would have said that he never shied away from giving a kid an autograph, his loyalty to his family and to his friends was unbelievable and he was a giving fella. It didn't matter if you had a hole in the bum of your strides or if you wore a suit, he treated everybody the same. I would have said a lot of things like that, but thankfully I didn't have to.

ARDRI VANDERHEYDEN: Nerissa was really worried and I said, 'There's no way he's gonna go. He'll be all right.' It was a different set of circumstances to mine, but I'd been through a coma and I thought he'd be OK. These days, they can keep you alive in intensive care where years ago I would have died and Jason probably would have too. I was confident that he would survive.

JAN MCCARTNEY: The doctor finally came back to us with the news that we all wanted to hear: 'He's back to normal; he's stable.'

I can't describe how relieved I was.

I said to the doctor, 'OK, you can go home now.'

He introduced us to a doctor who was taking over from him, and I said, 'Is he as good as you?'

I must have said some shocking things to the doctors, but they said they all still liked me.

IAN MCCARTNEY: In the back of my mind I thought, 'Nothing's gonna happen to him because he's such a big, strong bloke,' but a few days later, it did sink in. When the doctor came back and said he'd be right, it was a huge relief.

COREY MCKERNAN: Within about 45 minutes, Nerissa rang me and said, 'He's all right now; he's going to be fine.' To say I was relieved is a massive understatement.

DR CON MITROPOULOS: I don't think they would deny that an unhealthy person who was a smoker or a drinker probably wouldn't have survived. But Jason was an AFL footballer, a thoroughbred, with super-healthy lungs, a great heart, and a super-fit, healthy body. That's what really got him through.

NERISSA: That night, I wrote a letter to Jason. It was my way of talking to him. I needed to put my thoughts down so I could get some sleep.

Well, honey, today had some huge ups and downs. I thought they were going to take the tube out of your mouth … but they changed their minds … It was so disappointing because I was really looking forward to you waking up and opening your eyes! But I understand that all the decisions are for your benefit and a successful recovery.

When you do wake up, I wonder if you ever heard me talking to you?

Sometimes they lighten the sedation and you wake up a little and you move your head and arms. Tonight the nurse asked me if I wanted to put the cream on your face (they put it on every few hours) — so I did! It felt so good doing something for you and it was so nice to just rub your face and have that special contact with you. I loved it!

During the time that Corey came to visit, you had some problems. Your blood pressure dropped suddenly and fast, and the doctors were very worried — I was so scared!

I don't want to lose you Jason, we have so much to look forward to. This is so hard, I need you back here with me. It's hard being strong. My heart hurts, I love you, I believe you will get through this.

BRENDEN MCCARTNEY: I couldn't sleep, so I got up at about two in the morning. I had to drive the truck to Adelaide for work. Driving a truck was probably one of the worst jobs Steven and I could have had during that whole period. There's the isolation, miles and miles of nothing and you're left alone with your thoughts. It wasn't very easy at all.

I hadn't heard anything, and it just got the better of me, so I rang Dad at 5.30 in the morning and said: 'What's going on?'

Dad said, 'He's going all right. He's holding his own. The doctors are happy with everything.'

NERISSA: Sometimes they reduced the drugs that kept him in the coma. They would ask him, 'Jason, can you wiggle your toes?' or 'Jason, can you open an eye? Can you wiggle your fingers? Lift your left arm.'

But he never responded. At one stage, they were worried that maybe there was some type of delay. That was a bit scary.

They said, 'We might have to lighten the drugs and see whether we get a better reaction.'

So they tried again but didn't get a reaction. They said, 'We'll have to do a few tests.'

They took him for a scan of his head just to check that everything was OK. I never believed there would be a problem in that regard.

I would grab even the smallest positive. Even the smallest little comment from the nurses. If he twitched, it would be a massive achievement in my eyes. That would really excite me when times were tough and I was at my lowest ebb.

Our house was full. There was me, my mum, and Jan and Ian staying there sometimes, along with Brenden or Steven. I was sharing my bed with my mum and she said that she would never sleep at night because she was so worried about me; every night I would toss and turn and throw myself around the whole bed. I said, 'Mum, I can't remember doing that.'

She would say, 'My poor little baby. You would throw yourself around every night.'

I couldn't remember my dreams. It was probably best that I didn't. Sometimes I would wake up hot and sweaty. I'd have to have a quick shower and go back to bed again.

I was on a one-way street, being positive. I didn't do much dwelling on things. When I did I would cry a lot. But all you can do is just ride with it. I don't know how I did it though. I just don't know.

Certain songs always seemed to play on the radio when I was on my own and especially driving home at some late hour. I would be hysterical when I drove home from the hospital. I'm lucky I didn't have a car crash. One of those songs was Creed's 'One Last Breath', which talks about a guy who's down to his last breath calling for his lover to stay with him.

JAN McCARTNEY: We told the boys, 'When you go in to see him, touch him and say, "It's Brenden," or, "It's Steven." Make sure you get your mouth near his face. And tell him things like you would normally.'

I remember telling him, 'You're back in Melbourne. The doctors here are just the best, so you don't have to worry about anything. You won't be getting any of that go-go juice they gave you in Bali.'

I don't know what I said half the time. The nurse would come in and say, 'Jason, your mum just told us a joke.'

Nerissa and I were telling jokes one night and I don't know if he heard us but he certainly moved around a bit. I said to Nerissa, 'Don't say anything bad.'

BRENDEN MCCARTNEY: I never thought I'd ever have the courage to walk up to my brother and tell him that I loved him but when he was in the coma, I told him every day. I'd sit there just rubbing his head and telling him he was strong enough to pull through it. I'd talk about footy and what it was going to be like when he got back and played again, the wedding and what was going on at home — anything. I thought, 'He's listening, he's just asleep.' I was hoping like mad that he'd pull through.

STEVEN MCCARTNEY: We'd walk in and say, 'How are you going?' We felt a bit stupid talking to someone that didn't even look like a person. We were sort of talking to nothing.

NERISSA: At one stage, I wasn't allowed into his room because they were tidying it up or something, so I was sitting in the waiting room. It was early and I was by myself.

We received so much mail every day — it was just amazing. A lady came in and said, 'Hi there. Here you go.' She sat another 50 letters and cards on the table in front of me and said, 'Something for you to do.'

I said, 'Thank you.'

I'd sit there and open them one by one and read each of them. Some of the messages were wonderful and really picked me up. Others brought home some truths about what was happening. Sometimes I wouldn't let myself think about the harsh realities; I'd just ride with the situation. It was like I was numb the whole time and that's how I coped. So when I read a letter from someone stating plain as day what had happened, I would fight it because I could just feel all that emotion coming up. I experienced anxiety so many times. I felt pains in my chest. I would just fight it and think, 'That's a lovely card but I'm not going to let it get to me.' The next thing I would know, tears would be dropping onto the card.

Then Jason's cousin, Andrew McCartney, walked in. His brother and his brother's best mate were there because they'd been in a car accident. In my typical way of pretending to be strong, I quickly wiped away the tears and said, in a grunted voice, 'Andrew, get over here and help me open these cards.'

That was another way of coping — acting as though I was strong and tough. So Andrew sat there and read cards with me. He'd say, 'This one's from so-and-so,' and, 'Whoever wrote this is really nice.'

He also said, 'Would you like me to record the addresses so we can reply to them?'

I said, 'Andrew, if you can reply to them for me I would be so grateful.'

Little did I know that there would be so many cards and letters it would be virtually impossible to reply to them all.

JAN McCARTNEY: They didn't have any support for his feet, so we asked them what they would do about them. They came out with a pair of big snow-boot things to keep his feet straight.

It was funny one night when Steven, Nerissa and I were there. A fax came through from Aussie singer Renee Geyer. Steven turned up his nose and said, 'I don't know her music.'

One of the nurses said, 'I'll bring in a CD.'

One of the other nurses had a CD player, so we got the CD going in the room. I think it was one of Renee's hits from the 1980s. It was pretty loud. Jason was in an isolated unit so it didn't matter. Steven was holding onto these big snow boots that were on Jason's feet, dancing with him while he was in a coma.

STEVEN McCARTNEY: Everyone was fairly upset about the whole situation, so it was important to try and keep the spirits up a bit and have a joke.

JAN McCARTNEY: Nerissa and I were sitting by his side one time, telling him how much we loved him and so forth. Then one of the doctors said something like, 'I think he might have done his dash with football.'

With that, Jason's arm shot straight up, as if to say, 'I'll fix you.' Then his arm slowly dropped down by his side again.

Nerissa and I said, 'I suppose that answers the question. Don't you dare say that.'

NERISSA: I thought, 'Bloody typical. Here we are telling him we love him and we're getting no response. The second the word footy gets mentioned, we get a reaction.'

MEL PACQUOLA: I don't know how he heard it. Nerissa and I looked at each other thinking, 'Where did that arm come from?' It goes to show that you don't know what patients can or can't hear when they are in a coma. He doesn't remember it but he must have heard something.

DR CON MITROPOULOS: I said to his dad, 'If he gets through this, he'll play footy.' I was very, very confident that once he got out of this state, he'd come back and play footy. Knowing the kind of guy we were dealing with, I never ever questioned his ability to come back and play footy. He was always going to do it, whether it was three months, six months or twelve months. But that wasn't my concern at that stage — it was whether he'd make it out of intensive care because he was really very, very sick.

DREW PETRIE (YOUNG KANGAROOS TEAMMATE): We were told we weren't allowed to go and see Jason at first, so we felt really helpless. His condition was a pretty tough thing to take.

When I first went down to the club at the end of 2000, Jason was the guy who took me aside and showed me the ropes. When I got named to play my first game in the seniors in 2002, the first guy to congratulate me was Jason, and he gave me a bit of advice about what it was going to be like. I really appreciated that; I looked upon Jason as a role model, so I took it pretty hard.

NERISSA: Jason regained consciousness very slowly. It wasn't a case of bang, he's awake. I would stay as late as I possibly could because I wanted him to see me when he woke up. I was worried that if I wasn't there when he opened his eyes, he would think that I was never there. He would be devastated. But the nurses were always sending me home. I'd always say to the nurse that was looking after him, 'You have to call me if anything happens. I don't care what time it is. You have to call me.'

They'd be like, 'Yes, OK, OK.'

There was a guy that would look after him and he rang me at one stage and said, 'I have lightened the dose of the drugs and he is moving around a bit, but it's still not worth you coming in. He's opened his eyes every now and then but he has no understanding of where he is.'

When he was waking up the next day, I'd keep speaking to him loudly saying, 'Jason, you're in hospital. You're safe.'

I tried to reassure him because when he would wake up, he'd shake his head, try and move his arms. They would say that he was either frustrated or scared or didn't know what was happening. It was really upsetting to see him shake around and try to wake up.

Dear Jason,

My sweetheart, I really don't know how to put things into words. This is so hard, but it is a way for me to cope with not being able to talk to you or simply look into your eyes. I long for these things — and many more — hugs, kisses, to hear your voice and to look into each other's eyes. I miss you, more than you could ever understand.

I sit beside you all day and night and just watch you — it's like I have this huge amount of hope that you'll just open your eyes and smile at me.

I experience so many emotions in one day — every day. I cry, I feel numb, angry, I feel empty and hopeless, even guilty. Sometimes I wonder if you'll wake up and still love me? The pain inside is so bad.

JAN MCCARTNEY: Ian and I were in there when they were trying to bring Jason out of the coma to wake him up. It was really scary. He was shaking and making noises. They'd say, 'Calm down, calm down.'

They'd put him back under and then slowly try to bring him back again.

What we went through, I wouldn't wish on anyone. It's so hard seeing your son, your own flesh and blood, lying there like that. The worst thing is that you can't do anything about it. All you can do is wait.

People say, 'We know what you're going through,' and they mean well, but no one can say that until they've been there. You can't even begin to imagine what it's like.

It took me about six months to get back to being half normal. I couldn't concentrate on anything else. I was like a zombie for at least three months.

I don't think I'll ever get over it completely or have closure on it. Even when he strips off now, I think, 'What have any of them done to deserve that?'

When I finally emerged from the coma, I felt a little drowsy but well rested. I knew I'd been looking at the insides of my eyelids for a while, but I didn't know exactly how long.

I looked at Nerissa — the princess who must have been there all along. She was teary, but glowing.

'Gee, I've had a good sleep. I must have slept for a whole day.'

Nerissa started to cry. 'Try a week.'

I couldn't believe it. A week? I thought Nerissa must have been taking some of the drugs they'd pumped into me.

'Rubbish,' I said. 'What day is it?'

'It's a week after I spoke to you on the phone when they were going to put the tubes in,' she said. 'Remember?'

I did, but only vaguely.

Sure enough, I had lost six days of my life. But I wasn't disappointed. I felt, and still do, like I've got a second chance. Six days was a small pay-off for that chance.

11

Out of danger

Although my life had been on the line, I hadn't felt any pain. It was everyone else who endured the real hardship. They were aware of everything that happened throughout the whole ordeal. They lived it every minute of every hour of every day — and suffered all the way. It must have been soul-destroying. I dealt with a lot of physical pain after the Bali bombings, but Nerissa and my family dealt with an equally crippling amount of emotional pain.

DR CON MITROPOULOS: The concern when Jason came out of his intensive care-initiated coma was that, since his brain had been out of action for a number of weeks, he might end up with some permanent brain damage. He could have a stroke, or one of many sorts of micro-trauma to his brain, or there could be swelling of the brain, which might contribute to subtle problems with his speech or ability to function. You're always worried when you bring someone out of significant long-term anaesthetics like that. Initially, Jason was very slow and slurred his words, and his brain was very uni-lateral — he was just focused on what had happened and nothing else.

Within a week, his brain function, his motivation and his personality were back to normal. Everyone around him was in tears and he was the one cracking all the jokes.

He couldn't even lift an arm up and there'd be kids coming into his room asking for his autograph and he wouldn't have a problem doing it. He'd say, 'Yeah, no worries.' Nothing fazed him.

It took a little while to comprehend the fact that I had been asleep for six days. Like most people, I love my sleep, but no one loves it that much.

Six days had been taken from me that I would never get back. But it had saved my life and revitalised me. Many other people who were in Paddy's Bar or the Sari Club on October 12 did not have that luxury.

Although I hadn't been for a run in the three weeks between the end of the AFL season and the bomb blasts, my fitness level certainly helped me throughout my entire recovery process. Hughesy was a footballer, but hasn't done anything to any high degree of fitness since he retired ten or twelve years ago. He was in a coma for two weeks. Nashy, a bigger, older bloke, was in a coma for three weeks. There must be something in this fitness thing.

One of the people I made a point of calling when I got out of the coma was Corey. I left a message on Corey's mobile phone: 'Mate, I'm all right. I've been asleep for a while, but I'm back!'

I was quite touched when Corey told me that it was one of his greatest moments. I'd also heard through some mutual mates that his eyes had welled up when he had confided in them.

COREY MCKERNAN: I was in a nightclub in Port Douglas. I had a missed call and a message on my mobile phone. It was Nerissa. She said, 'I've got someone here who wants to talk to you,' and then Jason got on the phone. His voice was real weak and it sounded like he had been sapped of all his energy, but it was great just to hear him talking again. Here I was, in the toilets of this dingy nightclub, with tears running down my face, half-laughing, half-crying. I ran out and told everyone around the table, 'He's talking again.' It was a great feeling.

We're all macho footballers — at least, we'd like to think we are — but through this tough time, it hit the sensitive side of people and all of a sudden, it was OK for grown men — tough men — to cry. It had always been OK for blokes to cry; it just wasn't totally accepted. (Footballers usually don't readily admit to being Sensitive New Age Guys.) And when the waterworks did flow, it was done behind closed doors.

TONY AUSTIN: I left a few messages on his phone when I heard he was out of the coma and breathing on his own. I'm a zoo-keeper at Monarto Zoo in Murray Bridge in South Australia — I look after the rhinos — and I was driving to Adelaide to pick up some feed for the rhinos when my mobile rang. The screen said 'Jason McCartney' and the relief that came over me was unbelievable. We only spoke for about 30 seconds because he sounded quite weak — not quite fit enough to play on a half-forward flank or anything like that — but it was just an awesome conversation.

His first words were, 'Oogy Austin, how you goin'?'

I said, 'Bloody hell, how are you, mate?'

He said, 'Oh, getting there.'

I said, 'Mate, you've been to hell and back.'

He said, 'Mate, I've been to hell and back.'

I said, 'Well, you'll have to put the wedding off.'

He said, 'Nah, we'll be right, Oog.'

It was one of the greatest moments of my life, right up there with getting married and becoming a father. After I got off the phone, I bawled for half an hour. It was just my love for a mate coming out, knowing that he was going to be OK after being right on the brink.

Although I was out of danger in a mortal sense, I entered a horrible mind space — the world of nightmares. They tormented me. It seemed that every time I closed my eyes, visions of violence and disorder took hold. In my dreams, I'd be walking along a street and there would be wild gangs attacking each other all around me. Although I had been injured in a violent attack, I had been spared many of the gruesome sights that others like Mick and Febes had seen. While I was lying on the stretcher in hospital in Denpasar, I could see that there had been terrible carnage. I assume that my mind was taking a wild guess at what must have been going on around me in the smoke and darkness of Paddy's Bar, and across the road at the Sari Club.

The nightmares were definitely a side-effect of the drugs that had been pumped into me for an extended period of time. They had achieved their primary aim of numbing my pain, but they had also created havoc in my brain.

Whatever the cause of the nightmares, I wanted a cure. I knew, though, that I would just have to ride it out until the drugs were slowly flushed out of my system.

It got to the stage where the dreams became so upsetting that, despite my tiredness, lethargy and crying need for rest, I tried to stay awake. I felt like one of the characters in Nightmare on Elm Street who were scared of falling asleep because Freddy Krueger would terrorise them in their dreams. I too was afraid of dreaming. For the first time in my life, I craved insomnia.

NERISSA: He had been given the drugs for so long that they set in his system. They had to give him a lot because he's such a big guy. Then they started saying, 'When the drugs start to wear off, it's going to take quite a while for him to come back to normal because they're well into his system.'

They were right. It was a hard time — really scary. When he'd wake up he'd react strangely — he just wasn't Jase.

While he was in a coma, the nurses had always said to me, 'Go home now and get some sleep. You need to sleep as much as you can now because this isn't the tough time. The tough time is when he wakes up. He's going to need all your strength when he wakes up.'

I always thought to myself, 'No way. That's going to be great, that's going to be easy.' But in hindsight, they were right. It was just as hard, if not harder when he was awake because the emotions were so much stronger. He was awake, he was showing his emotions and his frustrations and I had that to cope with as well as trying to stay positive and be there for him.

Dear Jason,

I know you'll pull through this, you're amazing. I am so proud of the person you are, and what you are capable of doing, and what you have done!

Your strength, courage, love and optimism are just some of the true qualities that make you the extra special person you are — I love that person so much. I love you, honey — and I am so glad you are here!

I found comfort in holding Nerissa's hand at night. Apparently, she wasn't meant to but she'd sleep in a big fold-out chair next to me. Just knowing she was there and that I could feel her hand was an enormous comfort. I'm not ashamed to admit that, at times, I was basically reduced to the mental state of a little boy. I was shy, uncertain, frightened of the dark and in desperate and constant need of reassurance.

NERISSA: The nurses would bring in this massive old movable chair that folded down into a bed. They'd put sheets on it and I'd lie there right next to Jason's bed because he just wanted to hold my hand as he went to sleep. There were times when I was really uncomfortable. I'd have my arm on his bed and he'd be holding onto it and when I'd fall asleep, my hand would lose its grip and fall back on me. When that happened, Jason would wake up and scream my name: 'Nerissa! Nerissa!'

I'd say, 'Yeah, I'm here; I'm sorry, I'm sorry.'

I tried to stay awake all night so that my arm wouldn't fall away because he was the one who needed sleep and I didn't want to deprive him of it.

He would also need things in the middle of the night, or get frustrated, or need to go to the toilet, so I never really slept because I wanted to be able to act immediately when he needed me.

Sometimes, I'd be half-asleep and would hear Jason calling my name. He'd have to call it maybe eight times before I'd realise that he needed me. I felt so bad. I wanted to be there at a click of the fingers every time he needed me.

At one stage, if I'd leave the room to get something to eat, he'd want the nurses to go with me. There was one time there when he didn't want me to leave the room at all because he was scared that someone would hurt me.

Despite my frail mental, and physical, state, I wasn't past being funny — however unintentional the humour.

NERISSA: Two nurses were talking at the end of Jason's bed when Jason yelled, 'Mods!'

I'm like, 'What?'

He kept yelling out, 'Mods! Mods! Mods!'

I asked, 'Who's Mods?'

He said, 'Tony Modra,' who used to play with at the Crows.

I replied, 'No, he's not here.'

He said, 'Yeah, he is. There, at the end of the bed. Just there.'

'No, it's not him,' I said.

He said to me, 'Just get him for me, would you?'

I said, 'It's not him.'

'Just get Mods for me.'

He was getting louder and louder, so I went up to the male nurse that Jason was talking about and I said, 'Can you just turn around, please?'

He turns round and Jason said, 'Oh, oh, who are you?'

The nurse replied, 'G'day, mate, my name's Simon. I'm going to be your nurse for the next 12 hours.'

Jason asked me once, 'Have I got a new face?' or 'Is my face all right?'

'Yeah, your face looks fine,' I assured him.

He said, 'Are you sure?'

'Yeah.'

'I don't know whether it was real or whether I was dreaming but they did an operation to replace my face.'

I said, 'No, sweetheart, your face is fine. They haven't touched your face.'

'Must've been a dream then. I dreamt that Mods heard my face was burnt so he came in and donated his face. And now I've got his face.'

I just said, 'No, Jase, you're fine. I can get you a mirror if you want.'

'No, no, no, it's all right,' he said.

I started to giggle inside but when I realised he was serious, I thought, 'Oh, my sweetie, he must be so confused.'

I wasn't joking. I truly believed that Tony Modra, one of the game's glamour full-forwards, had generously agreed to undertake an operation that sounded like a scene from the movie *Face Off*, starring John Travolta and Nicholas Cage.

I wish! Unless you're Tom Cruise or Hawthorn captain Shane Crawford, any bloke would be happy to trade in their face in for Mods's.

It could've been worse — I could've dreamt that Mick had offered to donate his mug!

But I was determined not to have any more operations — full stop.

BRENDEN MCCARTNEY: Before they operated on Jase, Dad had to sign forms. After he'd had three or four operations, Jason put his hand on Dad's hand and said, 'Don't sign any more of those forms for a while.' He'd had enough.

The drugs were so potent that even helium balloons — the type that bounce along the ceiling — caused me problems. Sentiments like 'Get Well Soon' were emblazoned across them, but they may as well have said 'Get Lost' for all the good they did me. I had to get Nerissa to take them all down because they gave me nightmares. They would move, albeit ever so slightly, in the dark and I thought there were strange people in the room. I was hallucinating. But there was no psychedelic sixties fun in it for me. I was on a trip ... to the dark side. I hope you never have to experience it.

NERISSA: He had balloons in the room because we put up as much as we could to make it a bright and happy place. The nurses would say, 'No, Jason, this is a balloon. It's OK, see, I'm touching it.'

But he wouldn't have any of that.

He still couldn't cope with them being in the room, so we had to put them outside.

Without doubt the saddest reflection of my state of mind — which by this stage could almost have been diagnosed as a drug-induced psychosis — was my reaction to a photograph on the wall in front of me. I 'saw' and 'heard' the two people in the photo talking to each other, pointing, laughing and joking at my plight. Like real smug bastards. I already felt terrible. I didn't need my nose rubbed in it. I wanted them out of there.

I turned to Nerissa, shaking with a mixture of fear, anger and paranoia. 'Stab it!' I screamed.

As it turned out, it was a photo of Nerissa and me that was taken at a party a couple of months earlier.

NERISSA: I had put pictures up of family, and I'd blown up a picture of myself and Jason and put it at the end of his bed on the wall — about 3 or 4 metres away from him. I put it there so he could see it because he couldn't turn his head to the side very well.

He started looking at it saying, 'Who's up there? Who are those people? They're laughing at me. They're making jokes and they're saying things.'

I said, 'Who? Where? What are you talking about?'

He said, 'There they are! Look! They're saying they're going to get me! You've got to get rid of them! Get them out of here!'

I repeatedly asked him, 'Who? What? I don't know what you're going on about.'

He said, 'There! Those two people! Look! Look!'

When I realised it was our photo that he was directing his anger towards, I was so upset, but I didn't show it at the time.

'Get 'em down! I want to kill 'em! I want to stab 'em! Stab 'em! Stab 'em!'

I might only be 11 months older than my brother Brenden but I've always towered over him *(above)*. I must get my height from my grandfather, Mum's dad, Vic Deckert, who was about 188 centimetres tall – before he shrunk! While I used to give Brenden a ride on the back of my tricycle *(right, top)*, he learned how to drive before I did. He used to annoy me because he's always been good with his hands and I've always been useless. He'd be making things, while I'd have a football or a cricket bat in my hands, or a mongrel pup produced by one of the family dogs, our labrador, Cindy *(right, middle)*. Although I grew up as an Essendon supporter, I wore the Kangaroos' colours at an early age *(right)*.

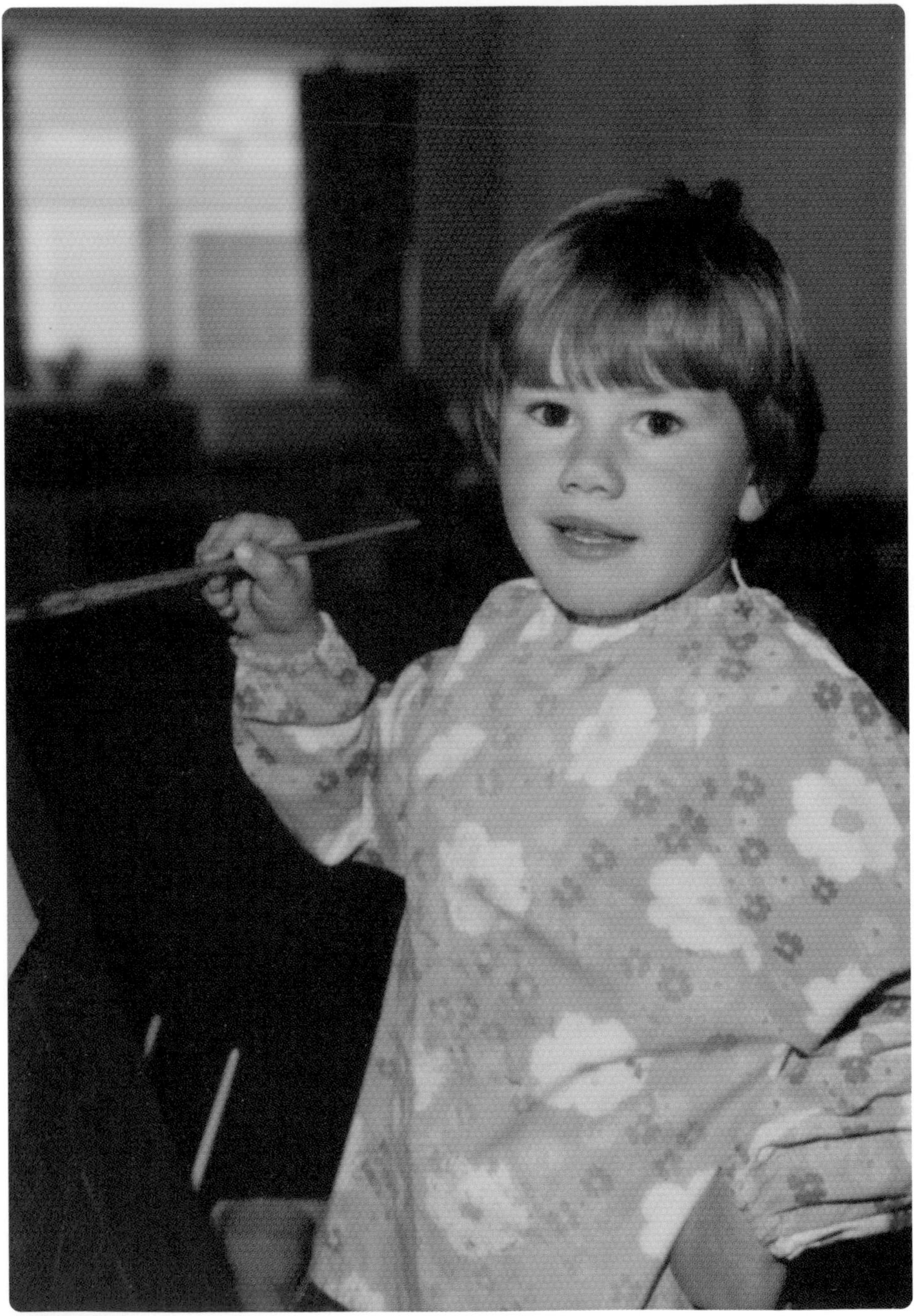

This is a treasured photo for the simple fact that it was the last time I attempted anything artistic. The floral art smock is a pretty ordinary fashion statement.

A triumphant day. All three McCartney brothers – Brenden *(back row, far right)*, Steven *(front row, third from right]* and me *(back row, middle)* – and a cousin, Michael McCartney *(directly on my left)*, pose for a happy snap before helping Nhill win the under-14 premiership in 1987. We played two 10-minute halves at half-time of the senior game and won by about 15 points. I kicked two goals, but the happiest person was Dad, who coached the side.

One of many backyard Test matches. Brenden *(out of picture)* bowls a short one that I nudge uppishly past Steven at short-leg, while Dad, complete in flannelette tank-top, stubby shorts and Blundstones, does his best impression of former Australian wicketkeeper Rod Marsh.

The Australian Under-15 Schoolboys' Carnival in Hobart, Tasmania, 1988. I'd never been on a plane before and was more anxious about that than playing. But all went well and I made the All-Australian side after kicking five goals against South Australia and six against Western Australia *(left)* in the last game. Among my Victorian teammates were others who made it to senior AFL ranks: Anthony Koutoufides *(third row, far left, who went to Carlton)*, Matthew Croft *(third row, second from left, Western Bulldogs)* and Anthony Banik *(back row, second from right, Richmond)*. I'm in the second back row, second from right.

A Sunkick final at Melbourne's Waverley Park before the qualifying final replay between Collingwood and West Coast in 1990. I'm wearing the big W of the Wimmera League. Shane Watson, who would become a teammate of mine at Collingwood, is on my right. I roosted a torpedo 50-odd metres but miskicked my other attempts. The bloke on the far right looks a lot more nervous than the rest of us.

This was among a series of photos taken for a story by Rohan Connolly of *The Age* in the lead-up to the 1990 National AFL Draft. Love the hair.

All-Australian, 1990, *(back row, fourth from right)*, this time at AFL under-17 championship level, with coach Denis Pagan, a man who would later have a huge influence on not only my football, but my life during my years at the Kangaroos. His assistant coach, sitting direcetly to his right, was Graeme Gellie, who coached at St Kilda. My teammates included Anthony Koutoufides again *(back row, second from left)*, Glen Jakovich *(directly on my right)*, who became a champion at the West Coast Eagles, Gavin Wanganeen *(front row, third from right)*, a Brownlow Medallist at Essendon and a great at Port Adelaide, Paul Williams *(middle row, second from right)*, a star at Collingwood and Sydney, Duncan Kellaway *(middle row, far left)*, Richmond stalwart, Darryl White *(back row, far right)*, a triple premiership player with Brisbane, Mitchell White *(middle row, third from left)*, a premiership player with West Coast Eagles, who finished his career at Geelong, and Julian Burton *(middle row, fourth from left)*, who suffered burns to 20 per cent of his body in the Bali bombings.

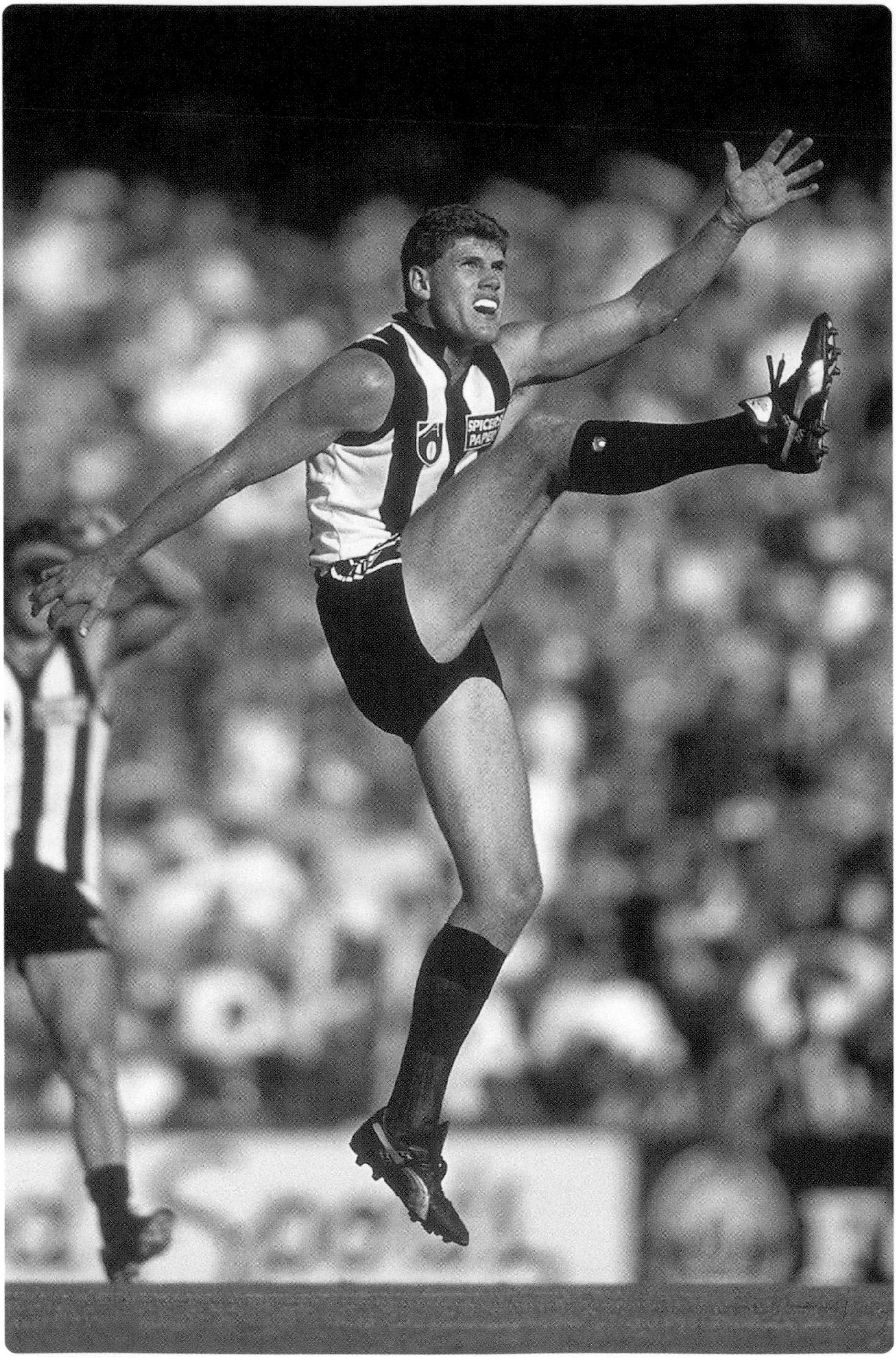

An afternoon to remember. We were in strife at the last change against Fitzroy at Victoria Park in 1994 when coach Leigh Matthews swung me from centre half-back to centre half-forward in the last quarter. Here I am having one of my four shots at goal – I kicked 3.1 on Paul Roos, a 300-game champion and later coach of the Sydney Swans. We managed to win.

I had a good player-coach relationship with Robert Shaw during his time at the Adelaide Crows (1995-96), a relationship which was probably borne from the fact that we were both 'outsiders', both having joined the club after leaving Melbourne. 'Shawy' was later one of the first people to visit me at the Alfred Hospital. People wrongly believed that Shawy encouraged me to be an enforcer with the Crows, which resulted in some undisciplined play. Truth was I tried to throw my weight around a bit because I thought the side lacked a bit of physical presence.

Leaving the AFL Tribunal after being suspended for four matches for striking Brisbane's Clark Keating in the 1999 preliminary final. The ban meant I missed out on playing in a premiership side for the Kangaroos. I thought it was the worst thing that could happen to me. How wrong could I have been?

This is how I'd like Kangaroos supporters, and football followers in general, to remember me – honest, reliable and hard at it.

I was never one of the most skilful players in the AFL, but what I lacked in polish, I made up for with determination, a trait which would hold me in good stead after the Bali bombings.

I had tears running down my face, but I was trying to talk to him. I said, 'It's not, Jason. It's just a photo of me and you.'

I took it down and showed him. He said, 'Oh, God, I thought they were going to hurt us. OK, all right, you can put it back then.'

I put it back, but then it happened all over again, so we just took it down and got rid of it. That was a really hard thing to go through.

It seemed so minor but, with everything he'd already been through, it was really hard to cope with. I often looked at him and thought, 'My poor baby, what is going through your mind?'

He would say lots of really scary stuff that just wasn't him and I would just be in tears. I would think, 'What's going on? What's happening to him?'

No matter what the nurses or anyone else says about it being a normal bi-product of the drugs, I worried like hell and wondered if he'd ever come back to his normal self again.

It was tough sometimes because I was trying to help him cope with all of this stuff and then I had to try and cope with it myself. It took a lot of strength.

Even the news on TV seemed to be conspiring to make me miserable. The whole program seemed to be taken up with doom and gloom. They were still examining what had happened in Bali, but there were also the shootings at Monash University and the tragic siege in a Russian theatre that resulted in the deaths of many hostages, among a seemingly endless series of bad news days.

I also saw an episode of *60 Minutes* that disturbed me and added to my fragile state of mind. They referred to a story they'd aired the previous week showing Hughesy putting on a brave face despite his poor condition. He had since gone into a drug-induced coma in Adelaide and I was naturally concerned about him. After seeing this bloke with a swollen face on the TV, I turned to Nerissa and frowned.

'They said that was Peter Hughes,' I said. 'That's not Peter Hughes.'

Nerissa started crying. 'It is,' she said.

It was a shock to my system.

'That can't be him,' I said, trying to convince myself. 'It just can't be.'

It's no coincidence that the nightmares and scary thoughts slowly went away as my daily intake of drugs was reduced.

12

Small steps

Although Nerissa was with me around the clock, and my family and friends were regular visitors, I felt very much alone. Try as they might, no one else knew exactly how I felt.

This all changed when Nerissa's dad Ardri visited. He and I hadn't done much bonding since Nerissa and I had met — Nerissa's parents have been divorced for some time — but he gave great support. Ardri had once been in a coma and intensive care himself, so he knew exactly how I felt. He intimately knew the function of all the machines I was hooked up to and could answer my questions. Although our circumstances were poles apart, he was someone I could relate to — he had endured and conquered it to lead a normal life.

ARDRI VANDERHEYDEN: It's a life-altering thing being in a coma, and you can't help but look at life differently after it. You've been given another chance. And then you start thinking, 'Well, what am I going to do with this second chance?' I found my calling and that was art and I made the decision to pursue it. Jason seems to have found his calling too. He's motivating people and helping them to help themselves.

Something Ardri hadn't had to contend with though was a nasty infection. It seemed that no matter what the doctors tried, I couldn't shake it.

My body was healing satisfactorily, apart from my legs, which were ravaged by putrid infection. Although there was never any danger that I would lose either of my legs, the doctors were concerned and frustrated by the mystery infection. I also had an unusually high temperature and a fever that lingered on for weeks. It wasn't common knowledge at the time, but about 90 per cent of the Australians burnt in Bali contracted this particular infection — hardly a startling revelation when you consider that we were in a Third World country, we had open wounds, and it took a few days to get home to the sterile conditions of Australian hospitals.

When you think of it in those terms, it was almost inevitable that bugs were going to get into our systems.

The doctors racked their brains and explored various avenues to find the cause of the nasty bug. At one point, they thought it might have been due to some minor shrapnel wounds in my backside. They X-rayed me every day to find out what they could.

Perhaps the most petrifying moment for me was when the doctors told me they wanted to perform an ultrasound on my heart.

'It's easy,' one if the docs said. 'We stick this tube down your throat and it's all over in 20 minutes. If there's an infection in there, we can cure it with antibiotics. If that doesn't work, we'll have to do some surgery.'

I wasn't having any of it. Apart from the fact that it's only natural to get twitchy about anything relating to your heart, the prospect of having another tube down my throat repulsed me. A dry tube in a gravel-dry throat meant friction, discomfort and pain. I also tend to gag on such things.

I was already highly strung because I was so tired and from the effects of drugs. I didn't need this. Sometimes I just wished they'd leave me alone.

After the coma, I thought I was out of any major danger. I was starting to feel better each day. But then this infection issue raised its ugly head. I accepted that I was burnt but I didn't even consider that something might have been wrong with my heart. I probably overreacted, but only because I was scared out of my wits.

I had a panic attack when I spoke to Nerissa and her dad.

'This is garbage!' I said firmly. 'There's nothing wrong with my heart. There's nothing wrong.'

Soon after, I directed my frustration at the doctors. 'You've got no hope of doing that,' I growled. 'You'll have to knock me out.'

They did.

I really had no alternative. It was a necessary procedure to find the source of the infection. I'd just have to summon the patience and will-power to get through it. Just as I suspected, everything dried up and I gagged on the tube. I felt like I was choking.

When I woke up, Nerissa and her dad were there. Nerissa had one of those smiles you'd crawl a mile to see. 'Your heart's OK,' she said. Apart from the night Nerissa agreed to marry me, I don't think I've been happier with something she's said.

But the infection was still with me and that meant I had to be thoroughly bathed. The two nurses who were keen to do the bathing, Mel Pacquola and Jill Saville, thought it would be good for the infection as well as general hygiene. I knew it would be too, but I knew it was going to bring enormous pain.

MEL PACQUOLA: The first day Jill worked with him was a tough one. It was hard because Jason is so tall and the bath wasn't made for people his size, so he didn't fit into it properly. We flooded the whole room.

We bathed him in an antiseptic solution to try and get rid of the infection. We had to get rid of a lot of dead skin so that the new skin could come up and it took a long time because we had to do his legs, his arms and his face. It was a painful experience for Jason.

I told Jill to go on her break and when she came back, she said, 'Oh, my God.' She'd been crying. It's quite hard to watch people like Jason who are in so much pain and knowing that you have to keep doing what you're doing for their benefit. You feel terrible, but you know there is no way around it.

But Jason was amazing — he was so positive from the word go. I never heard him say, 'I can't do this,' except one time in the bath when he'd had enough.

In his whole time in ICU, he had only one bad day — and he apologised for it. Most patients in ICU have a bad day every second or third day. He said, 'I'm really sorry, I'm having a bad day.'

I said, 'About bloody time. It's normal.'

He found strength that very few patients in ICU find because often they get depressed and start thinking, 'What's going on? Am I getting better or aren't I?' Jason never let it get him down. He'd turn any negative into a positive.

After the bath, I drifted off to sleep and dreamt about football. An hour or two later, Dad told me that Shaun Rehn, my former Adelaide teammate, had been appointed coach of SANFL club West Adelaide. As soon as Dad said, 'Rehny's been appointed coach of Wests,' I said, 'I already know.'

Dad was confused. 'How can you know? No one knows. I'm just telling you now.'

It was like I had heard it in a dream, in yet another out-of-body experience. But perhaps it was a telepathic thing because Shaun had called to find out how I was.

Before I'd gone away on holidays, Shaun came to my house to see what I would be doing with football the following year. He wanted me to join him at whichever SANFL club he got a gig at. But my injuries put an end to any hope he might have had of luring me back to Adelaide.

I had problems with my lungs. They were struggling to function. Although burns victims need to drink a lot of water to prevent dehydration, I might have overdone it. Rather than keeping me fresh and hydrated, the fluid had clogged up my lungs. When I came out of the coma, the only thing I wanted was to drink water, but I wasn't allowed to for a day or so because of the excess fluid.

I was allowed ice though. It became my new gold. I ate so much ice that there would have been enough to form an igloo in my stomach.

I munched and crunched my way through so much ice that my teeth became sore. The nurses tried to wean me off my frosty diet by telling me that the ice machine was empty.

When a new nurse started her shift, I thought, 'Here's a soft target.'

'Can you please get me some ice,' I pleaded, putting on my best puppy-dog eyes.

'No, we haven't got any,' she said, straight-faced.

'Damn it,' I thought, 'she's awake to it.'

I was excited when I was told that I would be rationed water. I thought that I might get a glass of water an hour. Imagine my shock when I was rationed what seemed like an eye-drop of water every five minutes. At the time, it was great just to get that much because I was so dry in my mouth and throat. But no matter how much I was rationed, I had an unquenchable thirst. They could have almost put a funnel in my gob and poured gallons of the stuff down my throat and reckon I still would have been thirsty.

NERISSA: He was only allowed to have 2 ml every five minutes. He was getting so angry and frustrated. I felt for him so much.

I wanted to give him the whole cup that was sitting there, but the danger was that it could've gone into his lungs. After he had those two big, garden hose tubes draining his lungs, I thought, 'He cannot go through that again. I'm not going to let him go through that again.'

He got angry with me because I wouldn't give him more, and I'd get upset and frustrated as well.

But every now and then, I'd relent and put an extra half a mil in. He'd say, 'Right, five minutes is up.'

I'd say, 'No, darling, it's only been about three.'

It was really tough.

When I was finally able to drink an unlimited amount of fluids, Nerissa got me a lot of soft, frosty ice-creams. She fed them to me and it was great because it was so soothing.

I wasn't able to eat properly for a couple of weeks. I was fed intravenously, 24 hours a day, because I was wasting away. Tubes pumped energy and dietary supplements like Sustagen into my system. The most annoying thing about the process wasn't the method of feeding, or the food itself, but the constant sound of the breathing machine. I panicked when I first heard it. You see hospitals scenes on TV shows and in movies and usually a noisy machine means bad news. I thought the worst when I heard it beeping. But I soon worked out how it worked. It was particularly annoying when my liquid food ran out because it would beep until it was attended to. It wasn't so bad when a nurse was sitting there with me in the room but if they left the room, which they often did to look after other tasks, the squawking of the machine could drive you crazy. I became immune to it after a while.

I was a very inquisitive patient, forever asking questions like, 'What's this for?' or 'How come you do that?' I basically harassed every doctor and nurse in the vicinity. When they swapped at the end of shifts, or if I got a different one, I'd open up with my verbal rapid-fire. 'How am I looking? How am I going? Do you reckon I'll be right? I've got to get married on the 14th of December.'

I did it to get as many different opinions as possible. But they wouldn't give anything away. The standard line they gave me was, 'One day at a time.' I'd heard lines like this before. I felt the frustration of a reporter when they ask a player or a coach a question and receive such a completely bland answer.

But then again, chances are if they told me what they thought — 'No, I don't think you'll be right for your wedding' — I would have used it as an incentive to prove them wrong.

NERISSA: I was quite happy to delay the wedding because of everything we'd been through. All I thought was, 'He's alive, he's awake, he's getting better. The wedding doesn't matter right now.'

I told him, 'We can postpone the wedding, it doesn't matter.' He wouldn't have a bar of it.

I told one of the counsellors, 'He won't accept that we can postpone the wedding. The doctors don't think he'll get there. It's really frustrating me because it really doesn't worry me.'

She said, 'Nerissa, you have to give him that because he's probably scared that if you don't get married, you never will. He's probably scared you're going to leave him.'

I said, 'But I won't. I've told him that.'

She said, 'Yes, you know that, but he might be worried. You have to give him that goal — it's something that is important to him.'

I agreed, 'Yes, you're right, but I am scared he'll push himself too hard.'

Everything the nurses did for me was ultra-positive. They wrote on a whiteboard the time that certain activities, like bathing and dressings, were to be done. I found it very positive because I like structure. I like to know what's happening and when it's going to happen. The structure and discipline of playing football, knowing what your week will consist of — it changed depending on what day we played — certainly helped.

The whiteboard, which acted as my diary while I was in intensive care, also noted any other important events. There was always something to look forward to and keep my spirits high.

One such event was a special visit by the Federal Opposition Leader, Simon Crean.

I felt honoured that Mr Crean, who is also the Kangaroos' No. 1 ticket-holder, took time out of his busy work schedule to see me. Unfortunately, because I was heavily sedated, I almost forgot his name. Fancy that. I'd met him before too, and even called him 'Creany'.

SIMON CREAN (FEDERAL OPPOSITION LEADER AND NO. 1 TICKET-HOLDER AT THE KANGAROOS): Jason and I had met before, but we hadn't spent a lot of time together. It was down in the rooms after a game with the usual banter of football. It was over at the presentation of the guernseys and that type of thing. I remember him during the celebrations of the premiership in 1999 when he couldn't play because he had been suspended the previous week. But he didn't let that get him down, and he got a tremendous cheer from the crowd nevertheless.

There's no doubt you take a greater concern about the overall horror when you know the people involved. It's the personal side of it. It doesn't matter if it's a bushfire tragedy or a road accident — they're all horrors. But if you know the people, you can't help that not impacting on you more.

Before I saw Jason, I had the opportunity to talk to the nursing staff, who I had also gone there to see, and to visit the burns unit. But none of that discussion prepared me for what I saw. Jason was laid out on his back, hardly able to move. I don't know exactly what I had expected to see.

I'd seen the picture of him lying on the trolley where his face looked really bad. What I hadn't expected was the extent of the burns to his body. My initial reaction was shock but I didn't show that. I wanted to talk with him to see how he felt, rather than judge that by the way he looked.

He said he wanted to do three things: make the wedding date, get back on the footy field, and get back up to the Gulf of Carpentaria where he'd been with mates.

It was very hard for him to turn his head, but he pointed to a photo on the wall. He said, 'Can you see that photo?' He couldn't turn to look at it. It was a photo of a big fish he'd caught on that trip.

He could move his arms but he couldn't move his body. He was all bandaged up and only part of his face was exposed. His attitude was very positive in terms of making the wedding and surviving, but he seemed to have real doubts as to whether he'd make it back onto the football field. That deeply concerned him because he loved the game so much and (pre-Bali) he had a few seasons left in him. I wasn't in the position to judge whether he would in fact make it back, but I thought to myself, 'Gee, this is going to be a miracle if he does get back on the field again.'

He also had real self-doubts about what he would do if he couldn't play football again. He was concerned about what it meant in terms of income and what he would do.

What also struck me while I was there was his fiancée Nerissa's constant attention and the soothing of ointment into his body. She was clearly a real power of strength for Jason. She was fantastic.

I felt good after speaking to Creany, but soon after that I almost hit rock-bottom. Nerissa had been sleeping in the room with me, even when I was in the coma — especially when I was in the coma — but you're not really meant to. The nurse was concerned about Nerissa burning herself out.

'She needs to go home and have a sleep,' she said. 'There's a long haul ahead and she needs all her strength.'

'It's all right,' I explained. 'When I get out of hospital, Mum's going to be around for a while, so it will be all right if Nerissa's struggling a bit now.'

But the nurse had obviously seen it all before.

'Right, this is it,' the nurse said. 'Nerissa can stay the night but after tonight she can't stay overnight again. It won't be able to happen when you go up to the burns ward.'

I lost it. I didn't want to waste time arguing. The simple fact was that I needed Nerissa with me. She was my security blanket. She been there to hold my hand and tell me it was all right when I went through my nightmare phase. Whenever I'd been conscious, she'd been there with me. I cried and screamed. I'd hardly slept and I got so upset and frustrated that I can't even remember what I said.

NERISSA: I'd actually out popped out to the toilet or gone somewhere for five minutes, and when I walked back into the room and saw Jason hysterical and looking so scared, it alarmed me. It was like the day I found out that he was involved in the bomb. I was so angry. I thought, 'What the hell is going on?'

He grabbed me and said, 'She said you can't stay. I need you here.'

He was so upset I could have wrung the nurse's neck. I gave her this dirty look and said, 'What's going on? He shouldn't be upset like this!'

I know that the nurse was doing what she had to do, but I just felt it was so thoughtless. I was furious because all I wanted for Jason was to be happy and positive because that is what would help him to get better. Jason was in intensive care — he didn't need any stress, especially over something so minor. I tried to calm him down the whole time. I was saying, 'It's OK. We can handle this. I'll stay until you fall asleep and then I'll come back before you wake up and you won't even know I was gone.'

I rang my Aunty Sue, one of Mum's sisters who I'm very close to — she's more like an older sister than an aunty. We've got a very special bond, and I'm also close to her teenage kids, Kirsty and Jayden.

Aunty Sue lives in Portland and hadn't been able to visit me at that stage. She comforted me and said that she and Jayden would get to the hospital some time soon. She tried to say that they must be doing it for a reason, and that they were looking out for my best interests. It certainly didn't seem like it at the time though.

SUE DECKERT (JAN McCARTNEY'S SISTER, JASON'S AUNT): It was the first time I had heard Jason's voice since he'd come back from Bali. As soon as Jason started talking, he started crying. He was so upset that he had to keep putting me on to Nerissa so that he could calm himself down a bit. We all ended up balling our eyes out. We spoke for about 20 minutes. Apart from when I first found out that he'd been hurt, it was probably the hardest 20 minutes of my life.

He was really upset that one of the nurses had said that Nerissa had to go home that night. He just couldn't cope with the thought of her not being there.

I tried to make light of it. I said, 'Put the nurse on the bloody phone. I'll sort her out. If that doesn't work, I'll come down there myself.'

He was trying to have a laugh but he was still upset.

He and Jayden spoke to each other and balled their eyes out.

Jason said to me, 'I want to see you.'

I said, 'We'll get down there as soon as we can.'

He kept saying to both of us, 'I love you guys so much. It's so good to hear your voice.'

After I got off the phone and had a really good cry, it was like a weight had been lifted. To hear his voice, to know that he was OK and that he was going to survive was all that mattered.

He's like a little brother to me, and he's like that with my kids too. They adored him long before he was a footballer. They always used to dote on him when they were little tackers.

Kirsty was so little as a kid and even back then Jason was fairly tall, so she would get a sore neck looking up to him when she spoke. Jason would lift her up and hold her in front of him, so they were eye-to-eye, and they'd continue the conversation. He was so rapt when she started to grow. He'd say, 'It's good to be able to talk to her without having to pick her up.'

He's always been great with kids. Whenever the kids have wanted to do something, I don't think I've ever heard him say, 'No, I can't, I'm busy.' He'd always set that time aside.

It doesn't surprise me at all that he gave up his spot on the plane for other people in Bali. But when I saw how crook he was in hospital, I thought, 'You moron. What did you do that for?'

We don't see each other very often because we live a fair way away from each other but we're on the phone a lot and we all just pick up where we left off.

NERISSA: The nurse said, 'Jason, would you like something to help you sleep?'

I said, 'Yes, that would be good.' They gave him something but it certainly didn't work because he was so worked up. I sat there gently rubbing his head and talking to him until he fell asleep. It was really hard leaving.

On my way home, I rang Jan. 'You should have seen what he was like,' I screamed. 'If they make him upset like that again, I'll take him out of hospital myself.'

I woke up shortly after and when I noticed that Nerissa had left, I freaked. I nagged and pestered the nurse who was in charge of me to allow me to call her at home.

'Come back,' I pleaded. 'Come back.'

NERISSA: I'd only just got home and was getting ready for bed when the phone rang. Jason was really upset. I jumped back in the car and went straight back to the hospital. They gave him some more tablets. I sat with him for about an hour after he'd dozed off, so that I knew he was really asleep. I promised him I'd be there before he woke up, so I went in extra early that morning because I didn't want to disappoint him.

I didn't need any proof about the quality of person Nerissa was, but it just reinforced in my mind that I had a real beauty — mind, body and soul — here and I didn't want to let her go.

We had a pretty special bond right from the start. We got engaged after only six months. I never needed any confirmation that she was the one.

There were times together in hospital that I told her exactly how I felt. 'People might think I'm strong doing what I'm doing,' I'd say, 'but the truth is that you're the strength behind all this. If you weren't here for me, I don't know whether I would have the fight to keep going.'

NERISSA: If I wasn't around, he would've had other reasons to fight and to live. Sometimes I feel that I haven't done enough for him. I want to do more all the time. I look back and I think, 'How did I cope?' The number one thing that made me cope and be strong was Jason. He says that about me too. With love comes strength, and a real willingness to do whatever it takes to make sure the person you love so much is going to be all right.

Nerissa provided me with so much strength by simply being there. She was with me through the good and bad times and kept me sane. She was my rock and, undoubtedly, the gutsiest person in my recovery.

NERISSA: At one stage, Jason said something like, 'Do you still love me?'

I nearly cried.

I said, 'Yes, I'm always going to be here.'

That broke my heart. I didn't want him thinking like that. I said, 'I'm going to be here for you all the time. I love you.'

I couldn't even begin to imagine what I would have been like if I hadn't had Nerissa by my side. For starters, I would have struggled to find the strength to survive. If I did make it out of that endless tunnel, what hope would I have had of finding a partner for life? With all of my burns and injuries, which could have been looked upon as disfigurements, how would I have gone trying to form some sort of relationship? I reckon I would have been on the shelf for a while because some women would probably be afraid or repulsed about even going near me.

But here I was set to marry this wonderful woman on 14 December — in just a month and a half. My major dilemma was making the date. I was hell-bent on doing everything in my power to ensure that our big day went ahead exactly as planned.

MEL PACQUOLA: If someone said that he couldn't do something, he would set out to prove that he could. He was told while he was in ICU that he had to stay in bed. When I was on night duty, he'd say, 'Come on, just help me to sit on the side of the bed.'

I said, 'You're not supposed to get out of bed.'

He said, 'No one will know — it's night time.'

I said, 'Well, I'm only half your size. How am I going to be able to get you out of bed?'

I ended up getting one of the boys to help meet him on to the side of the bed.

He was so sick of being in bed that he needed a change. He said that sitting on the side of the bed was the best thing ever. You could tell that he was in pain, but he was so determined. He would always push the limits and I think that's why he recovered as well and as quickly as he did. He was such an inspiration as a patient and a person — you can learn so much from him.

After speaking to people at the hospital about him, the common theme was that they would never forget his fantastic attitude. It made me really evaluate my own life and goals. I thought, 'Here Jason is with all these obstacles and challenges to overcome.' He really motivated me to ask myself, 'What am I doing to achieve my own goals?'

13

Getting better

In my last days in intensive care, I started calculating the days and weeks that were left before the wedding. I knew I couldn't get out of hospital one week and then expect to get married the next. I would be too weak. I had my heart set on being discharged at least a month beforehand, so I'd have time to get some strength back and, while I might not look my best, I'd be somewhere in the ball park — that way, at least I wouldn't look like death warmed up.

A few doctors had told Nerissa — they didn't tell me, but she relayed the information — that I would be in hospital for a minimum of eight weeks. That would mean that I'd be in hospital right up to the time of the wedding. They thought we should postpone it.

I kept telling Nerissa, 'Let's just wait. No need to postpone it yet. It'll be right. Things are improving.'

But I knew I had a lot of hard work in front of me if I was to prove the doctors wrong.

My condition steadily improved, and on 29 October — 17 days after the bombings — I was moved out of the intensive care unit and into my own (thankfully spacious) room in the burns ward. I wouldn't have the one-on-one attention that I had received in intensive care (where two nurses worked alternate 12-hour shifts to ensure I was looked after 24 hours a day), but the fact that I'd made such progress warmed my heart and gave me belief. It was another step towards recovering enough to go home.

'I'm gonna beat this thing,' I thought.

We immediately inquired about as to whether Nerissa could stay in the room with me. Thank God the answer was a resounding, 'Yes, of course.' Without delay, a roll-out stretcher was supplied.

The move to the burns ward coincided with my first session in a pressure, or hyperbaric, chamber, which the doctors believed might cure the infection in my legs and help my body heal quicker.

The beauty of hyperbaric treatment is that it supplies pure oxygen at high air-pressure and increases the amount of oxygen carried in the blood to the organs and tissues in the body. It activates white blood cells to fight infection and fast-tracks the healing process.

Sounded good to me.

DR HEATHER CLELAND: Jason's legs weren't getting any worse, but they weren't starting to heal either. We sent him to the hyperbaric unit because there's evidence that hyperbaric treatment can knock off the bugs and increase the activity of the white cells and improve the immune system in the patient. It's not routine therapy but it can't hurt. I've certainly sent patients that I've been at my wits end with for a bit of hyperbaric treatment, and sometimes I think it helps.

A doctor checked and cleaned my ears to see whether I'd be able to handle the below-sea-level air pressure of a hyperbaric chamber. I still had a perforated eardrum but I was given the all clear.

The Alfred Hospital boasts a massive hyperbaric chamber that can accommodate either 20 people or four beds. I didn't have any second thoughts about having the hyperbaric treatment. In fact, I jumped at the chance. It was something that I'd heard about from teammates. 'Footballers have it when they're injured,' I thought. 'It'll be a breeze.'

It wasn't a breeze, but it was certainly a lot easier to bear than bathing.

When I got in the hyperbaric chamber, a nurse put a ring around my head and placed a clear-plastic cap on my head. It was like a helmet. I felt claustrophobic.

Even in that first session, it didn't take long for the novelty to wear off and for me to become bored. Mind-numbingly bored. Time crawls when you're in pain or recovery mode. It's a mixture of boredom and restlessness. It was a relief that I wasn't the only person in there. I was joined by another first-timer — a man with a busted ankle. We spent about an hour in there. We couldn't talk though because of the headgear we were both wearing. I knew immediately that I would need to be patient to get the full benefits from such treatment.

After that I had a two-hour session in the hyperbaric chamber every day for the next week. I could feel myself improving and getting stronger every day.

DR HEATHER CLELAND: Jason started to show signs that the skin cells on his legs, instead of just sitting there and doing nothing, were starting to multiply and spread over the wound. All his grafts were also taking and his donor sites were healing, which may or may not have been helped by the hyperbaric sessions.

After my hyperbaric sessions, the routine was to bathe in the monstrous spa. It was high and bubbly and enabled me to stretch out. It was the complete opposite of the small, portable bath that I'd been subjected to in intensive care, which invariably resulted in water being splashed over the side and my room being flooded. There was also a television up there.

But bathing could sometimes be frustrating. You had to book your session because a number of patients needed to use it. It took time because the bath had to be cleaned; you couldn't just hop into the same water that other people had used. The routine of having a hyperbaric session, a bath and then cream and dressings applied would knock over half a day and keep me occupied. I wasn't bored.

After that first bath in the burns ward, I needed painkillers just to get through the process of cream and dressings. It hurt so much it made me cry. So much for being a big, tough AFL footballer.

It took so much out of me that day 2 was an absolute nightmare. I took a newspaper into the hyperbaric chamber but I couldn't read it because my fingers were still a mess. They weren't nimble enough to flick through the pages, so, after reading the front and back pages, I turfed it to the side. I just stared at the clock for two hours. It was tough. I've always been someone who's found it hard to sit still at the best of times; I have to be on the go, doing something.

One of the patients in there with me was an old guy who was a veteran of hyperbaric treatment. He knew how everything worked and didn't seem to mind the monotony. I don't know how he did it.

The staff were worried because I sweated so much that my mask fogged up. It was purely due to my anxiety — in truth, I was petrified — about being in a confined environment. After all, I'm a country boy who craves the open spaces. All of these factors compounded so that by the time it came to have my bath, I was completely drained. Delirious almost.

The process of getting into the bath wasn't a simple one. The nurses would take my dressings off, roll me onto a bed which jacked up, swing me around into another room and then lower me into the bath. But it didn't work like that on this particular day. I didn't think I needed any painkillers, which was to be a mistake. I was so wobbly and dazed that I nearly fell off the bed, which would have dropped me six feet to the hard, cold floor.

When I was lowered into the bath, I was totally exhausted and irritated. The hot bath drained me even more. I was dizzy and desperately wanted to get back to my bed to sleep and rest. I wished everyone would just leave me alone.

Normally I'd try to help them clean off the dead skin, by lifting an arm or a leg or moving slightly to enable them to get at an area that needed attention. They'd wipe me with a face washer and I could see the new skin coming through.

They'd say things like, 'Oh, the legs are looking better.'

I tried to bend my left leg and, in doing so, I got the shock of my life. I looked underneath and what can only be described as a hole in my leg. It was the first time I'd seen it.

'Holy hell!' I said.

I felt ill.

It was so deep that it was like a chunk the size of a golf ball had been ripped out of my leg. I was half expecting to see light shining through from the other side. And this was after it had healed a little in the previous fortnight. It must have looked a real mess initially. I knew I had a shrapnel wound in the back of my leg, which I initially self-diagnosed as a torn calf as Mick and I ran away from the bombsite. But this was far more serious than I could have ever imagined.

'I ran with that hole in my leg,' I thought, shaking my head.

MEL PACQUOLA: The hole in his calf was quite deep, and it was a new thing for all of us. We'd seen quite a few burns but none of us had ever seen shrapnel wounds, so that made it all a bit more real for us. We all thought they'd be a bit of a scratch and we didn't realise how big or deep they could be. We didn't think they'd be any bigger than a 10-cent coin, but some of them were just huge. It was a reminder that he wasn't just another burns patient.

The 14- or 15-year-old scar that I sustained on my right leg after being caught under a mate's ute had been burnt off. In a way, I had been attached to that blemish. It had been with me for half my life until that point. It was certainly a story to tell when people caught a glimpse of it and asked how I got it. But there was no time for sentiment. The childhood scar had been replaced by what was certain to be a longer-lasting memento. And I will be fielding questions about its origins long after it fades.

Something else that was partially burnt off me was a 15-centimetre by 5-centimetre tattoo of Roadrunner, the cartoon character, above my left ankle, which I got after the Adelaide Grand Prix in 1993. I regretted having it done and had already tried laser treatment to get rid of it, so I was glad when the doctors granted me my request to graft over it. I certainly went about tattoo removal the hard way.

I was lucky my leg wasn't blown off, or at least broken. People lost limbs in Bali after being hit by shrapnel. It was also lucky that I was hit in the calf and not a little higher, in the side or stomach, or a little lower, in my Achilles tendon.

I was lucky in a lot of ways. But at the time, I felt anything but lucky.

The next morning I struggled again in the hyperbaric chamber. I even got Nerissa to put up the 'Sleeping' sign at about 4 p.m. That was unusual because I loved having visitors. I thrived on them.

My mind was made up: no more sessions in the hyperbaric chamber. I decided that I had to make my feelings known.

NERISSA: He was coming back from the hyperbaric sessions upset all the time. I think that was the one moment when he really just wanted to give up. He didn't want to do it and he didn't care. He just wanted to get home.

I was trying to tell him, 'But it's really good for you and it's helping you heal.'

He was saying, 'Well, what is it really doing?' and telling me how horrible it was.

Then I said, 'Yeah, I agree. You don't have to go through that. I'll go and sort it out.'

I went and spoke to the nurse at the head of the ward and said, 'Jason doesn't want to do the hyperbaric sessions any more, he's not coping with it and he needs some time out.'

She said, 'OK, I'm going to have to send one of the burns nurses in to explain how important it really is.'

I was pretty stern with the nurse, but she was just as adamant. 'Well, do you want to play football again?' she asked.

'No, I'm not even bothered about that,' I said, meaning every word.

She went a different tack. 'Well, when you have kids, do you want to be able to run around the park and kick the footy with them? Do you want to be even able to run after your kids?'

Her words really hit home. Kids had always been in the plan for Nerissa and I. What good would I be if I couldn't even have a run around with them, like Dad did with Brenden, Steven and I? There was only one solution. 'I just have to do it,' I thought. 'I'll just have to grin and bear my way through it.'

We decided on a plan to try and alleviate some of the general tiredness that I attributed to my hyperbaric sessions. I hadn't slept well at night and being in the hyperbaric chamber at 7 a.m. only made me more tired and grumpy. I would now enter the chamber in the afternoon. It worked. I was more rested and in a better frame of mind to confront the remainder of my recovery process. These sessions were delayed a couple of times because helicopters are constantly flying in with emergency patients who need to be rushed into the hyperbaric chamber.

Nerissa wasn't sleeping well either. On top of the stress of having her fiancé in such an immobile condition, the fold-out stretcher she had been sleeping on had developed a bow in it. Dad was one of the culprits. He hates sitting around, he's always on the move — I must have inherited that from him — and sometimes when I'd come back from a hyperbaric session, he'd be flaked out on the fold-out bed. Nerissa would get annoyed though when people came in to visit and they'd make themselves comfortable on her bed. It wasn't their fault though; there was simply nowhere else for them to sit.

I almost felt like getting replacement limbs at times. My legs, which, it was hoped, would benefit most from the hyperbaric sessions, were still a reddish-purple colour and very raw. The nurses continued to firmly wipe and almost scratch away the dead skin and the light, milky film that formed due to the infection.

It was like pulling off scabs all over my body. They had to be firm but they didn't want to go so hard that they'd make it bleed. They also took out staples that had been inserted during my skin graft operations. I was pretty naive to think that the skin that had been grafted from another part of my body would be held together with stitches.

We found staples all over my body in those first two or three bathing sessions. They were only small but they were everywhere. It was like someone had gone to town on me with a stapler. It was a weird feeling because these little pieces of metal, these foreign objects, had been literally holding me together.

My left arm was a mess but it didn't hurt because the staples would simply fall out. It was a different story removing staples from my legs because when the nurses hit one of them, I would almost jump through the ceiling.

Skin was removed from my body with a big potato-peeler. Before they grafted my legs or arms, they stretched the skin through a machine that can stretch it to four or five times its original surface area. Initially, there was a meshy, chicken-wire effect in certain areas.

It's all flattening out now thanks to the pressure garments. That took a bit of getting used to at the start. It was like I had pieces of skin from other people, when in fact it was my own skin, which had been relocated to a different part of my body.

The doctors and nurses often commented on how good the grafts looked.

I'd eye them with suspicion. 'You're not just being nice, are you? All due respect, but they look pretty ordinary to me,' I'd say.

'No, trust me, they look good,' they'd say.

I just wanted the truth. Honestly. Even if it was brutal. I might not agree with it, but I could handle it. Always have.

I also wanted to tell the truth to the public and set people straight on the 'hero' tag that had somehow become attached to my name. Many people believed that I had single-handedly 'saved' the Woodgate sisters, Samantha and Leanne.

I first realised that this was a common misconception when I received some amazing letters from a primary school in New South Wales. The pupils wrote about how 'those girls from Melbourne must be so proud of you. You showed so much courage to run back into the burning building to save them.'

Even Nerissa's brother, Shane, said, 'How good was Jase, running back into the fire and pulling people out?'

I thought, 'That sounds like a great scene from a movie — something that Arnie Schwarzenegger or Sly Stallone might do in a Hollywood blockbuster — but it didn't happen.' Although I'd like to be able to claim such things, I couldn't. And it's not through any sense of false modesty that I admit this. The fact is that I only helped Samantha walk out of Paddy's Bar, and she probably helped me just as much. We escorted each other out. Nothing heroic about that.

If Nerissa had been with me and I'd come out and she hadn't, I probably would've put the Superman kit on and run back in. But it was so hot and dangerous that it would've been virtual suicide.

I cringed every time I was asked about how I felt about being regarded as a national hero. I wanted to set the record straight and whenever I was confronted with the hero thing, I said, 'I just grabbed whoever was next to me. I didn't know who it was. It just happened to be Samantha.'

Sometimes I wonder, 'Could I have done anything differently?' Another question I ask myself is, 'If I was just walking by and hadn't been hurt in the blasts, how would I have reacted?' I've heard stories about onlookers getting in and passing injured people over the fence at the Sari Club. That's true heroism. Aside from the fire and the debris, there was still the threat of more bombs. Would I have helped? Or would I have left the scene for fear of more explosions? I don't know the answer. I don't think there is a right answer either, as both courses of action have their merits and are completely understandable. You don't know how you'd react until you're in that situation.

My small room could only accommodate a couple of people at a time, so when quite a few friends and relatives visited one weekend, most of them were forced to sit in the waiting room. One of the nurses had a remedy.

'We can put you on this big fold-out chair and we can actually take you out there,' she said.

I thought, 'This is great. I can get out of the room.'

So I went out to the waiting room, where it was warm and bright with sunlight and smiling faces. I thoroughly enjoyed it. Another step forward.

JAN MCCARTNEY: There were a few people there that day. They weren't expecting to see Jason; they were there for a bit of moral support for us. They wheeled him out to see where we'd been virtually living our lives. He only stayed about ten minutes and then he wanted to go back. It was a bit uncomfortable; he was a bit tired. Everyone was saying hello to him. One of my nieces, Kimberley, who's always been like a little sister to Jason wasn't handling things too well. She broke down. Jason said, 'I think I'd better go back.'

I had to take 'Kimbo' for a walk to calm her down. I said, 'He's OK now.'

She said, 'Are you sure, Aunty Jan?'

'Yes, he's fine.'

Her parents didn't tell the kids that we nearly lost him until he was well recovered.

Aunty Sue and my cousin Jayden had made the four-hour drive from Portland to see me. I was rapt to see them.

SUE DECKERT: It shocked the hell out of me. He looked like death warmed up. In a lot of ways, he probably looked great to anyone who had seen him in the previous couple of weeks.

I saw him the week before he flew to America with his footy teammates. He'd been to Millicent and was driving back to Melbourne. I was working but I spent a couple of hours with him and we went to lunch.

So I the last time I'd seen him, he looked great — he was fit and healthy. I couldn't believe the difference in the space of a couple of weeks. But, at the same time, I knew he was the same lovable person inside.

I'll never forget the look in his eyes. I worded Jayden up. 'Don't be frightened because Jason will be looking to you for your reaction.'

Jayden was very strong about it, held his emotions back and it wasn't until we had a bit of a break and went downstairs that he let his emotions out.

When we walked back to Jason's room, I said, 'How are you going, gorgeous?' and gave him a kiss. That's the way I've always been with him. I make things light-hearted, give him heaps and he gives just as much back.

My thinking was, 'Well, he knew he looked different and that he'd lost weight.' But looks are only skin-deep and Jason knew I'd be the last person to judge him on his looks.

But it was the most trying time I've had in my life.

One of the many moments of truth in my recovery process happened one night soon after. I'd had a gutful. I was on a blow-up bed, which limited my manoeuvrability. It annoyed the hell out of me. I decided to have a chat with the male nurse, Simon.

'Do you reckon I could sit up?' I asked. But before he could answer, I rephrased my question. 'No, actually, do you reckon I could stand up.' (I imagined footy commentator Denis Cometti trotting out his famous line, 'That's ambitious.')

Simon, a funny guy in his mid '20s, responded with, 'Hmm, Jason stand up? Jason stand up? … Let me think about that.'

He walked out of the room to think about it.

'Jason stand up?' he repeated. I hung on his words with baited breath. 'Come on, come on,' I thought.

'OK.'

OK? 'Terrific,' I thought. 'Let's get this show on the road.'

Simon enlisted Nerissa's help. They rolled me to one side, which was painful because I was brushing my burns.

They tried a similar technique to grant me my wish of standing. It didn't work. Too difficult; too painful.

Plan B was far more successful. They sat me up and moved me to the foot of the bed so that my feet dangled over the end. Just getting to that point had taken a lot of energy out of me. I thought, 'Bloody hell, I'm light-headed.' I was so dizzy I could have fainted. This nausea convinced me not to try to stand. I let my feet touch the floor though. They tingled as blood rushed through them for what seemed like the first time in months.

It was a moment of enlightenment, something I took for granted in my former life. Up until that time, I had seriously doubted whether I'd walk again. I had to pinch myself. I thought, 'My feet actually touched the ground.' In many ways, they've barely touched the ground since.

Splints had been strapped to my feet to keep them at right angles with my legs. My leg muscles had been idle and it was important to have some tension in my calves so that they didn't go to waste. They were tight and my feet were swollen and sore, but if such measures weren't observed, it would take longer for me to walk — when, and if, the time came.

Splints were also strapped to my hands to keep them straight and outstretched.

Occasionally, I got a little depressed because I was worried I wouldn't be able to bend and move my limbs again. I'd been like that for two weeks — I couldn't even move myself around in bed — and I'd become far too used to inactivity for my liking.

As I sat on the side of my bed and I caught my reflection in the window. I was covered in bandages: arms, legs, torso — everywhere except my head and face. I didn't need a reflection to know that. But what I didn't know was that my ears were patched up and bandaged and I looked like Dumbo the elephant.

I had already seen parts of my face in a little mirror they used when they shaved me. They let me see it because the skin on my face was improving. It was still peeling and there was some redness but there weren't any scabs. It was new skin. In those limited viewings, I hadn't seen the big ear patches though.

I jokingly lectured Simon, the male nurse about it.

'You're kidding me,' I said with a laugh. 'You mean to say I went out there to see my mates and my 'relos' with these big puppy dog ears? And you let me do it. You mongrel.'

Despite being on the brink of death just days earlier, my ego was still as prominent as ever. I must have been getting better.

14

Walk the walk

I was still pretty weak and tired when I was visited by the Kangaroos' new coach, Dean Laidley. I wondered whether I would I actually make it back to play under him. We talked about a lot of things, not so much about footy.

It was pointless for me to talk too much my football prospects. I was simply trying to make a full recovery and get the hell out of hospital. Playing footy seemed like a pipe-dream. My main concern was the wedding.

And pre-season training hadn't started yet, so I didn't feel like I was missing it. Obviously my teammates would have been miles in front of me in terms of fitness and general well-being at that point, even if they had sat on the couch for weeks eating donuts and guzzling beer and soft drink. And I knew that by the way Dean played his footy — tough, courageous, uncompromising — a return to footy wouldn't be handed to me on a silver platter.

DEAN LAIDLEY (KANGAROOS COACH): My first memory of Jason was when we were playing against each other on a wet, cold night in Adelaide. He was with Adelaide and I was with the Kangaroos. We were having a go at each other and I said, 'You weak so-and-so, you couldn't get a kick at Collingwood, so you changed clubs.'

He said, 'Hang on, what about you? You've done the same thing.'

I thought, 'Oh, yeah, I forgot that' because I'd started with the (West Coast) Eagles. So I just shut my mouth and decided to concentrate on the footy.

Ultimately, Dean was the bloke who would decide: a) whether I retained my place on the Kangaroos playing list, and b) whether I should get a game.

DEAN LAIDLEY: When I first walked in, I didn't recognise him. It was a real shock. I thought, 'Nah, that's not him.' But when I really looked, I could tell it was.

His hair and his face was all singed, but it still had a shine to it because of the cream they'd put on. He had sunken eyes, difficulty breathing. Nerissa was sitting next to the bed, just looking at him.

We talked mainly about him getting right for the wedding. He was very upbeat, very positive. Even then, he was saying, 'I should be right for the first game.'

I thought, 'There's no way.' I didn't think he'd ever play again. But I didn't tell him that, of course.

I was actually supposed to be in Bali myself, but I had to cancel it because my father died. I was in Perth and woke up to the news of what had happened.

Dean had delisted Mick, whom Denis Pagan later drafted to Carlton. I was barely conscious when Mick visited me.

MICK MARTYN: When I saw him, I thought, 'That's not the Jason I know.' He was swollen and looked pretty ordinary. He was pretty with it but I don't think he would have remembered that though because he looked like he was still in shock.

It drove home the fact that there was no discrimination about who got killed, who survived, who was injured and people like me who got out of it with minor injuries. There are a lot of 'what ifs?'

It could easily have been me lying there instead of Jason. The cold reality is that we're lucky we walked out alive. I'm extremely grateful for that. Other people didn't get that chance.

You can't get away from the cold hard fact of the matter that any or all of us could have been killed right there and then. That hits you between the eyes — even now.

The club's chief executive, Geoff Walsh, and the football manager, Tim Harrington, were also among my visitors.

GEOFF WALSH (KANGAROOS CHIEF EXECUTIVE): Like everyone else, I had read about and seen pictures of burns victims, but I didn't really know what to expect when I saw Jason. I don't think Tim did either. One of the things you tell yourself is, 'Irrespective of how he looks, you don't want to show him your reaction and perhaps upset him.'

TIM HARRINGTON (KANGAROOS FOOTBALL MANAGER): As we were about to walk into Jason's room, Geoff said, 'We'd better be prepared for anything here. He might be a bit under the weather.' I thought I was prepared because I'd been to plenty of hospitals before.

My first reaction was, 'Oh, he's sharing the room with someone,' because the person I looked at wasn't Jason. I quickly looked around the room, thinking, 'Where's Jase?' and realised that this was the only person in the room and it was him.

He'd lost a lot of weight, he had no hair — it was shaven off — his eyebrows had been burnt off and he was pink. Normally, Jason is a robust, dark-skinned, healthy-looking bloke.

I think he noticed my reaction — I went 'Oh, God' — and he looked away from me too.

GEOFF WALSH: I thought, 'We're in the wrong room,' because he was totally unrecognisable. It was a shock to see him in that condition and I suppose that hit home to me just how horrific burns can be. He was conscious and talking and calm, but his injuries were pretty severe.

TIM HARRINGTON: I didn't say it aloud to anyone but I thought, 'There is no way that he'll play footy again.' I didn't feel bad about thinking that to myself because I thought, 'This bloke is going to struggle to survive.' Footy didn't matter. I also thought, 'How are the burns going to affect his movement? Will he be able to walk again? Will he be able to function normally?'

GEOFF WALSH: It was hard to see at that time how he was going to get up and play. We were just hoping he'd pull through, and weren't even entertaining any prospect of him playing footy again one day. I thought, 'What sort of quality of life is he going to have?'

Several groups of teammates also made their way into my room.

LEIGH COLBERT (KANGAROOS TEAMMATE): I went to see Jason there with three or four of the younger guys. Walking in, I was thinking, 'How are we going to approach this?' I met Jan in the corridor and she said, 'Just be ready, he's not going to be the Jason you recognise.'

I walked in and said, 'How are you mate?'

We gave each other a bit of stick. The next thing I said — for some reason, I still don't know why — 'Oh, mate, did they burn the tattoo off?'

He replied, 'It's the best thing that's ever happened to me because they had to do skin grafts and the tattoo's no longer there.'

His Roadrunner tattoo on his ankle was gone, so he thought that was great. It broke the ice and I think it just made it easier for the three or four younger guys there because I think they were relying on me to be the one to actually say something.

It was a shock to see him like that, but we went through what he was going to have to go through as far as rehabilitation with his physio. It was just a huge thing he had to take on.

DREW PETRIE: Jason was pale and his skin was all fragmented. He put his hand out to shake hands and you could see where his hand was all burnt and blistered. I just felt terrible. To see what Jason was like before, it was almost like he was another person. It was sort of scary. I didn't know what to say because his eyes were really wide open, so I just wished him well.

I didn't think he'd make it back to footy. Knowing Jason and what he was like, you'd never give up on the bloke, but I didn't give him much chance.

STUART COCHRANE (FORMER KANGAROOS TEAMMATE, NOW AT PORT ADELAIDE): It was scary — we didn't know what to expect. We were sweating about going in and we were worried whether we could handle it or not because we'd been told a few stories. When we got in there, Jase looked pretty much like a skeleton. He didn't look like the same person. You could see in his eyes he still had the same spirit, but his body looked totally different.

DAVID KING (KANGAROOS TEAMMATE): I wasn't super keen to get in there because I'm not real flash with that sort of thing. I remember seeing the scarring on his back and the backs of his legs and just feeling sick.

The club's hardman, Glenn Archer, also visited. From the look of shock on his face, I don't think 'Arch' was prepared for what he saw.

GLENN ARCHER (KANGAROOS TEAMMATE): When I walked in I got the shock of my life — and I didn't see him at the worst. When I saw him, it was like he was going to pass away in front of me. His hands, I couldn't stop looking at his hands, it was shocking, he'd had the grafts and all that but they just looked terrible. He had tubes coming out of him and he was struggling to breathe.

I thought footy was out of the question. I thought, 'He can't even walk, let alone be able play footy.'

While Arch is as tough as everyone says — he'll hate me for saying this — he does have a genuine soft side. He and his wife, Lisa, have got three little kids and, would you believe it, Lisa rules the roost at home. So while he's an angry man who you wouldn't want to cross on the football ground, he's anything but away from the game.

I had a TV in my room that I was quite happy with, but Arch, in his wisdom, decided that it was too small.

'Look, Jase,' he said. 'I've got a mate who could get you a bigger telly, a PlayStation and some DVDs. Do you want 'em?'

I didn't want to seem ungrateful to the hospital staff who had supplied me with this TV to help alleviate my boredom, but I didn't want to disappoint Arch either. He insisted that I let him go ahead with his plan to set up an entertainment system for me.

I relented. 'OK then, just ask the nurse if it's all right,' I said.

Arch nodded and smiled. 'No worries, mate,' he said. 'I'll ask on the way out.'

Within minutes of him leaving, he rang me on his mobile phone. 'It's all ready to go,' he said.

Next morning, sure enough, Arch and another teammate, Adam Simpson, came in with a huge, 68-centimetre TV, a PlayStation, some games and a box of about 20 DVDs, half of which were the property of our Kangaroos teammate

Johnny Blakey. 'Blakes' had ordered some DVDs from Arch's mate months before, and it certainly didn't seem like he was going to get them for at least another few months. Arch giggled with a mischievous glint in his eye. 'Stuff Blakes,' he said. 'He can wait a bit longer to get 'em.'

ADAM SIMPSON (KANGAROOS TEAMMATE): Jason was in one of those wheelchairs where you don't really sit down, you're sort of standing up — like Hannibal Lecter.

I couldn't recognise him when I saw him. He stuck out his hand to shake it — of course, I did. Under all that, he was still the same bloke, cracking jokes straight away.

His weight loss struck me the most. His face was very drawn and faded away. He looked in pretty bad shape but his attitude from the first time I saw him was pretty good.

He didn't have a lot of energy so we couldn't really hang around for too long, after five minutes he was pretty buggered.

I thought there was no way he'd play footy again.

Blakes, who was hoping to escape Melbourne for the sun of Brisbane, popped in. He had just retired after 18 seasons and 359 games. Talk about a marathon man. He was about to go up to Brisbane for an interview for an assistant coaching role with the Lions, a position that he started in 2003.

JOHN BLAKEY (FORMER KANGAROOS TEAMMATE, NOW AN ASSISTANT COACH AT BRISBANE): Jason could hardly move. I couldn't believe his face — it was red and still weeping from the burns. He looked like a different person. I didn't want to act shocked or anything like that.

Nerissa was continually applying cream to his face to keep the moisture on the skin.

The family was in there. I probably stayed for about half an hour. We just talked about footy. Even then, he was determined — even confident — that he was going to get back and play. He was unbelievable. His whole body was heavily bandaged — only his head was sticking out the top of the bed — and I thought, 'If this is any indication, he's got a long, long road back.' I didn't think that he would get back.

I filled him in on what the boys were up and I reassured him that we were there if he wanted anything from us.

You could see he was getting tired very quickly. They took him out again, just because he was so tired from the effort of sitting there and talking to a group of about ten of us.

Johnny was one of the best prepared, most professional footballers I've had the pleasure of playing with. I prided myself on my professionalism, preparation and self-discipline as well. That meant adhering to a stringent diet. Strictly no junk food. As someone who has been an elite athlete for ten years, I naturally associate healthy food with healthy living.

Imagine my confusion when dietitians at the hospital started drumming into me that I needed to eat anything and everything. My previous experience with dietitians was all about low-fat and high carbohydrates. The fact was I needed to eat more to regain my strength. I was being fed intravenously, but that wasn't enough on its own. I struggled to follow these orders because the nasal-gastric tube gave me a sore, dry throat, making it painful to swallow.

Hospital food is traditionally and notoriously bad. It was no different at the Alfred. No disrespect intended, because you can get by on it, but it just lacks the natural, freshness of 'real' food. You get sick of hospital tucker sooner than you can say, 'Gee, that tastes crap.'

Dom Camillo's café-restaurant in West Melbourne — a popular haunt for AFL footballers, including myself — generously offered to deliver food free of charge for us. I usually like to try and get by without too much help, but I had to take Dom's up on their offer. They delivered pasta meals, which were hard to swallow, but I was willing to put myself through the discomfort for the taste-treat sensation.

I also broke my own rule and succumbed to the lure of KFC and Subway. Normally I wouldn't go near either of them, but doctors' orders prevailed.

I had spaghetti every morning which, early on, I struggled to eat because my throat was so sore. Fancy not being able to slurp down spaghetti.

I thought I was doing a great job of devouring anything and everything that was edible — until the dietitian did a calorie check on me. I was still way down on what was needed.

I was wasting away. My face was drawn and bony, like He-Man's nemesis, Skeletor, except with skin. When they weighed me in the burns ward, I featherweighted the scales at 86 kilograms. I'd lost 9 kilos from my playing weight of 95 kilograms.

I noticed my weight loss when I bathed in the huge spa. My whole body had lost power and definition. I was glad, then, when I was introduced to Henrietta Law, a physiotherapist from Hong Kong. I was told, 'She's the guru.' It didn't take long to find out why. She certainly knows her stuff.

HENRIETTA LAW (SENIOR CLINICIAN PHYSIOTHERAPIST, ALFRED HOSPITAL): I was actually in Auckland at the time of the Bali bombings and I didn't know a lot about what had happened because New Zealand didn't have a lot of coverage of it. The first day when I got back — 28 October — it was eight o'clock in the morning and the nurses in intensive care called me. They said, 'We've got Jason here. He's really enthusiastic to get out of bed and wants you to be down here.' As I'm a very low-key person, I didn't know Jason was a footballer. I don't usually look after intensive care patients — it's not my area — but I went down there around lunchtime.

I had a look in his record and saw that he had been very unwell. Up to about that day, he had a very high temperature of about 38 or 39 degrees. On the 24th, it had actually risen to about 40 degrees. He had been through quite a dramatic process. But despite having a very high temperature, Jason was in very good spirits and he didn't actually look that unwell.

One of the first things I noticed about him was how organised and tidy he was. In many of the rooms in the hospital, people have clothes on the floor and so on. His room was so tidy. I thought, 'It's probably not him; maybe his fiancée is very tidy.' Later on, when he was an outpatient, he rang Nerissa at home becase he wanted her to find a document. He said, 'Go upstairs, go to this drawer on the filing cabinet, go to file whatever and then you should find the document.' I thought, 'This man is very organised.'

Henrietta started me with some hand therapy. My hands were both stiff and the skin was tight. I was a little tentative with my right hand, which had minor grafts, but I had no hope of clenching a fist with my left because the whole hand, including the fingers, had been grafted.

Henrietta brought in some dumb-bells for me to do a series of little exercises — intense but not too strenuous — that would increase the flexibility and strength in my hands. She had me squeezing balls — the type that you play sport with — and playing some computer games that tested my thinking and reactions. I also had to do things like pick up nuts and bolts to work my fingers.

NERISSA: The first day that Henrietta came in, we thought that she was a very interesting character. She didn't focus on any negatives; she was a hundred per cent positive. She was a really amazing person. The first thing Jason told her was, 'I have to be ready for my wedding day.' Henrietta realised immediately that this was something that had to be done and she was ready to help him as much as she could.

She was upfront and honest. She said, 'I know, but we're going to do this first,' and she explained everything to us. She took the guesswork out of it.

As soon as she left, about two hours later, Jason said, 'I want to stand up.' Henrietta seemed to flick a switch inside him that said, 'I can do this and I'm going to. I have to achieve these new goals every day.' Every day she came in, he just grew to love her, and so did I. She is one of the reasons that he has been able to reach his goals: the wedding, the football comeback. She was phenomenal.

HENRIETTA LAW: My rationale is that each day we will work them to the maximum capacity. But they have a goal each day, they have a gain. So they see an improvement, but they still have enough energy to work just as hard the next day.

I understood that athletes like Jason have very high expectations of themselves. I used to work with athletic teams, so I know athletes with serious injuries will continue to play.

In Jason's circumstances, I also realised that we had only a very limited time — there were only six weeks to Jason and Nerissa's wedding.

Jason had 50 per cent burns. Generally speaking, you require one day in hospital for every one per cent of your burns. If people do well, they might be doing 2 per cent a day, so their hospital time is cut in half.

It didn't take her long to increase the strength and flexibility in my legs either. A major development on this front took place on 31 October, less than a fortnight after I almost died in a coma. Henrietta told me that it was time I stood up. I looked at her with disbelief. 'Are you sure?'

Henrietta nodded. 'Yes, you'll be fine,' she said.

HENRIETTA LAW: When we allow a patient to stand up, we bear in mind how thick the burns are, how debilitated the patient has been and we consider the time of rest. Many a time we need to sit them down for at least an hour beforehand, just to get the blood system used to it, so when they stand up, they won't be extremely dizzy.

Henrietta got me on the side of the bed and I slowly, painstakingly, stood up for the first time. Unlike the previous attempt where I just let my feet touch the floor, I had the full weight of my body on my legs. I was elated. But, at the same time, I was shattered.

'I'm never going to walk again,' I thought.

I was so weak and dizzy that Henrietta had to help me sit down on my bed after only 30 seconds.

HENRIETTA LAW: He did better than I expected — a lot of people are so woozy they just can't handle standing up.

While it had been a quantum leap for me to stand, walking seemed like a shimmering mirage in the distance. The unattainable.

'I'm not going to be able to do this,' I thought.

It was going to be an uphill battle. 'I'm going to struggle,' I thought.

The next morning, we were at it again. Round 2. But this time I was determined not to sink to the canvas. I resolved that I would push myself to the limit. I'm not the first person to face such things, and unfortunately I won't be the last. I wanted to meet it head-on. Bugger self-doubt — it only drags you down and impedes your progress. If you're determined enough, you can overcome and conquer anything.

Henrietta helped me to stand again. I felt that familiar tingle.

I'd been this far before. It's funny how something so simple for able-bodied people, something I took for granted pre-Bali, could be such a huge personal achievement.

Henrietta thought the logical progression from the day before would be to simply walk out the door. I was hesitant, but excited. Blood flowed to my extremities; adrenaline coursed through my veins. It was like the start of the 1998 Grand Final all over again. I had to harness that nervous energy. Control the moment; don't let the moment control you.

Henrietta brought over a walking frame, which she called a 'four-wheel drive'. Normally, I would push it away. Most people would if they thought they could walk without it. But I couldn't walk without it. I didn't know if I would even be able to walk with it. But, by God, I wasn't going to die wondering. I would give it my all.

No matter how much I wanted to, it was physically impossible for me to do it on my own. In some ways, it was emotionally impossible for me as well. While I was desperate to do the Aussie thing and 'have a go', I was so gangly and wobbly that confidence was hardly warranted. Hopefully that would come later, in time.

Henrietta had to hold me in case I fell. She had to protect me from any mischief I might cause myself. The last thing I needed was a broken arm or leg.

Initially, I plodded rather than walked. Left, right, left, right. Each step was a mini-triumph. I gained confidence with each movement. I was a little shaky but I became steadier as I went.

I not only walked out the door, but I walked about 60 metres beyond it! It took me a couple of minutes this time — it seemed like a couple of hours — but I couldn't have been happier. I even raised a genuine sweat; not a sweat borne of infection, but one that came from hard work. It felt great. Exhilarating.

HENRIETTA LAW: Generally speaking, it depends on the fitness of the person, but his was actually a very good walk for the first walk. Then we went out of the ward in a wheelchair and did some other work because his left hand was the other area that was extremely important.

It was like a new world opened up to me. Once I could walk with the frame, I treated it like a form of fitness training. Small steps and improvements in the short-term would become huge improvements in the long-term. It was like I was building a brick wall: each session or exercise was another brick in the wall. I had to work hard, make sacrifices and be patient. The same values had sustained me throughout my AFL career.

I was like a dog with a bone and I wouldn't let go. Although Henrietta didn't work on weekends, I virtually demanded that she spend as much time as was physically possible with me. It was selfish, I know, because she had other people to attend to, but I was on a mission. I had to make it in good shape for my wedding day. Failure was not an option.

'You've got to come and get me in the arvos,' I said to Henrietta. 'You've got to either wheel me down to the gym in the chair or I'll try and walk to the lift and then walk into the gym and we can do some light weights.'

Henrietta tried to contain my excitement a little but she said she would do what she could. The next day, I doubled that effort. I did a lap of the block — about 120 metres of it — in five or six minutes.

HENRIETTA LAW: Jason wanted to walk again in the afternoon, but when he'd had hyperbaric treatment and all the dressings, he was far too exhausted. There was a physical factor.

The next day, when I get up to the ward in the morning, he'd already walked with the nurses, so he was already showing off.

Usually when I came to work, he'd say, 'Hey I've done the walk already.' So he was very focused. He wanted to shift the goalposts every day.

His attitude was quite refreshing because burns can be very depressing for the person who suffers them. It's actually one of the worst injuries that can be inflicted on someone.

Many a time, patients who have been burnt and then in intensive care for a long, long time, it's almost like they have had heart bypass surgery. It's very challenging for the heart system. It's important that you have them very well conditioned.

There were never any problems with Jason. Most patients want to have a sleep-in because their body energy level is fairly low, but he was awake at 5 o'clock.

I repeated the 120-metre walk for Mum and Dad. Dad had been in Nhill for a couple of days and he hadn't these developments. Mum had. She said, 'You've got to do some walking when Dad's here.'

I don't think Dad believed me when I told him about the progress I'd made. He couldn't believe his eyes when I got out of bed and walked a lap of the block. Dad followed me with the chair just in case I felt weak. But not once did I take the soft option of a rest in the chair. To Dad, it must have been the equivalent of watching me take my first steps as a toddler.

IAN MCCARTNEY: It's fair to say I was a pretty happy man that day.

Mum and Dad, like a lot of friends and relatives who saw me in my early stages in hospital, couldn't envisage me ever running around or being very active again. They knew I'd be healthy, which was the main thing, but anything above that would be a bonus.

HENRIETTA LAW: I needed to get him out of the four-wheel frame that was supporting him. There's no way Jason would have gotten out of the hospital with that, and there's no way he could walk down the aisle like that either.

We went to the gym and I did a dance with him. It was a very funny thing because I'm so short and Jason's so tall. He put his head on my shoulder and we did some side walking and then front walking. I gradually handed my role over to Nerissa. That's how he actually got off the frame.

The next day, Melbourne Cup Day, we just kept practising that. The day after that, he was walking by himself, and saying, 'I'm going home.'

My old mate Corey McKernan, who had held grave fears for me, was pleasantly surprised to see me walking. I walked up on my toes because my calves were still weak through under-use. They were stiff and I didn't feel that I could force my heels to the floor. My left calf was tightest due to the chunk that had been blown out of it. Corey joked about my bouncy gait. 'Mate, you're Johnny Blakey reincarnated!' 'Blakes' always walks up on his toes.

BRENDEN MCCARTNEY: He was really proppy with the walking frame and I thought, 'He's never going to be able to get his heels on the ground. It's going to be a long road back.'

But I knew how dedicated he was to his training and I thought, 'Nah, he'll be right; he'll do it.'

He'd have his gown on and he'd be about to take off with the walking frame and he'd say to Henrietta, 'Have you covered up my bum?' We were cracking up.

STEVEN MCCARTNEY: I couldn't believe it. Within three weeks, he went from being a body just lying there with no movement at all, to being up and walking around. I reckon our nanna would have beaten him in a footrace, but it was truly amazing. He was walking along with the frame, just taking little steps and I suppose it would've been about 50 metres up the end of the corridor and back again.

Another indication of my progress was the fact that the nurses no longer mummified me in bandages. I only had a couple of patches on my left elbow and my legs. I started to think, 'Hey, it's not all about getting the bandages and dressings off. My injuries don't have to fully heal. If I can start to walk properly, get out of bed myself and become mobile, that's when they'll let me out. As long I'm well enough and my weight is starting to come back.'

I saw that as my chance. I would go at it like a bull at a gate.

I drew inspiration from a patient named Kylie, a girl from Perth, about 17 years old, who was waiting for a suitable donor for a kidney and lung transplant.

She was going through her training program as well and occasionally I'd visit her. We struck up a bit of a friendship. It opened my eyes to the fact that, 'Hey, I'm 28, I've played football at the highest level, been overseas many times, experienced the love of a partner, and yet this poor girl is just starting out in life really and, if things don't go her way, she won't get to experience any of those things.' It was very sobering. It proved that, no matter how harshly done by you feel, there are always people worse off than you.

My condition improved rapidly. To my infinite relief, the doctors decided to reduce the amount of time I had to have a nasal-gastric tube — which fed me throughout my stay in hospital — in my throat from 24 hours a day to 18 hours. Although my throat was still dry and sore, I had started eating.

A few of my teammates came to see me on separate occasions. My captain, Anthony Stevens, saw me after he got back from the USA. I should have told him that one of my saviours in Bali, Tim McGill, was almost a dead-ringer for him in both looks and personality. 'Stevo' is such a modest person, he probably would have responded to that with something like, 'Poor bastard. I wouldn't wish that on anyone.'

ANTHONY STEVENS (KANGAROOS CAPTAIN 2002–2003): Some of the news reports said Jason wasn't too bad and other reports had him close to death, so I didn't really know what to expect. It was a shock to see him laid out with burns all over. He showed me a fair few of them. I didn't know what to think, I didn't know what to say — I was just glad the big fella was still alive and still kicking.

I definitely thought he'd get back playing footy. One thing about Jason is that he's very determined and he's worked very hard throughout his whole footy career. I just wasn't real sure how long it would take him. He never expressed any doubts to me, but that's one of the qualities about Jason — he never talks in negatives, he's one of the most positive guys I've come across.

JOHN BLAKEY: I went back and saw him and I couldn't believe how much he'd improved in that week or so. He was being able to sit up a lot better and talk a lot more. I started thinking, 'Maybe he can make a comeback.'

A visit from the former Governor-General of Australia, Peter Hollingworth, and his wife, Ann, on Melbourne Cup Day, was a nice break from what had become a daily grind. I would have thought they would be lapping up the festivities at Flemington Racecourse. But no, they were doing the rounds in hospital, trying to foster spirit and hope among those that were less fortunate than themselves. They were lovely.

The next day, Wednesday, 6 November, I was having my daily bath when Dr Heather Cleland checked on my progress.

'Your legs look good,' she said. 'You might only need a couple more sessions in the hyperbaric chamber.'

Dr Cleland seemed like the type of person who didn't make big statements, so this was a major development. My excitement was palpable. I felt like a little kid who had been given a big present.

Over and over in my mind, I analysed what Dr Cleland had said. 'She said "a couple" more sessions,' I thought. 'Hey, that's only two. Two more and I'm outta here.'

I approached my last two hyperbaric sessions with a far more positive outlook. I knew I had broken the back of this thing and I was on the home stretch.

It was an enormous relief because I had almost been at breaking point the previous day in the hyperbaric chamber. Instead of completing the session lying down in a bed, I tried to do it sitting in a chair. Initially there was a delay because the chair I originally sat in wasn't hyperbaric-proof, so they had to manoeuvre me into another chair, which was bloody uncomfortable. I was forced to sit there and wait for 45 minutes — I timed it on the clock — before I could enter the chamber because they had to clean it out. That, in addition to the two-hour session, was a real struggle.

The staff there said to me, 'Look, we know you're a tough bugger, but you've got to go back to the bed. We can see you were doing it hard on the chair.'

All I could do in the hyperbaric chamber was think. I couldn't read because of the state of my hands, I couldn't sleep because I couldn't relax. It drove me crazy. It was like I was in solitary confinement. Alone, with only my thoughts to comfort me. I didn't want to think any more. I wanted to do.

I managed to grit my teeth through those last two hyperbaric sessions and got through it. Another mission completed.

After the last session, I started sounding off to the staff about how good I felt. 'Boys, I don't have to come back here any more,' I said with a cocky grin. 'This is it for me. It's been great, but you won't be seeing me again.'

A specialist said everything seemed to be healing well. I pointed to the hole in the back of my left leg. The specialist didn't appear concerned. 'That'll be all right. We can graft over that.'

But it wasn't all right. I thought, 'I've done a lot of walking, I've used the treadmill in the gym. I'm still wobbly on my feet, but I'm rebuilding my confidence in my body. I'm even able to push the walking frame in front of me and take a few steps on my own. 'If I get this leg grafted, it could set me back five days in my recovery. I can't do that.'

I decided against the skin graft. I was told it would heal on its own eventually anyway, but that there might be an indented scar. I could handle that.

BRENDEN McCARTNEY: Each day you saw him, he'd show you something else he was able to do. We walked with him down the corridor one day and he said, 'Have a look at this' — no walking frame. We surrounded him because we thought, 'He's gonna go arse-over here.' But he didn't. It was a real sign that he was coming on in leaps and bounds.

HENRIETTA LAW: I always had confidence that he would play football again. You get a bit of a gut feeling about your patients. He had a positive goal, so he would heal, and he had a lot of other components that would get him playing again. I always said, 'Give it six months. I think he has a fair chance.'

Jason wanted me to say that on day one. He always asked me whether he would be able to play again. Of course, in the medical profession, I can't really make guarantees like that.

MEL PACQUOLA: Everyone was saying, 'He's doing too much exercise,' mainly because he had gone well and truly beyond anyone who was recovering from burns. None of us had seen anyone push themselves to do so much and cope with it.

On Wednesday, 6 November, the doctors gave me the news that I'd been desperate to hear ever since Bali. They told me I could go home in five to seven days. As soon as they said that, I started thinking about halving that time. 'I'll be out on the weekend then,' I thought. It was like the doctors could read my mind.

'We know you're pretty determined,' one of them said. 'We don't want to put a specific day on it because we know you'll try to undercut it.'

Slow and steady progress is the best progress and all that.

HENRIETTA LAW: He actually got out of the bed without us helping him, only supervising, and he walked about 100 metres. His body capacity had improved a lot.

BRENDEN McCARTNEY: One day, Jase said, 'Have a look at this.' He jumped out of bed — he had a bit of spring about him — and pretended he was on the speedball like Rocky Balboa.

After passing the physical tests they put before me, I thought that a few words in the right ears would certainly give my campaign for release a decent push along. My powers of persuasion — or desperation — worked a treat.

I was allowed to go home on the Saturday morning.

To be out of hospital five weeks before the wedding was ideal. I knew I'd need at least three weeks to build my strength up enough to enjoy the special day, so to have an extra fortnight was a godsend. That meant I would have four weeks of physio and rehab to get myself in tip-top condition. It was going to be a long haul but I've always been up for a challenge.

The nasal-gastric tube, which fed me constantly for most of my stay in hospital, was only in action overnight during my last two days there. To help me put on and sustain my weight, I was given a dietary supplement to have in between meals. It tasted like crap. As a result, I hardly ever had it.

I got Nerissa to buy plenty of strawberry Big Ms in the cafeteria downstairs. The Big Ms and other milkshakes contained full-cream milk — weight-gain material. Normally, I'd never dream of drinking such things.

I had dreamt, though, about leaving hospital and going home. That dream came a step closer to a reality on the morning of Friday 8 November when the nasal-gastric tube was removed from my throat — for good. 'Good riddance,' I thought.

While I was desperate to have the tube removed, I didn't want to gag again when they were taking it out, as my throat was still sensitive. Thankfully, it was a quick and painless procedure.

The doctors couldn't believe that I was getting out. Some of the doctors that treated me in ICU visited me and said, 'You're unbelievable. When you came in, we thought, "minimum eight weeks".' Here I was getting out in three and a half weeks — less than half the time they had forecast. I was pretty happy with that, ecstatic in fact.

But perhaps the doctors hadn't taken into consideration what I did for a living. Rehabilitation and working hard on my body was part of my job as an AFL footballer. I'd done it seriously for 12 years, and spent another decade before that preparing myself for it. While the wedding was my major focus at the time, I wanted to get back to work as soon as I could.

HENRIETTA LAW: Just before Jason left hospital, he had started on the treadmill. So we go from walking like an old lady, who you more or less worry about stumbling and falling over, to walking with a machine at 3 kilometres an hour. That's reasonable progress.

Also we started bouncing on the Fit Ball, which increases your lung volume and works your arms. It's very good cardiovascular training.

On his third day at the gym, he did a one-hour session, which is actually a lot for a burns patient. Most burns patients, on their first day at the gym, might just walk there and do two or three minutes of training before they give up.

I think I told him that he would be running in two weeks. But for him to start running, he would have to get to at least 8 kilometres an hour on the treadmill, he still had to improve a lot before he started running.

One morning, he walked all the way out to the end of Commercial Road to Nerissa's car park, and then all the way back. That's was about 200 metres. Then, in the afternoon, just to prepare him to go home, he felt he really wanted to do more treadmill. I think that attitude is part of being an athlete. He increased his speed on the treadmill to five kilometres an hour, and he did it for five minutes.

I wasn't about to tell Henrietta or any of the doctors that I lived in a double-storey townhouse and that our bedroom was upstairs. I thought that they would detain me until I was a competent stair-walker and I presumed it would add about a week onto my departure time. Somehow, Henrietta found out about the stairs. But then I virtually forced Henrietta to give me some stair work. I was pleasantly surprised when I conquered them within a day and was able to walk, unassisted, up stairs.

HENRIETTA LAW: He did two flights of the stairs and he was fine — no problem at all.

In normal circumstances, I wouldn't have suggested that I should walk up stairs. I didn't think I had the strength or balance. But the power of positive thinking, combined with a sense of urgency and purpose, can produce positive results you don't think are possible. In a nutshell, if you have a go, you never know what might happen. The same theory that applies in footy when you find yourself up against a top quality opponent who you're not expected to beat. This time though, my 'opponent' was someone I knew inside out. My opponent was myself.

I'm sure that the doctors and nurses were glad to see the back of me, and not just because I had recovered sufficiently and was out of danger. I had constantly asked them — nagged and harassed would be a more accurate description — whether they thought I'd be right for the wedding.

DR HEATHER CLELAND: Jason and his family are pretty sensible people. They were all very reasonable in their concerns and took an intelligent interest in what was going on. There's absolutely nothing wrong with people wanting to try to understand what was happening. The whole thing is completely alien to the average person. Asking questions and being curious is a natural part of that education process.

Jason wasn't bad at all. He was very sensible and took a very pragmatic view of everything. He wanted to know what was going on and why things were happening, but he was not in the slightest bit tedious.

He seemed to have a lot of self-discipline. When someone like him, with an elite sporting background, is faced with something like this that requires a lot of discipline and hard work, they naturally do it because they've been doing it for years. Jason understood that that's what you've got to do to get back to where you want to be.

I thought it was a tremendous effort. He was very focused and disciplined all the way through his acute treatment and rehabilitation. He wanted to do anything he could to make sure that he got as well as he possibly could.

People do the most remarkable things when these appalling things happen to them.

I've got no doubt that the wedding played a significant role in my rapid recovery. It was a huge motivational tool. I couldn't afford to just sit back and accept my predicament.

I drew enormous confidence from my earlier-than-expected release. (I make it sound like a jail term. I suppose in some ways it was.) It proved to me that I could overcome most things — perhaps everything. Such self-belief was to help me face the challenges in the months ahead.

My last night was a memorable one for many reasons — not just for the fact that I was leaving hospital the next morning. My brother, Brenden, was there. His beautiful daughter, my niece, Tarlie, was two in March (2003). When Brenden and her mum, Ange, came to Melbourne, they left Tarlie to be looked after at home in Nhill. They were afraid that if she saw me wrapped up like an Egyptian mummy, it would give her nightmares. But even though she was so young and no one had told her anything, she knew something was wrong because her parents were suddenly away a lot more. Ange says that whenever Tarlie was asked how her Uncle Jason was going, she'd hunch her shoulders, cross her arms across her chest and say, 'Ooh, Uncle Jase sore.' How cute is that? Kids obviously understand a lot more than we give them credit for sometimes.

Brenden brought in Tarlie's Lego box, which I thought was strange until he opened it to reveal about a dozen stubbies of VB that he'd smuggled into the hospital.

BRENDEN McCARTNEY: There were a couple of nurses up there, so I made Tarlie carry the box because it would have looked a bit sus if I was carrying it. She was battling; she nearly dropped it on the floor. No wonder — I'd jammed six or seven cans of beer in there and put half a bag of ice on top.

Not to be outdone, Corey brought along some food and a bottle of wine in his footy bag. Nerissa was just hanging for something like that because she just needed to release the pressure valve after what she had endured over the previous three and a half weeks. It was good to finally see her relax a little.

A couple of mates also came in and there was a bit of a celebration. I just settled for a strawberry Big M — an unusual celebratory drink, I must say. But it was refreshing to bring some happiness to the faces of people I cared about.

I was so excited that I hardly slept. A bit like I felt before my first game of AFL footy. I was wide awake at 5.30 a.m.

Looking back, going home was just another brick in the wall to full recovery. But at the time, it was an enormous thing. It had been a huge carrot dangling in front of me, which, at first, appeared unattainable, but, with each skerrick of improvement, had suddenly come within an arm's length.

Every emotion I felt in hospital was amplified. I had lived outside the real world, in a virtual cocoon, for four weeks. Twenty-eight days. It doesn't sound like such a long time, but when you've taken an emotional roller-coaster for that long, it seems like 28 years. It was certainly long enough to transform all that was familiar to me — football training, driving, even walking — into unfamiliar, unfathomable acts, while things that were once blissfully foreign — intense rehab sessions; laying idle in bed for hours on end; being unable to fend for myself — frustratingly became part of my day-to-day routine.

None of this was a reflection on the level of treatment I received while in hospital, as I can't speak highly enough of the expertise, honesty and optimism of the doctors, nurses and physios who helped me during my stay. They made every effort to make me comfortable. It was just that, in my condition, no amount of care was going to make me completely comfortable. As much as I enjoyed their company, I was desperate to finally go home.

My parents arrived at 7.30 a.m. It was time to go.

JAN MCCARTNEY: Jason just strolled down the ramp as casual as can be. I thought, 'This is really something.' I'll never forget it.

IAN MCCARTNEY: It brought tears to our eyes. The way he walked out, if you hadn't known, you would have thought the only reason he was at the hospital was because he'd been visiting someone.

NERISSA: It was like a scene from a movie. I walked out first and I looked around to make sure there was no media or anyone. As we walked out, I remember saying, 'Let's go home,' and giving a big sigh of relief. We were all really excited. We were happy too that the media weren't there to potentially spoil the moment.

Mum, Dad and Nerissa loaded the cars with boxes full of cards, letters and balloons. Lucky I had a Toyota Prado four-wheel drive because we also had to transport the TV and the PlayStation that Arch and Simmo had brought in. The bigger vehicle also made it easier for me to get into and stretch out a bit. I might have struggled to get down low and fold myself up into a normal sedan.

NERISSA: Jason went with Jan in his car and I went with Ian. I was just watching Jason's car, knowing he was in it on the way home, just thinking, 'This is so great.' But I was also very unsure about what life was going to be like from then on because I'd have to do a lot more for him and help him put his clothes on. I was very nervous about that.

But it was a huge relief, and I had a huge amount of pride in Jason because he had worked so hard and he had made it.

I thought, 'Now I'm going to be really strong because I'm going to have to be there every minute of the day. I'm going make his life as comfortable as possible while he's at home.'

DI LLOYD: We thought, 'How can we get Jason out of the hospital without 50,000 people waiting outside for him?' He came out unexpectedly, but soon everybody found out. You can't keep anything quiet in Melbourne.

JAN MCCARTNEY: When he got in the car and we drove off, he said, 'That was easy, wasn't it Mum?'

I said, 'Very easy compared to what we've been dodging and weaving for the last four weeks.'

I was so relieved. A frustrating chapter of my life was over. I had a fresh start. A new beginning.

15

Home again

We got home at about 9 a.m., and Dad went to the South Melbourne market and bought plenty of eggs, bacon and sausages. With my throat improving, I decided to follow the instructions of the hospital dietitian to eat whatever I could. I felt like a glutton, but I also felt empowered. I still didn't eat as much as I would have pre-Bali because my stomach had shrunk a little after being forced to survive on liquid food, but I gave it a fair nudge. I never thought I'd say this but it was good to be onto the greasy food.

The simple fact was I had to put on weight. I was 9 or 10 kilograms below my playing weight. I was doing light weights but I thought, 'There's no way I'm going to be able to put that weight on with muscle straight away. The best way to go about it is to eat fatty foods. I'm never going to become obese.' Then at least I would have something to work with when I got back into serious footy training in January. I would still be a few kilograms under my playing weight, but at least I'd be somewhere near it. It was a better option than going in skinny, training and doing weights, but being weak and feeling tired throughout.

I started thinking about football almost by instinct, but I didn't want to get ahead of myself. My number one priority was being fit for the wedding. Next on my wish list — indeed dream list — was to play AFL football again. I didn't know if I was going to make it back to that level, but I needed to continue my rapid recovery to give myself the best possible chance.

I'd put so much effort into getting out of hospital — it took me back to when I had my appendix removed at Nhill Hospital at the age of 11 or 12. The doctors then didn't expect me to be out for another week, but I put on a big front that I was OK. I strutted around the hospital in my jocks, visited other patients and generally tried to mock the fact that I was in hospital. When they asked me how I felt, I looked at them cocky and brash as ever and declared, 'I'm fine; I'm ready to leave.' They relented and let me go home. When I got home, I couldn't move and felt terrible because I was still sore. I wasn't as bad this time —in the 16 or

17 years since, I had actually learnt something — but I'd used so much energy and put on such a brave front that, when I got home, I was physically and emotionally exhausted. In horse-racing parlance, I couldn't raise a gallop.

JAN MCCARTNEY: During the two weeks I stayed there — my sister Wendy also stayed for a week — we made cheese-and-bacon scones and Chinese food and whatever else. I couldn't believe my eyes when I saw him eating all these different types of junk food — he'd always watched what he ate. But he sent Nerissa and me all over Melbourne to buy different food that he wanted. The more we made, the more Jason ate. Wendy had never seen him eat like that before. She said, 'He's like a pig.'

I said, 'Let him go. He's got to put plenty of weight back on.'

While I expected the food overload to give me more energy and strength, it actually had the opposite effect. When I went to the toilet I became light-headed and had to lean against the wall for a minute to steady myself. That's when I realised just how weak I was. My energy had been sapped.

The same thing happened the next morning when I had a shower. I nearly passed out. After that, I'd ask Nerissa to make a bowl of cereal for me so that I could go into the shower with some energy. I was accustomed to eating energy food before football matches, but now I had to 'prepare' myself for a shower.

Whenever I'd strip down in those first few weeks, I'd look at my reflection in the mirror and think, 'Gee, the body's a bit of a mess.' But I soon tempered that by thinking, 'With time and the use of the pressure garments, the redness and the scars will fade. Other people died, so what are scars?'

I did wonder if Nerissa would be repulsed by my body.

NERISSA: I'd seen all of Jason's wounds in the hospital. When they first changed his dressings, I thought, 'Oh, my goodness.' But I've never thought, 'Oh, gross.' I really felt for him and how he might cope with it all.

People commented about how bad the burns are and when Jason would show someone, they'd go 'ooh'. I look at Jason walking around the house naked, and I think 'Hey, baby, come over here and let's have some fun.' I don't even look at the scars. I look straight through them. I see the man I love. When you're in love with someone, you don't really care about their appearance.

BRENDEN MCCARTNEY: Jason's always been a big, strong, bulky bloke, and he always got around with his top off at training. Whenever he'd come home at Christmas time during the break in pre-season training, he'd get around without a shirt — he hardly had a mark on his body. I thought, 'Well, he's not going to be able to do that again.

He's going to have to keep covered up and he's not going to like that.' I was really feeling for him because there were a lot of things that were new to him that he was going to have to get used to. He accepted it pretty well though.

I was ready to read through the hundreds of cards, letters, faxes and messages that I'd received while I was in hospital. Nerissa had tried to read some of them to me in hospital, which I really appreciated. But I couldn't focus on anything for long, the cards included. I was too scatter-brained.

At home, Nerissa and I separated the cards into three categories: family, friends and people neither of us knew. It was a tiring but worthwhile exercise. It gave me something to focus on, occupied my idle time and made me feel like I was doing something useful. It took forever, but it was well worth the effort. I read all of them and was completely overwhelmed by the lengths people had gone to.

Just when I thought I was making progress through the boxes of letters, Nerissa would come in with another box in her arms and say, 'Here's another lot for you to go through.' I'm glad I went through them all individually though. I've got a good memory too, which comes in handy. Sometime later at Tullamarine airport, I bumped into a couple whose son I went to school with in Nhill. Although I hadn't seen them for a long time, I said immediately, 'Thanks for the card.' I could tell they appreciated the recognition.

In hindsight, I wish I'd replied to all of the well-wishers. But it was physically impossible. My hands were still healing and weren't nimble enough. I had no choice but to simply rip the envelopes open. If the sender hadn't written their address on the card, it was gone.

NERISSA: Jason and I feel guilty about not replying to all those people. At one stage, I said to Jan, 'I think we should, as a family, put something in the paper to thank everyone because it's too hard at this moment in time to send something back to all these people.' They were putting their addresses on the back of the cards, so I thought, 'Did they want a reply?'

We put a little thank you piece in the *Herald Sun*. That was the best we could do. Replying individually would have been too emotional.

One parcel in particular choked me up. It was from a three-year-old girl named Olivia Johnston, who I had never met before. In her letter, she said that she had been born prematurely and had undergone a few operations. She also sent me her favourite raggy bear to hold on to and be comforted by. All she asked was for me to bring her bear back when I recovered.

Olivia's parents were quite shocked when I rang a few weeks later and told them I wanted to return Olivia's bear to her. Nerissa and I drove out to the Johnstons' Ferntree Gully home in Melbourne's eastern suburbs. Although she was only a toddler, Olivia impressed me as a very intelligent girl who had an unusually acute awareness of her surroundings. I half expected the family to be Kangaroos' fans, but they weren't. Olivia's parents told us that she latches on to anything relating to the human spirit that she sees on TV. She had endured some traumatic times in hospital herself, so when she saw someone else doing it hard in hospital, she developed an emotional attachment to them.

All of the messages are in boxes at home. A steady stream of them arrived at the footy club while I was on the comeback trail and another flood came in after my retirement from footy. I'll keep them forever.

There have been times when I've opened a box and found myself getting sidetracked flicking through some of the messages. Everything comes flooding back. I always find one or two messages that I'd overlooked. I don't want to live in the past, but the messages inspire me and give me a better perspective on things.

DI LLOYD: We were getting letters and cards and phone calls and emails. It was a huge response — and it didn't stop from the time that Jason was injured until well after his comeback match. I was trying to work out whether it was coming from the traditional AFL states or if it went further than that. But it was the whole country. We got a lot of things from footy clubs at all levels.

DR ALLEN AYLETT (KANGAROOS PRESIDENT): The amount of interest in Jason McCartney was unprecedented. Not only in Melbourne but all over Australia. People would come up to me and ask, 'How's Jason McCartney?' Even when I was walking the streets of Hong Kong — I've got family there — during the week that I was there, I was stopped half a dozen times by Australian people. The first question they asked was, 'How's Jason McCartney?'

PAUL CONNORS (JASON'S MANAGER): The most out-there request came from a group of people exiled from a Middle-Eastern country. They wanted to present Jason with a shield of honour. This is coming from people who are exiles, and they wanted to give him a bravery award.

When you're the subject of such an outpouring of emotion, it's easy to feel overwhelmed. I knew there would be a lot of support from my family and friends and the footy club, but I never counted on getting cards from total strangers from all around the country, and even some from overseas.

That's when the realisation hit me: 'I'd better keep fighting this thing; a lot of people are counting on me.'

Being an AFL footballer meant that I got more support than the other survivors because I was already a public face. Although I've never been one of the big names in footy, that didn't seem to matter. People knew how to contact me too — either through the footy club or at the hospital.

There is no escaping the fact that it gave me a huge lift. The positive response alone probably took a few days off my stay in hospital.

I actually feel lucky. Lucky to be alive. Lucky to get a second chance. Lucky to have such a loving family, a wonderful wife and a rock-solid bunch of mates. Lucky to know the depth of feeling that certain people have for me.

I'm sure a lot of people die without knowing how others truly feel about them. In a way, what I've gone through is like turning up at your own wake.

I don't lose sight of the fact that I have been blessed in areas that many people can only dream about. For that, I am eternally grateful.

GLENN ARCHER: Jason rang me up and said, 'I'm at home. What do you want me to do with this TV?' I thought he was joking at first. Only days before, he was just taking his first couple of steps. But he said, 'A couple of days later, something just clicked and I was flying.' So it was a bloody amazing comeback.

On Thursday, 13 November, I was ready to tell people exactly how I was going. My manager, Paul Connors, took me to the Kangaroos' traditional home at Arden Street to see my teammates. The club had a trauma counsellor on hand for the players after the bomb blasts to help them work through any issues they had.

I addressed the players as a group and tried to reinforce the old message that your career passes by very quickly. I was told the exact same thing when I was 17 or 18 and I thought, 'That's crap; I've got ten or 12 years in front of me.' But it's true. It really hit home that if I was an 18-year-old kid, the Bali bombings would have ended my AFL career before it started.

I also told the boys that while they were training their butts off and were getting pretty fit, they wouldn't get too far ahead of me because I was doing daily physio and rehab, and couldn't wait until I ran out with them again.

LEIGH COLBERT: When he said, 'I'm going to play again next year,' I didn't doubt him one little bit. Just knowing the bloke, and how fiercely determined he is, I knew he was going to do everything in his power to get to the line.

BRENT HARVEY (KANGAROOS TEAMMATE): I thought, 'It's not going to happen.' I wanted it to happen as much as anybody, but I really didn't think it would.

The next day, after I'd completed my daily physio and rehab session, I had a press conference.

DI LLOYD: There was a huge demand from the media for interviews with Jason. But right from the start, he said, 'I'll do (interviews with) everybody. I'm not going to do one person, I'll do the lot.'

You look at that attitude and then you look at some other instances where people have been thrust into the spotlight by accident and really cashed in on it. He could easily have chosen to go down the same path. I had a fairly cynical attitude, having been in the newsroom at the *Canberra Times* during the Thredbo disaster. So it was nice that Jason had a different attitude. He certainly made my life easier.

PAUL CONNORS: He got thrown money from a number of people to do exclusives. They certainly offered enough bucks to make it pretty enticing for Jason, given his football salary had gone from 200 thousand to 40 thousand. He knocked back dollars from other networks to do exclusives, and then proceeded to do *Today Tonight* and *The 7.30 Report,* and he did them all for free. He was adamant about that.

While I was prepared for the type of questions that would come my way from reporters — my friends and family had asked most of them at one time or another, and Paul prepped me for 15 minutes immediately beforehand — I wasn't prepared for the amount of interest attracted by the event. Cameras and reporters were everywhere. I don't think I've ever seen so many people in the Kangaroos Social Club. It was standing room only.

The photos from the press conference are not pretty. I had a bony, drawn look and it was hot because of the lights. People ask me whether I sweat much as a result of being burnt. I've always sweated a lot and I don't sweat any more than I did previously. But the skin on my face was new like baby skin, and it was greasy and shiny. With the lights on me for 45 minutes, my pressure garments on and all of the questioning, I was glowing.

I made a point of thanking the Australian public for their support through trying times. I also promoted the Red Cross Bali Appeal race meeting to be run by the Kangaroos in conjunction with the Moonee Valley Race Club. I didn't realise it at the time but the Fox Footy channel, which obviously isn't too busy at that time of year, broadcast the entire press conference.

Until then, I'd only ever dealt with the sports media. This time hard news and current affairs reporters were there too. Afterwards, I did interviews with Channel Seven's *Today Tonight* and the ABC's *The 7.30 Report*, posed for photos for the newspapers and filmed a TV commercial for the race meeting.

DI LLOYD: I don't know how Jason coped with it. The room was packed and it was hot. After the press conference, I threw him another T-shirt to change into before the other interviews because he was drenched in sweat. But he handled it all with great aplomb, as we've come to expect. In the months to come he was asked the same questions 50,000 times over and always answered them with a smile.

I was completely drained that night.

Two surprise visitors were my former captain, Wayne Carey, and his wife Sally. They were all set to move to Adelaide the next week. Duck had been traded to the Crows, where he would resume his AFL career after leaving the Kangaroos. I'd spoken to him a couple of times over the phone since the bombings. He didn't need to speak to me that much because he'd been kept in the loop by his sisters and Mick. He was very positive. He said, 'Mate, I know this is a huge battle, but you've had some pretty big battles along the way. There's no doubt you'll get there.'

WAYNE CAREY (KANGAROOS DUAL PREMIERSHIP CAPTAIN, NOW AT THE ADELAIDE CROWS): I just wanted to see Jason, make sure he was all right, let him know that my thoughts were with him and, if he needed help with anything in any way, to let me know. I told him to keep his chin up.

It was a bit of a shock. He's a big strong bloke, so I was surprised at how thin he looked. He had bandages on, so you couldn't really see how horrific his injuries were. But considering what he'd been through, I thought he looked quite well. But that's the way the guy is, strong and playing it all down a fair bit.

Jason's always been a great competitor. We had a few duels when he was at Collingwood and Adelaide and I always found him to be a good opponent. There were some good battles where we had a few wrestles and so forth, but it was always in the right spirit.

I remember when Denis Pagan called me and said, 'What do you think about us going after Jason McCartney?' I didn't really know Jason as a guy then, but I knew he was a great competitor and he'd always give 100 per cent for the team. That's obviously come out in his normal daily life.

We've all had personal struggles throughout our lives, but when something like that happens, it puts everything into perspective. Just knowing that so many people were caught up in such a tragedy — not just Jason, but everyone involved — you can really draw a lot from it.

But I think I'd probably be lying if I said I thought he could get back to play in the AFL. He's always been a fairly determined, strong, hard-working guy, so it certainly wouldn't have surprised me. But if I was a betting man, I would have said no.

I think people might have told me positive things thinking that maybe this battle was a bit too big, and that I probably wouldn't overcome it. But I'm glad they were positive. The last thing I would have wanted was people saying, 'Mate, you've got no hope. You're not going to be able to do anything.'

The fact that I was surrounded by so many positive people helped me. You soon forget any self-doubts you might have, and their positive attitude rubs off on you, almost without you realising. It's infectious.

Self-doubt and pessimism had actually threatened to ruin my AFL career. During my three seasons with Adelaide in 1995–97, my confidence almost completely deserted me — a major handicap for a professional sportsman. In my first two years with the Crows, I missed a lot of footy through suspension. Silly stuff. I was in my early twenties and thought I had to play aggressively. We didn't have many big blokes and, even though Mark Ricciuto is an intimidating and fearless player, I thought I had to take on the role of enforcer. It wasn't my natural game and I got exposed for it. People sometimes say the coach, Robert Shaw, encouraged me to play that way, but he didn't. Like every coach, he wanted me to be aggressive, but the problem was I didn't do it the right way. I lost my cool, lost my focus and my place in the team.

It was to get worse. At the end of the 1996 season, I allowed myself to become involved in a regrettable incident. After running amok on 'Mad Monday' — the traditional post-season drink with your teammates — and following it up with 'Terror Tuesday', it promised to be a 'Wild Wednesday'. That promise was delivered.

End-of-season celebrations get out of hand at the best of times, but this particular year there was an added edge to our revelry. Malcolm Blight, who'd led Geelong to three losing grand final appearances in six years, had been appointed as the new coach. You didn't have to be Einstein to figure out that, after we'd finished 11th, 11th and 12th in the previous three years, 'Blighty' would take a hard line towards turning the club's fortunes around. This was confirmed at the post-season review on the Wednesday when we were told, 'You blokes get six weeks off a year, two of them are at Christmas; you've got four now, so you've got to be back for training three days after the AFL grand final.'

It was a ridiculous situation because the SANFL grand final took place the week after the AFL grand final, so there were some players on our list who were still playing while we had started pre-season training. (Nothing like today, with the AFL Players' Association's Collective Bargaining Agreement stipulating an eight-week break at the end of the season.)

We went out that Wednesday night and got fairly drunk, as young blokes tend to do. I thought, 'I'll just drop into the ex-girlfriend's place on the way home.'

I had been going out with a girl from Horsham who had moved to Adelaide. After a strong, four-year relationship, we broke up. It was an amicable split about a month before. I'd seen her earlier that day to give her a card to pass on to her two sisters, who had just had their second children days apart. We were pleasant to each other.

Anyway, I knocked on her front door and she let me in. Her bedroom door was shut, but I pushed it open and a bloke was in there. I was shocked because I didn't expect anyone else to be there. I went into a rage and whacked the bloke a few times. She jumped on me and knocked me off the bed, and the bloke left. I think a neighbour called the police because they heard screaming. I got a taxi home and didn't think much of it.

The next morning, the club's footy manager, John Reid, called me for an explanation. Someone had called the club and told them that I had been involved in an incident.

The fact that I'd been drinking wasn't an excuse — I realise that you've got to take responsibility for your actions — but it certainly didn't help. I was charged with assault, went to court and was acquitted, but I had to pay damages and undergo anger-management therapy.

It was reported in the newspaper, which is fair enough, but the way the story was written sounded like I may have hit my ex-girlfriend. Where I come from, hitting a girl is one of the worst things you could do. That wasn't me.

I didn't want to show my face anywhere. I became a recluse. I just wanted to hide from the world. Away from prying eyes and malicious whispers.

The next weekend, a mate of mine from Nhill who lived in Adelaide wanted me to go to the basketball with him. I was dead against it. I was worried about being recognised and perceived as a girl-basher. But somehow he persuaded me that it would be OK. When we got there — I should have known this would happen — people were looking at me and talking to the people beside them. (I wasn't imagining it; I heard them.) I was worried about what their kids would have been thinking when their parents told them, 'That's the bloke from the Crows who belted his girlfriend.'

It took a long time for me to recover from those mental scars. It battered my self-esteem and I went to a well-respected counsellor and activist named David Bonython-Wright for advice. I felt comfortable with Dave, and he soon became a trusted friend. I'd leave a session thinking, 'Bloody hell, I've told this bloke a lot of stuff here.' But he played an important role in my maturing process. I'd left home at 16 for the bright lights of the AFL, and there were a few issues that came with that — the pressure to perform and to be a public figure, the homesickness, girls and so on. Dave was the first person I poured my heart out to.

It helped that Dave was a well-rounded individual. He wears almost as many 'hats' as Eddie McGuire. An Australian volleyball representative from 1975 to 1982, he works with indigenous prisoners in jails, has an involvement in politics, calls Midnight Oil lead singer Peter Garrett a friend and is a consultant to many different bodies and organisations.

DAVID BONYTHON-WRIGHT (JASON'S COUNSELLOR, ADVISER AND FRIEND): Jason was very easy to work with. He was open and honest — that's all you can ask.

My disillusionment with life spilled onto the football field. I played the first six games in Blighty's first year, 1997, and didn't get a look in after that, despite playing some good footy with South Adelaide.

Although I knew I wasn't in Blighty's plan, I didn't dislike him or anything. That was just the way it was. I was big enough to accept what he was trying to do, and the proof is in the pudding — he won the flag that year and repeated the effort the next year.

However, during our second round match that year against Richmond at the MCG I disliked Blighty intensely. We played insipid football and were lucky to lose by only 28 points. It was the day that Blighty labelled my then teammate David Pittman as 'the most pathetic ruckman I've ever seen in my entire life in footy'. But I remember that autumn afternoon for an entirely different reason.

During one of the breaks, Blighty grabbed me and delivered a stinging rebuke. 'They tell me you're tough,' he said, eyeballing me with disdain. 'I reckon you're as weak as piss!' It was the angriest I've been on a football field and I wasn't angry at the opposition, the crowd or the scoreboard.

I've always been taught to treat the coach's word as gospel and follow his instructions carefully. Not this time. I had to stop myself from hitting him. How would that have looked? The headlines wouldn't have been 'Pathetic Pittman'; they would have screamed something like, 'Crow stones coach!' or 'Knockout of coach a Blight on the game!' I later laughed about it with the Kangaroos property steward, Aub Devlin, who has been at the club for years, including Blighty's era as a player. Aub said with a grin, 'I wonder what Malcolm thinks now, after you've been through all this.'

But hindsight has 20/20 vision. I understand some things said in the heat of battle can be either over-the-top, untrue or unintentional. I know this only too well after playing under Denis for five years. He had to restrain himself occasionally after games and say, 'I'll talk to you about it during the week; if I talk to you now, I'll regret it.'

16

On the run

When it came to my rehabilitation, I didn't want to have any regrets. I didn't want to leave anything to chance. I wasn't going to miss the wedding by a day or a week simply because I didn't do an extra few minutes on the treadmill, or because I couldn't be bothered putting my compression garments on.

While I focused on the bigger picture, I was also mindful of the smaller but no-less-significant challenges that I had to face, and conquer, each day.

On my last day of hospital, we worked out my rehab routine. I could get a district nurse to come around and change my dressings, but that way I'd be stuck at home all day because they don't come at a definite time. Or I could have a personal trainer. Or I could go to the Alfred every day and continue my association with Henrietta Law. I knew how to do a rehab session but I didn't know what to do if there was a bit of pain. With muscle tears and so forth, you can push through it, but I didn't know if you could do the same with burns.

Initially it was going to be Monday, Wednesday, Friday, and I'd get my dressings done as well. But on that first Monday, we decided to do it every morning, Monday to Friday. I'd go in at about 8.30–9 a.m., go through hand therapy and general physio, then I'd go up to '6 West' in the burns ward, where a nurse would look after me. I wouldn't leave until about noon. I'd be pretty knackered for the rest of the day, especially by about Thursday. When I got home each day, I'd plant myself on the couch, watch DVDs and have a siesta.

I felt like a first-year draftee at an AFL club who was still adjusting to the new workload. A lot of teenage rookies are dead-tired in the afternoons after their training sessions.

At first, I was so weak that I went from being able to do 50 proper push-ups, touching my chest on the ground each time — in peak physical condition — to not being able to do one 'girls' push-up' on my knees.

Henrietta gave me hand therapy, which consisted of exercises and squeezing to strengthen my hands. I also took it upon myself to do some extra hand work on my own. I would break shelled peanuts for a lot of my spare time away from the hospital. There would be remnants of peanut shells all over the couch and the floor, like at the front bar of a Lone Star restaurant. I felt myself getting stronger all the time.

My main focus, though, was to improve my walking and start running again. I'd clocked plenty of time on the treadmill and I steadily built up from 6 kilometres an hour for ten minutes.

HENRIETTA LAW: Jason would start each day warming up by bouncing the Fit Ball 50 times. Then he would go on the treadmill and each day, he could either increase by one minute, or 0.5 to one kilometre, as he saw fit. The third group of exercises on the work stations were to work the pectorals, biceps, triceps and, if he was up to it, quadriceps, because his lower limbs were a bit fragile.

In his last couple of days in hospital, Jason started on the stepper machine and did 50 steps the first day and 150 steps the second, which really exhausted him. I dropped him back to 100 steps, which he started to increase by ten.

He also did quite a lot of stretching with the Fit Ball and some quad core work, which is actually abdominal work.

Initially, most of the time after he exercised, he would be very thirsty. He actually sweats a lot, so he had to replace what he had lost.

Henrietta would also include Nerissa as much as possible.

HENRIETTA LAW: I found that while Jason was doing all of this work, Nerissa was standing there, not knowing what to do. On the second day, I said to Nerissa, 'Tomorrow you can bring your gear so you can do the same together.'

We always try to not only look after the patient, but their family as well. I think that definitely helped them because by putting Nerissa into some form of exercise, it had not only a calming effect on her, but was very good for her well-being. They started to achieve things together.

I was hoping that they would do sessions that lasted one hour, but they usually did one and a half hours. Then Jason became very hungry and they would take a short snack break, so their sessions went a long time. But he never complained.

By the end of the week, Jason was running for up to 12 minutes at 6.5 kilometres an hour, and his weight and everything else had increased. One of the problems we confronted early on was that his calf was quite tight, partly because of the left leg shrapnel wound, which was still healing, so we had to hold back a bit on that. We concentrated quite a lot on stretching.

In week 2, he was running up to 12 minutes at 7.5 kilometres an hour. He started doing three short one-minute jogs in between.

Usually he was a bit slow to get going on a Monday because there was no exercise on the weekends and he was not so well stretched. He was OK on Tuesdays, he might improve a bit on Wednesdays, and then Thursday was usually the climax day. He actually built up to that day and he'd usually do his best effort. Sometimes he was a bit tired on Fridays.

We used a heart-rate monitor from the hospital that I think was due for a service. Pre-Bali, my resting heart rate would be in the 50s or low 60s per minute; now it was in the mid-90s. When we'd walk across Commercial Road to Fawkner Park, which wasn't very far or very strenuous, my heart would pound away at up to 100 beats per minute. There was a hell of a job ahead of me if I was to return to my former fitness level.

Each time we went, Henrietta would pack a little medical kit, consisting of heart monitors, first aid, even an oxygen mask in the event that things got out of hand. I said to her, 'Gee, thanks for building up my confidence.'

HENRIETTA LAW: I was cautious and conservative, but I knew that with his body build, his previous health condition and his age, he would be very safe.

Henrietta would also panic when I crossed the road to the park because I'd cross even when the traffic lights hadn't changed. I suppose I was a bit like a little kid — OK, a big kid — going on his first school excursion. I wanted to get there as soon as I could. Henrietta would say, 'Jason, Jason, be careful, I'm at fault here.' It was like one of those old pedestrian safety commercials for kids that preached, 'Look left, look right, look left again and then cross (the road).' (Maybe the medical kit was actually for Henrietta in case I caused her to have a heart attack!) I understood Henrietta's concerns though. Obviously we were outside the hospital grounds and if anything happened, it was on her head and the hospital would be liable.

HENRIETTA LAW: I must say it is a very, very unusual thing that we run with a patient outside of the hospital. There are legal implications. I ran it by my boss and he said, 'If it's part of therapy and you're comfortable with it, do it.'

I started with a walk in the park. It was only 100 metres, but it was anything but easy. It was a strange thing to ponder, considering I'd done thousands of 100-metre sprints in my time as a footballer.

Henrietta did a few tests on my heart, lungs, flexibility and so on. One of them was a two-minute walk. I went 260 metres the first time and stretched it to about 300 metres two weeks later. I couldn't have walked any faster; in fact, I felt like

I could have broken into a running stride. It was amazing considering that I hadn't been able to walk at all only three weeks earlier. Progress is a wonderful thing.

TIM HARRINGTON: He said, 'I'm going really well,' and I was saying, 'God, take it easy. You've got plenty of time to do all this.' But he was pushing and pushing. I started to get a bit concerned when he said, 'I'll be right to be at training.' I started thinking things like, 'God, we'll have to have a specialist at training when the time comes.' I was ready to have an ambulance there.

I heard how other Bali victims were going with their recovery and testing, and, like anyone with a shred of competitiveness in them, I was determined to beat them although I was really only competing against myself.

I was even competitive with Henrietta. At first, I couldn't keep up with her, but as I improved, I powered around the corners. My longer stride, due to a 30-odd centimetre height advantage, certainly helped.

I'd often say to Henrietta, 'How about another lap?'

'Jason, mate,' she'd say, 'you've got to take it slowly.'

When I felt confident enough — and with Henrietta's approval — I started jogging and increasing both the distance and intensity of each session. It wasn't long before the time had come for me to run. I was nervous. I knew it was another moment of truth. But I also knew that it was a natural and logical progression.

My first official run was over 100 metres, at about half-pace. I felt like a newborn foal or giraffe — raw and gangly, legs sprawling all over the place. Not quite sure of how everything was supposed to move, but moving it nonetheless.

I couldn't run flat-out — I've never been a racehorse anyway — because I was hesitant to put too much weight on my left calf. It still felt like someone was jabbing me with a knife. Like a lot of things, my mind was faster than my body. It was a new fact of life that I had to become accustomed to.

HENRIETTA LAW: We did a 150-metre, which he did in 43 seconds. He didn't anticipate that running on the flat ground would be harder than running on the treadmill. I actually ran with him. It was a hard run for him. He was a little bit awkward on the first 15 to 20 metres, and then he got into the swing of it.

When we went for the first run, his heart rate before we started was 79, which is actually quite normal. Then when we finished, it was 129. That's reasonable, but the thing is if it doesn't come down, then I would be worried, because 129 is a very fast heartbeat. To work out someone's maximum heart rate, you subtract their age from 220. In Jason's case that means it's about 190. He says his usual heart rate doesn't go above 180. When you get to 180, that's his break point. So you've got to be ax bit careful.

I recovered well from my first run. I was a little stiff and sore, like after any early football training session. A couple of days later, I jogged a slow half-lap of the track, which is about 800 metres around, and then I walked a brisk lap.

With my footy background of time trials and gut-busting running and circuit sessions, it didn't feel like I was doing enough. Although Henrietta assured me that I was doing plenty, I craved more. That was strange in itself: while I've always enjoyed footy training, a part of me has always sighed with relief when the last sprint or the last push-up or sit-up has ended for a particular session. Not this time though.

Two 100-metre strides and an 800-metre walk isn't a lot in anyone's language. But I realised I had to stop relating it all back to what I did pre-Bali. I had to accept the fact that it would be a long process to regain my fitness. I felt like a dodgy computer: my mind, as well as my body, had to be re-programmed.

Henrietta would make sure I didn't push myself too hard or do too much, so I started calling her 'Handbrake Henrietta'. The problem was that I was only thinking about the effect training was having on my skin and my calf, rather than the most important parts — internal organs like my lungs and heart. With my resting heart rate a lot higher than usual, and vaulting even higher when I exercised, a conservative approach was best. I couldn't go too hard, otherwise there could be consequences that could jeopardise my chances of playing football. I couldn't risk that.

I must admit that after I got the hang of running again, I felt like Forrest Gump. Running made me so happy that I could have run, and run, and run — out of the park, out of the street, out of the suburb …

Within a week of leaving hospital, I had put on 3 kilograms and hit the scales at 91 kilograms. My 'add-weight-quickly' campaign was working. I was rapt, whereas normally I would have been mortified. I stabilised after that — I was stuck at 91 kilograms — because my training with Henrietta began to burn a few calories.

I was also making headway with the dressings on my wounds. After about ten days of getting the dressings re-applied, there wasn't much left to dress except for my left calf. Then we were finally able to get a compression garment over it. Nerissa had to put it on and take it off for me at home — it took about half an hour — because my fingers weren't strong enough. We put the skin-coloured garments on my hands and then my arms.

It was another step forward, but I started to worry. I thought, 'Everything's fine now because Nerissa is with me all the time. But what's it going to be like trying to put garments on both arms and both legs — by myself?'

'And what about when we're playing footy interstate. How am I going to be able to get my arm garments on?

I can't have one of my teammates having to help me. That's too much of a burden for blokes who are trying to concentrate on their footy.'

But steadily, as the strength returned to my fingers, I was soon able to do it all myself, and those fears were erased.

You don't get a second look from people when you wear compression garments. If I wear pants and a long-sleeved top, most people don't even notice. All they can see are those that cover my hands. Whereas scars attract stares and curiosity.

But they're called compression garments for a reason. I'd worn full-length tights at footy training before, but these are tighter than tights. They're like tight, thick stockings. Hardly manly. But after you get over the initial shock, they're quite comfortable.

My surgeon, Dr Heather Cleland, jokingly said, 'I'd like to see you wear them for the next four or five years.' Apparently, kids with burns would not wear these garments in the past, but since I've worn them and played footy in them, they're cool among young burns victims. You can get them in different colours. Doctors love it because they don't have to push the issue with kids now. Kids are saying, 'Oh, that footy player wears them, they must be all right.'

HEATHER CLELAND: They're not all that much fun to wear. Sometimes they can make people more comfortable, because they actually give support and put a bit of pressure on the scars which relieves the itching. But often people find them pretty tedious. No matter how hard we try to tailor them to the patient, they're hard to get into, they're hot in the summer and they tend to rub around joints. They're not something that you can just throw on. They need to be looked after too.

The other thing is that people, especially the younger ones, feel self-conscious about wearing them. So Jason was a great example of someone who said, 'I'm going to do what I need to do to get the best possible results.'

Mum and her sister, my Aunty Wendy, stayed at our place for the first two weeks and ensured that Nerissa and I were all right. They were a huge help.

JAN MCCARTNEY: I burnt one of my fingers getting a big, glass, roasting dish out of the oven. It hurt a lot. I gritted my teeth and whispered, 'Oh, bloody hell!'

Jason was sitting on the couch, looking at me. I tried to hide it and pretend that nothing had happened.

My sister-in-law, Karen, said, 'What have you done, love?'

I said, 'Oh, nothing, nothing.' I whispered to her, 'Shut up!'

I was thinking, 'This thumb could drop off and it wouldn't be anywhere near what we've witnessed with Jason.' Having said that, it was sore though. Three big blisters came up pretty quickly. I picked up a tea towel and it was damp, so that eased the pain a bit.

I took Jason's roast over to him, and he said, 'What did you do to yourself, Mum?'

I said, 'Oh, I just burnt myself.'

He patted me on the back and said, 'Welcome to the club.'

Nerissa had her hands full as my carer, helping to dress and shower me — basically being my personal maid. And she did it all with a smile. Mum and Aunty Wendy took over most of the other duties like cleaning and cooking. It was a huge weight off Nerissa's mind and helped create a largely stress-free environment at home.

NERISSA: It's easy caring for someone that you love. It's unconditional love — it's not an effort because it's a natural thing to do.

The hard part was controlling my emotions. It was harder putting his garments on him. Beside the fact that they were very difficult to get on, I had to be so careful not to touch the burns or the grafts. Sometimes he flinched. I had my hair hanging over my face and tears were running down my face while I was putting them on. But I wouldn't let him see that because I didn't want him to feel bad about it. It was hard to be really strong. The nurses were correct in saying that I'd need my strength when Jason came home. To care for someone when they are still recovering is even harder than sitting by their bed when they are in a coma. But you do it because you love them and you want to make their life as normal and comfortable as possible.

I was also very grateful for the support of Father Geoff James at my school who gave me the last term off. I'll never forget that. Unfortunately, Father Geoff died suddenly (in mid 2003). He is sadly missed.

I don't know how I would have coped if I'd been a single bloke and didn't have such a dedicated support network to drive me on.

Talking of driving, Nerissa drove me all over the place. That's despite the fact that we've got an automatic car. We had planned to go to Millicent for a weekend in late November to do a few things for the wedding and I decided that it would be the perfect time for me to get behind the wheel again. I thought, 'I'm going to drive.' It doesn't sound like much of a development but I was as nervous as a kid doing their driving test.

I thought, 'If I'm going to drive, I may as well do the city driving,' so I drove the first leg of the trip from Albert Park.

With all the physio I'd been doing in the mornings, I was usually really tired and in need of a nap by 2–3 p.m. We headed off at about 1 p.m. I only lasted about 40 minutes, as far as Rockbank, a little town in Melbourne's western suburbs.

Maybe the extra concentration brought that tiredness on a bit quicker.

'I'm knackered,' I said to Nerissa. 'You're going to have to take over.'

I pulled over at a service station in Rockbank where we swapped seats. I had a snooze for a couple of hours. We stopped at Ararat and I thought, 'Gee, I haven't had a meat pie for a while. That'll help put some weight on me too.' Strangely enough, the pies must have energised me because, about an hour later, I had another go at driving and lasted two and a half hours.

Lucky we had an automatic car and not a manual. Although my legs were moving again and becoming stronger by the day, pushing the clutch might have presented a few problems.

Driving a car was another step towards regaining my life, and normality. I was able to drive again. I crossed it off the list.

Driving was an achievement considering I had trouble simply lying in bed without discomfort. My right leg was fully grafted under the knee, while my left leg was partly grafted under the knee and more on the side, so I needed to sleep with my legs outstretched. The skin in the grafted areas was so inflexible at that stage that if I dozed off with my legs slightly bent and then tried to get out of bed and walk, I would have to endure a series of what I can only describe as 'Chinese burns'—torture techniques kids administer to each other in the schoolyard—before the skin would stretch to accommodate a full range of movement. It was a pain because I'd always liked curling up in bed, as I'm sure most people do.

It got so bad that even if I sat in a chair for five minutes without straightening my legs, I'd have to stand on the tips of my toes and slowly, very slowly, put my heels to the floor. I started to think, 'Am I going to be like this for the rest of my life?' I asked my specialist about it and he said, 'It'll gradually get better.' He was right. It took about three months for the Chinese burns to stop.

It took at least that long for questions about my well-being to slowly die off. Thank God for that; it was driving me crazy.

When I got out of hospital and ran into people in the street or people at the footy club, it became worse. It got to the stage where people would just have to say, 'How—' and I'd machine-gun my reply, 'Yeah, no worries, I'm good.' Although I understood that people were only asking out of genuine concern, I wanted to be positive about the whole process. I wanted to avoid pessimism.

My former Adelaide teammate Shaun Rehn, who had a couple of knee reconstructions during his stellar AFL career, would quickly tire of such questions. He once said that he wished he had a tape to play back to people. The only question he seemed to get was, 'How's your knee?' It was like a broken record. I know exactly what he means.

Hard work and a positive attitude were instrumental to everything I did.

At the end of some days, I would get a burst of self-satisfaction and confidence in the knowledge that I had approached my day in the right way. I was giving myself the best possible chance to achieve anything. The sky was, and still is, the limit.

The more I got into my rehab and exercise program, the more I regarded my appearance at the wedding — in good health as well as good spirits — as a fait accompli. I also became more confident about returning to football for the 2003 season.

The *Herald Sun*'s chief football writer, Mike Sheahan, came to the hospital, along with photographer Wayne Ludbey, and I spent half a day showing them how I went about my rehab.

I wanted to show them how far I'd come in such a short time, so I ran a full lap, faster than I'd done it previously, but still at a relative snail's pace. I was exhausted at the end of it — as though I'd just completed a 5-kilometre time trial — but I tried to act as though I got through it OK. After all, Mike Sheahan was writing a story about me that would be read by the footy world.

After my session the next day — which marked four full weeks of rehab — Henrietta surprised me with morning tea. It was a kind of graduation ceremony.

HENRIETTA LAW: He probably only did six runs in total, building up from 100 metres to about 800 metres. That's a big step up from where he was. It was quite demanding for him.

When Jason graduated, my little present for him was actually a drinking bottle.

It was one of the first times that I reflected on how far I'd come. Before that, I'd simply concentrated on the challenges that I would face that day. But here I was, looking at the bigger picture. I liked what I saw. I thought, 'If I keep going and keep improving at this rate, I'll play footy next year.'

MIKE SHEAHAN (CHIEF FOOTBALL WRITER, *HERALD SUN*): The stark reality of what had happened in Bali hit me as soon as I saw Jason. I had mixed emotions at how unfortunate he'd been, but how lucky he was to still be with us.

In our world (football journalism), everything comes back to footy, and I thought, 'Jeez, it's impossible to see him play again.'

I was just stunned to watch this bloke, as terribly injured as he had been, start running through this park. When he did that, my admiration for him was immense. His resolve was incredible. Clearly it was a massive task for him, but he overcame it. I thought, 'Jeez, athletes are fantastic with their discipline and their courage. Their minds are so strong.'

Nerissa was fantastic too. She was just so bubbly.

I never heard Jason say anything like 'poor me'. I know that if I had've been the one in his position, I would've been thinking, 'How could this have happened to me? Why me?' But I never detected that from him, and the people around him were very positive because of his spirit.

I was in Ireland, on the International Rules tour, when the bombs went off in Bali. I don't think that those of us over there understood its impact and how it had shaken the country. All the blokes were worried because the Melbourne and Kangaroos guys had mates that were involved, but it was just so far away and so unlikely. The whole essence of what we heard was just so improbable that, subconsciously, you just think, 'It can't have been that bad.'

Jason was the only Bali victim I've seen in the flesh. I'd never had a lot to do with him as a footballer. I think I'd actually been a bit critical of him at different times. I used to suspect that, 'Oh, he probably doesn't like me much because I've written some stuff that he didn't like.' But this sort of thing just transcends it and I was full of admiration and sympathy and respect, for what he'd been through, and how positive he was during his rehabilitation.

It's unusual that in a hospital, where there is so much pain and suffering — and this may sound paradoxical — Jason, as crook as he was, was almost the morale officer. Because people knew him, they gravitated towards him. He had this magnetic personality in the hospital. He was so positive that it seemed everyone in his orbit was much more positive about what had happened to them because of his inspiration.

For about a month, I felt guilty about all the things I had written about him in the previous ten years. I can remember thinking, 'We say things about these blokes and we criticise them professionally and yet when it's all laid bare, there he was, just so brave and so strong.'

By the time Mike Sheahan's story, along with a cover photo of Nerissa and me, hit the newsstands, we were in Perth visiting Hughesy and his son, Leigh.

Hughesy had just been released from hospital. I'd spoken to him but I hadn't seen him since we stood next to each other in Paddy's Bar on 12 October. Strange as it sounds, considering Hughesy and I are such close mates, I was actually nervous about seeing him.

I'd seen him on TV and noticed that he'd lost a lot of weight — 14 kilograms, in fact. He'd always been harping on about how he'd wanted to lose weight, but I'm sure this wasn't the way he had intended to do it.

He actually looked like an old man. That wasn't the Hughesy I knew. I mean he is an 'old boy' — I've poured bucketloads on him about that — but he's not an old man.

I knew he was going to struggle to attend the wedding, despite his heartfelt assurances to the contrary. I hoped like crazy he'd get there, but I thought, 'In the off-chance that he doesn't, at least we've seen him the week before.' It wouldn't be ideal, but it would be some consolation. Hughesy had burns to 54 per cent of his body and also suffered shrapnel wounds.

When Nerissa and I arrived at Perth Airport, Channel Nine reporter Mark Readings interviewed us. Ironically, Mark was one of the first reporters to break the news of the bombings back to Australia. Stranger still, he had actually been at the front of the bar at Paddy's when Mick, Hughesy, Nashy and I went in, and left shortly before the blasts. Lucky bloke.

Hughesy and Leigh picked us up and it didn't take long for them to start arguing with each other. I cracked up laughing. Leigh turned to me and said, 'What are you laughing at, Jase?'

I said, 'If you two are at each other's throats again, Pete must be getting better. Nothing changes, does it?'

Hughesy is so laidback that I think Leigh gets frustrated by him sometimes. Hughesy likes to be one of the boys and mix with people Leigh's age. Leigh assumes the role of father figure and occasionally reads him the riot act. It's quite funny.

I had seen footage on *60 Minutes* of Hughesy in Royal Adelaide Hospital, hugging Leigh and telling him how much he loved him. It's not a macho thing to do, but Hughesy did it — on national TV. It brought a tear to my eye sitting at home watching it, and I'm sure would have had the same effect in many lounge rooms around the country.

It was good to finally be in Hughesy's presence. We were probably next to each other in Royal Darwin Hospital before I was transferred to Melbourne and he to Adelaide, but were unaware of it at the time.

It was good for Hughesy to see how far I had progressed with my rehab. I was well ahead of him — largely because I was younger and fitter — but it gave him something to aim at, and proved that a full recovery was possible.

He had only been out of hospital a few days and chose to have a district nurse come to his house each day to dress his wounds and help him with his rehab. His foot was swollen and blood seeped through his compression garments in places. There was definitely a hint of frustration about him. He wasn't the easygoing Hughesy that I knew.

I was sitting with him on the couch when the phone rang. It was ABC Radio in Adelaide, which had a pre-arranged interview with me. I literally jumped up to answer the phone. Nerissa told me later that Hughesy's reaction was, 'Bloody hell! He's normal; he's walking normal. What's going on?'

Nerissa explained to him, 'You'll get to that stage too. He's obviously fitter and a bit younger. Just remember, he's been out of hospital for four weeks.'

Hughesy and I spent a lot of time talking that weekend — about Bali, recovery and life in general. I told him, 'Things will improve pretty quickly if you just stick at it.' That gave him even more of a kick along and made him even more determined.

Hughesy said that while he was in hospital in Adelaide, Leigh stuck up a newspaper article about me on his bedside wall. He thought, 'That's where I want to be' and actually drew inspiration from it.

LEIGH HUGHES: I put it there to inspire Dad. Because he couldn't see Jason, that was the closest he could get to him. He'd read it when he did his physio and think, 'I'm going home before Jason's wedding.'

PETER HUGHES: After Bali, Jason had a lot of impact on me. In a sense, I've regarded him as a hero. He's helped in my rehab and my thoughts and my life in general. I know that if I'm having a bad day, all I have to do is think about Jase.

We also caught up with one of my old mates from Nhill, Greg Waugh, who has since relocated to Perth.

GREG WAUGH (CLOSE MATE): Jason said, 'Come round to Hughesy's for a BBQ and we'll catch up.' I said to Toni, my wife, 'Look, whatever you see, just say he looks better than we thought he would, he looks all right, he's made an amazing recovery and all that sort of stuff.' We got around there and he couldn't step on his heels. Later on, he just ripped his bandages off and I nearly lost it. I said, 'Jesus, Jason, you look bad, mate.' Then seeing pictures of him running, I got a bit overwhelmed by it all. I couldn't believe that he was able to do that.

We also accompanied Hughesy to a function raising money for him at Perth Football Club, which he had represented in the WAFL. Being the larger-than-life personality that he is, Hughesy arranged for a limousine to take us to the ground. There was a good crowd at the club, so we — or should I say, Hughesy — got a very warm reception. We auctioned Corey McKernan's Carlton jumper, one that was worn by his Blues teammate Anthony Koutoufides and another from St Kilda's dual Brownlow Medallist Robert Harvey. It was great to share such an occasion in Hughesy's company, and to finally finish the drink we'd started seven weeks earlier.

The four of us went to a restaurant in Victoria Park for dinner that Sunday night. It was warm, the windows were open and we were in a relaxed mood. It was a similar mood to what it was like on that fateful night in Bali.

And suddenly there was a loud bang. Hughesy and I both flinched. My heart almost missed a beat. I thought, 'Oh no, here we go again.'

A car had backfired directly outside the restaurant. Hughesy and I looked at each other as if to say, 'I know exactly what you're thinking.'

PETER HUGHES: We both stood up as one. It was quite ironic that both of us were in the same place at the same time when it happened. Jase and I were still pretty raw out of hospital at that stage, so we were on tenterhooks and trying to regain our confidence.

It scared the hell out of us at the time but we had a laugh about it later on though.

After composing ourselves, Hughesy said he had his flights booked for the wedding and was raring to go. He couldn't wait to celebrate our special day with us. I was desperate to have him there.

Leigh was a bit concerned when his dad's foot swelled, so he rang the hospital. He was told, 'That's normal; you'll have to get used to that.' We all thought, 'Well, that's OK then; it shouldn't be a problem', and didn't think another thing of it.

When we were in Millicent on the Tuesday — just four days before the wedding — Hughesy rang me to confirm that everything was set to go. But when he called the next day, he was nearly in tears. The swelling in his foot had actually been diagnosed as an infection and he wasn't allowed to fly due to cabin pressure. I fully understood his situation. We were both disappointed, especially after he was told that it was a normal reaction. He felt that if he had been treated immediately he might have been OK for the wedding. However, Hughesy was always going to be with us in spirit anyway. That wasn't any consolation for Hughesy though.

PETER HUGHES: I was very upset. Devastated. I got an infection on the day I was meant to fly and I wasn't going to tell anyone because I was trying to get on the plane and get to the wedding. But it was just too painful.

It was one of those occasions when you think you're going OK and all of a sudden something like that happens.

It was really bad timing.

I was a few weeks behind Jason in terms of getting well and I thought, 'What else will go wrong?' It was a low part of my life. It would have meant a lot to me if I had've got there.

17

Falling in love

Nerissa and I met at, of all places, Joplin's — one of Adelaide's most notorious nightclubs. It was 28 April 2001 — a date I could hardly forget. Earlier that night, I'd played my 150th game of AFL football, for the Kangaroos, against the Crows. Although I upheld my end of the bargain by playing well, we got beaten.

I'd been single for a while, so I was on the prowl. I wanted to find my perfect woman. I was beginning to doubt whether she'd ever appear. I was thinking, 'Where is this girl? Does she exist?'

I was ready to settle down — with the right woman, of course. I'm sure I probably scared some girls away because they could sense my desperation.

My Kangaroo teammates and I hadn't planned to hit the town that night; originally, we were just going to have a few quiet drinks at the Hyatt Hotel where we were staying. But after some arm-twisting — I think mainly on my behalf — a group of us decided to sample some of the Adelaide nightlife before we flew home to Melbourne the next morning.

I was with Corey, Wayne Carey and a couple of mates from Adelaide. We went to the casino for a while before we bit the bullet and decided to go to Joplin's.

As usual, it was packed with people. Action upstairs, action downstairs. Plenty of energy in the air. When people see 'Duck' (Wayne Carey), that energy generally tends to escalate.

Corey and I were downstairs where a band was playing. We were pretty flat due to the loss, but after a couple of beers and a few cool tunes from the band, our spirits lifted. We went upstairs to look for Duck and the other boys.

I clamped my eyes on a strikingly attractive girl with a Hawaiian leis around her neck. She was running around like a ball of energy and dancing the house down. I thought, 'Gee, she's all right; I wouldn't mind getting to know her.'

NERISSA: I'd been at my brother Shane's 21st birthday party that night. I'd been drinking with him and keeping up with him the whole night, so I was pretty merry by the time we got to the nightclub.

One of my closest girlfriends, Donna Jarrad, and I were dancing around and having a great time. We were both single but neither of us was really looking for anyone.

I saw a guy standing near the dance floor and I thought, 'He looks cute; I like him.' I just grabbed him and started dancing with him. I can't really remember, but I think we kissed there and then.

I was determined that I wouldn't say anything about being a footballer. My occupation is a turn-off for some women because they automatically think that footballers only care about their mates and are always cheating on their women.

I asked her, 'What do you do for a living?'

Nerissa will hate me revealing this, but in her inebriated state, she replied, 'I'm a primary school teacher. You probably think all primary school teachers are quiet and boring. But you know what, we're not all like that.'

She asked, 'So where are you from?'

'Melbourne,' I said.

'So what are you doing over here?'

'Visiting family.'

OK, so I wasn't being totally truthful, but I wasn't lying because Mum and Dad had driven to Adelaide for my 150th game. Nerissa went back to her friends, danced around a bit and came back. We struck up some good conversation, a little more relaxed than the usual, stilted small-talk.

Duck innocently came over for a chat. Nerissa knew who he was, but she looked at Duck and said, straight-faced, 'Do you mind? We're talking,' before focusing back on me. She wouldn't even let him into the conversation.

I was rapt with that — so was Corey, who started clapping and laughing — because everyone knows Wayne Carey. At the time, he was the biggest name in AFL football, and had been for several years. And Nerissa had completely ignored him.

NERISSA: I recognised Wayne Carey. I don't remember exactly what was said. When he left us, I asked Jason, 'How do you know him?'

He said, 'We're good mates.'

I thought, 'Hmm, that's interesting', because I was trying to find out whatever I could about Jason.

WAYNE CAREY: We were standing there having a beer and Jason left us and went over and started talking to Nerissa. They got along like a house on fire straight away.

One of Nerissa's girlfriends recognised me and took Nerissa away to talk to her. That spelled trouble.

(From left) My two younger brothers, Steven and Brenden, me, and my parents, Ian and Jan, at Brenden's wedding in November 1999. The disappointment of missing the 1999 Premiership was still churning in my stomach and people wanted to know how I felt. My standard response was, 'It's upsetting but I can't let that hold me back.' I didn't. The next year, 2000, I played my best season.

Paddy's Bar, 12 October 2002 11.08 p.m.

Jason McCartney's recollection of the events of that fateful night and beyond.

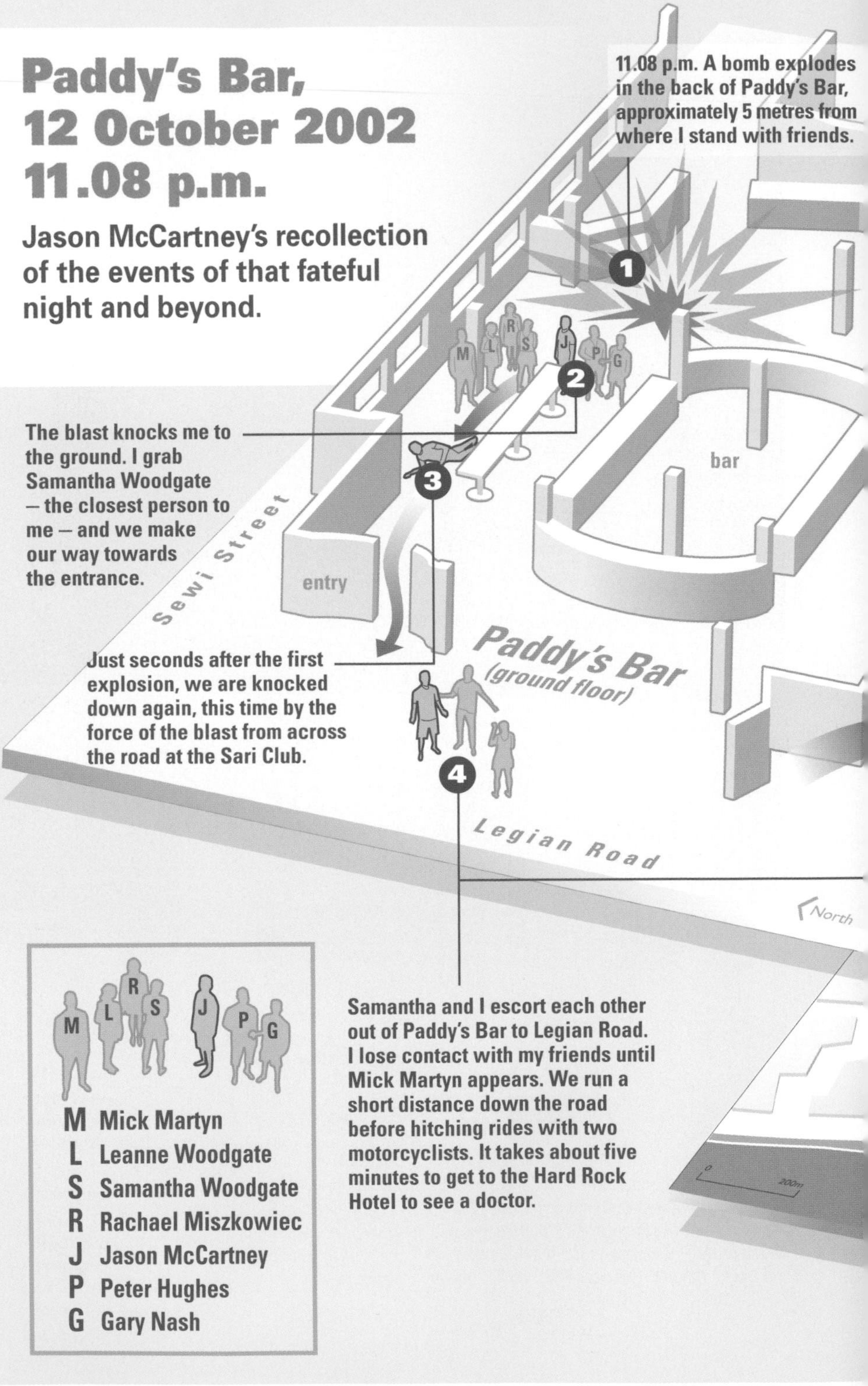
11.08 p.m. A bomb explodes in the back of Paddy's Bar, approximately 5 metres from where I stand with friends.
1
M L R S J P G
2
The blast knocks me to the ground. I grab Samantha Woodgate – the closest person to me – and we make our way towards the entrance.
3
bar
Sewi Street
entry
Paddy's Bar (ground floor)
Just seconds after the first explosion, we are knocked down again, this time by the force of the blast from across the road at the Sari Club.
4
Legian Road
North
0
200m
Samantha and I escort each other out of Paddy's Bar to Legian Road. I lose contact with my friends until Mick Martyn appears. We run a short distance down the road before hitching rides with two motorcyclists. It takes about five minutes to get to the Hard Rock Hotel to see a doctor.
M L R S J P G
M Mick Martyn
L Leanne Woodgate
S Samantha Woodgate
R Rachael Miszkowiec
J Jason McCartney
P Peter Hughes
G Gary Nash

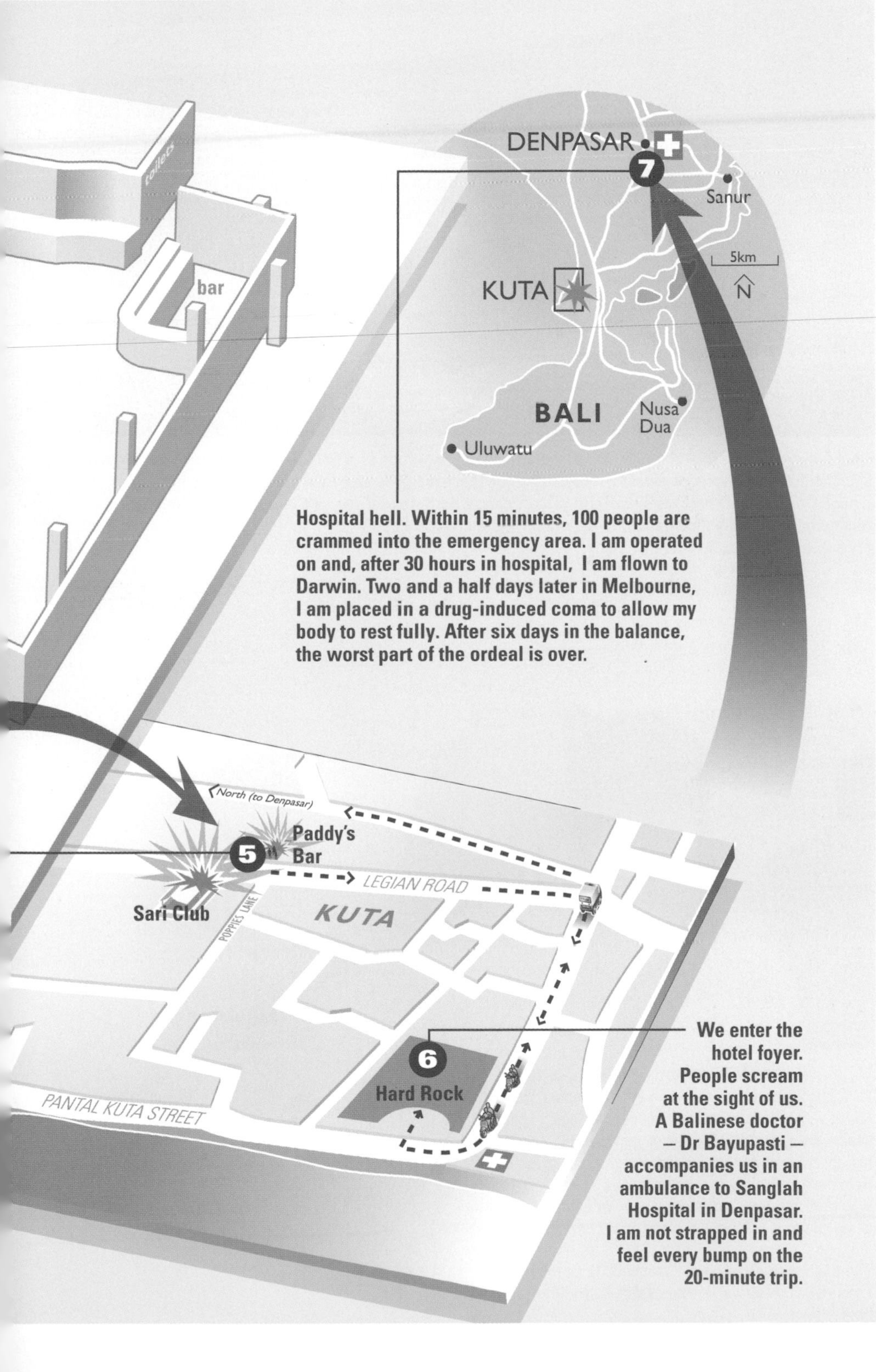

Hospital hell. Within 15 minutes, 100 people are crammed into the emergency area. I am operated on and, after 30 hours in hospital, I am flown to Darwin. Two and a half days later in Melbourne, I am placed in a drug-induced coma to allow my body to rest fully. After six days in the balance, the worst part of the ordeal is over.

We enter the hotel foyer. People scream at the sight of us. A Balinese doctor – Dr Bayupasti – accompanies us in an ambulance to Sanglah Hospital in Denpasar. I am not strapped in and feel every bump on the 20-minute trip.

Mick Martyn and me after the 1999 Grand Final when the Kangaroos beat Carlton. Mick was saying something like, 'You're part of this,' but while I was there for the boys in Grand Final week, on the day and in the celebrations, I didn't feel like I was part of it. It was a hard day for me, but I was rapt that the boys won because I knew how much it hurt to lose to my old club Adelaide the year before. Three years later, Mick consoled me for vastly different reasons, when I needed it most.

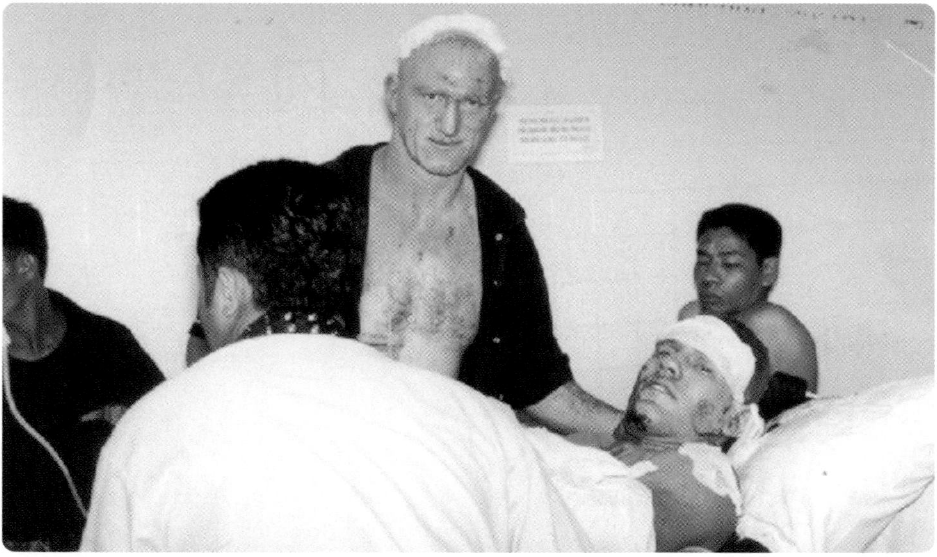

My trusty mate, Mick Martyn, and Balinese doctor Dr Bayupasti stand guard over me in Sanglah Hospital. Mick and I thought there had been a gas explosion. While the sight of Mick with a cloth on his bald head, his shirt missing all of its buttons and half of his chest hair burnt off gave me some comic relief, the reality was that this could very easily have been the last photo of me alive. PHOTO COURTESY OF *BALI POST*

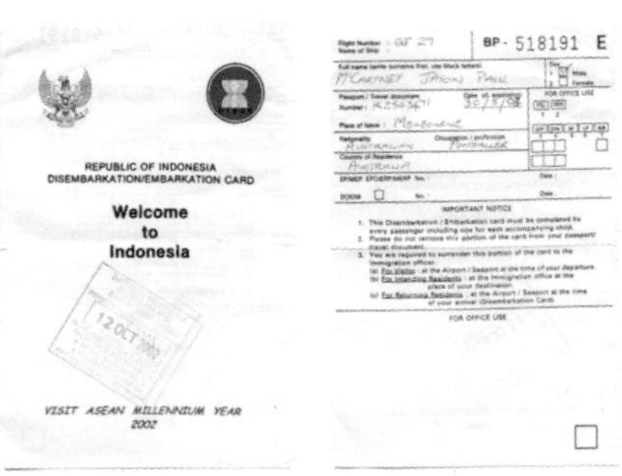

REPUBLIC OF INDONESIA
DISEMBARKATION/EMBARKATION CARD

Welcome to Indonesia

12 OCT 2002

VISIT ASEAN MILLENNIUM YEAR 2002

BP - 518191 E

IMPORTANT NOTICE

FOR OFFICE USE

The disembarkation card – stamped 12 October 2002 – I received on arrival in Bali. Eight hours later, all hell broke loose.

The extent of Jason McCartney's injuries

THE RECOVERY PROCESS

OCTOBER 2002

- **12** — Injured in bombings. Rushed to Sanglah Hospital. Excision of burns (EB), dressings applied.
- **13**
- **14** — Flown to Royal Darwin Hospital. EB and change of dressings (COD).
- **15** — Admitted to Alfred Hospital Intensive Care Unit (ICU). EB, split skin graft (SSG) and COD. Removal of shrapnel and wound cleaning.
- **16**
- **17–18** — EB, SSG, COD. Treated for respiratory distress, intubated and put on a respirator. Placed in a drug-induced coma.
- **19**
- **17–20** — Body almost completely shuts down. Close to death.
- **21–22** — EB, SSG, COD.
- **23** — Emerge from coma and taken off respirator.
- **24**
- **25** — COD.
- **26**
- **27**
- **28** — COD.
- **29** — Leave ICU, move to burns ward. Begin hyperbaric therapy, physiotherapy and rehabilitation.
- **30**
- **31** — Stand for the first time.

NOVEMBER

- **1** — First steps with walking frame.
- **2**
- **3**
- **4**
- **5**
- **6** — First walk unassisted.
- **7**
- **8**
- **9** — Released from hospital.

GRAPHIC: JO GAY

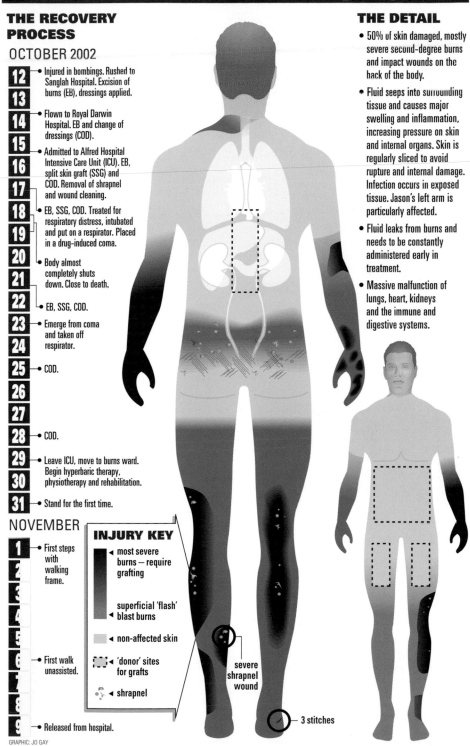

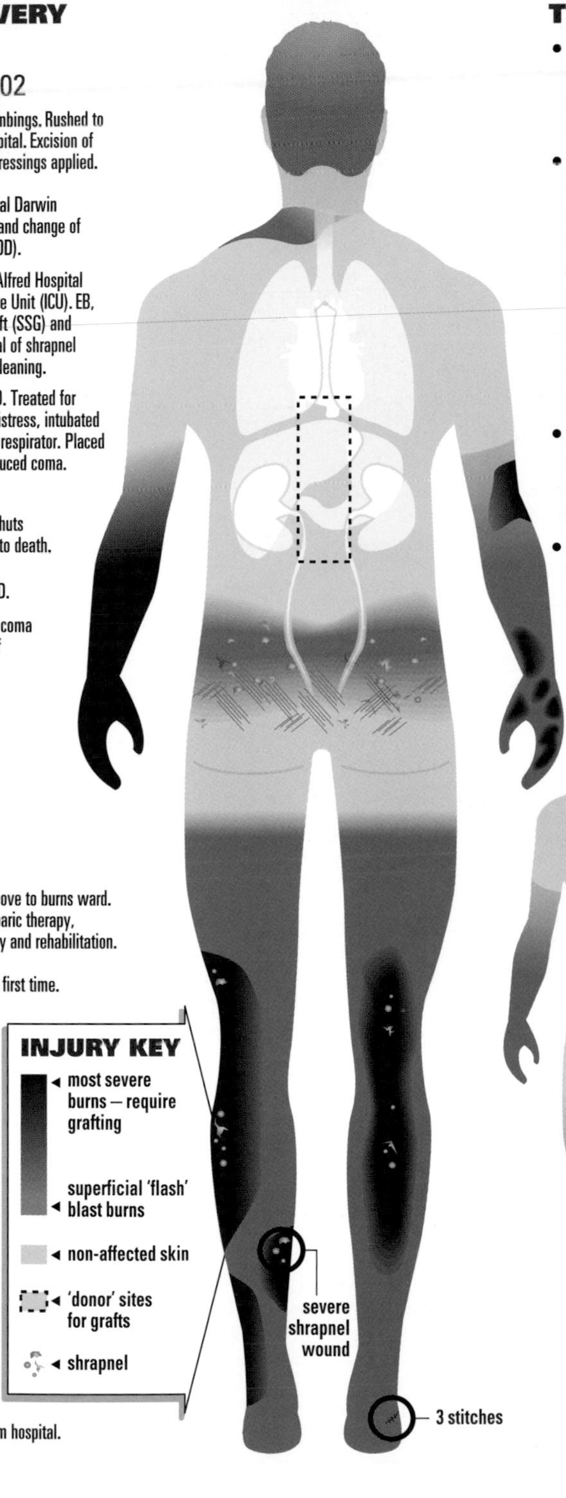

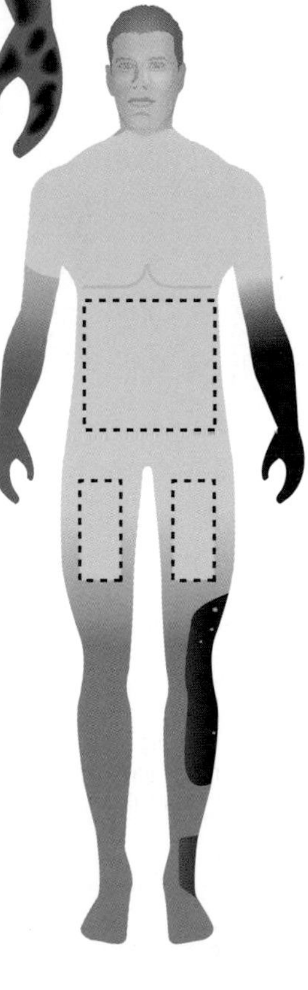

THE DETAIL

- 50% of skin damaged, mostly severe second-degree burns and impact wounds on the back of the body.
- Fluid seeps into surrounding tissue and causes major swelling and inflammation, increasing pressure on skin and internal organs. Skin is regularly sliced to avoid rupture and internal damage. Infection occurs in exposed tissue. Jason's left arm is particularly affected.
- Fluid leaks from burns and needs to be constantly administered early in treatment.
- Massive malfunction of lungs, heart, kidneys and the immune and digestive systems.

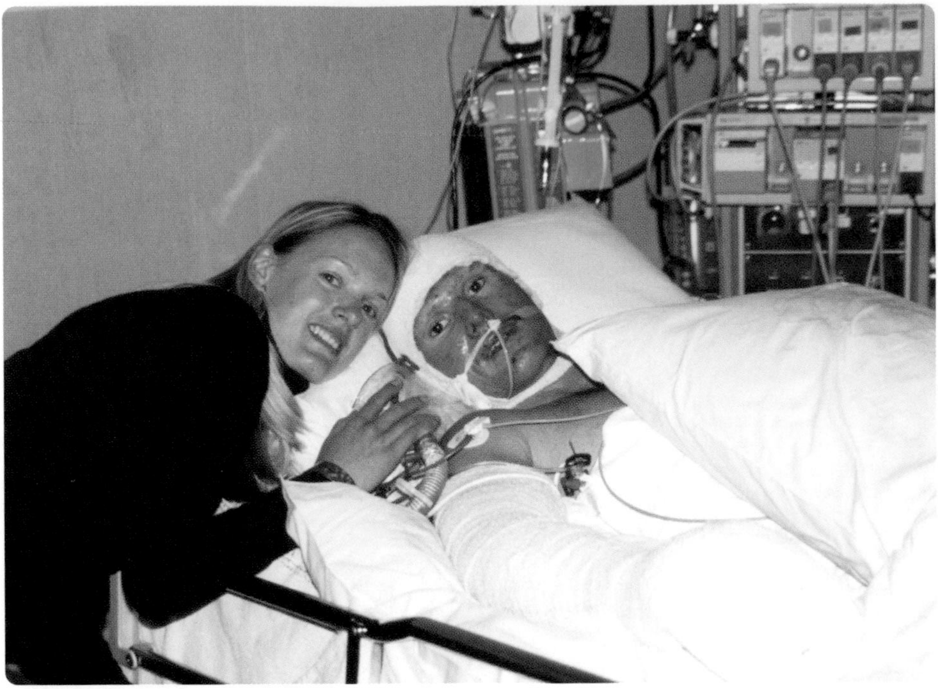

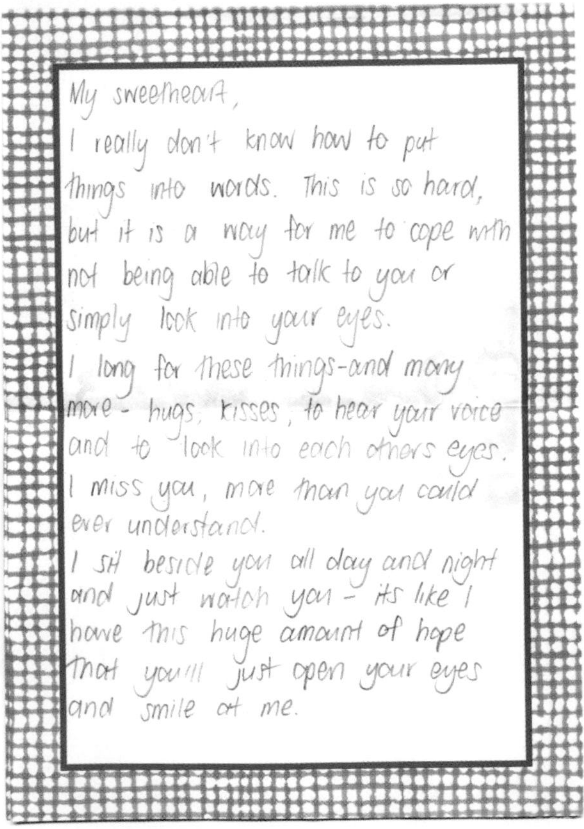

My sweetheart,
I really don't know how to put things into words. This is so hard, but it is a way for me to cope with not being able to talk to you or simply look into your eyes.
I long for these things-and many more- hugs, kisses, to hear your voice and to look into each others eyes.
I miss you, more than you could ever understand.
I sit beside you all day and night and just watch you - its like I have this huge amount of hope that you'll just open your eyes and smile at me.

With my then fiancée, now wife, Nerissa, days after I emerged from a six-day, drug-induced coma, during which I was on the brink of death. My face is swollen and red, my body virtually mummified. A lot of family and friends still didn't recognise me.

This is one of several letters Nerissa wrote to me while I was in a coma. It's hard for me to read them even now without becoming misty eyed. It was a hellish ordeal for Nerissa and my family and the hardest thing they had to deal with was the uncertainty of whether or not I'd survive. I wasn't in any pain when I was comatose; they were enduring all the pain.

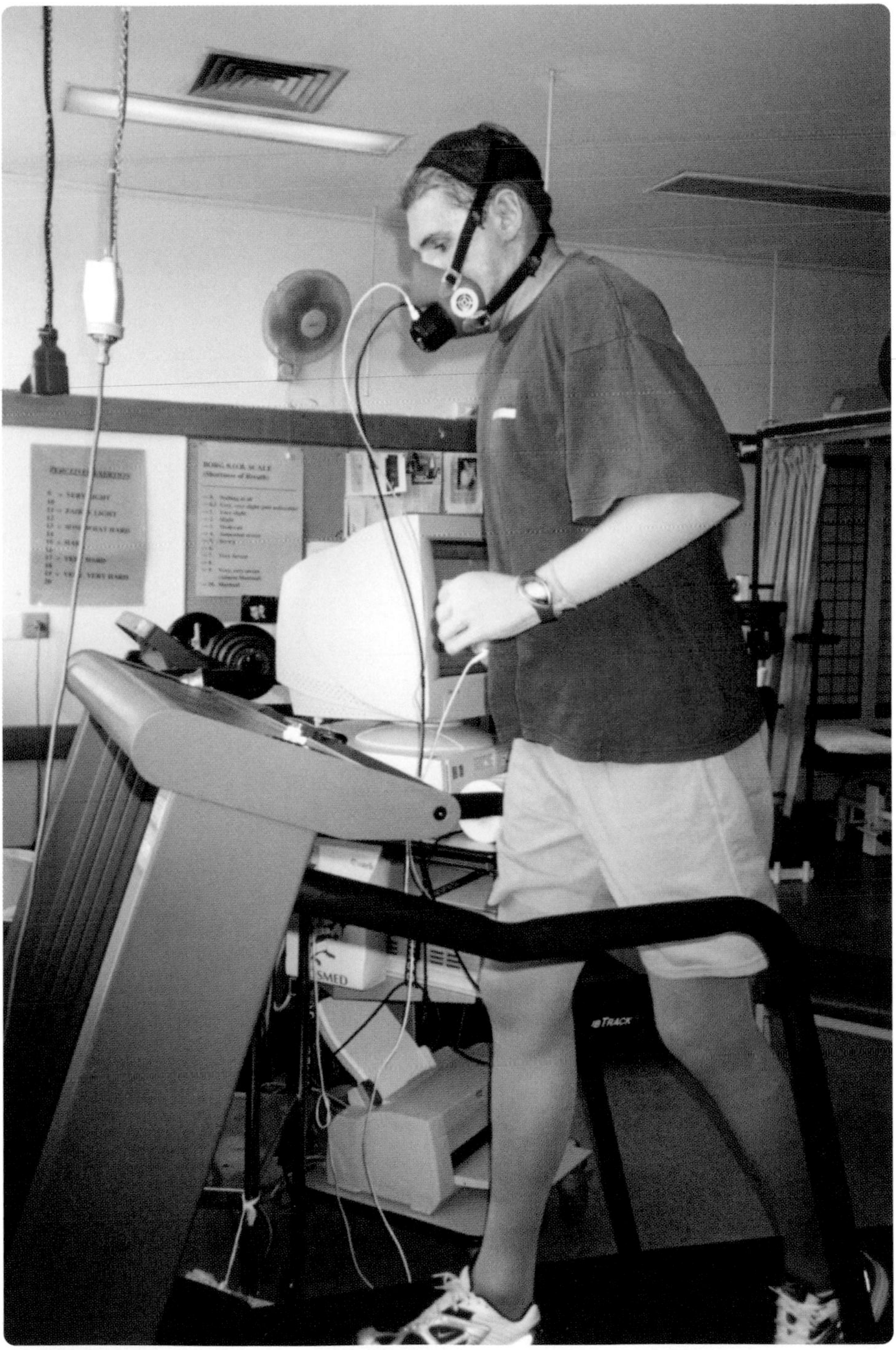

It's 16 January 2003 – three months after the bombings – and I'm on a treadmill at the Alfred Hospital doing a VO2-max test to gauge my fitness and lung capacity. After being a little apprehensive because of the strength and conditioning I'd lost, I was rapt to find that I was still above the fitness of an average person and only 20 per cent below my peak fitness. I still had a lot of ground to make up before returning to AFL football, but I was on my way.

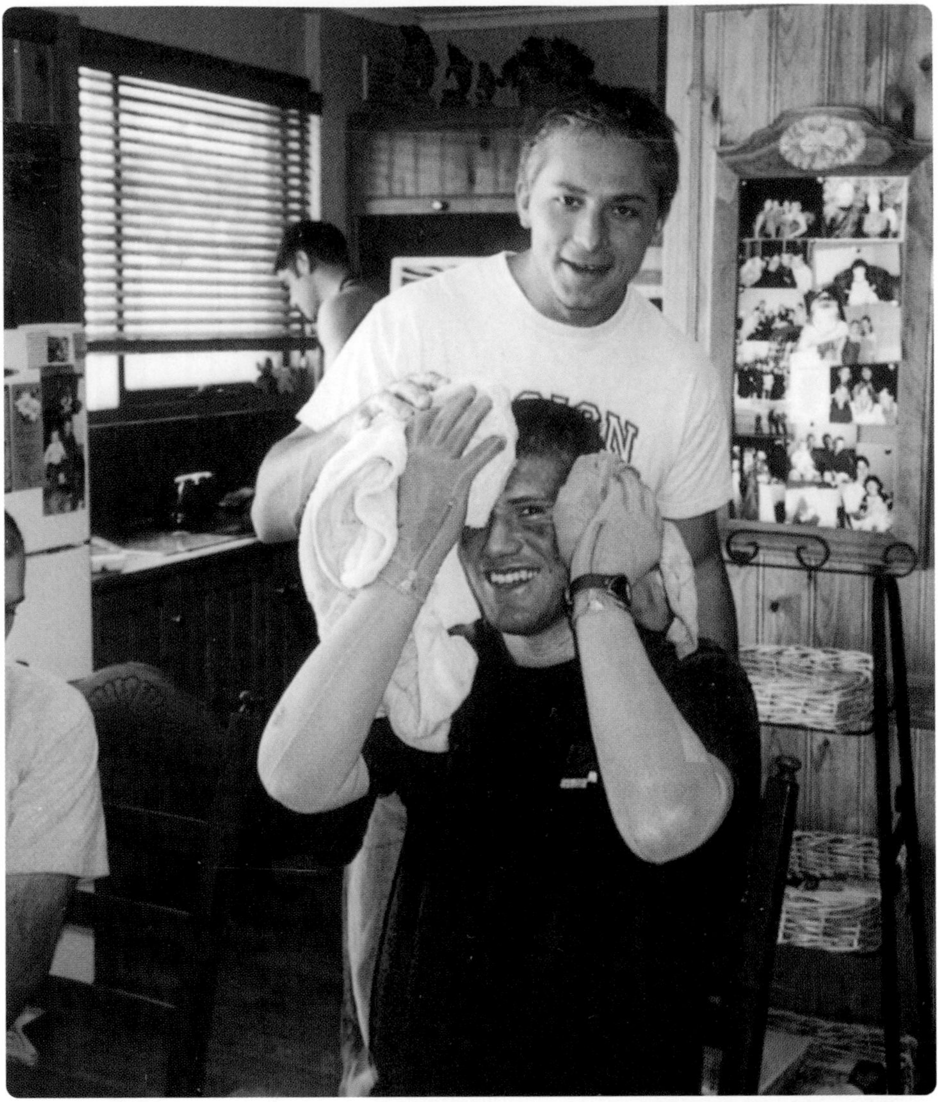

Mini-drama on the wedding day. I'd had too many drinks the night before, vomited and burst a blood vessel in my face, which made it look like a beetroot. Kangaroos doctor Con Mitropoulos *(behind me)* made a house call and gave me an antihistamine. Nerissa then got her make-up artist to weave some magic.

Mum pins a flower on my suit *(right)*. She's been a huge support.

Getting ready for the wedding *(far right)*. My wounds are red, raw and still tender.

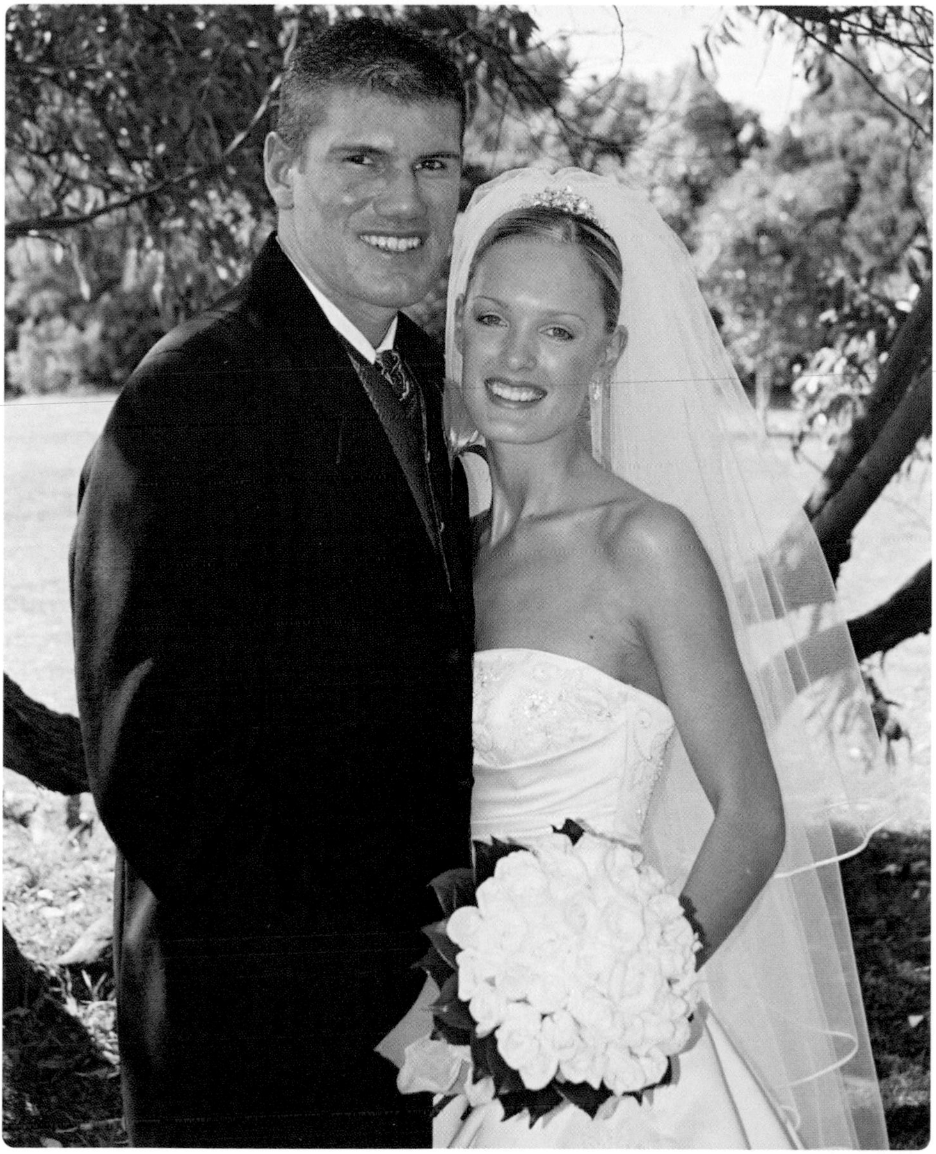

One of the proudest moments of my life – I have married Nerissa, the woman of my dreams and the person who became my full-time carer when I was discharged from hospital in November. Words can't describe how stunning she looks. The day had more than the usual sentiment that accompanies weddings because of what we'd been through just to make it there.

PHOTO COURTESY OF *NEW IDEA* and LINDSAY KELLEY, INSTYLE STUDIOS

Hamming it up for a photo shoot on the beach at Southend, South Australia. I also wanted to show off in front of my best man Corey McKernan, my brothers Brenden and Steven, and fellow groomsmen Tony 'Oogy' Austin and Greg Waugh.

PHOTO COURTESY OF *NEW IDEA* and LINDSAY KELLEY, INSTYLE STUDIOS

Team photo shoots can be a bit monotonous, but I felt like an excited teenager when I donned my full kit, including a new long-sleeved jumper, for the 2003 Kangaroos team photo. There were many times when I doubted whether I'd actually be among the 44 players in this shot. I'm forever indebted to the Kangaroos for giving me that opportunity.

I stand in exactly the same spot, at exactly the same time (almost five months later), that the bomb exploded about 5 metres behind me at the site of Paddy's Bar, Kuta.

Reunited with Balinese doctor Dr Bayupasti, five months after the bombings. 'Dr Bayu', as I called him, accompanied Mick Martyn, myself and another woman caught in the blast to Sanglah Hospital in an old ambulance. He stuck to my side as long as he could.

The media kept the public updated on the latest developments in the Jason McCartney story. During the week of my comeback to AFL football, there was back and front page news coverage. I couldn't believe it.

(Above) I'm slightly embarrassed that people would make banners with me in mind. It was the first time that any banners featured my name.

(Above right) A pivotal sequence of events: *(top)* taking a strong mark in front of Richmond defender Andrew Kellaway, *(middle)* kicking for goal and *(right)* celebrating a crucial six-pointer.

Announcing my retirement in an interview with Channel Nine's Tony Jones. The crowd at Telstra Dome heard the interview via the public address system. I was physically and emotionally spent.

(Above) What a way to finish my AFL career – chaired off by teammates Drew Petrie, left, and Shannon Grant, to a standing ovation. *(Left)* A special moment with Dad who, along with my brothers Brenden and Steven, encouraged me to pursue a career with the Kangaroos in 1998 when I considered playing in the SANFL.

My counsellor and friend David Bonython-Wright *(left)* and me with Australian Prime Minister John Howard during a special trip to Parliament House in June 2003.

The standing ovation I received during a lap of honour at the MCG on AFL Grand Final Day had me almost bubbling over in tears several times. After missing out on playing in the 1999 Premiership side due to suspension, it was some consolation.

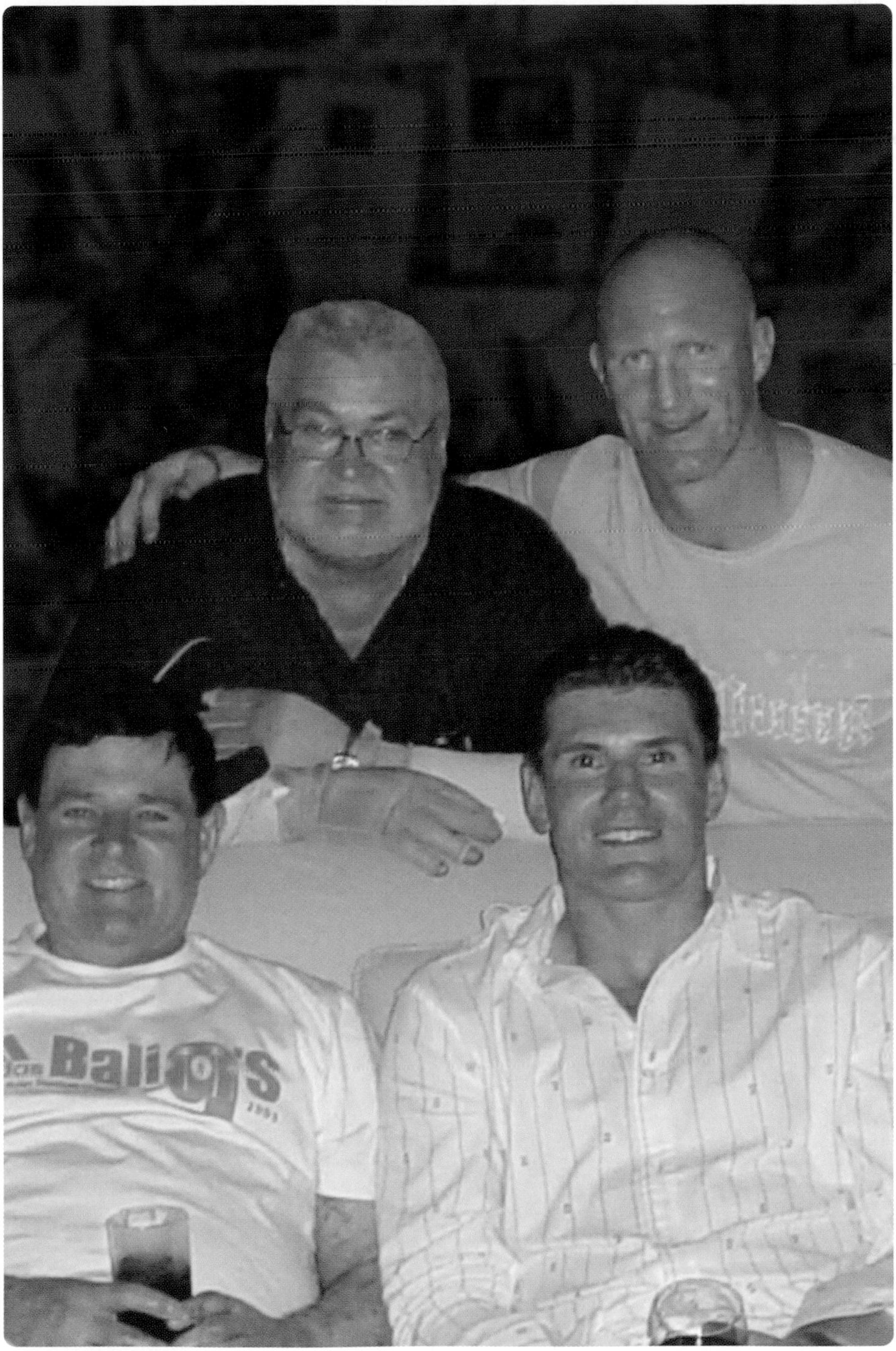

Bonded forever. *(Clockwise, from back left)* Gary Nash, Mick Martyn, me and Peter Hughes back together again in October 2003 for the first time since the bombings. We had all been standing within a few metres of each other when the first bomb exploded. Nashy was in a coma for three weeks, Hughesy for two weeks and I was comatose for six days – each of us coming close to dying after suffering burns to at least 50 per cent of our bodies – while Mick received superficial burns.

October 2003 – one year on. Nerissa and I stand in front of the monument that commemorates the innocent people who lost their lives in the Bali bombings. The victims came from 22 countries – a fact I am still coming to grips with.

(Above left) Hundreds of flowers, cards and tributes fill every available centimetre of the fence around the former site of the Sari Club, while *(above right)* banana trees spring up where the original Paddy's Bar once stood. A cross shows roughly where I was standing when the first bomb went off.

NERISSA: Donna said, 'Do you realise who that is?'

I said, 'Who?'

She said, 'He's a footballer. He plays for North Melbourne.'

By the look of annoyance in Nerissa's eyes, I thought I'd blown it.

'You can get stuffed!' she said. 'Don't think you're getting anything out of me. I know what you do — you play footy.'

I thought, 'I've no chance with her now.'

NERISSA: I said, 'You're a liar. You said you were seeing family. You're just after one thing ...'

He said, 'No, I just want to get to know you. Let's just have a drink and a chat.'

I was somehow able to sweet-talk my way out of it and, at about 3.30 a.m., Nerissa came back to the hotel with me. There weren't any ulterior motives; I just wanted to spend more time with her. Ricky Olarenshaw, who was rooming with me, was in bed after ripping his hamstring — yet again — in what turned out to be his one and only game for the Kangaroos. Ricky hadn't slept because he'd been in pain, and he hadn't even contemplated going out with us that night because drinking alcohol is a big no-no when it comes to treating injuries. (I'm sure Ricky, who's now a player manager, would have had a few sips though if he'd known it would be his last game of AFL football.) He was happy to have company. He made us coffee.

Nerissa mentioned that she'd better get going because her mum was staying at her house. I thought, 'I'd better get her phone number then.' When she gave it to me, I thought, 'She's pretty smart, this girl; she's probably given me a dodgy number.'

NERISSA: I said, 'You won't call anyway.'

Like hell I wouldn't call. In fact, I decided to give it an immediate test run. When Nerissa wasn't looking, I keyed the number she had given me into my mobile phone and rang it. I was rapt when her mobile started ringing.

NERISSA: I said, 'Everyone be quiet, this'll be my mum.' I thought my mum might have been worried because it was so late.

I picked up my phone and Jason cracked up laughing ... I thought, 'That's a good sign; he's checking that I've given him the right number.'

At least I knew that I'd be able to contact this beautiful girl who had made such a big impression on me. She must have felt that something meaningful might eventuate.

Nerissa got a cab home at about 4 a.m. 'She's pretty special,' I thought. I was aching to be with her. It was like that catchy Kylie Minogue song: 'Can't get you out of my head.'

NERISSA: I didn't expect to get a phone call until about Wednesday — that's the usual with guys, to show they're keen but not too keen.

The next night, I was on the couch, consoling myself because I had a hangover, when the phone rang. I lived with my sister Jodie and another girl from Millicent. I picked up the phone and I couldn't believe it, it was him. From then on, he rang every single day. He was keen.

The best thing about it was that we got to know each other so well. Because we weren't face to face, we weren't afraid of asking personal questions. That was a great basis for a long-distance relationship.

He rang later in the week and asked, 'Can I come over and take you out on a date?'

I said, 'OK, that sounds nice.'

We happened to play Richmond the following Friday night, so after our Saturday morning recovery session, I caught the first available flight to Adelaide. We weren't due back for training until Monday afternoon, so I had plenty of time to play with. The fact that I was able to get the AFL rate and book into the Hyatt was a bonus.

NERISSA: That was really nerve-racking. I remember sitting at the airport thinking, 'I hope I remember what he looks like.' You've got to remember that I'd had a few drinks when we met on the previous Saturday night and my recollections of the night weren't 100 per cent clear. But I did recognise him because I remembered that he was tall, dark and handsome.

It was a bit uncomfortable at the start. Because we'd spent every day that week on the phone to one another, and we'd got to know each other fairly well, so there didn't seem to be many more questions to ask.

I said to him a few times, 'You haven't started on the right foot here; you lied to me.'

I think he wanted to make up for that. He was saying, 'Yes, but it's unfair. People always judge footballers like that and I didn't want that to happen. That's why I kept it from you.'

It was quite funny.

After he checked in at the Hyatt, we agreed to walk to Rundle Street to find a place to eat. We were talking so much that we walked up and down Rundle Street about three times before we even decided where we were going to eat. I said, 'I love Indian.' He didn't seem too keen. That's when I first learned that he was really fussy with his food. I said, 'No, they have some good food. Come on, we'll go in here.' It was the Taj Tandoori.

The food and wine were great and we talked the whole time. He was really doting. He did nice things like hold my hand across the table. I thought, 'Oh, my God, I can't get over how quickly things are moving here.' I was overwhelmed because I didn't expect anything to come out of it. When I first found out he was a footballer, I thought, 'Here we go.' I wasn't keen on having a full-on relationship with a footballer because the perception was, 'don't trust them'.

After dinner, we went to the Stag Hotel and sat at the bar, just the two of us.

A few people came up to him and said, 'G'day, Jason, what are you doing over here?' I was a bit taken aback by that. I thought, 'Is this what it would be like? Would I have to put up with this type of thing all the time?' It didn't necessarily annoy me, it just made me a little uncomfortable. But we had the best night.

We told each other all about our past relationships. He said to me, 'Look, I've got to tell you something because I know people will tell you things, and I want you to hear it from me first.' So he told me about what had happened with his ex-girlfriend and how he had a blue with her new boyfriend. He was really open and honest about it all. It told me a lot about his character and him as a person. I thought, 'This guy's honest and he wants people to believe in him.' I was really impressed.

It also proved to me that maybe he does want this relationship to go somewhere because he's laying everything on the table.

We hit it off better than I could have ever imagined. It was probably the first time I'd gone for a drink just with a girl. Usually you'd either go out for dinner and go home, or you'd go to a pub with some mates and their partners and you tend to mix with the boys while the girls chat amongst themselves. But this was just Nerissa and me, one on one — two young people enjoying each other's company. It was like a new world had opened up to me. I'd had a taste and wanted more.

NERISSA: The next day, we went down to Glenelg and got some sandwiches and sat on the beach. The whole weekend was just perfect — I'd never had such a wonderful, special time on a first date with a guy before. I thought, 'This is looking up.'

A lot of people told me not to get involved with Jason because of what happened to him when he was at the Crows. I had friends saying, 'He's meant to be real aggro.'

I thought, 'If that's what he was really like, he wouldn't tell the story to a girl that he liked on the first date.'

Donna, being a concerned friend, rang me and said, 'I heard that he did this and that.'

I said, 'He's already told me.'

Everyone was really surprised because every time someone went to tell me something I already knew about it. I was proud to stand up and defend him when people said something.

I'd say, 'I can tell you the whole story if you want it. Have you heard his side of the story? You've only seen what's been in the media.'

Even my dad had been talking to a few people he knew in Adelaide and he said, 'Well, I've done a bit of research on this guy and I heard this.'

I said, 'Well, he's already told me. He told me on our first date — he explained everything to me. So I'm going to put my trust in him and believe him.'

There was, of course, the stereotype of AFL footballers as womanisers. One of my sisters even said, 'Well, just keep your eyes open.'

But, right from the start, he was very romantic. After our first date, he sent me a dozen red roses and a card saying how he'd had a wonderful a time and that he couldn't wait to spend more time with me. I couldn't believe it. He really put in the effort. I thought, 'This must be it because he's not going to give up.' I didn't feel any pressure though. Everything he did just said to me that he wants this to go somewhere, whereas I was being careful because he was a footballer.

From that point on, a long-distance relationship developed. The phone bill skyrocketed, but I couldn't care less. I had no doubt that I would be repaid many times over, as I realised very early on that she was 'the one' for me.

NERISSA: He rang every single day — without fail. I remember saying to him one time further down the track, 'You don't have to ring every day, you know. We'll run out of things to say. We can ring each other every second day.'

But he was adamant. He said, 'No, no, no, we'll ring every day.'

I made an effort to fly to Adelaide every two or three weeks, or, ideally, fly Nerissa to Melbourne. Due to my footy commitments, it was difficult to find time together, but, as they say, 'where there's a will, there's a way.'

When the 2001 football season finished — the Kangaroos didn't make the finals that year for the first time in Denis Pagan's ten-year reign at the club — I spent three or four weeks with Nerissa in Adelaide. She was teaching at the time, but it was a good test for our relationship, and we passed with honours.

When the school holidays came along, I took the girl I love to the place I love — Bali. The holiday took our relationship to another level again. She had to get back home, so I stayed on for another week with Hughesy and Leigh. While I had my usual amount of fun with the boys, this was tempered by the fact that I missed Nerissa dreadfully. I pined for her. I couldn't imagine life without her. I felt compelled to make a lifetime commitment to her. I wanted to marry her. I hoped she felt the same way.

I had an inkling that, deep down, Nerissa was half-keen to live with me in Melbourne, and I knew that we'd done the long-distance relationship thing for long enough. It would've been too emotionally and physically draining to do it for another year. I felt the time was right.

During 2001, it had a negative effect on my footy too. It sounds terrible, indeed unprofessional — Denis would shake his head — but it got to the stage where I wasn't even looking forward to playing footy. I was always looking forward to seeing Nerissa.

My mind was made up. As soon as I got back to Nerissa's house, I asked her sister Jodie for their mum's phone number. With Nerissa's parents being divorced, I hadn't spent much time with Ardri, so I thought the proper thing to do was to call Marleen instead. When I asked her if I could have the honour of Nerissa's hand in marriage, she got very excited. 'Yes!' she said. 'Of course you can.'

I went straight to a jeweller's shop to look for an engagement ring. I was like a fish out of water. Like most blokes, I had no idea when it came to jewellery. I could feign my way through it if I was getting a birthday or Christmas present, but the stakes were much higher this time. I was about to purchase something that Nerissa would hopefully wear for life. That fact made it an even more nerve-racking experience. While I wasn't shaking or stuttering, I wasn't far off it. Thankfully, they helped me select a ring that I was happy with — and, more importantly, one I thought Nerissa would be happy with.

There was no time to waste. The next, and most important, part of my plan — the proposal — would go into action that night.

NERISSA: When I got home from work, I was really excited to see him. I had begun to realise that 'this was it'.

He said, 'How about we go to that Indian restaurant, Taj Tandoori, for dinner.'

After working all day, I just said, 'We don't have to go there; we can go somewhere more casual, like the pub down the road.'

He said, 'No, no, no, we'll go there.'

I said to my sister, Jodie, 'Come with us, Jode, come on, it's really yummy food.'

She was like, 'No, no, that's OK.'

Jason said, 'No, just us two.'

At the time I thought, 'That's really sweet. That's Jason being Jason, doing something sweet because he's been away.'

Phew! At least I didn't have to drag her there kicking and screaming. That would hardly have set the mood for romance — or a positive response.

When we got to the restaurant, I decided that we would sit at a quiet table in a corner. Nerissa wasn't impressed. 'It's too dark here,' she complained.

'No, this is all right,' I assured her.

Shortly after we sat down, ten people arrived and sat at a big table right next to us. Just my luck. This wasn't going according to plan.

After dinner, I tried to get down to business.

NERISSA: I was so excited to see him, I was talking at a mile a minute, and asking him plenty of questions. Then he said, 'Can you just shut up for a minute? I have something I want to say.'

I said, 'Oh, OK,' not knowing what to think.

No matter how hard I tried, I couldn't get the bloody words out. My nerve deserted me. I became misty-eyed and emotional.

NERISSA: He started going red and teary. I thought, 'What's going on? Oh no, he's done something and he feels really bad about it. He's cheated on me.' I started getting really nervous and I sort of wasn't listening to him. He wasn't talking anyway; he was just stumbling over his words. I thought, 'When he tells me, I'm just going to grab my jacket, tell him I never want to see him again and walk out.' I was planning my escape. But then I thought, 'No, he's not that type of person. He wouldn't do that to me.'

I worried about him and the typical footballer stereotype. But he rang all the time and he also had flowers delivered while he was in Bali. He was, as usual, quite romantic and keen to impress me.

Nerissa had been sitting opposite me, but she moved round and sat beside me. That was good because she blocked out the noisy table behind her.

NERISSA: I got closer to him and said, 'What's wrong? Just tell me; just say it.'

He was all teary and it was obviously really hard for him to tell me. I leaned forward and said, 'Just whisper it in my ear.'

Finally — thankfully — I regained my composure.

NERISSA: He leant forward and he whispered in my ear, 'Nerissa-Lee Vanderheyden, will you marry me?'

As I delivered the big question, I slid the box with the engagement ring in it under Nerissa's arm without her knowing. Despite the fact that I had become a blubbering mess right before her eyes, Nerissa didn't seem to think I was serious. 'Are you for real?' she said.

'Well, have a look under your arm,' I said.

NERISSA: I just grabbed it and looked at it and said, 'Oh my God, oh my God.' I took it out of the box and put it on. I said, 'It's beautiful.'

The ring fitted perfectly — but that was the least of my worries. Nerissa hadn't said anything. After a few anxious seconds, I prodded her. 'So, is that a yes?'

She started crying. 'Yes,' she gushed.

We kissed and wiped each other's happy tears away. We could barely contain our excitement.

NERISSA: It was wonderful. The fact that he was very emotional just made it seem more special. We were both so excited. I said, 'Let's re-live our first date. Let's go down to the Stag now.' So we did. We wanted to ring everyone. I think everyone he rang was more shocked. My friends had been saying to me, 'Yeah, you'll be getting married soon', because I'd say, 'I got another bunch of flowers', or, 'He's taking me to Bali.' When I told my friends that we were engaged, they said, 'I told you.'

It was amazing. You have thoughts like, 'Is it too soon?' but you could be in a relationship for a long time where nothing ever happens, so I just rode with it because I loved him and didn't want it to stop. Admittedly, everything moved quickly but it just seemed so right from the very first date. We're both born in March, both Pisces, both from the country, both sensitive and caring people.

His family was so wonderful to me and my family.

The first time we went to Nhill after we'd been engaged, we walked in the door and Jason's dad opened his arms and gave me a big bear hug, and the first thing he said was, 'Welcome to the family.'

I said, 'Thanks.' I got along with them so well, which is important.

And because Jason's such a friendly, down-to-earth person, even when we went back to my hometown for him to meet people, everyone just loved him. He could get along with anyone. Some people thought that someone of his stature would be stuck up or think they're better than them, but that's not Jason. He got along with all my friends really well and even my closest girlfriends and their partners. That made me happy, and added to the long list of things I loved about him.

It just felt like we were meant to meet. It was fate.

As they say, when you fall in love with someone, you know it. I'd never loved anyone like I love Jase.

18

The wedding

When we got to St Alphonsus Catholic Church for wedding practice at 6 p.m., we were confronted by a Channel Seven news crew from Melbourne. The problem was that while I was in hospital, *New Idea* had approached my manager, Paul Connors, who arranged a deal that allowed the magazine do a story while I was in hospital, and cover the wedding — exclusively. Although we were paid for the privilege, money was a side issue. But I didn't want to be seen to be cashing in on a tragedy, so, with $5000 of that money, I sponsored a race at the Red Cross Bali Appeal race meeting, which was held at Moonee Valley Race Club. The reality was that the extra funds would come in handy because of the money I would lose by not playing footy. I would have been mad to knock it back.

The idea was that it would keep the rest of the media away and that it wouldn't develop into a bunfight. Well, that was the intention anyway.

When I saw Channel Seven there, alarm bells started ringing in my head. After all, a deal's a deal and it's important to stick to what has been agreed upon. The next edition of *New Idea* wasn't to hit the magazine stands until a couple of weeks later, so the last thing we wanted was photos all over the next day's news. It would have been a waste of time *New Idea* doing a story then. Corey spoke to the news crew and they seemed to understand our position. It was always going to be the newspapers that would pose the problems.

After wedding practice, we went across the road to the Sportsman's Hotel, where Nerissa had booked for about forty people. That figure swelled to about 80 or 90 by the end of the night as family, friends and footy mates descended on the town.

We had the run of the back bar area. Everyone started arriving. There was real excitement in the air. Occasionally, I'd look around the room and marvel that, 'Gee, it's been a hard, long road, but it's really going to happen now.' It was a magnificent realisation.

The girls went back to Marleen's house at about 10 p.m., but the boys hung about. I thought, 'This is ideal: I'll have a few more drinks, nothing too serious and get to bed at a reasonable hour. Everything will be sweet.' Besides, my groomsmen were there to look after me; they wouldn't let things get too out of hand.

My Kangaroo teammates Shannon Grant and Glenn Archer mixed with my old Crows mates Ben Hart, Peter Caven and Peter Vardy, along with Mark Richardson from my Collingwood days. I indulged in a bit of fantasy. 'I wish these blokes all played their footy with me at one club,' I thought.

When we got back to Nerissa's sister Rachel's place, I went straight to bed. My groomsman, Oogy, stayed with me. As soon as my head hit the pillow, the room started spinning. Almost immediately, I needed to rush to the toilet, but before I got there, I vomited — on the newly-laid carpet. Rachel, quite understandably, wasn't impressed.

They cleaned me — and my mess — and put wet towels on my face.

Steven got upset too because the reality of how badly I'd been hurt hit him.

STEVEN McCARTNEY: Jason didn't have a top on, so seeing him like that, with all the scars and everything, caught up with me a bit.

Rachel soon became even more concerned. 'Jason, you've got a rash all over your face,' she said.

TONY AUSTIN: It was like a big, port-wine birthmark. He said, 'What's it look like, Oog?'

I said, 'Not too bad, mate.'

I was lying — it looked shocking.

I got up at about 6 a.m. and felt fine. I thought, 'I've managed this pretty well.' That was until I looked at myself in the bathroom mirror. Uh-oh. The left side of my face was purple, and there were red patches on the right side as well. It was like a corked thigh, except on my face. Here I was, set to get married in eight hours, and I had a face like a beetroot. I thought more sleep might do the trick.

Wrong.

I called Kangaroos club doctor, Dr Con Mitropoulos, who had only just arrived in town for the wedding. I got him to make an urgent house call. I thought he might be able to give me some pills to clear up the rash.

We put ice-packs on my face, thinking that it was just a heat rash. Wrong again.

Con's diagnosis was that I must have burst a blood vessel in my face — the skin was still new and fragile — when I vomited. I had slept on my left side, so all the blood had pooled on that side of my face.

Con gave me the news that there was nothing he could do or give me that would make the redness disappear before the wedding. In fact, Con said, it probably wouldn't disappear for a couple of weeks. 'Just what I wanted to hear,' I thought.

DR CON MITROPOULOS: To be honest, I was quite happy because initially I thought he'd had some serious ailment or done something to his skin, but it was self-inflicted.

I rang Nerissa. I was pretty emotional. I sobbed as I broke the news to her that, 'Honey, we can't get married. You should see my face.'

All I was thinking of was the photos. But she talked some sense into me.

NERISSA: I said, 'Don't worry about it, I'll get Mum to pick you up and we'll get the make-up artist to fix you up.'

BRENDEN MCCARTNEY: I told Jase, 'Don't worry about it, mate. People are going to accept that you're not 100 per cent anyway and that your face is going to be marked because you're still recovering. You've had 50 per cent burns.'

I shook my head. 'Yeah, but a hundred people saw me last night and I was spotless,' I said.

Shane Chambers, whose wife Kylie was one of Nerissa's bridesmaids, put his own spin on the situation. Shane's a cray-fisherman and a big knockabout country bloke and he said, 'Jase, you've had a tough couple of months, haven't you mate?' He put a Crown Lager stubby right in front of me and said, 'You may as well have this.'

I laughed, but Shane was right: what could we do?

Marleen took me to the make-up artist who had been helping the girls. She did a sensational job and no one could tell.

TONY AUSTIN: The make-up artist should have been nominated for an Academy Award.

The red-face debacle soon became only a minor drama. I didn't know where the hell my groomsmen were. They were all supposed to stay with me at Rachel's place, but had obviously found accommodation elsewhere. I made some phone calls and told people that if they saw my groomsmen, 'Tell them to get here and get ready.'

My panicky mood wasn't helped when I found out that the drivers we had appointed — Nerissa's brother Shane and Rachel's husband Steven Thiele — had decided they would do a spot of cray-fishing in a little boat before the wedding. I thought, 'This is going to be a disaster.'

At least we were blessed with a great day — a sunny 25 degrees, and not a breath of wind, after the weather had been ordinary all week — and our master of ceremonies, my good mate Brad Flood, had his act together. When Brad popped in — he was another person I hadn't seen since the blasts — I only had shorts on, minus the compression garments. The scars were still a bit raw in places and they must have been fairly confronting for poor Brad. He was also pretty nervous about his gig.

BRAD FLOOD (CLOSE MATE): I couldn't believe the extent of the damage that had been done to his body. I said to him, 'Jeez, you must have been in a bad way.' I started asking questions. 'Is this going to heal?'

When I saw how much he had been burnt and how deep the scarring was, I was in a state of shock. You don't know how the human body can get through that sort of trauma.

Finally, the boys arrived and, funnily enough, were ready before me. But obviously I had to do a few things that they didn't have to worry about, such as putting on garments and creams and so forth.

It seemed to take me an eternity to get ready, much of which can be attributed to nerves. I had a shower and I sweated a lot after that.

It felt strange because it was the first time I'd had to put on a pair of pants in a long time. I'd been getting around in just thongs, shorts and a T-shirt during my rehab. When we were in Perth the week before, the dressiest clothes I wore were a pair of baggy cargo pants.

Although my left hand had been extensively grafted and it looked like a plastic hand — stiff and shiny — I decided that I wouldn't wear my gloves. It would be a symbol that terrorism wouldn't stop me from living a normal life. And I wanted to feel my wedding ring on my skin. I even practised slipping it on and off the previous day, so that I might prevent any embarrassing moments when the time came. It went over the glove fine, but I thought I'd be fine without them so I put the gloves in my pocket.

TONY AUSTIN: The drive to the church was great. Finally, after all the trauma, we had him in one piece and it was all going to happen.

We said hello to our guests before moving to the altar, where we waited for the girls. I felt like I was fighting back a tidal wave of emotion. My mind raced back to Bali, and what had happened. 'I've actually made it; I'm here.' I wrestled with these thoughts for a few minutes and I was barely able to maintain my composure.

When the music started, I felt a huge lump forming in my throat. I lost my focus. I'd been to wedding practice, so I should have known what was going to happen next, but somehow part of what I'd learned had been erased from my memory.

I expected Nerissa to come down the aisle first, but I forgot that the five bridesmaids would lead her out. I hate being out of control. Then I remembered that I could just relax and watch. But it didn't stop me from wanting to break down and bawl my eyes out.

I looked at Mum and Dad and wondered what they were thinking. My brothers and best mates were standing there with me. We were all brothers at that moment.

To keep my emotions in check, I focused on my niece, Brenden's daughter, Tarlie, who, at the time, was still a few months off turning two. Tarlie looked like a little princess. She was so excited that she was standing up on her seat and yelling out to her dad: 'There's Dad-a! There's Dad-a!' Each time I thought the lump in my throat would turn into tears, I'd focus on Tarlie. She'd make me laugh and I'd relax again. She was a great distraction.

I had a few pre-wedding jitters — just the normal amount of butterflies doing laps inside my stomach — but never any doubts. Nerissa had brought out the best in me as a person, and hopefully I had had the same effect on her. I wanted us to continue to evolve as people — together.

One of my favourite moments was when Nerissa finally made her way down the aisle, on her dad Ardri's arm. It was extremely moving for me because from about ten minutes after the bomb in Bali, I had wondered whether that moment would ever come. I felt like the luckiest man on earth. I knew Nerissa would look stunning, but she exceeded all of my expectations.

COREY MCKERNAN: When we saw Nerissa walking down the aisle, that was as good a moment as any. It was a victory. Nothing was going to stop Jason from doing what he wanted to do.

ARDRI VANDERHEYDEN: To walk down the aisle and give Nerissa away on a day that meant so much to her and Jason and everyone else who was there, was very special. The word 'special' doesn't really come close to describing it. I was enormously proud and honoured. She's in love with him, he's in love with her and they're such a great fit. I was very happy with her choice of husband. I love them both to bits.

Throughout the whole service, Nerissa and I didn't stop looking into each other's eyes and smiling. It was an eye-lock that neither of us wanted to break. Saying 'I do' was a minor detail as far as we were concerned.

STEVEN MCCARTNEY: When they said, 'I do,' that got a pretty big response. A big cheer went throughout the church. The eyes were watering a bit.

NERISSA: I thought, 'You're amazing. You've done it; you've made it here.' It was really special.

I was so nervous that I was moving around. Jason whispered, 'Stop swaying,' but I couldn't quite hear him, so I was trying to work out what he was saying while the priest was telling me what I had to say. Then Jason said, 'Speak.'

I went, 'Oh.'

I'd completely missed what I had to say. Everyone in the church laughed.

The Millicent Italian club, which had received a total make-over, looked a treat and provided a cosy atmosphere for our guests for what turned out to be a ripping reception.

Brad announced our arrival as 'Mr and Mrs McCartney'. It was the first time we'd heard that, so it was another realisation that, 'Yes, this has really happened.'

BRAD FLOOD: It was the first time I'd done public speaking and the fact that it was such a big event meant the pressure was certainly on me.

The main thing that Jason wanted me to stress to the guests was that it was a day of celebration and what's past is past. The wedding had been his inspiration and he wanted to celebrate the day and not to worry about the past. He wanted to get that across particularly to people like me who hadn't seen him between the bombings and the wedding. That was something he felt had to be done.

Corey and I both delivered emotional speeches — they weren't intended to be emotional; they just came out that way.

COREY MCKERNAN: Jason made one of the all-time great speeches. It was real and it was raw and had all the style of the laidback country boy that he is. When he described what it all meant to him after all that had happened, there weren't many dry eyes in the place.

I spoke about mine and Nerissa's journey: how we met, how I knew she was the one, and how she had stood by me. I really lost it when I spoke about my parents: how they'd been there right through, and how Mum had helped me move to three AFL clubs, supported me, and then how, like Nerissa, they had spent four weeks sitting beside what was almost my deathbed. Being the eldest of three boys, I've never openly shown emotion, and affection, towards my family. I always knew that I was loved — and I'm sure they knew I loved them — it's just that we didn't put it on display.

The Bali tragedy and the wedding represented a kind of 'coming out' in that regard. It was like bursting a bubble.

I became emotional when I looked down and saw a telegram with the letterhead from Hughesy's roofing company. Most people there knew that Hughesy was alive, but I became so tearful it might have seemed like Hughesy had actually died. Leigh, who's a tough young bloke, feigned annoyance with me afterwards because I had him crying. But there weren't many, if any, dry eyes in the place.

LEIGH HUGHES: I was there representing Dad as well. It got pretty emotional during Jason's speech. I also felt for Nerissa big time. We were chatting a fair bit through the whole thing, especially when it got pretty dodgy for Jason and Dad. We've become closer through all of it. We counselled each other a fair bit. I never thought that Jason would make the wedding date. It was a huge effort.

GREG WAUGH: Brenden's speech was an absolute cracker. He was trying to be really emotional, saying, 'It's fantastic that Nerissa and his mother never left his side,' and just as he was about to break down, he said, 'because when I spend more than ten minutes with him, he gives me the shits.' It broke it up a bit because it was a very emotional day. He had everyone in stitches.

My crying probably contributed to the make-up rubbing off my face, and exposing the red rash. I probably needed more applied, but I didn't bother once all the official stuff was over with. It was the happiest night of my life.

NERISSA: It was more of a celebration than a wedding. It was a really special event.

We had a lot of positive comments afterwards. It made us realise that, yeah, everyone saw it as the celebration that we wanted it to be — a celebration of our love and life because of Jason's recovery and then being able to get married and stick to that date.

JAN MCCARTNEY: The wedding day was as emotional as his (comeback) game of footy later on. I was just so proud that he'd set his mind to something and achieved it. And, of course, we're pretty happy with his choice — Nerissa is a lovely girl and we're very proud to call her a daughter-in-law.

IAN MCCARTNEY: It helped everyone along a bit. It helped them get over what had happened in Bali because there had been a lot of stress and worry and tears after Jason got hurt.

It was going to be a big day, no matter what happened, and it turned out that way. It wasn't just a wedding. We were celebrating that we still had him. It was a celebration of life.

19

New beginnings

The natural encore to a dream wedding is a dream honeymoon — and that's exactly what we had planned. We wanted to soak up the culture of Thailand for a fortnight, and welcome in the New Year with Hughesy and Leigh at the Perth Cup races. But that was the pre-Bali plan.

Travelling to an Asian country was not an option as far as I was concerned. The odds of being involved in another terrorist attack were slim but I didn't want to take any chances. And there was no point going anywhere that would be hot either because I wasn't allowed to expose my scars and raw skin to the sun. I could still get sunburnt through my pressure garments.

While I was in hospital, we threw around a few honeymoon options. Noosa? Port Douglas? But I thought, 'I'm not going to enjoy either of them — they're too hot.' In the end, we decided on the Barossa Valley. Before we went there though, we wanted to recreate our first date from 19 months earlier.

We stayed at the Hyatt hotel in Adelaide on the first night, as I had on that special night. We were keen to eat at Taj Tandoori, our favourite Indian restaurant — where I also proposed to Nerissa. But it was closed due to renovations.

It was 40-plus degrees every day in the Barossa Valley — so much for dodging the heat. And so much for marital bliss. I stayed indoors in front of the air conditioner most of the time, which, understandably, frustrated Nerissa. I was just so hot. I didn't even stick a toe in the pool. It was fair to say that I was pretty grumpy too, which was also understandable. But after an ordinary beginning and the odd wine tour, we ended up having three or four great days together.

On the honeymoon, I also took completed my final assignment for the AFL Players' Association's Level 2 Coaching Course. Coaching had appealed to me before Bali. I had planned to play a couple more seasons at AFL level, then maybe return to Adelaide and get my coaching career underway, with a view to eventually landing a job at a SANFL club. I had received positive feedback throughout the course from some credible sources.

The AFL's game development manager, Ross Smith — St Kilda's 1967 Brownlow Medallist — was positive about my coaching prospects. He said, 'You could do all right.' I also received an encouraging phone call from Richmond assistant coach David Wheadon, who has vast experience as an assistant at several AFL clubs. He said he would be happy to provide a reference. But the bombings had put these plans on the backburner.

However, I was determined to clear the decks, just in case I felt like pursuing coaching at a later stage. When I was in the burns ward at the Alfred Hospital, I asked Nerissa to bring in the papers I needed to complete the assignment. I told her, 'I want to finish this assignment while I'm in here to get my mind going again and to think about something else.' But for one reason or another, I didn't get around to it in hospital. While I sweltered in the heat of the Barossa Valley, there was nothing worth watching on TV, so I got stuck into my assignment. I posted it a couple of days before Christmas.

LAWRIE WOODMAN (THE AFL'S NATIONAL COACHING DEVELOPMENT MANAGER): Other than those who were actually coaching at the time, Jason was the first one to complete all of the set tasks and submit them on time. He was really well organised and seemed to be achievement motivated. He got things done when, for a lot of blokes, it was all too hard.

The final part of the assignment was due on 20 December. I got back to work after the Christmas-New Year break on 6 January and waiting for me was an Express Post parcel. Jason had posted it from his honeymoon in South Australia, to meet the deadline. He must have completed most of it while recovering from his injuries. After all that he'd been through, I thought there was a possibility that he might not complete it at all, let alone submit it on time.

On the way back from the Barossa Valley, we spent a night at the Grand Hotel in Glenelg. It was there that I was reminded about how curious people are about my injuries. When I went to the men's toilets, I could physically feel eyes on me as I relieved myself at the urinal. I can understand people thinking, 'Well, he's got burns to 50 per cent of his body; I wonder if his old fella is OK.' It's only natural, I suppose. But I must admit that it was an uncomfortable situation, trying to take a leak while blokes are trying to get a sneak peek at your private parts. I almost got stage fright! I turned to a few of them and said, 'No, it's all right, boys — no problems there,' and we had a bit of a laugh.

Gradually, laughter and smiles replace the tears. Christmas Day was indicative of this. We had breakfast at Marleen's that morning before embarking on the two-hour drive to Nhill, where about 35 relatives visited my parents' house at different stages of the day for lunch and dinner.

20

Back to work

Motivation comes from within. Others might say and do things that inspire you but, ultimately, it has to come from you. You need to set a goal and be prepared to put in the hard yards to achieve it. It's no use having a goal without a work ethic because that would be pie-in-the-sky stuff; and it's no good working without an aim or a sense of direction, because you could be wasting your time. Having a goal is the easy part; it's putting in the hard work that really tests a person's strength of character.

I took this approach to make it to my wedding day in good condition and felt the self-satisfaction and contentment that comes with reaching a goal.

My next goal — admittedly, it seemed more like a fantasy at times — was to play AFL football again. I so desperately wanted to run through the Kangaroos' banner, soak up the atmosphere of a big crowd, put my body on the line for my teammates and celebrate a win. That would indeed be a dream. If I could do it, I'd be a happy man.

But I knew that it would be no easy mission. In fact, there was a chance it would be aborted before it even got started if the Kangaroos didn't renew my playing contract. I was out of contract at the end of 2002. My immediate football future was uncertain. And that was before I was almost fatally injured in Bali.

The club was in an awkward position. Should it retain a bloke who might not play again — not even at suburban or country level, let alone at VFL or AFL level? The hierarchy would also have been aware that if they delisted me, they might have to endure a backlash from supporters, which I personally think would've been unfair. I believe I had given the club good service in my five seasons there, and I'd won the Best Clubman in 1999 and 2000, which I thought would give me a chance.

But in today's game, where there is little room for sentiment, I wouldn't have been surprised if the Kangaroos decided to give my spot on the list to a youngster. After all, Dean Laidley said early on that he would go with youth.

GEOFF WALSH: The Best Clubman Award at the Kangaroos takes into account on-field contributions as well as off-field stuff. It takes into account attendance at social functions, attitude to training and value as a role model for their teammates. It is a very coveted award. I know that Wayne Carey, who is one of our most decorated players, was always keen to win the Best Clubman Award. For Jason to win it twice was a pretty big effort.

But his training regime was impeccable, he was a great example on the track, his preparation was faultless and he's always been popular amongst the players. He always presented himself well. We were always happy to use him as someone who could promote the club and represent the club in public pretty well.

IAN MCCARTNEY: When Jason got back to Melbourne, he said, 'Dad, you'd better go down to the Kangaroos and see what you can sort out.'

I went with his manager, Paul Connors, and Corey to a meeting with the club. I always thought they'd keep him on for another year and that's what happened. The club was real good. There weren't any hassles, and they were happy to have him on board.

PAUL CONNORS: Jason was coming off a pretty healthy contract to start with. Our thought was that Dean Laidley was probably moving in a different direction and Jason had done it pretty tough the previous season.

When he went to Bali, it was basically up in the air whether the club would keep him or not. But to the club's credit, they stood by him in the hard times. And not only did they supply him with a football contract, but they gave him an opportunity to work within their marketing department. They had no idea whether Jason would recover enough to play any football, or whether it would work out well for the club. It did in the end, but they didn't know that, so they put themselves on the line.

DEAN LAIDLEY: People with good character, especially those who have worked hard around your football club and earned the respect of everyone at the club, you need to look after them — no matter what happens to them. You need to make sure that they're all right. That was certainly the case with Jason.

I thought that a lot of our younger players would learn a lot by having Jason around during his rehabilitation, even if he didn't play a game. Our younger blokes could learn a lot from the way he approaches his footy, challenges and adversity.

Being a new coach, I needed a fair bit of guidance on a whole range of things, and I got great guidance from Geoff Walsh and Tim Harrington. We were trying to make decisions on players, and trying to do trades, and then this happened with Jason. I was worried about how to handle it. We'd always talked about what we needed to do, and Geoff and Tim can take a lot of the credit for the way Jason's comeback was handled.

I owe the Kangaroos a great debt for giving me that chance. If they hadn't, you might not be reading this book.

I was offered a base contract — $42,000 plus $2100 for each AFL match — like those given to first-year draft picks. The club was good enough to employ me in its branding department — a part-time job that boosted my pay packet to about $70,000 — to ensure that my life wasn't thrown into upheaval off the ground. I appreciated that; it was a heartfelt gesture and reinforced to me just how special the Kangaroos Football Club is.

It was a drastically reduced contract compared to my previous one, which was close to $200,000 a year. I had no qualms about it though. Beggars can't be choosers. I would have received a downgraded contract if I'd been fully fit anyway after my below-par performance in the 2002 season. But money was a side issue. The most important thing was that I had another shot at playing AFL footy again — a longshot, but at least it was a shot. As much as I desperately wanted to play at some stage in 2003, I expected it would take a full year to build my body to anything like its former strength.

I had a lot of work ahead of me. When Nerissa and I were in Millicent on New Year's Eve, I decided that I'd go for my first run in a couple of weeks. Nerissa came with me. I had started to get some flexibility in my left calf but when we took off, at no more than a leisurely pace, it became very sore. I struggled even to jog. I cracked it.

'Stuff this, stuff New Year's Eve,' I said gruffly. 'We've got to go home tomorrow. I've got to get back into the hospital and get my physio started up again. This just isn't right.'

Nerissa, always the voice of reason, said, 'No, come on, let's just walk a bit.'

NERISSA: He started saying negative things, so I coaxed him on by saying, 'You're pushing yourself too much too soon. We shouldn't have run first. You need to walk first, stretch it out, then we'll run. If you feel it pulling a bit more, we'll just walk. You need to remember what we did with Henrietta. We'd walk a lap to start with, then we used to run a quarter and then walk the rest. Then we used to run half and walk half. It was a slow build up.'

I learnt a lot from Henrietta because when she was working with Jase, I would listen intently. I used that when we were on our own and he needed someone to help him think positively again. That day, I tried to talk him through it the way Henrietta would.

Nerissa was right. We walked a bit and then I started jogging again and feeling much better than I had just minutes earlier. We went over to an oval, walked some more and started jogging again. When I did some strides to stretch out a bit and loosen up, Nerissa seemed fearful that I might overdo it.

'Be careful you don't do too much,' she said.

She'd been through all the rehab with me at the hospital and she wasn't about to see all that hard work go to waste.

NERISSA: I was very wary of how his heart would react because he'd experienced a lot of trauma. Henrietta had always kept an eye on his heart rate. They were actually more worried about his heart and lungs than his skin condition. I was a bit paranoid about it. When he would do sprints, I could hear the heart monitor beating and I'd check it and it would be sky high, and I'd be like a personal trainer and say, 'Stop now.' But he'd keep pushing himself.

'Don't worry,' I assured her, 'I'll be right.'

I actually tried to race Nerissa up the middle of the ground, over a distance the length of a cricket pitch, and I couldn't, for the life of me, keep up with her.

NERISSA: He'd get frustrated because when he started to slow down, I would continue to push myself. I thought I was doing the right thing by helping him along, but then one day, he said to someone else, 'Nerissa just keeps going; she's doing better than me.' Then I realised that when he stopped, I should stop too.

Not only was it a blow to the ego, it was shattering my hopes of playing football at the top level again. I thought, 'Maybe I won't be able to make it back. Maybe this is something I won't be able to overcome.'

When I tried to stride out, I didn't seem to have any power in my legs. I felt weak. If I trod on a rock or on uneven ground, I'd lose my balance and nearly fall over. I was exhausted too. It was like I'd completed a gruelling time-trial, but this was nothing like it.

I was angry with myself, or, more to the point, angry with my body. My mind was willing, but my body was slow to take up the challenge. I was determined to jolt it into action. I lifted the intensity. My attitude was, 'I've got to do more: I've got to go harder, I've got to go further.' Gradually, I felt better, more fluent, but still more awkward than I was before Bali.

'That's it,' I said to Nerissa. 'I want to be there at training when the boys start on the sixth of January.'

I wasn't expected at training until 13 January, but we'd had a long enough break anyway — we'd been away for three and a half weeks. Although I had put on some weight, I knew it wasn't muscle.

The night before my first training session, I felt like a little kid before his first day of school. I put my new Kangaroos training outfit on — runners, socks, tracksuit and cap — and asked Nerissa how I looked.

She shook her head and laughed. 'You look great, honey,' she said.

I was irrepressible.

'I'm ready to go,' I declared. 'I'm going to training tomorrow.'

I was so excited that I hardly slept a wink that Sunday night. This was another momentous day that I'd been waiting for.

When I got to training, a few people said, 'You're not supposed to be back until next week, aren't you?' I like surprising people.

People talk about how the smell of the liniment and the leather affects you and it's true. You don't realise how much you miss it until it is almost taken away from you.

The boys were jogging a couple of laps to warm up before they were to run a time trial at Princes Park. I thought, 'I'll just join in and then I'll jog over and watch them do their time-trial.' It sounded like a sensible plan — in theory. But I should've known that I wouldn't be able to help myself.

For a few days after my New Year's Eve run, I'd been stiff and sore in the legs, but strangely — pleasantly — I felt good, refreshed even, after this part-session. I don't know whether it was due to the extra comfort of my new running shoes, or the fact that I was running on grass rather than road, but I craved more. In the end, I clocked up almost 4 kilometres, which I completed in stops and starts throughout the session. I'd only done half that, at best, in my previous running sessions.

It was the first time the players and coaches had seen me since some of them visited me in hospital when I was a skeleton with skin. I literally saw a few jaws drop and eyebrows raise.

PAUL HAMILTON (KANGAROOS ASSISTANT COACH): When he first came down to training and started doing a little a bit, he was hobbling, and the coaching panel felt he had no chance. It was a case of 'Should you tell him or should I?' I saw him on the track and thought, 'Oh, Jason.' All the other guys had just gone through a massive pre-season and were as fit as anything and here's Jase, struggling to run without a limp.

TIM HARRINGTON: There were a couple of times where he had to lift up his body suit or shift the garments, and some of the people around the club were seeing him stripped for the first time; it was just amazing. The general reaction was, 'Oh, I didn't think it was that bad.' He'd had skin-grafting too, so where his skin was good, they'd taken big squares and rectangles off it. I suppose it was a bit of a patchwork quilt.

BRENT HARVEY: When I first saw him, it knocked me back a bit. I didn't really know what to say, but he was in great spirits when he saw us.

GLENN ARCHER: His posture wasn't too bad and he was walking around OK but he didn't look like he was a sportsman or anything. I didn't think he'd be able to come back. But Jason's always been a really hard worker, really dedicated to his training, and he worked twice as hard as he usually does. That's pretty hard to do because half of us didn't train as hard as Jason had before he was hurt.

LEIGH COLBERT: I called him 'Skins' because of the body suit. I told him he should patent it and make a few dollars, and about halfway through the year, Australian Test cricket captain Steve Waugh stole the idea. It was a bit of a running gag, but that's the way we've always approached each other and that was the first thing that came to mind — Skins McCartney.

Early on it was really hard, especially for the younger guys, because they hadn't been around him or spent any time with Jason. We tried to break the ice a bit for them — not that they sat and back and laughed or anything — but at least then they felt more comfortable around him.

LEIGH BROWN (KANGAROOS TEAMMATE): I'd just come across from Fremantle, so it was the first time I'd met Jason in person, and it was actually a great honour. It was amazing how normal he was. You wouldn't have known that he had been through such an ordeal. He was very welcoming to me, being a new guy to the club. I was interested, more than anything, in understanding what operations he'd had and all his rehab, and whether there was anything we could do to help. He was very open about everything that had happened and I don't think he was in any way trying to hide his scars or wounds.

ROGER MOORE (KANGAROOS PHYSIOTHERAPIST): The first day he got to training, I told him that I'd been on a holiday to Mildura.

Jase, as quick as a flash, replied, 'I wish I'd come with you.'

He was certainly able to maintain his sense of humour.

GORDON MCDONALD (KANGAROOS PHYSIOTHERAPIST): He just fitted straight back in. He didn't ask for any special treatment. With guys like Jason, you don't know how much pain or discomfort they're in because they don't say anything.

SHANNON WATT (KANGAROOS TEAMMATE): When Jason first turned up at training, I didn't think he looked too bad. I thought to myself, 'Was it really that bad?' I thought he'd made a miraculous recovery.

Then I saw him getting changed and some of the scars he had and I thought, 'Oh my god, how did he come back?' because it just looked horrific. He must have a lot of ticker. He could quite easily have decided he'd had enough of footy, to get better in his own time. It was an achievement in itself that he was training.

PAUL HAMILTON: It was fantastic to have Jason in the gym because I could say to the younger guys, 'You think you're doing it hard, just have a look at that guy.' He was an inspiration like that and certainly made the coaches' jobs easier. And some days it was pretty hot and guys are thinking they're hot and sweating and here's Jason running around in a wetsuit.

I thought the media that had followed me for the previous two months would finally ease off — at least until I got closer to playing. I couldn't have been further from the truth. The media was there in force at the next session two days later. Cameras were trained on me for the entire two hours. Everything I did, which wasn't much — stretching, running, basic skill work, talking casually with coaches — was captured on film. I was shocked — embarrassed even. That type of thing is usually reserved for the superstars — Michael Voss, Nathan Buckley and James Hird — not a normal country bloke from Nhill. OK, so my situation wasn't entirely normal. But fate had decided that.

Now I certainly have a greater appreciation of what these guys, including my old skipper Wayne Carey, have had to put up with for most of their careers. And I can understand why Tony Modra has become media-shy and a virtual recluse.

TROY MAKEPEACE (KANGAROOS TEAMMATE): This may sound funny, but it was like having a superstar turn up to training. I felt kind of nervous around him — I'm sure I was more nervous than he was. I just shook his hand — I didn't want to shake his hand too hard — and I tried to let him go about his business. I didn't want to be in his face asking questions. Everyone was just rapt, firstly, that he'd pulled through. To have him back at training was amazing.

I was reminded about why I had become the flavour of the month when Ros Grant from the Australian Federal Police (AFP) visited me to formulate my impact statement to assist in the prosecution of the Bali bombers. It was an interesting two-hour exercise. I examined the floor plan of Paddy's Bar and quickly pinpointed where we were standing when the bomb went off. Several images of that night flashed through my mind; it was like a camera clicking in my head.

Ironically, while Ros was there my front door slammed shut and made a loud noise. It spooked me a little, but I kept myself under control. She said, 'You're all right. I was at someone else's place the other day, the same thing happened and they jumped on the floor.'

At that stage, the AFP thought that a bag that had been placed on the dance floor had exploded in Paddy's Bar. They didn't think it was a suicide bomber. Initially, I thought, 'No way, that can't be right. If someone left a bag under a stool, you wouldn't notice it; but a bag sitting on the edge of the dance floor would have been very noticeable. I would have seen it.'

When we found out later that it was, in fact, a suicide bomber wearing a bomb-vest, I battled through a couple of tough, soul-searching days. I kept going through it over and over in my head. 'Did I see him? He might have brushed past me when I had my back turned. Could we have done something?' But what could we have done — grab the bag and blow ourselves up?

Football training was a good therapy to take my mind off such things. Sweating it out on the track and sharing a few jokes with the boys, that camaraderie, was better than anything any doctor could order.

After a week back in light training, Dr Con Mitropoulos came with me to see a specialist at the Alfred Hospital. I received a good report. A few days later, I had lung function and VO2 max tests at the Alfred and was ecstatic that I was only 20 per cent down on peak fitness. Even at that early stage, I was in much better shape than an average person.

DR CON MITROPOULOS: For a guy to be in the normal range after being unconscious for a week and having had such terrible trauma in intensive care, it was already amazing.

That was a load off my mind. I was nervous about the outcome of the examination because I didn't want anything to have an impact on my dream of playing for the Kangaroos again. I couldn't afford any interruptions to my preparation if I was to make it back. My teammates — and my opponents — were already miles in front of me. They were so fit that they could've played games in January. While I knew I would never catch them, I had to bridge the gap as much as possible.

I had my skin-fold measurements recorded for the first time since the footy season too. I was anxious about the result, but was pleasantly surprised to measure 87 mm. I usually played at about 50 mm, but I was sure I would've cracked the ton. Remarkably, I'd was in worse shape when I joined the Kangaroos in late 1997. Although I trained with the Crows throughout the finals series, I wasn't playing. Add to that the fact that the Kangaroos had made the preliminary final that year, which meant that training hadn't started until mid-November — I'd virtually had a 12-week break, and I hadn't done much in that time. My skin-fold reading then was a disgraceful 114. I gained confidence from that knowledge because only a few months after that I was playing good football.

After receiving the medical all-clear, I was raring to start the steady build-up to what I hoped would be a successful return through our VFL side, Port Melbourne.

The Kangaroos' new fitness and conditioning coach, Jarrod Egan, with Con's help, devised a six-week training program that was aimed at gradually building endurance, speed and strength — and making up the 20 per cent I needed to regain peak fitness.

DR CON MITROPOULOS: Given that Jason had lost an incredible amount of weight and muscle mass because of his burns and his time in intensive care, we really had to get his body built up. I made it up as I went along really, but I put a bit of a plan together, so that by the time the season started, he would be training properly with everyone and handling the ball.

It was going to take six weeks of strength work and running, and then another six weeks of football — a good three months for him to really come back. A lot of that was just buying time to allow his skin to heal and his grafts to take.

My main concerns were his shrapnel wound in his calf, the wasting of his hamstrings, and whether the skin behind his legs was actually going to be good enough for him to land on, twist, pick up the ball, kick and do all that kind of footy stuff.

I did say to Jason at the start that the one area that would probably be his downfall would be his calf, the left one, which had the shrapnel wound. I thought that somewhere along the way he would either tear it or it would cause him grief.

Before he even started to run on it, I gave that shrapnel area an ultra-sound because I knew that somewhere along the way we would end up having another scan look at it. I wanted to see what it looked like because if it was to re-tear somewhere along the journey, I could at least have a comparison and say, 'Well, actually, it's through the scar tissue or it's in the muscle above or below.'

I loved the fact that my fitness program — my road back to AFL football — was all mapped out for me. It comes back to that structure thing. I stuck the program up on my fridge so I had a constant reminder of what I would be doing the next day.

I was to do 17 sessions (17 hours) a week and, as the program stipulated, the longest distance I would run in the one session would be my warm-up jog of three laps. Then I'd stretch for about five minutes, jog two laps, stretch, jog one lap. This type of training was all new to me because I didn't feel like I was putting enough miles in my legs. But it didn't take too long for me to shake the 'unco' running style.

Then I'd run sets of about 80 metres: jog 20 metres, build up for 20 metres, stride 40 metres and then ease down. We'd put a stopwatch on each 40-metre stride. As expected, I progressively improved. I started striding at 50 to 60 per cent intensity and slowly increased both the intensity and the distance. Although it didn't feel like it at the time, it gave me a good base of fitness to work with.

I wore a heart-rate monitor at every session so we could track my progress. I uploaded all the sessions on my computer and diligently charted the results. I was my own homework project.

DR CON MITROPOULOS: I considered Jason the best prepared footballer I'd come across — without a doubt. Where other players might roll in at 10 a.m. for a bit of physio, he'd be there at 7, and he'd already been down to the beach for a walk.

Even before Bali, I used him as the classic example for all the young kids. When these kids got injured they'd never come in to the clinic to get treated, and then they'd complain that they were sore. I'd say, 'Here's your classic example, a guy like Jase, who doesn't even have an injury. He's in here twice a week, nice and early, having his rubs and his treatment.' He always took very good care of his temple, which is his body.

Even without any injuries at all, he would regularly see the physios. He was always meticulous in his preparation. He wasn't injury-prone but we used to see a lot more of him than anyone else because that was his way of maintaining his body. That's probably the reason he's done so well since Bali.

During his whole recovery process, he really didn't do anything different from what he would normally have done as a healthy footballer.

BRENT HARVEY: Sometimes you go to training feeling pretty ordinary, like you don't really want to be there, but then you see Jase putting on his skins and doing all the stuff he has to do before training, and not moaning one bit. You think to yourself, 'Why am I complaining?'

I wouldn't have been able to run 5 kilometres — at any pace — but at least I was starting to get some condition. Occasionally I had a general feeling of mild tightness throughout my body — it wasn't soreness; more an awareness that I was steadily pushing myself. I almost welcomed it in a way because it meant that I was getting closer, ever so slowly, to achieving my goal.

DR CON MITROPOULOS: Jason worked very, very hard to get his range of movement back because he naturally ran very stiff-legged. He was always called 'The Robot' because he used to run like a robot. Nothing had changed.

TIM HARRINGTON: I was still in a state of shock that he was training. During the pre-season, we had to be really careful because we train in the morning — in the heat. I was thinking, 'The sun's going to get to him, he's going to dehydrate, he's going to be no good.' He had to take a step back a couple of times because he'd probably done a bit too much, but his fitness came on really quickly. I was really surprised. I thought, 'God, I didn't think his body would cope with this.'

ADAM SIMPSON: It must have been excruciating for Jason on the hot days, but he never once complained and never took the smile off his face. From what I've seen, 99 per cent of the population wouldn't have been able to do what he did.

JESS SINCLAIR (KANGAROOS TEAMMATE): Everyone's going, 'How bloody hot is it?' and here's Jason in tracksuit pants and a tracksuit top running round. That's one thing I immediately took out of it — just to face life, don't complain, get on with things.

DAVID DUNBAR (PORT MELBOURNE COACH 2000–2003): The Kangaroos were doing some early morning sessions and while the main group was doing their work, Jason was off to the side doing his bits and pieces to slowly build up his fitness. He had a long-sleeve skivvy on and body stockings. I knew it would be a bit of a battle for him then. He had to be covered up from the sun even at eight o'clock in the morning. I thought, 'How's he gonna go at 2 o'clock in 30-degree heat in the practice matches?'

I thought that maybe he could be a good contributor for us at VFL level. I didn't think he'd get back to AFL level. I don't think I was alone in thinking that way either. Playing AFL was a million miles away at that stage, so I didn't really consider it.

ALLEN AYLETT: I had a quick word to him at training one day. After that, I had no doubt that he'd get back into the side at some stage. I said, 'How's it going?'

He said, 'Fine.'

'How are you feeling?'

He said, 'Feels good.'

I said, 'You'll make it.'

I've been around football long enough and you just develop a sixth sense.

DEAN LAIDLEY: Initially, we were actually thinking of putting Jason on the long-term injury list — we had two rookies who would probably come onto the list. But that didn't happen, only because Jason was improving at such a huge rate.

When he first came down, he looked very stilted, he was still very weak, but it was fascinating to see him evolve and improve bit by bit, inch by inch, every day.

BRENT HARVEY: Just to watch Jason recover was absolutely fantastic. It was inspiring.

A lot of people would ask, 'Is Jason going to play again?' and I'd say, 'Yeah, he's training well,' but deep down I really didn't think he'd get back.

DAVID DUNBAR: Here's a bloke who's been in a near-death situation and to actually be able to get up, walk, run around and start training and playing again, I think he would have to rate himself one of the luckiest blokes on earth to have the chance to play footy again. People lost their lives, lost limbs and suffered horrific burns, so he was lucky to be alive, let alone playing footy.

Despite all his AFL experience, there were never going to be any problems with him coming back and saying, 'I'm an AFL player, I'm above this.' Because of what he had been through, he was on a clear mission to get the best out of himself as a footballer. He still had the opportunity of playing AFL again, and playing for Port Melbourne in the VFL was a necessary part of that, which he accepted. I knew he would try to make the most of every opportunity.

I had a chat with him one morning in pre-season training. We had a new alliance between Port Melbourne and the Kangaroos in the VFL, and he told me about how he'd experienced a bit of that under Malcolm Blight at Adelaide when he had to go back and play in the SANFL. In the initial set-up with Port Melbourne and the Kangaroos, he was the fella who really made it work. We had a couple of meetings in the pre-season with the younger Kangaroos boys who were likely to play a fair bit of footy at Port Melbourne. Jason sat in on those meetings. I had my say about how things had run during the previous alliance with Port Melbourne and the Sydney Swans, then Jason would talk about how Blighty had selected players if their form was good in the SANFL. Jason really put the blokes at ease about the whole situation. The Kangaroos youngsters had an enormous amount of respect for him.

We slowly introduced some agility work into my training — football movements like twisting, turning and jumping — which would ultimately determine whether I would be able to match it at the highest level.

I didn't want to spend too much time doing skills sessions at that stage because I knew I had a lot of work ahead of me in building my fitness. I did basic skills and a lot of stationary drills just to get my body used to kicking and handballing again.

TIM HARRINGTON: When he started getting involved in the kicking drills, I had a kick with him one morning just to loosen up. He wasn't supposed to be doing too much. He said he'd lost a lot of power in his legs. Even though he was running well, the kicking was testing him out a bit. But it wasn't long before he was joining the group.

I knew I would have to wear some gloves for the ball work because my pressure gloves are so slippery that I wouldn't have been able to grip the ball. I couldn't lay my hands on any football-specific gloves so I bought a pair of netball gloves instead — there's not a lot of difference between the two — and cut the fingers out of them. But I initially made the mistake of taking my pressure gloves off and only wearing the netball ones on their own. It made marking painful. In the summer heat, it didn't take long for my hands to became swollen. They became even hotter and more swollen as my body temperature increased due to the physical activity. The skin and scars on my hands, especially my left one, were still fairly raw. Every time I tried to mark the ball in front of my eyes, it felt like I was banging my hand in a car door. But I tried not to let on that I was in pain. Imagine saying, 'Oh, my hands hurt' during a training session at an AFL club. I don't think the blokes would have bagged me or thought any less of me, but the fact was that if I wanted to play with these blokes again, I had to act like them.

I did just that in a simple passing drill and was surprised at how cleanly I marked the ball. But it was a different story when it came to jumping and judging the flight of the ball. My coordination was completely off.

I could handball on my right hand OK, but I had to perfect the old flick pass on my left because there was no way I could hit the ball with a clenched fist. I could barely make a fist with my left hand.

I'd always been loud on the training track — encouraging, supporting, instructing. It's an important aspect of being a valuable team member. But I soon discovered that I had to retrain my voice box. It was another part of my body that needed strengthening. My voice would often be croaky in those first few weeks as I readjusted to the vocal requirements of the game.

I was limited in a lot of ways, but the limitations only extended as far as my mind allowed. While it was a purely physical thing, I believed that a strong and prepared mind might help me overcome some obstacles. It certainly helped me accept the fact that I would have to work almost twice as hard as everyone else to make the grade.

I also had to wear twice as many items of clothing as my teammates. Along with the hand and arm pressure garments, I had to wear custom-made tights, similar to wetsuit material, with the crutch cut out of them to release some of the tightness. I thought, 'Am I going to rip holes in them? How many of these will I go through?' I did end up sending them back to the manufacturer for repairs sometimes.

In the second week of training, I went swimming for the first time since the bombings. We went to the beach at Albert Park, just two minutes from home. It was weird to start with because the skin was tight on my left arm and I couldn't straighten it. It felt like my left arm was a foot shorter than the other because it was constantly bent. (If I swam, I would have gone in circles — or sunk like I usually did.)

The salt water felt good on my body though, quite soothing, and it wasn't long before my skin began to stretch. While I enjoyed having a paddle, I gave the swimming away fairly quickly because it was too time-consuming. I had to get my pressure garments off before I went into the water, and then put them back on when I got out. It was too much of a nuisance if we had to go to a session or a meeting at the club. I didn't want to miss any sessions, or parts of sessions, but it was a common-sense decision. I'm not the greatest swimmer anyway. Another reason not to swim outdoors was the risk of being sunburnt. It was more practical for me to go to the gym and get on an exercise bike or a rowing machine.

I also had my first massage in three months. I'd gone from being massaged two or three times a week — often by Leanne Woodgate — to going cold turkey for three months. But, boy, did it feel good. It felt different from the way I had remembered it. Different depending on which area was being massaged, as the masseur's hands moved from the smooth texture of 'normal' skin to a grafted area. It felt particularly soothing in the grafted areas. I was itchy in these spots too, so the rubbing smothered that itchiness.

LEANNE WOODGATE: I was able to compare how Jason's body coped before the ordeal and how it did afterwards. His skin was so fragile and marked with bumps. He was still going through the healing process, yet he was playing football.

Massage is an important part of healing. You have to do things a little differently because there is a lot of scar tissue to break up and try to thin the burns out a bit.

The first time I massaged him after Bali, I didn't go as deep as I used to because his skin was so tender.

When we initially saw him, we were shocked because we didn't know how severely he'd been burnt.

I got most itchy when I hung upside down, did push-ups or certain types of weights. I would be so itchy that I was almost in pain. I took tablets to ease the all-over itch and the urge to scratch. Although I no longer need the tablets, I still get itchy if I stand still for long enough, whether it be when I'm public speaking for half an hour or standing in a long or slow line at the supermarket.

DR HEATHER CLELAND: Even once their wounds are healed, patients get a lot of problems with pain and stinging. The most persistent and troublesome symptom a lot of people have is itching. Severe, persistent itching can drive people around the twist. It stops them sleeping, it means that because they're always itching and scratching — even if they're scratching subconsciously and in their sleep — their grafts tend to break down and get oozy and weepy. It varies from person to person, but it can be terribly distressing. They don't feel all that flash for months and months.

21

Feeling my way

Team photo sessions are normally a chore. Sure, you have a bit of a giggle as blokes crack gags, but you want to get it out of the way as quickly as possible. However, the Kangaroos team photo shoot on 31 January 2003 was, for me, a great honour. It had always been an honour but this was extra special. To once again wear my full match-day gear — including a new long-sleeve jumper to further protect my more tender spots — with all of my teammates was another sign that I was moving closer to achieving my goal of playing AFL football again. It was still a long way off, but it seemed possible.

But before I could move forward with my football, I had to move back in time.

On 1 February, about twenty-five bomb victims — survivors and people who had lost loved ones — were flown to Sydney to participate in a forum for *60 Minutes*. Hughesy, Nerissa and I went together to the luncheon in Woolwich Road, Hunters Hill. The property had breath-taking views of Sydney Harbour, the bridge and the city. If there was a perfect backdrop for a reunion of people whose lives had been affected by tragedy, this was it.

Before we went inside for the forum, we mingled around the pool for a casual barbecue. There were many familiar faces — some I'd met, others who I'd only read about or seen on TV.

It was the first time that I'd spoken to people who had lost their friends or family in the bombings. People like Phil Britten, who lost seven mates from Kingsley Football Club in Perth. Or Eric de Haart, who lost six mates from the Coogee Dolphins rugby league club. Or Hannabeth Luke, who lost her boyfriend, Marc Garjado. Devastating stuff. Earlier in the recovery process, I doubt whether I would've been able to handle such a situation. Sure, we survivors had been injured — some of us horrifically so — but at least we lived to tell the tale. With these poor people clearly suffering and grieving, I wasn't sure how to approach the situation. In the end, I didn't have to. They asked a few questions and then they opened up. I didn't have to pry.

I already knew how lucky I was to be alive but this event reinforced that I needed to make the most of my second chance at this precious thing called life.

We traded our personal stories and compared injuries, percentages and garments. While each person had a different story to tell, most of us could relate to each other in terms of treatment and recovery. We each knew the pain the others had endured and the impact that burns have on your life. That was refreshing in a way because sometimes I felt isolated and almost alone during my recovery. Now I was among kindred spirits.

People kept telling me, 'You've been such an inspiration.' It was a difficult compliment to accept because virtually everyone there had been inspirational in one way or another. There were so many heroic and selfless acts, so to single me out would be unfair. I have received a lot of media attention that I feel should have been bestowed on all of these courageous people.

I didn't set out to inspire anyone, or champion any cause. It wasn't a conscious thing at all. My sole aim was to get myself healthy again. Having said that, I'd be happy to claim that I inspired someone, or that someone took some positives from my experiences. I suppose that I have helped others by helping myself.

Fittingly, the forum was hosted by Peter Overton, a reporter who had developed a genuine and emotional attachment to the victims of the Bali tragedy. Overton did a story on Hughesy for *60 Minutes* a few months earlier when Hughesy was in a coma and teetering somewhere between life and death. Even after the story screened, Overton regularly called Leigh for updates. So when Overton said he felt privileged to attend the reunion, we knew he meant it.

It was an amazing experience. I think many of us felt privileged to be there.

We were asked questions about everything from our recovery progress and our feelings towards the bombers to our thoughts on sending Australian troops to fight in Iraq, which some people saw as a knee-jerk reaction to the Bali bombings. The feeling of spirit, passion and emotion in the room was so strong you could almost grab it. Everyone openly shared their emotions and opinions. It was very therapeutic — for me at least.

The most emotive issue was whether or not the death penalty should be invoked to deal with those responsible for the bombings. For a couple of minutes, the group seemed overcome with anger. Some wanted the perpetrators to suffer like we did and be burnt. I started thinking, 'We're getting into some really sensitive areas here, and we're starting to sound a bit like the Ku Klux Klan.' A lot of raw emotion and bottled-up anger was spilt that day. Hannabeth brought some reason to the debate by saying something along the lines of, 'No matter what you do to these guys, it won't bring back my boyfriend.' She had a totally different perspective and helped to broaden our thinking.

NERISSA: It was an emotion-filled day, but it was good to meet partners and family members. It really lifted my spirits to know that even though we'd been through hard times, we weren't the only ones. Everyone there was an inspiration in their own way.

If people who have been injured or lost loved ones can be very positive and get on with life, so should the rest of us. It really teaches you not to complain about little things in life. The people we met that day are going to be a special part of our lives from now on.

That night, when the anger subsided, about twenty of us went out for dinner and a few beers at a pub. We must've looked like Dad's Army as we hobbled up the street. Some were on crutches, one of the guys from Queensland, Andrew Csabi, was in a wheelchair and everyone had bandages wrapped around them. There were only a handful of people, loved ones like Nerissa, who looked 'normal'. But we couldn't have cared less.

Although we may have different views on certain topics, we share a special bond. Always will. We were victims of terror, and most of us will bear the scars for life, but there is no denying that we are all survivors. Real Aussie battlers. We're like an extended family.

A couple of days later, I joined my other extended family, my Kangaroos teammates, in a skills session for the first time. I completed the first 20 minutes — the basic warm-up of lane work, kicking and handball drills — of a 40-minute session. I felt rigid and because I trained in runners, without ankle-strapping, I had the turning circle of a small ship. But I certainly didn't disgrace myself. In fact, I thought I went well, all things considered. I was puffing and sweating a lot but I thought, 'In a country league, I would have to be right up with the best players, or maybe even ahead of them in terms of preparation.'

I was almost 29 years old, hardly an immature youngster — I'd like to think I was a seasoned campaigner — but it was hard to contain my excitement. I was transported back to the time I was a junior at high school and I was asked to train with the seniors at Nhill. Even I was amazed with how everything was coming back to me. It was like I'd had football amnesia and my body was slowly remembering how to play the game. I rang my manager, Paul Connors, that afternoon. 'I know I've got a long way to go mate, but I think I'm ready to play.'

I soon discovered that maybe I had overestimated my progress. By this stage, I had built up to training almost the full 45–50 minutes. I ran to the right spot and received the ball on my non-dominant left side. Normally I would have kicked with my left foot, but I was running so fast — well it seemed fast — that I couldn't coordinate everything. I knew where I wanted to deliver the ball but I would've had to kick across my body, about 30 metres, to get it there. I didn't want to do that because I was worried about tearing a groin.

My left hand still wasn't in the greatest shape either, but my options were limited, so I attempted a handball with my left hand. The result wasn't pretty. It was actually one of the worst handballs I've ever executed. It only travelled about 5 metres, and dribbled along the ground to no one in particular.

In the space of a few seconds, my confidence had been shattered. I felt like a burden on my teammates. Self-conscious. Nothing came naturally to me. I didn't want to stuff up their drills. I had a genuine fear of failure each time I grabbed the ball. And this was only training. I thought, 'If I'm like this at training, what am I going to be like under pressure in games?'

At the end of the drill, Dean called us all in. 'What we want, fellas, are thinking players, smart footballers,' he said. 'You've got to remember, you blokes, Jason isn't quite up to speed here. He's only just started training and his execution's not going to be the same, so you don't go offering yourself bloody 30 metres away on his left hand. But the idea was right.'

That was some consolation.

'That's a good lesson for everyone,' Dean added. 'It's about knowing your teammates better — their limitations and capabilities, which foot, which hand.'

I thought, 'Gee, this bloke's going to be a good coach.'

DEAN LAIDLEY: He was coming back from something pretty horrific and we had to understand his limitations. He was going to take time to regain touch as his body re-adjusted to training. But that didn't just apply to Jason McCartney. He might have been the example I was using at that particular time, but you need to understand the limitations, and strengths, of every player in your team.

I was also frustrated because I'd played under Denis Pagan for five years, and I knew every training drill and every facet of his game plan intimately. The long-kicking, physical style of play that Denis demanded from his players suited me. If you gave a hard contest and played common sense football, Denis was happy. I had a strong body and prided myself on playing the percentages and attacking the ball, so I felt comfortable in that environment. But, all of a sudden, I had to learn new and more complicated drills that my teammates had already been working on for a couple of months, and a new, free-flowing game style. This was all foreign to me.

In a way, I didn't feel part of it because I didn't know what they were doing. I felt like a teenager just starting out. I tried to think my way through each drill, which isn't ideal because football is very much an instinctive game. I started thinking, 'It's true what they say — you can't teach an old dog new tricks.' The fact that my body wasn't where it needed to be only compounded my lack of confidence.

That same session, I confided in Stevo. 'Mate, I don't know if I'm going to be able to do it,' I said.

Stevo was as supportive as ever. 'You'll be all right, mate, you'll be all right,' he said.

I couldn't see how my fortunes would improve. But then again, I've always been a deep thinker prone to over-analysing things. In my earlier years at AFL level I was probably a bit of a pessimist, a 'worry wart'. Some blokes are able to switch off from football and put it to the side. Corey is like that. I wished I was that way inclined, but it wasn't in my make-up. If I played or trained poorly, it would eat away at me until the next session. Denis must have been able to sense it. 'Let's get some highlights of all your good stuff,' he'd say, 'and you can watch it at home. You'll be all right.'

He was brilliant like that. He directed another of his favourite sayings my way a few times too. 'You know, son,' he'd say in his fatherly way, 'an old coach once said to me when I was playing down back, "If you've got the ball in your hands, your opponent hasn't got the ball."'

It took the pressure off me and, almost invariably, I'd perform better the next chance I got.

At the end of 1998, my first season at the Kangaroos, Denis said something that will ring in my ears forever. He asked me, 'Who's your toughest opponent?'

I thought about the season I'd just had and there was a day when Western Bulldogs star Chris Grant stitched me up in the second half of a match. I looked at Denis and said, 'Probably Chris Grant.'

Denis shook his head. 'No, son, who's your toughest opponent?'

I shrugged my shoulders. I thought, 'Is this a trick question?'

Then Denis, the old master, said, 'I'm looking at him right now — he's the No. 5 for the Kangaroos.'

And he was right — as usual.

I was now faced with a similar scenario. I was battling myself. I was battling my body, as I had done throughout my recovery, and I was battling my attitude towards change.

One aspect of the new regime that I was ecstatic about was the concept of a pre-season camp. In the early to mid 1990s at Collingwood and Adelaide, such camps were merciless exercises in gut-busting. At the end of 1994, my first pre-season with Adelaide, we did a commando-style camp, with players divided into teams and performing ludicrous acts like carrying people on stretchers and paddling across a huge dam on surfboards.

But there was to be no such lunacy when we headed to Canberra for a four-day camp in the first week of February. On day one I couldn't join the boys for a swim because of the threat of sunburn. Day 2 was a rest day, so I stayed in my hotel room at the Hyatt (much better than huts and tents) with a couple of teammates and watched videos. We had a smorgasbord of food every night and I thought, 'God, years ago I'd come home 5 kilograms lighter, but this time I'm going to go back 5 kilograms heavier.'

MATTHEW BURTON (KANGAROOS TEAMMATE): I roomed with Jase. The first morning we got there, he got up before me and had a shower, and then I had a shower. I said, 'I'll wait for you.'

He said, 'Nah, mate, don't wait for me, I'm going to be another half hour or forty-five minutes.'

He had to moisturise and put the skins back on and then get his clothes on. So I took off for breakfast and he was right, he came down ages later. That's the way he started his day and ended it, which meant he basically had about an hour less each day than the rest of us. He was great to chat to. He was just being the normal Jase, writing his diary, writing down his thoughts and the things he'd done. Jase has never avoided the issue of what happened in Bali.

While we were there, the club held its first intra-club practice match. Although my fitness was steadily improving, I wasn't quite ready to play a full-scale match. The thing that struck me most was the youth of our playing group. I wasn't the only one who noticed it. When one of the sides ran onto the ground, one of our Canberra-based supporters asked me, 'Is this just the young guys? Is the other team more senior?'

I said, 'No, the other side will be similar.'

It reinforced in my mind just how tough it was going to be to get a game in the senior side. Even without my injuries, I wouldn't have been a walk-up start.

However, my confidence lifted after a team meeting that focused on goal-setting. We decided that our buzzword would be 'JUMPER', and we came up with a characteristic for each letter. J for Journey, U for Unity, M for Mateship, P for Pride, E for Every time, and R for Respect. I was taken aback when Matthew 'Spider' Burton came up with the idea that we present an award each week during the season to the player who best exemplified these six traits — the prize being a jumper signed by all of the players, with my No. 5 on the back. My jaw dropped. I was shocked. Utterly humbled. The awards you rate the highest are those that come from your peers.

MATTHEW BURTON: We all signed it because we felt Jason lived all those values. We carried the jumper everywhere. It was at all our meetings, right next to the coach's board. We have a board in our players' room where the winner's name went up. I won it in round 7 in my first game back this year. I was rapt.

I knew it wasn't out of sympathy either because, without bragging, I knew that I'd carried out those values to the letter. I'd built my career on them.

I soon realised that I could also build a career in public speaking. I addressed a crowd for the first time at a sportsmen's night in Seymour, in country Victoria, as part of a function attended by Dean Laidley, Geoff Walsh and club chairman Allen Aylett. I was the main topic of interest and, for about ten minutes, I answered questions about my experiences in Bali. Often you hear mumbling in the back of the room when someone is speaking, but they listened intently. I tried to break it up with a one-liner about Mick but it went straight over everyone's head. No one dared to laugh. Perhaps they didn't think it was funny, but I suspect they felt that laughing would have been disrespectful.

ALLEN AYLETT: I've heard Jason speak at several functions and he's been just outstanding. He's kept everything in the right context and he's clearly ambassadorial. He knows how to carry the flag. He's kept his feet on the ground and he hasn't done a thing wrong. He comes from a strong family, tough stock and good citizens. He's also a product of the discipline of the football environment. I'm certain both of those things helped him overcome adversity.

DAVID KING (KANGAROOS TEAMMATE): Jason's become a fantastic public speaker. His ability to portray the message that he's carrying, and put it across in an emotional way, is something I never knew he had.

An elderly couple approached me. They had lost a son in Bali. Another lady there had lost her best friend. I gained the impression that, in a way, I was their 'great white hope'. It was times like that when I felt under pressure. 'I'd better make this work and get back to play footy,' I thought, 'otherwise I might let a few people down.' But no one could have placed more pressure on me than myself.

As the (reluctant) public face of the Bali tragedy, a different kind of pressure was placed upon me. Steven Febey and I met with Richard Middleton, a lawyer from Alabama in the United States, and Mike Hourigan, a lawyer from Adelaide. They wanted to launch a class action on behalf of the victims of both the Bali bombings and September 11 terrorist attacks in the US. And they wanted us to be the faces of the campaign to get other people on board and make a united stand against terrorism.

Our initial concern was that we could be targeted by terrorist groups. Nerissa and I wanted to travel overseas and the last thing we wanted was to be kidnapped or 'knocked off'. It might sound a bit extreme, but terrorist networks are widespread. However, Middleton and Hourigan impressed upon us that fact that terrorists act on large groups of people, not individuals.

STEVEN FEBEY: I've been happy to comment about my experience in Bali, but because I wasn't physically injured, it has been hard. My injuries have been psychological — the sights, sounds, smells. I hung around the site for about twenty minutes and probably saw more than Jason and Mick did.

Without saying 'no', I wanted to move on with my life. I didn't want to keep digging it up. Sometimes these cases can drag on for four or five years.

I joined the cause — but not as a figure head. I was swayed by two things. The first was an aim to hit the terrorist organisations where it hurts — in the hip-pocket. You can't stop terrorism but I held the hope that maybe we could stifle the flow of dirty money that funds terrorist training camps and propaganda. The second factor was compensation. Although I don't expect anything to come from the class action, I'd be upset if people started receiving compensation payouts in five years and I missed out because I didn't sign a piece of paper. Nerissa and I deserved it as much as anyone.

I caught up with my counsellor-cum-advisor-cum-mate Dave Bonython-Wright on 23 February. Dave is more mate than anything else now. He flew over from Adelaide. He and Nerissa hadn't met before, so we chatted for a couple of hours over breakfast. It was meant to be a simple case of friends reuniting, but it turned into a very worthwhile two-hour counselling session. A couple of touchy subjects were raised that Nerissa and I hadn't really explored together.

A few people had floated the question to Nerissa, 'Why were Leanne, Samantha and Rachael in the bar with Mick, Jason and Hughesy?' Nerissa hadn't been concerned about that until a couple of people also speculated about what might have happened between me and the girls if the bomb hadn't gone off that night. The fact is that we knew the girls through Leanne being our masseur. Sure, we were friendly with one another but it was purely platonic.

It was never a big issue but I knew we needed to address it to expel any smidgeon of doubt that Nerissa might have had. Nerissa didn't want to look stupid standing by me through all of this if I was playing up on her. I know it sounds self-righteous, but the truth is I'd never even consider cheating on Nerissa. Never have, never will. She's my soul mate. Why would I put myself in a position to lose someone so precious to me?

I'd never heard such rumour-mongering first-hand, but a couple of the older ladies at the Kangaroos told me how they had told a woman to 'butt out' when she mentioned it. I thought, 'Gee, I was only talking to the girls for a minute.'

Whenever I was asked about the girls — in interviews or normal conversation — I probably went over the top in explaining that, 'Look, Leanne and Samantha are sisters and Leanne is my masseur, she works at Carlton Football Club.'

I felt like I had to do it every time. I didn't have to prove anything to myself, but with the rumours and innuendo that get bandied around in footy circles, I was keen to point that out immediately. That was the last thing Nerissa and I needed.

NERISSA: It started with a newspaper article that had a glamour photo of Leanne and Samantha, along with a photo of Jason, saying they had been drinking together in a bar. Jan said to me, 'Look at this article!'

I said, 'Oh, great,' and threw it aside. I thought, 'I'm not going to worry about it.'

But then people started saying things to me like, 'So, he was in Bali without you and he was drinking in the bar with other girls.' At first, I'd say, 'Yeah, so? People talk to other people. He knew them anyway, he's friends with them.'

But when it kept going, it eventually wore me down. I thought, 'This is ridiculous,' so I questioned Jason about it. He got really frustrated — understandably too — because he'd done nothing wrong. He explained to me, 'It's the stupid mindset of people who stereotype footballers like that.'

I said, 'So, you expect me to sit back, take it all on board and just believe you?'

He said, 'Yeah, you have to because that's the way it is.'

I trust him, so I believed him. People still carry on about it and I think, 'After all we've been through, how dare you bring up stuff like that?'

I didn't care in the end. I thought, 'People are going to think what they like anyway and it's something too trivial to worry about.'

DAVID BONYTHON-WRIGHT: The test of all relationships is how you handle the heavy stuff. If you can survive those things without them busting up your relationship, chances are you'll be better for it. Jason and Nerissa have had to endure a lot of hardship and trying times but they've been able to stay strong together.

Dave also helped us through the loneliness Nerissa felt when I returned to football training full-time in January. She was on holidays because school wasn't due to resume until February, and, of course, I was often at the club all day. So Nerissa went from being run off her feet with visitors to being alone. She really struggled for a little while. She'd been so strong for so long that it really took its toll. I didn't know about how she felt until she broke down one night.

NERISSA: There was a really bad stage when Jason started going back to training, actually leaving home and doing things on his own. I found that really hard to cope with because I was on holidays and had nothing to do — I didn't have to look after him any more. He'd say, 'I'll be home at 5.30 p.m.,' and if he'd get home at 5.45 I'd be hysterical. I felt I needed him with me, so when he got home I'd be angry with him.

Sometimes I'd cry all day because I needed to release some of the emotion that I'd kept inside me. If I didn't let it out, I would've gone crazy. It wouldn't even be a matter of something triggering it — I'd just cry and think, 'Why am I crying?'

I'm much more emotional now — if something happens to someone I care about or if I watch a sad movie, I cry. I think I'm still releasing a lot of emotions.

Dave has also introduced me to a simple form of yoga. When he first mentioned it, my mind cast back to the time when I was at Collingwood and all the players had to sit around and hold hands in the dark. Denis Banks ran outside and started making ghost sounds in a pipe. We also did something similar at the Kangaroos where we were humming, but Stevo could never concentrate — he would just piss himself laughing.

The technique Dave taught me was: close my eyes, slow down my breathing and allow my mind to drift off into a happy memory, which, for me, was enjoying a beautiful sunset with Nerissa on a balmy evening in Bali. This simple technique has been very effective. It certainly helps me to overcome stress and the pressures of daily life — which, at that stage, included trying to return to AFL football and coping with my phone ringing 40 times a day with people asking me to do various things.

During the discussion with Dave, I mentioned that we wanted to go back to Bali. I needed to come to grips with my emotions and confront some fears, but, more importantly, see how the Balinese were coping. Dave said he wanted to come with us as a support. I earmarked 8–10 March as the ideal time to go. I told Tim Harrington my intentions and he supported me. It was difficult booking flights because there weren't as many planes going to Bali due to a fear of repeat terrorist attacks, but I sorted everything out.

But before flying out, I made an unscheduled appearance on the football ground. When I heard that Port Melbourne's reserves side would play a practice match on the Friday night — just hours before I'd leave for Bali — I saw it as the perfect opportunity to get some long-awaited match practice. I cornered Tim Harrington. 'Port Melbourne seconds are playing Friday night,' I said.

'Yeah, that's right,' Tim said. He must have known what was coming.

'I think I'm ready to play,' I declared. (I knew I was ready to play.) 'I'm doing all the training, I've completed all of the hard running sessions, I've done competitive work.'

They agreed to let me play, but only a quarter — broken up into maybe two 15-minute bursts or three of ten minutes. I couldn't care less how much game time I had — short of running onto the ground for the last two minutes of the match — because the main thing was that I was back.

I'd done body-on-body duels with some big blokes like David Hale and Drew Petrie and didn't get out-marked, which was encouraging.

The Thursday night before I returned to Bali, I was a guest on the *The Footy Show*'s first episode of the year. Despite my affiliation with Eddie McGuire and Channel Nine, there was no way I would give even the slightest hint that I'd be playing the following night at Optus Oval. I told all the boys at training to respect my wishes and keep it quiet because the last thing I wanted was a media circus railroading my attempts to get a kick. As if I wasn't under enough pressure without the spotlight.

And to top it all off, it was my birthday on game day. But that was almost an afterthought. I was focused on bigger milestones.

I was relaxed throughout the day (Friday) but that soon changed when I arrived at Optus Oval. Crews from Channel Nine and Channel Ten were there. 'Damn it, the secret's out,' I thought. But I should've expected that; after all, there are no secrets in AFL football. (Sounds like another 'Paganism'.) There wasn't a large media contingent though — at that stage.

God, I was nervous. But then I've often been nervous before matches, even when I played junior footy in the country. It's funny because I wasn't all that nervous playing in the seniors at 14 but I got quite jittery when I went back to the under-16s. That was because a lot more was expected of me. A fair bit was expected of me on this particular night too. I wasn't worried about my body holding up; I was more concerned about getting a kick and not making a fool out of myself. I'm sure some people expected me to get hurt or not even get a touch, just so they could bag the Kangaroos' decision to keep me on the list. I was determined to repay the club's faith.

I tend to urinate a lot before a game, and this was no exception. It would be nothing for me to relieve myself eight or nine times in the half-hour before I ran onto the ground. It was due to a combination of nerves and the fact I'd drink copious amounts of water and energy drinks to prevent cramping. Another cause for anxiety was the fact that I didn't know any of my teammates. I just hoped that they would give me the ball when I called them all 'Mate! Mate! Mate!'

There was to be no working me into the game off the interchange bench or getting an easy kick as a loose man floating across half-back. I was thrown straight into the fray — into the centre at the first bounce. That was ideal because I could go at my own pace, rather than chase around an opponent at centre half-back or be chased by an opponent at centre half-forward.

I got an early touch when I picked up the ball, went for a little run and dished off a handball. I felt sheer relief when I got that one out of the way. It was like shaking out the cobwebs.

I was a pretty loose centreman and didn't chase too much but by the 15-minute mark, I'd gathered six or seven disposals and taken a couple of marks. But instead of taking a break, I decided to play the entire first quarter. Then I thought, 'I'm going all right here; the calf feels OK. If I only play a quarter, I'll probably have to play a full game in the VFL reserves next week. I'll keep going.'

At quarter-time, I spoke to the coach, David Rogers, and convinced him that I was OK to play another quarter. I only had three touches in the second quarter but I ran up and down the ground as much as possible to give myself a thorough workout. I came off the ground a happy man.

DAVID DUNBAR: He didn't know any of his teammates on the night, he hadn't trained with any of them, so he just rolled up and he did quite well. I was reasonably surprised because I had no idea how his body was going to hold up.

DR CON MITROPOULOS: He didn't even think twice when it came to doing the contact work, tackling, hitting the ground and testing out his skin. It wasn't an issue. These guys break their jaws and once their jaw is set, they're right back into putting their heads into packs again. He's no different. He didn't even blink an eye when it came to testing out his body. He was chomping at the bit to get out there and once I allowed him to join the rest of the group and get involved in the contact stuff, he never looked back. It was as if nothing had happened.

STEVEN FEBEY: It was ironic that I was there to see Jason's first practice match for Port Melbourne's reserves at Optus Oval. Melbourne had played the game before it. There was a bit of hoo-ha out there. People had got wind of the fact that he was going to play.

After watching him play his first quarter and a half, I didn't think he would get back to playing AFL standard. There was a bit of apprehension and uncertainty about the way he moved. He was very robotic. But if you look at the way Jason played before Bali, he was never a silky-smooth player — he was never Darren Jarman-like, put it that way. He had the long-sleeve jumper on and the tights, but I was uplifted and motivated by it.

My body work and spoiling were fine, but jumping for the ball had posed a few problems. Instead of landing on a slightly bent leg with a bit of 'give' in it, I'd land with a straight leg and my knee would flick back dangerously. I thought, 'I'm going to do my knee here.' But I soon got that technique flaw ironed out.

However, I couldn't completely iron out a problem with the back of my left leg where shrapnel had ripped a hole. It seemed to be healing OK but it was still tight and it restricted my stretching. I was shocked when an x-ray revealed that the scar tissue had calcified. In layman's terms, it had hardened like bone. It was like a spur growing out the back of my leg.

I quickly put my performance into perspective. A lot of the youngsters who I played with and against were just testing themselves at the next level and probably didn't even get a game in the VFL reserves. Nonetheless, it gave me enormous confidence. I didn't feel out of place and, from all reports, I didn't look out of place either. 'I can still do this,' I thought. 'And at least I know that if this doesn't all work out with the Kangaroos, I can still play footy somewhere.'

I'd also gotten through the game with barely a scratch. That was the unknown factor for me. I didn't know how my body would cope with the bumps, tackles and (accidental) scratches.

TIM HARRINGTON: Before the game, I thought, 'He's going to be really scratchy and this will be one of quite a few games that he'll play in the Port Melbourne reserves.' If your match practice is under scratch, like Jason's was, you generally don't judge the flight of the ball well, you don't position yourself well and it's hard to get into the flow of the game. But he wasn't like that at all. He was judging it well, he was standing under balls that were floating everywhere. It was a pretty ordinary standard practice game, but he just stood out. I thought, 'God, this is amazing. He's amazing.' That was his only game at that level.

When I emerged from the change rooms, a gallery of reporters and cameras were waiting for me. Little did they know that the real scoop was that I was flying to Bali the next morning.

22

Back to Bali

Plane flights can be boring and tiresome. They can also be nerve-racking when you are travelling to an important engagement. But strangely enough, I didn't feel any apprehension on the flight to Bali. Nerissa and I spent some time talking about smells, sights and sounds that might trigger my emotions. In some ways, I prepared for it like I was about to play a football match. I was confident that nothing would catch me off guard. No surprises.

Almost as soon as we'd dropped our bags in our room at the Hotel Padma — just out of Kuta on Legian beach, about a kilometre from the Hard Rock Hotel — Nerissa, Dave and I set off on the 2-kilometre walk to the site of the bombings. On the way, we stopped at an Aussie bar and had a chat with two Balinese brothers and a couple of Melbourne women who recognised me. We then went across the road to a little bar that Nerissa and I had frequented 17 months earlier. We talked to a few more locals and told them what I was doing. They gave me some offerings and incense sticks to place at the site.

By this stage, all I wanted to do was get to where the Sari Club and Paddy's Bar had once dominated the district. We passed some Balinese salesmen, who gave us the standard fare: 'Come and have a look in my shop. You want hat? T-shirt?' Buying some bargain basement items was the last thing on my mind. As soon as I told them my intentions, they became deeply and genuinely concerned. They actually wanted to come with us. I thought, 'This is good because they can show us around.' In days past, you could walk past the Sari Club and not realise you'd gone past it. But you couldn't miss it at night because its sign towered above everything else in the street and stood out like a beacon. Now, in daylight, although it doesn't actually exist any more, there is no mistaking where it once stood.

All of a sudden, it seemed, we were there. It hit me with the force of a steamtrain. A green fence separated it from the street. There were plenty of flowers, many of them dead, and incense strewn across the ground. Stuck to the fence like a cotton tombstone was a white sheet, about 20 metres long and about

1.5 metres wide, on which were written countless heartfelt messages of hope, despair and inspiration. Many were in foreign languages, confirming the world-wide impact of this human tragedy.

The crater — 4 metres wide and 1.5 metres deep — that was caused by the car bomb out the front of the club had been filled but not levelled off. I thought about the poor bouncers who'd been standing out the front of the club, just a couple of metres from the car. They would have been dead before they knew what was going on.

Although I hadn't been at the Sari Club on the fateful night, it had been my night-time hangout in Bali every year for a decade. I'd had some of my best nights there. All remnants of the club had been cleared, but I was able to walk sombrely across the site. Several emotions rushed through me at once. Sadness. Disbelief. Anger. The power of the place was like nothing I'd ever experienced. There was a real eeriness about it and a strong sense of loss. It was like a black cloud hovered over the site.

NERISSA: When I walked onto the site, I was struck by a very heavy feeling of sadness. I just couldn't control my emotions. I thought of all the people who had died there. I couldn't control my emotions, and tears were just running. I wasn't crying hysterically, but the emotion was pouring out. Then I looked at Jase. I thought, 'How is he coping? What's going through his head?'

DAVID BONYTHON-WRIGHT: It was really emotional. I'd never been there and what I felt at the sight was very powerful. You could feel vibes from that place. Even talking about it gives me goosebumps.

Nerissa tried to hug me but I shrugged her off. I needed a minute on my own to enable my brain to process the mass of information that had flooded its way.

NERISSA: That made me feel like I wasn't doing enough for him and it made the day even harder. I said to him afterwards, 'I hope I'm doing everything right. I hope I'm doing as much as you want me to do, to support you.'

He said, 'Of course you are. Why are you saying that?'

I said, 'Because I went to hug you at the Sari club and you just kept walking.'

Then I realised he needed to be on his own, and he didn't know whether to kick the ground or to let it all out and cry.

I walked towards the back of the site and saw the remains of an old beer chest. I went to sink my foot into it, to release the pent-up anger that was boiling inside me, but I pulled back a bit on impact. (Imagine returning to the club with a broken foot!)

All three of us had heavy hearts. Understandably, I was the most affected. So much for being emotionally prepared.

NERISSA: In the end, I said to Jase, 'I need to get out,' because I could not control the sadness that I was feeling. As soon as I stepped off the site, I could feel it lift from me and I started to feel better.

We wanted to leave a message on the sheet but we didn't have a texta, so we used a pen. (We returned a couple of days later to go over our message with a permanent marker.) We went across the road — a short pass away — to the site of Paddy's Bar. I showed Nerissa and Dave exactly where everyone had been standing when the bomb exploded. It was easy to work out because you could see the base of the brickwork in the ground where the oval bar had been.

Strangely, although I'd nearly lost my life in Paddy's Bar, I didn't feel as emotional as I had at the site of the Sari Club. It was due to the fact that I'd had more history there, and more people had perished there.

We lit some incense at a small temple in the back corner of the site and one of our Balinese friends took us through a prayer.

Dave, always thoughtful, asked me, 'Do you want to just grab a rock or something small to take from the site?'

I did. I felt compelled to. I also took a rock from the Sari Club site.

We wandered across for a look at the Macaroni Club, where Mick, Hughesy, Nashy and I had eaten before we went to Paddy's Bar. It had been damaged in the bombings.

We went to the nearby Troppo Zone hotel for a cold beer — just what I needed after a very confronting experience. The hotel had a reputation for being an 18-to-30s club and was usually packed with Aussie party-goers. But there were only three people staying there at the time. (Business was slow for almost everyone in Bali because tourists were afraid to go there.)

We sat at the bar and chatted to some locals. We were amazed when they told us about a cleansing ceremony that was held at the sites. The aim of the ceremony was to send the spirits of the people who died there to heaven. Little kids started screaming and grabbing on to their parents because they believed they could see people with what looked like white sheets over them wandering the site and slowly floating away.

That night, we indulged in some heaven on earth: eating fish on the beach at Jimbaran Bay with a Balinese mate of mine, Jimmy, and his wife and kids. In this wondrous setting, I was overwhelmed with disbelief. I thought, 'How could something so terrible happen in such a beautiful, peaceful place as this?'

We didn't get back to the hotel until about 10.30 p.m. There was something else I desperately wanted — needed — to do: go back to the bomb sites at around the same time that the explosions had happened, and call into a couple of bars and clubs.

We walked over the sites again. We sat down on the kerb near where the car bomb exploded. We pondered.

We strolled to the nearby Apache Bar. It was small and crowded, mostly with Europeans. I didn't hear any Australian accents. Talk about having a few quiet drinks; these were sombre ones. Nerissa was talking to me but I was a million miles away. Over and over, I tried to find an answer for the question that kept repeating in my brain. 'How could this have happened?' It still perplexes me.

I looked around and watched the customers. They were cheery, happy, relaxed. Enjoying a presumably well-deserved break from life at home — as we had been on 12 October 2002. 'It was a night just like this,' I thought.

On the way back to the hotel we took a detour through Seminyak, a suburb north of Kuta, and were pleasantly surprised to be reminded of the Bali I knew — people were spilling out of the bars and restaurants and having a good time. The nightlife had shifted from Kuta to Seminyak. But, again, no Australians.

The next morning we had breakfast at a little Aussie bar and watched the Wizard Cup (pre-season) Grand Final. The combatants were my two former clubs, Collingwood and Adelaide. I barracked for the Crows because I'd played alongside more of their players, plus Wayne Carey was playing his first official game for the club. I found it amusing that whenever Duck went near the ball, the Balinese would say, 'The King! The King! Wayne Carey!' But they really cracked me up when they said, 'Where's Modra? Where's Modra?'

Another heavy-hearted experience was visiting the Sanglah Hospital in Denpasar. The staff there allowed us to wander around as we liked. As soon as I turned a corner to enter the emergency section, memories of the night came flooding back. We retraced the path along which I was wheeled on the stretcher from emergency to a waiting room outside an operating room. The waiting room wasn't much of a room — it was the holding pen that I recalled it being. Nothing modern, just a flimsy chipboard door. Being a Sunday, no doctors were on duty, so we didn't get to go into the operating theatre — not that I wanted to anyway.

I was a bit shy at first but no one seemed to mind when I took some footage with my video camera. They were as angry and upset about what happened as we were, and perhaps they felt they owed us something.

Nerissa and Dave were surprised by my clear recollections. I even surprised myself.

All three of us were surprised when we were allowed access to the hospital morgue. One of the staff took us there. Nerissa couldn't bring herself to go inside. She was thinking, 'It could've been Jase here in there.' I struggled too, but was determined that there would be no backing out. I'd come too far for that.

The morgue was smaller than I anticipated and was shaded with colourbond so that its interior was not visible to passers-by in the adjacent corridor. I was well aware that up to two hundred bodies had occupied this very same room only five months earlier. I was shown an area where the bodies were washed down. I was barely able to maintain my composure.

I was curious about five wooden boxes sitting on the floor.

'What's with the boxes?' I asked.

I was told that they held remains of people killed in the bombings. I was dumbstruck.

'How come? Why?' I asked.

Apparently the bodies had been identified, but, for whatever reason — breakdowns in communication, trouble locating families, etc. — they had sat untouched. (Unidentified remains had been cremated a couple of weeks earlier.)

I looked a little closer at the boxes and saw notes attached to them stating the name and country of the deceased person inside. One man was South African, another was from New Zealand. I felt relieved that none of the five was Australian. It was distressing enough that actual dead bodies were in the boxes, but it would've smacked me around even more if an Aussie was among them. It would have been too close to home. But, really, nationality was irrelevant.

I was hurting.

I walked out of the hospital feeling satisfied that I had done what I came to do. But I wanted to take it a step further — I wanted to go to the jail where Amrozi and Imam Samudra were held in custody. I didn't imagine doing much once we got there — I just wanted to see where they were being housed.

We spoke to some guards and police officers at the front gate of police headquarters in Denpasar, and I was astounded when they led us through to the back entrance. For a minute there I thought that we were actually going to see the terrorists. We probably got within a couple of walls of them. On the off-chance that I had been able to speak to these people, I would have simply asked, 'Why?' I just wanted to get inside their heads. But their head space would probably be a scary place.

That night we had dinner with the former owner of Paddy's Bar, a Balinese businessman named Kadek Wiranatha. When I spoke to him on the phone and started explaining who I was, Kadek said, 'I know all about you, Jason' and insisted that we have dinner with him at Ku de Ta, one of his restaurants. Kadek was deeply concerned about me and upset about the impact of the bombings. It had done enormous damage to his businesses, and he, indirectly, felt guilty because one of the bombs exploded in his 'house'. He told me, 'Whenever you want to come back for a real holiday for two or three weeks, there's always the use of my personal villa and a couple of plane tickets waiting for you.' It sounded like a pretty fair offer. He also arranged for a driver to be on call for us for the rest of our stay.

Kadek is supporting seven widows himself. They were the wives of cab-drivers and so forth who got their business outside his establishment. I have since met six Balinese widows, all of whom had relied almost solely on their husbands to make ends meet.

KADEK WIRANATHA (BALINESE BUSINESSMAN): I was worried that Jason was going to hate Bali and never come back again. He came to my nightclub, which I regard as one of my houses, and a bomb went off. I feel very sad for that. It would have been easy for him not to come back to Bali. I was very nervous about meeting Jason because I didn't know how he felt. But he put me at ease straight away when he said, 'It's not your fault, mate.'

I was very happy to see his open-minded attitude – he didn't blame the Balinese people for what had happened.

By an amazing stroke of luck, that afternoon we tracked down Dr Bayupasti — the doctor who took Mick and me to the hospital — on the phone. He was keen to see me, so we made plans to have dinner together on the Monday night before we flew home. When I told Kadek, he said, 'No problems. You can eat at one of my other restaurants. Consider it done.'

Nerissa became ill at the hotel. I was sure she had a bout of Bali belly. But after a huge 48 hours — and four or five days in which I hadn't had a decent sleep — I was too tired to get out of bed and care for her. Nerissa had also got sick the first time I took her to Bali. 'Bloody hell!' I complained. 'I'm never bringing you back here again. Every time you come here, you get crook.'

It wasn't exactly what she wanted to hear.

NERISSA: I was upset that he didn't seem to care that I was very unwell. I was shaking uncontrollably and was freezing cold, but I felt that he didn't respond to my needs like I had for him the whole time.

When I started feeling better myself, I couldn't believe how insensitive I'd been. Rewind the clock back a few months and Nerissa had sacrificed virtually every spare second she had to help me. She'd stuck by me when I'm sure many people would have walked away. I was ashamed of myself. I thought, 'How could I be such a bastard when she's done all this for me?'

Later, Dr Bayu sent word to us that he would not be able to make dinner but would see us at the airport. I couldn't remember what he looked like or even whether he was young or old. I was surprised by how young he looked — he was probably only my age. His wife and brother-in-law were with him and while we only chatted for about ten minutes, it was an emotional reunion. I thanked him for his efforts in helping to keep me alive, and Nerissa was pretty happy with him too. Dr Bayu smiled and laughed a lot, so I'm sure he felt the same way. He hadn't known for sure whether I had lived or not. 'You look well, you look well,' he repeated a few times.

DR BAYUPASTI: It was very good to see Jason looking so fit and healthy. I was so glad that he had made a full recovery because sometimes you don't know if they will. He had moved on with his life and got married. It was great.

We boarded our Air Paradise flight — upgraded by Kadek to super economy class — satisfied that we had done more than we could ever have imagined in three days. Everything had fallen into place. I hoped that trend would continue.

When we landed in Melbourne, two airport managers ushered us out a back exit to avoid the media. A photograph that was taken of Nerissa and me at the site of the Sari Club had been splashed on the front page of the previous day's edition of the *Herald Sun*. We were whisked away in a car, James Bond style. I was glad that my manager, Paul Connors, and Di Lloyd had made such arrangements because while I had every intention of speaking publicly about the trip, I was desperate to shield Nerissa as much as possible.

When I turned my mobile phone on — I didn't take it with me — there were heaps of messages from journalists. I called Di and asked to her to arrange a press conference for that afternoon so I could accommodate everyone in the one hit and get it out of the way.

No hiding or side-stepping; that's not my style.

23

Biding my time

As soon as we got home from Bali, I went straight down to the football club for a weights session. I hadn't exercised since playing four nights earlier, so I needed the work. More so when Dean Laidley took me aside and said I would be playing in Port Melbourne's senior side that weekend. I tried to contain my excitement — after all, it was still a level below the one I eventually wanted to reach. But it certainly vindicated my decision to play an extra quarter in the reserves.

While the window of opportunity was opening up for my football, many people thought that the return trip to Bali had enabled me to find 'closure' on the tragedy. When I was asked about it at the press conference that afternoon, I dismissed the closure concept. I personally believe it is a load of garbage. You can learn to cope with adversity and emotional pain, but you never get to the stage where you say, 'Right, that's over with; I'm not going to think about it ever again.' Hardly a day goes by when I don't think about what happened that night. Hell, I'm reminded about it each morning when I have a shower. Truth is, it will always be part of my psyche and will continue to influence the way I look at life.

It also influenced the way other people started looking at me. That night, at the Kangaroos' season launch, I was the only player to score a seat on the table designated for coach Dean Laidley, CEO Geoff Walsh and the club's major sponsors. I realised then that I had moved up in the world. Normally, after the formalities were over, I'd quietly leave such a function. But there was no chance of that on this occasion. To top it off, club chairman Allen Aylett, in his speech, said it was time for true Kangaroos people to stand up and become heroes, alluding to what happened to Mick and me in Bali. Mick wasn't there, so all eyes were focused on me. I was quite chuffed, but also embarrassed. I wanted to hide under the table.

There was also nowhere to hide when I played for Port Melbourne against Sandringham that week. I approached the game with the plan that I would play well enough to put my hand up for senior selection for the Kangaroos' season-opener against St Kilda the next week. But despite the fact that I played all but ten minutes of the game — I went off for a rest just before three-quarter time — that plan quickly came unstuck.

Often the second week after a lay-off is the real tester and that was the case here. I felt I ran to the right spots but it didn't quite happen for me; I didn't win as much of the ball as I would have liked. It was a reality jolt. Although I recognised that my preparation wasn't ideal due to the Bali trip, and I only knew a few of the Kangaroos-listed players in the side, self-doubt started circling like a vulture in my mind. 'Am I going to be good enough? Can I still do this?'

I also landed heavily on my left knee, where there had been some grafting. I looked at my stocking and could see the blood starting to pool. Not massive amounts, but enough to be of concern. With the strict blood rule in place, I pulled my sock up over my knee to conceal it. I was worried about what I would see when I took the stockings off, as the blood stain was half the size of my knee. I was relieved when I found that it was only a scratch, and that the garments had soaked up the blood and made it look a lot worse than it actually was. It stung like hell in the shower, though. It was like running hot water over an open blister.

I had to cover up even the smallest scratches otherwise they would continue to weep. I would soon get used to being the last player to leave the change rooms.

DAVID DUNBAR: We'd do our post-match review of the game, and it would take a fair while, but when we came out Jason would still be going through the process of having a shower and getting dressed.

Sometimes after games there'd be patches of blood on the bandages.

The scars on his body were horrific. I felt a lot of pity for the fella about what he'd gone through — and what he was still going through to play footy.

Even a couple of weeks after his comeback game (three months later), I saw him at Kangaroos training and asked him, 'How's the skin?'

He said, 'Oh yeah, it's still got a fair way to go.'

But he'd still kept training to keep the blood flowing, so he used that as part of the healing process.

DR HEATHER CLELAND: It was certainly a gutsy effort to get back into something so physical. I suspect he might have been splitting himself open a bit and knocking his skin grafts around. I'm sure it was tough-going because grafts are never like normal skin. Anything from twelve months to two years after the initial grafting, they can still be troublesome in everyday life. To go out on a football field and get knocked around — I wouldn't have been surprised if he'd been splitting bits open here, there and everywhere. I suspect he stayed away from me while he was playing football because he knew I'd be cheesed off.

Leigh Colbert: It looked like at any stage his skin was going to tear. I shared a locker close to him and the thing that stood out to me is he'd take his body suit off and there'd be blood in it just because the skin was so fragile and not ready for action. Any sort of rip and he'd bleed. It took a bit of time for that to go away, but not once did he complain. It looked like it was bloody sore though. When he was able to do some body contact at training, I think we blokes were a bit wary about tackling him because we didn't want him to fall apart.

Initially, you just shake your head and think, 'There's no way this bloke's going to be able to play at the required level,' but his improvement was unbelievable. I could even tell by the colour of his skin that it was slowly improving. He was getting some cortisone, which makes it more supple and helps it repair better. Over a two, three, four-month period it was showing signs of how much it was improving.

Nerissa: When I started watching Jason play, if he was tackled or he fell or someone fell on top of him, I'd close my eyes and think, 'I hope that didn't hurt him.'

But I know how strong he can be. I've definitely learnt that he'll put up with anything to get what he wants. He wouldn't show anyone else if he was hurt.

Every game I watched, I saw the bumps and bruises, and I knew where the skin grafts were and which were the most raw and tender parts of his body. Whenever he knocked one of those parts, I'd cringe and my heart would go out to him. I'd think, 'To be able to go through this, you're amazing.'

After games, he'd tell me, 'No seriously, I'm fine.'

It got easier to watch, but I still felt for him. I had great admiration for him the whole way through. To see what he was doing, and how far he'd come, it was very inspiring. I was so proud. Sometimes he'd have nicks and cuts all over him and I'd say, 'You've got to be more careful. Should you really be doing this? Maybe your skin hasn't healed enough.'

But as time went on, and those nicks and cuts subsided, he'd say, 'I must be getting better — I'm not bleeding as much any more and my skin's getting tougher.'

David Dunbar: He was a bit scratchy in the practice matches. He was obviously lacking some touch and match fitness, and there was still a question mark over him after going through the trauma that he had.

But there was no question about his commitment. When Jason came to Port Melbourne, he had no tags on himself. Even though he'd played a lot of footy, he took all of my instructions on board. You didn't have to tell him a great deal because he knew what he had to do. He really tried to help as much as he could to make it all work.

It seemed that whenever I felt like wallowing in self-pity, I would get a reality jolt that would give me an improved outlook on things. This happened when a young bloke named Nathan Hahn asked me to speak at the jumper presentation of his club,

University High School. Nathan and I had struck up a friendship when I was doing physio at the hospital. He suffered burns to 40 per cent of his body, including horrific burns to his head and neck, in a car accident on the morning of my wedding. Nathan was allowed out of hospital for a couple of hours to attend the evening.

Despite my improved perspective, I emerged from a couple of important hours of my own on the football ground — against Springvale at Port Melbourne — with my self-belief waning even more. The 27-degree heat sapped me of a great deal of energy with my stockings and long sleeves. I figured out very early on that my fitness level wasn't going to enable me to be very free running or creative. I got knocked around a bit too. 'That's two average weeks in a row,' I thought. 'I've got a long way to go if I want to make it back.'

I hoped that I would be able to go up a gear when the real stuff began the following week, and that's exactly what happened. But I had another less-than-ideal preparation for the round 1 VFL match against Geelong at Skilled Stadium. The night before the game, Nerissa and I attended a surprise birthday party for Leanne Woodgate, which had been organised by her sister, Samantha. Nicole McLean, who lost an arm in the bombings, also turned up and time flew with fascinating conversation. We didn't get home until 2.15 a.m. Although I didn't have a drop of grog, because of the lack of sleep I woke up feeling like I had a hangover. I had to leave for Geelong at about 7.30 a.m. because we were playing the curtain-raiser to the Geelong–Kangaroos match.

It was a perfect day again, the kind I had started to dislike because I knew I'd swelter. I was a bit flat-footed and sluggish at the start, but was happy with the way I worked myself into the match. Crucially, I backed into packs a couple of times and emerged with the ball. It felt good to wear a few bumps and bruises in a fair-dinkum contest. I even got a cut on my head and was forced to wear Rambo-like headgear. I was a walking mummy. But I got through the game well, we won and Dave Dunbar gave me a 'good' rating.

DAVID DUNBAR: He played all right. It was a big game for our club and he helped us win the game, so I was pretty happy with the way he was going along, improving all the time.

I was relieved to be given the chance to play down back. If they played me at centre half-forward, any hope I had of returning to the AFL would have been over before it began. It would have been a real battle just to contribute, much less play well enough to earn a promotion. I would have needed a miracle.

DAVID DUNBAR: With Jason's experience and his size, and the structure of the side, it was a natural thing for him to play down back. Coming from where he was, it also took the pressure off him a bit. He could get behind the footy, have an opponent take him to the ball and then he could use his experience from there.

A few days later, I was reminded that the fact I was alive was a small miracle in itself. I attended the opening of The Pub at Crown Casino, where, among a virtual who's who of Australian celebrities, I met Jess Hardy of *Big Brother* fame. Jess lost her brother Billy in the Bali bombings. We had a bond that we wished we never had, but we decided to make the best of a bad situation. We exchanged phone numbers and agreed to go out for dinner at some stage.

But first I wanted to gorge myself on leather. My next opportunity was Port Melbourne's round 2 clash against the Coburg Tigers at Port Melbourne. I was quite emotional before the game because it was the six-month anniversary of the bombings. I wore a black armband as a mark of respect for those who died.

It was dark and overcast, so, for the first time that season, I didn't have to cake sunscreen on my 'new' skin.

My form, and that of the team, was hot. I took three marks in the first few minutes of the match. I knew I was in for a good day because whenever I get decisive touches early, I generally continue that form for the entire match. I got another 'good' rating from Dave Dunbar.

DAVID DUNBAR: It was another step forward for Jason with his form and fitness, and that was a real pattern. Inch by inch, step by step, he got better and better.

But midway through the third quarter, Dave must have been tempted to downgrade me. I became frustrated with the umpiring — I was already on edge emotionally — and I unleashed an uncharacteristic spray on one of the men in white. I shouldn't have been thinking this way but, with the anniversary at the forefront of my mind, I thought, 'You miserable little man, you couldn't even begin to imagine what I've been through.' The umpire, quite within his rights, awarded a 50-metre penalty against me and Coburg kicked their only goal of the quarter. A team rule dictates that anyone who gives away a 50-metre penalty gets dragged off the ground, so off I went. When I reached the interchange box, I got on the phone and Dave Dunbar asked me, 'What happened there?'

I was still furious. I screamed down the phone what I had said. A loyal group of elderly ladies — ardent supporters of the Borough — cracked up laughing behind me. But Dave wasn't impressed.

'You're known as a leader around here,' he reasoned. 'You can't go doing that.'

'Yeah, I know,' I conceded.

It was the first time that I had really vented my spleen since the bombings.

Until that point, I had channelled all of my energy into my recovery and rehab — positive things. I hadn't had time to get angry. But this time I let rip. It was the wrong thing to do, and I'd never condone such behaviour, but I felt better for it.

That night, I was supposed to meet Nerissa at an engagement party but decided I was too weary and it was too far away, so I stayed home. I bought six stubbies of Bintang and listened to a compilation CD of Balinese music that was put together as a tribute for the victims of the 12 October bombings. I shed a few tears.

'I could've been dead,' I thought. 'I should've been dead. How lucky am I?'

I never lose sight of that fact.

Although I was well aware that I was going to need an element of luck to break into the Kangaroos side, which started the season well, I was giving myself the best possible chance by making the most of my opportunities. My form was stronger than I expected it would be so early in the season, yet I felt I still had a lot of improvement left.

I took the next step in the round 3 match against traditional rival Williamstown at Point Gellibrand Oval. I controlled my area of the ground in a fierce contest with the eventual premier and earned a 'very good' rating.

COREY MCKERNAN: Jason came around to my place in Port Melbourne after they'd played at Williamstown. It wasn't a super-hot day — about 20–21 degrees — but he only had his footy shorts and thongs on, after playing in a full bodysuit. Anyone who's played footy knows how hot you get running around, even when it's cold, let alone having to do it in a full bodysuit. His wounds still hadn't fully healed and he'd taken little nicks out of those, and there were little bits of blood all over him. To have that impact on your health and go through all that, you must really love your footy.

The next day I went to the Alfred Hospital and visited Therese Fox, a 30-year-old mother of two who suffered burns to 85 per cent of her body in Bali. I spent about 40 minutes with Therese and her mother, Dawn. After about 20 skin graft operations and an enormous battle to survive, things had slowly started to improve for her. But she was still unable to do many of the things that able-bodied people can do. It drove home the point that, no matter how bad you feel, there is always someone worse off than yourself. It's a great lesson and ensures that you don't take anything for granted.

In keeping with this theme, Anzac Day loomed large on my calendar. Not only would I be playing in my first game on this sacred day, but our opponent was the Northern Bullants, which was aligned with Carlton. I was sure that my former mentor Denis Pagan would be at the game to check on the form of players on the fringe of senior selection.

Football clubs try to invoke the spirit of the Anzacs and emulate their traits of courage and mateship, and some even try to go a step further and pump the game up as if it's a war, a life and death struggle. I've always been one to put my body on the line and take my footy 100 per cent seriously, but after what I'd been through, footy, relatively speaking, was a breeze. I saw it for the fun game that it is.

I certainly enjoyed myself that day in our win at the Cramer Street Oval. I took six or seven marks in the first quarter, ended up with a dozen for the match and enjoyed a reasonable afternoon.

DENIS PAGAN (FORMER KANGAROOS COACH, NOW COACH OF CARLTON): He was better than reasonable. As far as I was concerned, it was the same old Jason McCartney I'd coached for five years. His strength really showed out, the way he supported his teammates, how courageous he was in his marking. He was really like a playing-coach that day at Cramer Street.

I thought to myself, 'Gee, he's not far off getting a senior game.'

That was just before the Adelaide game and I thought, 'They might play him.'

With the Kangaroos suffering successive losses to Fremantle and Denis's Carlton side, I thought, 'I'm not far away from playing for the Kangas. I'm half a chance to play against the Crows. I might even play on Duck (Wayne Carey). It might help to defuse the thing with Stevo.'

My initial attitude was that no matter how well I played, I would clock up at least a month of solid footy in the VFL before I even considered putting my case forward for a call-up to the seniors. That month had passed, so it was time to speak up. I rang Dean Laidley. From his point of view, he had suddenly picked up another player who he didn't think he was going to have at the start of the season.

DEAN LAIDLEY: He'd been going really well. I'd seen a few of his games. We also get a highlights package of individual players on our computers by Monday or Tuesday, so I knew that he'd been in good form. He was getting close to senior selection.

LEIGH COLBERT: I thought he would be picked because he'd had a really good game at Preston, took 12 or 13 marks, and I reckon the only thing that kept him out of the side was the fact that we were actually winning games in the seniors and they don't tend to change the side as much when you're winning. The other thing against him was that we didn't have any injuries.

But I thought it was just going to be a matter of time before he got a game. He was just so determined that the injuries he suffered in Bali weren't going to hold him back.

24

Injured ... again!

The first trial verdict related — indirectly, I believe — to the Bali bombings caused a huge uproar. Silvester Tendean was sentenced to seven months' jail for illegal possession and sale of explosive materials after Amrozi bought a tonne of potassium chlorate from Tendean's chemical shop in Sarabaya. The chemicals were later used in the Bali bombings.

Many people suspected that Tendean knew what Amrozi was planning and, as a result, should have been given 20-plus years in jail, or even the death penalty. I heard some people say things like, 'He ought to be shot.' People were worried that the actual bombers might get off scot-free.

If Tendean was 'in on it' I would have advocated the strongest of sentences, but I don't think he had any idea about what was going to happen. He simply sold chemicals without a proper licence. People do it pretty tough in developing countries and I can't blame the bloke for selling the chemicals in good faith. He might have been suspicious about the quantity of chemicals Amrozi wanted but he wasn't a mind-reader. If he'd done the same thing in Australia, he would've been fined.

I had more pressing concerns though. I had pains in my chest and shoulder. Whenever I took a deep breath, I'd get a short sharp pain. I went to see Dr Con Mitropoulos.

DR CON MITROPOULOS (KANGAROOS CLUB DOCTOR): It was quite frightening because he was really training quite hard. The concern from the lung specialists at the hospital was that he might get a pulmonary embolus, which is a blood clot of the lung. That was always the concern, even after he got going with his rehab.

I had a good look at him, and he had some rib soreness, so I thought, 'Maybe he's just pinched a rib.' But he really was sick and he was very concerned about it. A guy like him doesn't complain about pain unless he's got significant pain. I sent him to have a special lung scan where they inject radioactive dye into your blood. This allows the doctors to have a look in your lungs to see if you've got a blood clot.

Jason had a lot of scar tissue because of the smoke inhalation. Breathing in very hot air causes burns to the lungs.

It was kind of ironic that the day I finally got into the senior meeting, I missed it anyway because I was having scans done on my lungs. It frustrated me even more. At least I knew I was in the minds of the selectors — finally. But I was on edge; I didn't know what the results were going to be. I panicked. 'My lungs have shut down once before,' I thought. 'If they give me more problems, it'll be too risky to keep playing footy. I'm probably not going to get my opportunity to play at AFL level again anyway.' I trained that night and was in a bit of discomfort, but I got through it all right.

DR CON MITROPOULOS: The scans came up clear. Once Jason heard that, away he went — at 100 miles an hour, as always.

Funnily enough, the perfect distraction from this health issue was an emotive football match — Wayne Carey's first match against the Kangaroos since he left the club a year earlier in unhappy circumstances. I was as excited as I'd ever been before watching a game. I was also excited because it was to be the first time I'd give special comments on radio 5AA. The media was an area that I wanted to move into after football.

I could feel the tension and the expectation in the air as soon as I got to Telstra Dome that night. In a sense, it was like watching a grand final — although you didn't know what was going to happen in the first quarter, you knew it would be worth watching. Obviously, I wanted the Kangaroos to win but, deep down, I wanted all parties concerned to have a good game. It didn't turn out that way — the Crows won by 54 points — but I'm glad it didn't explode, which was what many people wanted.

All parties handled themselves well. I don't think Stevo, Arch or Duck had ever had so much pressure on them before a game, grand finals included. The testosterone started flying in an amazing period in the second quarter. When the three of them were in the same vicinity for a few seconds, I started cringing because I didn't want any of them to come out of it with a broken jaw or anything.

We all know Duck is more than handy in a dust-up. Mike Sheahan once wrote that it was common knowledge that, if the gloves were off, Duck would punch holes in anyone in the AFL. That was a few years ago but Arch and Stevo, like everyone else at the Kangaroos, knew this only too well. Although things nearly boiled over on several occasions, they weren't silly enough to go down that path.

Much was made of the Kangaroos walking off the ground after the game without shaking Duck's hand. I think it was for the best because it had the potential to get ugly.

A lot has been said and written about the whole unfortunate saga but, personally, I didn't know what to think when the news broke out 13 months earlier, and I still don't know what to think. We'd all been close mates, especially when Mick and Corey were at the club, and Duck was the leader both on and off the field. With Stevo taking over as captain, all of the boys threw their support behind him. To Stevo's credit, he has never held anything against blokes who have kept in contact with Duck. That speaks volumes for the type of bloke he is. But it's a touchy one.

Although I was disappointed that the Kangaroos lost the match — the third in a row after winning the first two rounds and drawing with dual reigning premier Brisbane — I saw it as a great opportunity to stake my claim for senior selection. Even if I didn't make it back to the AFL, by playing with the VFL, I would have achieved more than a lot of people could have ever imagined after being in my position. But the way some people looked at it, they seemed to disregard the fact that there *was* a competition called the VFL. Whenever I went to a Kangaroos match, our well-meaning supporters would ask, 'When are you playing?'

I thought, 'Can't they go down to Port Melbourne on a Sunday and have a look?' In the end, I was short with them: 'Why don't you ask the bloody coach?'

I couldn't watch a game in peace. I'd get frustrated and angry. I'd come home to Nerissa and say, 'Bugger this, I'm not going to the footy again until I've played.'

I eyed the round 7 clash with Hawthorn the following Friday night as my best chance to nail down that elusive comeback game. But before that there was the small matter of playing well again for Port Melbourne against the Box Hill Hawks.

Things didn't go to plan from the start of the match. Box Hill coach Tony Liberatore, one of the smallest men to ever play AFL football, went with a short forward line and I couldn't find a good match-up so was moved to full-forward in the third quarter. Within minutes of the switch I took a couple of marks and kicked a behind, then a goal. I had a few inches and kilograms on my young opponent and I thought I was set for a big one. But that was to be short-lived.

I went to take off and felt a tear smack bang in the middle of my left calf — the one that had been literally ripped in the bombings. I tried to run but struggled to put any weight onto the leg. Although I waved the physio over to have a look at me, I didn't need him to tell me what I'd done. I feared the worst. My self-prognosis was, 'This'll cost me four weeks minimum.'

I was taken straight up the players' race and into the change rooms for a proper injury assessment. Dr Con Mitropoulos had a look at me. As always, he was very reassuring.

'Keep your chin up,' he said. 'Let's just wait and see how it settles down. Look after yourself and let's make sure we get this right.'

DR CON MITROPOULOS: That was probably the most devastated and negative I've ever seen Jason in all of the time I've known him. I've never known him to be tearful, worrisome, devastated or negative. Even when he was in intensive care and struggling with pain, he was always positive.

He said, 'This is too much now.'

That was the only reason I thought, 'Jeez, that's it for him.' I felt so sorry for him.

No amount of reassurance could lift my spirits. I was shattered, disconsolate — all those words that mean I felt crap. I thought, 'It'll be at least eight weeks before I'm even close to playing for the Kangas again.' All my hard work and good form, it seemed, had been for nothing.

TIM HARRINGTON: I went down in to the rooms to say, 'Stick at it, it's just an injury. You'll be OK.' He was really emotional about it and said, 'I was going all right. This is going to set me back.' I walked away thinking, 'Gee, he's not too flash here. He might be ready to throw this in.'

I went back in and said, 'Listen, mate, don't worry about it. I'll make sure that, whatever happens, you'll get a crack at it.'

He wasn't convinced, but he said, 'Yeah, all right.'

To see how much it meant to him, I thought, 'I reckon he can do it, but he's just got to hang in there. If I can keep him bubbling along, he'll get there.'

DAVID DUNBAR: I asked him, 'How did you do it?'

He said, 'Oh, I was only jogging from centre half-forward down to full-forward when I felt it go.'

I thought, 'Gee, that sounds a bit strange, because normally when you do a calf, you're trying to sprint or something.'

Up until that point, I thought he was going OK but I thought he needed to string a few more games together. I didn't have any doubt that he would make it back at some stage unless he was injured again.

ROGER MOORE: I saw him sitting with an icepack around his leg and he was almost in tears. He must have thought his comeback was over. His wife was shattered. It was the darkest day in his rehab.

NERISSA: When I saw it, I thought, 'Why did this have to happen?' We suspected that the calf injury may cause problems down the line, but he was always really careful with it, stretching it well and having rubs. Hughesy and I went down into the rooms to see him. He looked so disappointed, I had to hold the tears back. I didn't want him to see me cry because it would be like I was giving up too.

Hughesy came back to my place after the game and we had a chat over a few Bintangs. Initially, I wasn't going to have a beer because it would have broken the club rule about not drinking alcohol when you're injured. But then I thought, 'Bugger it, I'm stuffed. I can't give any more. I've had it with trying to do the right thing.' In the end, I decided to hedge my bets — I placed my leg on a stool so it was in an elevated position, but I still had four Bintangs.

Hughesy tried to snap me out of it.

PETER HUGHES: I said, 'You can't just sit back and say, "Well, this is it because of a calf injury." You've come too far to do that. You're not far away. You should've been playing your first game two weeks ago because you're back to where you should've been. I don't know why the hell they didn't pick you.'

He got more frustrated by that. I said, 'Jase, your calf's going to take two weeks. I don't get to Melbourne very often, so let's have a beer and a chat.'

I said, 'Hang in there, mate. If it takes all year, it takes all year. You should have no regrets. If you quit now, you will have regrets.'

Jase finally settled down to a point where he said, 'Well, yeah, I've come too far. I was one game away from it; I can get back to that.'

NERISSA: At first I thought, 'You don't need to prove anything. You're so much better and you've got your quality of life back.'

Jason had always spoken highly of Glenn Archer and Stevo and how they had supported him at the club, so I secretly text-messaged Glenn and told him what had happened, how Jason was feeling pretty down about it all and wasn't sure if he should continue. I asked him to give Jason a call later that night.

Glenn replied, 'Yeah sure.'

I was sitting and having a few beers with all the boys, thinking, 'When's Glenn going to call?' Then he did. Afterwards, Jason got off the phone and said, 'Gee, he's a good bloke.'

I was very grateful to Glenn. He made Jason feel a lot better.

JAN MCCARTNEY: Jason rang me and said, 'I'm gonna pull the pin. I've had enough.'

I said, 'You can't do that!'

He said, 'Why not?'

I said, 'Well, your first goal was to make your wedding on the day without altering a thing and you did that. Your second goal was to get back and play AFL footy. Even if it's just one game, hang in there.'

Ian and I were cheering him on the phone. 'Just hang in there. It'll happen. It'll happen.'

BRENDEN MCCARTNEY: I told him, 'You're not far off playing; you've got to hang in there. Everything you've done, all your recovery, the rest of your life will depend on this one game. You'll go out a hero if you make it back.'

He didn't say anything and I thought, 'I've got through to him.'

I'd overcome plenty of setbacks before. I'd been traded twice, missed selection in Adelaide's 1997 premiership, played in a losing grand final side against Adelaide in 1998 and, to top it all off, I'd missed the Kangaroos' 1999 premiership side due to suspension. I got four weeks for a late spoil on Brisbane ruckman Clark Keating in the dying minutes of a preliminary final that was safe in our keeping. It was a crushing blow at the time.

In the week leading up to that Grand Final, I tried to encourage and support the boys as much as I could. I kept training because I somehow wanted to feel part of it and add more positive energy to the group.

On the Thursday before the 1999 Grand Final — our last training session of the season — we were doing a cool-down lap at the end of training. I took it upon myself to say a few things. I said that I knew how much it had hurt losing the Grand Final the year before, that I wasn't going to be there through my own fault, and that guys were getting opportunities that they shouldn't let slip.

I had to stop because tears were welling in my eyes. Footy was my life. At the time, I thought it was the worst thing that could possibly happen to me. But, as subsequent events proved, I was a fair way off the mark.

BRENT HARVEY: It was so courageous for Jason to speak in front of the boys like that, admit that he'd stuffed up and say 'good luck'. He shed a few tears too. You realised just how much it meant to him. All the boys were around him, just patting him on the back and clapping him.

GREG WAUGH: I was with Jason on Grand Final eve. I remember staring over at him in Bells pub in South Melbourne. He was a lonely sight, sitting up there at the bar. He did that for ages. I thought to myself, 'This is a life sentence he's doing, not four weeks.' But obviously that was put into perspective with what happened in Bali.

DENIS PAGAN: The way Jason handled himself after that disappointment was nothing short of amazing. We were terribly upset for him. No matter what you do, you can't get that one back. His career is over now, so his chance of playing in a premiership side are gone and he should have been a premiership player. He had a very good year that year.

But I don't think anyone else could have done it as well as he did. After we won the premiership, he was up on the stage with the players, he was with them, he supported them. That was just special. And it really made us feel good that we made the effort to seek Jason out and get him to the Kangaroos.

ANTHONY STEVENS: It was pretty sad to see him after the game because he'd played all the year and missed out. But to Jason's credit, he was same old Jason, just rapt that we'd won.

TIM HARRINGTON: In a way, Jason has became more memorable because of the way he handled himself after missing out on the premiership than a few blokes who played in the premiership. Many people wouldn't remember that Scott Welsh or Cameron Mooney or Shannon Motlop even played, but they remembered that Jason didn't, largely because of the way he carried himself throughout the week, on Grand Final day and in the celebrations afterwards.

TONY AUSTIN: A week or so after they'd won the Grand Final, Jason rang me and I asked him how he was going. He said, 'I'm all right. There's a young fella at the club in a wheelchair who can't walk, so if this is the worst thing that happens to me, then so be it. I'm actually pretty lucky. A lot of people haven't done what I've done or been where I've been or met the people I've met.'

That character was there long for Bali happened.

I had plenty of experiences from which to draw strength and belief. Not all was lost. I saw Dr Con Mitropoulos the next day and he strapped my calf fairly heavily. It also helped that I wore my compression garment over the top of the strapping. Normally when you strain or tear a muscle, there is a fluid build-up that causes swelling. The strange thing was that there was no sign of swelling.

I was able to put some weight on the leg but I must have pushed it too far on one occasion because I buckled and nearly fell over due to the pain. It was like a knife was being driven through the muscle.

When I was at the club that day, Dean told me, 'You looked all right when you went forward.' I knew then that if I did make it back to the seniors, it would be as a forward — to start with at least — because the defence was pretty settled. When referring to my injury, Dean said, 'Well, you've come back from a lot worse than that.'

I thought, 'He's dead right, you know.' I walked away with renewed enthusiasm. I couldn't have been any happier, or surprised, with the results of the scan on my calf.

Con told me that while the shrapnel wound and the scar tissue around it was torn, the calf muscle itself was intact.

DR CON MITROPOULOS: Unfortunately, when you tear scar tissue, it bleeds, so he was really sore — he could hardly walk on it. But within a week, it had settled down and he was able to get going on it. He loosened up after that and felt terrific. He got much better range of movement in his foot and his ankle joint and the problem went away after that.

He'd actually done himself a great service. Instead of all the physios trying to stretch it out for him, he fixed it himself in one fell swoop.

It was another one of those devastating blows that somehow or another Jason managed to overcome. I don't believe in fate. I think you make your own luck. Jason's the kind of guy who will basically turn any situation into a positive one.

The free weekend gave me the perfect opportunity to do some more media work. (I could seriously watch the game 24 hours a day.) I helped call the Kangaroos–Hawthorn game at the MCG for K-Rock. It was a funny night. Former Geelong star Billy Brownless made his commentary debut that night and had the box in hysterics when he got over-excited and jumped up with his arms in the air — and his pants around his ankles!

One of my co-callers, Anthony Mithen, who is also a sports reporter for Channel Nine, caused a stir when he threw to an ad break with, 'Jason McCartney, on fire tonight with the commentary.'

Mitho went bright red almost as soon as he said it and apologised profusely. 'Sorry, mate,' he said.

It didn't bother me — I knew it was a figure of speech, especially in footy terms.

I said, 'If I get back and play, Mitho, you can call me anything you like.'

The next night, I once again broke the club's zero-alcohol-while-injured policy, which I had helped to implement. Nerissa and I went to dinner with Jess Hardy and her then-boyfriend, co-*Big Brother* housemate Nathan 'Marty' Martin, and we must've downed four or five bottles of red wine between us in a St Kilda restaurant.

I mentioned that if I did make it back to AFL level, I'd like to display something on my jumper as a mark of respect to all the people who died in the bombings. I didn't know exactly what I wanted to do, but possibly something showing the number of Australians who lost their lives. At that time the official death toll was eighty-nine.

Jess was a panellist on the breakfast show on Nova FM radio and she persuaded me to join her the next morning. I'd forgotten about it the next day — Mothers' Day — and I was having breakfast with Corey when Jess rang me.

She sounded as hungover as I was. We decided to do an on-air interview over the phone. She caught me off-guard when she asked me about the tribute concept. Thinking on my feet, I said, 'Maybe instead of my No. 5, I could have 89. Or that might be too much; maybe the 89 could be somewhere on the front.'

I thought nothing more of it.

On Monday afternoon at the club, Di Lloyd said, 'What have you said?'

'What about?' I said.

'Jumper.'

Media outlets had called Di numerous times and run with the story. The AFL's then chief executive Wayne Jackson commented on it, saying that the AFL couldn't consider the proposal because they hadn't received a formal request. That sparked a bunfight, with grief counsellors saying that it would be a disgrace if the AFL didn't let me alter my jumper. Even Rex Hunt said that if I was fined, he'd run a sportsmen's night to pay it.

But I knew that it was a formality and that the AFL would approve it when I made an application. However, I was never going to make that approach until the week I was selected because I would have looked like a fool if I made the request and didn't make the side.

There was something else I had been considering. I had mentioned to Nerissa that I wanted to play for the Kangaroos before we went back to Bali to give evidence at Amrozi's trial. If I made it back, I told her, I might hang up the boots. During my break my body felt unbelievably fresh and my scars and wounds seemed to mend faster. That's when I realised that playing and training was taking an enormous toll on me.

Dave Bonython-Wright opened my eyes to the kind of arrangements I might have to make if I did get the call-up to the seniors. I would have to get my hands on a heap of tickets to hand out to the appropriate people — burns victims, family members who lost loved ones, representatives of the various football clubs that were impacted, medical people.

It would be a lot of work but it certainly had the potential to be a very special event. Sure, we were dreaming, but this whole thing was about making dreams come true — making the seemingly impossible possible.

25

Lows and highs

My first game back from injury — against Werribee at Port Melbourne — couldn't have gone better. I played in my familiar role at centre half-back and the ball seemed to follow me — that's not false modesty, sometimes you have days like that — and I was awarded best on ground.

DAVID DUNBAR: He showed some solid form against Wade Skipper, who's played with the Western Bulldogs, so he had a good opponent. He was playing fantastic footy for us.

Although I was on a high, I knew deep down that one good game wouldn't be enough to earn a call-up, especially as the Kangas had a convincing 25-point win over Sydney in Canberra.

That high became a plummeting low a couple of days later when I wasn't invited into the senior team meeting — which comprised the senior side from the weekend plus six or eight other players from the VFL side. I was absolutely filthy about it.

NERISSA: Jason would come home and say, 'I wasn't bloody invited to the meeting again. What's going on? I can't believe this. What do I need to do?'

I'd get angry and upset too. I'd say, 'Just walk in there and say something to them. Have a meeting with Dean and tell them how you feel. Ask them what's going on.'

We'd come up with ideas and then we'd agree, 'We've got to soldier on.'

He'd played well and still hadn't been picked and I thought it was unfair for someone who had worked ten times harder than anyone else.

One time Jase came home and threw his bag and just got so upset. It would break my heart. I really felt like I was trying to get a game too. I could feel his frustration, knowing how hard it was for him to push himself all the time. I'm sure that Jase had to find every positive just to keep going, and keep thinking, 'I'm gonna do it.'

Every Monday night I would wonder, 'Was he invited to the meeting?' When he walked in the door, I'd know straightaway.

I was in an even fouler mood when I got onto the Internet that night and listened to some of Dean Laidley's comments made at a press conference that morning. I totally understand where he was coming from, but it riled me when he replied to a question about me with, 'What's the infatuation with having to play Jason McCartney?'

This was after much of the questioning in the post-match press conference focused on me, not on the fact that the Roos had recorded a great win against a Sydney side that had won four games in a row. Reporters wanted to know when I would make my return.

While I felt enormous pressure to perform, Dean seemed to be under just as much pressure to pick me.

I didn't look at it like that at the time though. A night's sleep didn't calm me; if anything I was even more furious. We had a 7.30 a.m. stretching session that next morning, during which I approached Tim Harrington.

'Tim, what's the bloody go?' I demanded. 'What more do I have to do to get a game? You've made yourself look good by keeping me on board when I was on my deathbed and used me to promote the club all year.'

Tim was quite understandably taken aback, but I continued to rant.

'Why didn't you just wipe me at the start?' I implored. 'You've had no intention of playing me all year, so what was it? "We'll make the club look nice and Jase will get some publicity out of it?"'

I was so angry that my thoughts twisted in my head before they came out of my mouth. I wasn't myself and I was completely out of line. I didn't have any untoward feelings against anyone. I was just getting so desperate to play, and I'd been so close once before. The pressure to play was so overpowering that I allowed my pride and personal interests to get in the way of my common sense. The trial was also on my mind.

Tim tried to set me straight. 'No, no, that's not right,' he said. 'Just calm down, calm down. That's not the case — you know that.'

I did.

TIM HARRINGTON: I thought, 'This is quite out of character.' I said, 'You've never been like this. Look, you're getting close, but don't judge your performance on the team. Judge your performance as you always have, on you. You just worry about your performance and get yourself right. I'll worry about the team.'

Tim added that it would take at least a couple of games — and very good ones at that — if I was to get back that quickly. 'Well, I've already played one good one,' I thought. 'I just need another one now.'

TIM HARRINGTON: At that stage, there was so much pressure on him. He was sick of it and so was I. Every time I answered a call from the media, it was, 'What about Jason McCartney? What did he do for training today? What did he have for breakfast?'

Dean was copping the same. I was saying, 'Hang on, Jason's not the only person at the club.' It was the same with Jason as well. By that stage, it had just got to him, so he teed off a bit. The next time we spoke, he was in my office laughing about it saying, 'It's all happening, isn't it?'

With Port Melbourne due to play at Frankston on the Sunday, I watched the Kangaroos game against the Western Bulldogs on the Saturday with great interest. The boys played pitifully in the first half but turned it all around to snatch the game by 11 points in a high-scoring game. I had a horrible feeling that I would be close to selection but not close enough — as had happened a month earlier. The other factor working against me was that the next AFL match was a Friday night game, which gave me only five days to prepare for the match — a less than ideal scenario even for a super-fit footballer, let alone someone who had been through what I had. I refined my aim even further: I wanted to play well and I didn't want to get any niggling injury that might prevent me from training at full pace. That would be no mean feat.

Dad and Brenden came down in the truck from Nhill and I picked them up from a truck stop in Footscray Road. It was a tense, hour-long drive to Frankston.

Everything went to plan. I started the game strongly and we built up a big lead, so I had the luxury of cruising through the last quarter and a half in self-preservation mode. I didn't shirk any contests — that wouldn't have impressed anyone — but I did play smarter. I didn't back into as many packs.

'I have to be a chance now,' I thought. 'I've upheld my end of the bargain. I've got the form on the board.'

BRENDEN MCCARTNEY: He played well — just like his normal self — and he was one of the best players again. I thought, 'They've got to pick him now.'

That week, he said, 'If I don't get in this week, that's it.'

I said, 'Just stick it out until you get a game.'

Anyway, after the game, Dave Dunbar patted Jason on the head and said, 'You're not far off, son.'

It was that day that we realised how tough it really was for Jase. We'd watch him getting changed in the rooms after games and he'd have little nicks where he'd been opened up a bit and they'd be weeping and there'd be a bit of blood about on the raw areas.

The rest of us play a game of footy, have a shower and we're right, but what Jase went through just to play a game of footy was amazing. Everyone else had left the rooms and

Jason was standing on his towel putting his pressure garments on, then he had to get dressed. And he did it every week.

Dad and I were trying to help him put things in his bag and do things for him to get him into the car. You could tell Jase had had a gutful of it.

While I didn't expect any concessions from the selection committee, I didn't need any. 'I deserve a game in the seniors,' I thought.

I spoke to Tim Harrington that night — there wasn't anyone from the match committee at the game because they were watching Essendon, who we were scheduled to play in two weeks. But they had already seen the match report and statistics. Tim said, 'Look, I could've guaranteed you a game after the way a few blokes played in the first half, but they've won, so who do we leave out? I'm pretty sure you're in the mix, but I can't say anything for sure until I speak to Dean.'

Dean called and didn't give away too much, as you'd expect. I knew the match committee would meet the next morning and that the side would be picked by lunchtime, barring injuries. That night, as I was lying in bed, I pondered just what a return to AFL football would mean to me. 'Triumph over adversity' and 'sense of achievement' were two things that immediately sprung to mind. But then I thought, 'Pull your head in. Don't get ahead of yourself. Calm down a bit.' I didn't want to set myself up for the big fall because I didn't know how I would handle missing the side again.

I had never been as keen to get to training on a Monday. The suspense was killing me.

IAN MCCARTNEY: I thought he was playing well enough to get a game in the seniors. I packed my bags and said, 'Jan, I won't be back for a week. I reckon he'll play this week.'

The next morning, I was talking with Stevo and Arch — our captain and vice-captain — when Dean called them into his office for a chat. I read the play. Being a new coach, Dean must have been asking them what they thought about the possibility of me playing. I knew Stevo and Arch would be in my corner.

ANTHONY STEVENS: Dean told Glenn and me that they were going to play Jason, so we were to support him and make sure all the boys were behind him because it was going to be a big week for him. I thought Jason was definitely ready. His form was sensational for Port Melbourne and he well and truly deserved a chance probably a month beforehand — when he was on the verge and then he hurt his calf.

I could see how frustrated he was because he'd worked so hard to get back to actually playing footy with Port and the effort he had to go through to get his body back to playing condition and make it tough enough to cop the knocks, especially with his skin. You'd see the frustration in him on occasions but the old positive attitude would come back again. He worked his butt off to get back in the side again and I was rapt to have him back.

GLENN ARCHER: Jason had really earnt his spot. My first reaction was elation. I'd watched him a couple of times playing for Port Melbourne and he was ready to come back. He was probably a bit frustrated earlier on because he was playing well in the seconds but he wasn't being involved in the senior meetings and all that sort of stuff, but I think that just made him work harder.

About half an hour later, I saw Arch in the gym and asked him what the chat was about. His face broke out into a big grin. 'It went well,' he said. Then, with a sheepish look on his face, he added, 'I'm not allowed to talk to you.' I tried to interrogate him some more, but he gave me nothing. He didn't have to say anything though — he'd given me an inkling that I would be playing. 'I knew Arch wouldn't be able to keep a secret,' I thought.

I did the same thing when I saw Stevo, but he gave absolutely nothing away. I wasn't so sure about it then.

Tim grabbed me and took me into Dean's office. My heart started doing somersaults. I couldn't read anything in the way Tim had approached me to indicate whether he was going to give me good news or bad news. I didn't have to wait long to find out.

I sat nervously in Dean's office for about a minute until he finished whatever it was he was doing. Dean eye-balled me. 'We're gonna play ya,' he said in his straight-talking manner.

I think I replied with 'Thanks,' when really I could've kissed him. I felt like jumping in the air the way they do in the Toyota ads. I'd truly earnt this moment.

DEAN LAIDLEY: Once Jason came back and played a couple of games, I thought, 'I want to play him. He's been through so much that to get back to the top would be fantastic for him, the footy club, and probably everyone.' His form had been good. The timing was right.

It was like picking a bloke for his first game.

I didn't think much about the future beyond that game. I picked him because I thought he could help us beat Richmond that Friday night.

Dean and I talked about how we were going to handle what was certain to be a massive week. We decided that we'd wait until Tuesday morning to tell the players. I was numb with excitement and I felt like a huge weight had been lifted from my shoulders. It was to be my crowning glory.

As soon as I got to my car, I rang Nerissa at work. She was sworn to secrecy but she was almost in tears when I told her. I was too. I also rang Dad. He was rapt. Making phone calls like that, sharing good news, is one of life's great joys.

IAN MCCARTNEY: It was a very proud moment. I didn't think he'd get back to that level and here he was, proving his old man wrong — again.

Someone must have spoken out of school though because Channel Seven reporter Craig Hutchison called and asked me if I was playing that week.

I tried to play it cool.

'I don't know, mate,' I said. 'I hope you're right though.'

'Hutchy' must have known, or taken an educated guess, because he broke the story on the Monday night news. The phone rang non-stop.

Paul and I met with Tim Harrington and Geoff Walsh to discuss how the week would run.

Nerissa and I hardly slept that night. Nerissa become very emotional because she knew how much blood, sweat and tears had gone into it.

Through hours of conversation in bed, it became clear in my mind that this would be my last game of AFL football. I was mindful of not taking the spotlight away from the team, but I thought, 'The focus will be on me anyway, so if I retire, it'll be on me for a couple more days after it, but then the footy club can go back to normal.' I felt that if I announced my retirement later in the year or at the end of the season, all the attention would be back on me again, and the side would miss out on using it in some small way as a motivational tool.

26

Farewell to footy

Although some of my Kangaroos teammates already knew that I was back in the side or at least had a fair idea, Dean Laidley officially announced my comeback to the players first thing Tuesday morning. Dean emphasised that we needed to keep our minds on the job and reminded us that we had failed in two other emotional games that season — the Carey / Adelaide game and the one against Denis Pagan's Carlton.

I knew the boys were behind me 100 per cent, but it was great to receive their heartfelt congratulations.

DAVID KING: I thought, 'This is going to be an amazing game for the club.' We were still right in the hunt to play finals footy and I just couldn't believe how big that week was going to be, and it was bigger than I expected.

Jason's got an amazing ability to put a lump in my throat when he speaks.

SHANNON GRANT (KANGAROOS TEAMMATE): I was rapt because I'd missed the previous two games with a hamstring injury and I was back that week. I would've been really annoyed if I'd been out for another week and missed the opportunity to run out there with Jase in his comeback match. He was absolutely ecstatic, as was everyone else in the team.

DREW PETRIE: I was thrilled that Jason was back in the side and I was back next to him. He's a reliable fella and someone you can really trust. I knew it would lift the team immensely.

MATTHEW BURTON: I had played the previous four games and had a broken foot. The doctor and I decided I should have a couple of weeks off, so I was really disappointed it coincided with that game.

TIM HARRINGTON: Jason came into my office and shut the door. I thought, 'This is unusual, it must be serious.'

He told me, 'I think this'll be it — my one and only game.'

I said, 'I'm rapt for you.'

We talked for quite a while. I said, 'Can you imagine what it'll be like if you kick a goal?' It was good to visualise what it might be like for him to get out there again. For a brief period, we forgot about the team and just thought about him.

It didn't surprise me that he wanted to retire, because it had been a huge effort to get himself up. I wasn't sure how much he had left in him. He'd gotten up in round 11. That was amazing. If someone had told me that he might scrape in for a game at the end of the year, I would have thought that was amazing. But he was spent by round 11.

DEAN LAIDLEY: When he told me he was going to retire, I thought, 'There's a man who's been through everything and he's reached the top again. It's obviously time for him to move on with his life.' I really respected that. At the time, I didn't understand exactly what playing footy was doing to his body. I knew it was hard for him, but I just didn't know how hard. I know now because I've spoken to him about it since.

That afternoon, I announced my comeback in a press conference at Telstra Dome. I stressed that while it would be a huge personal milestone, the most important thing was that we win the game, otherwise I'd feel like a burden.

The media wanted to get some shots of me on the ground, and I was happy to oblige. It felt great just to set foot out there again.

DI LLOYD: Funnily enough, Karen Lyon from *The Age*, who's a Kangaroos supporter, had been telling me for six weeks that she thought Jason would be back for the Richmond game. She just thought that he wouldn't come back for an interstate game and that he'd match up well. It was a pretty good hunch.

I spent part of the afternoon getting a massage from Leanne Woodgate. It was nice that she was helping me prepare for the game that would mean so much to her, Samantha and the entire burns 'family'.

I did a few interviews while I was there, including one with my former Adelaide teammate Andrew Jarman for Triple M Adelaide. The club and I decided that Tuesday would be the day that we would knock over all media commitments. That way we could control it and I would be able to concentrate solely on the game.

I also took time out to visit some staff and patients in the intensive care unit at the Alfred Hospital. I took my wedding album in with me for a bit of show-and-tell. I wanted to make sure that the staff weren't working on Friday night so they could accept my invitation to the football.

HENRIETTA LAW: When Jason visits, he gives a lot of patients a bit of a booster.

One patient wrote to Jason three times. To a lot of people, Jason is not only an inspiration; sometimes he's almost like a godsend, a lucky charm.

Sometimes we have patients who I feel might benefit from a little bit of Jason's input, which Jason is only too happy to give.

Whenever he comes to the hospital, he will pick up the phone at reception and say, 'Guess what? It's your favourite patient here.'

He's done a lot for the hospital and has also made my job easier at times.

Dr Heather Cleland: I've been very impressed with how Jason takes time to see patients who have been having fairly tough times, when the burns ward is probably the last place on earth he feels like being. Through having that type of consideration for what others are going through and being prepared to put himself out, I think he's shown himself to be a pretty decent guy.

I visited Kylie, the teenager from Perth who I had become friendly with during my rehab. She'd just had her kidney and lung transplant and was in recovery mode. She seemed to be doing well considering she'd just had a major operation.

I spent some time with Therese Fox and her mum Dawn, and asked if they would want — and be physically able to — go to the footy. They seemed happy just to be invited and said they'd see what they could do.

Therese had been in hospital for eight months. I can't begin to comprehend what that would have been like. She hadn't had an outing since the bombings. I wasn't sure whether a night match with a big crowd would be too scary for her.

Seeing people like Kylie and Therese, such strong and courageous people, is a very humbling experience. While I felt terribly sorry for them both, I drew strength and inspiration just from hearing their names. It made the football match almost pale into insignificance and made me realise that, when you strip it all back, footy's only a game. But I was also aware of just what this match could do for the spirits of people like Kylie and Therese.

Strange as it sounds, there was a definite buzz around the hospital during my four-hour visit. There was probably a great deal of relief among the staff — I was one of their star pupils, living proof that they'd done a good job. I walked down the corridors and people I had never met were saying, 'Good stuff, good luck, hope you do well.' There was also a buzz at the club the next day. We had a backline meeting and an opposition meeting. I thought to myself, 'This is too complicated for me. But I don't have to worry about it after today anyway.'

That night, Dad came along to watch what he knew would be my last training session for the club. In the back of my mind, I thought, 'Whatever you do, don't get injured.' That would've shattered me.

Dean had set my mind at ease about what was expected from me on the training track. 'You just do what you have to,' he said.

I knew exactly what he meant. I wouldn't go through the motions — that's never been my style — but I would certainly pace myself.

If I'd been retiring under normal circumstances, I think I would've been pretty emotional during that final session. But this was my last game and my comeback game, so the emotion was far outweighed by sheer excitement.

I was even more excited when Dad showed me the 120 tickets that Tim Harrington had handed him. All complimentary, they had arrived at the club courtesy of Ian Collins and his team at Telstra Dome. It was an incredibly generous gesture.

IAN MCCARTNEY: He said to me, 'This is the one and only. I won't be able to come up again after this.' You could see what was going to happen because Dean Laidley wanted young blokes, which was fair enough. Here was a chance to go out on a high. He had nothing else to prove. He'd made it back. We were 100 per cent supportive of whatever he wanted to do. We were just so proud of him.

BRENDEN MCCARTNEY: I pulled up in the truck outside a newsagent's in a little two-bit town somewhere. It was about 4.30 in the morning and I saw an old fella inside the shop with the light on. All the bundles of newspapers were on the footpath outside. I went in and said, 'Mate, I need a copy of the *Herald Sun*.'

He said, 'No, I don't open till seven o'clock. You'll have to come back then.'

I said, 'Mate I need one because I reckon there's going to be something in there about my brother.'

He said, 'Oh, all right, I suppose you can have one. I don't normally do this sort of stuff you know.'

There was a big photo of Jase in the paper and there were all these little messages from everyone. I sat in my truck reading them and I had tears in my eyes. I thought, 'Bloody hell, he's a hero for what he's done.' I also thought, 'Jeez, it's gonna be a big weekend, that's for sure.'

The next day, game eve, I started distributing some of the tickets at the Alfred Hospital. By this stage, everyone knew what was happening and there was an even greater sense of expectation in the air. I felt it all building up to a crescendo. I didn't know whether it was a good thing or not.

GEOFF WALSH: Emotions were pretty high in the 48 hours leading up to the game. Everyone wanted a piece of Jason at the time. The profile of the match was gaining momentum by the hour.

DEAN LAIDLEY: By the time Thursday came around, I was starting to crap myself. The hype surrounding the game was just getting bigger and bigger and bigger. I thought, 'What have I done?' I got really scared. This was my first season as coach, the first time I've had to deal with something like this. I thought, 'Bloody hell, how am I going to handle this?'

TIM HARRINGTON: We wanted to control all the outside things so that Jason could focus on playing. He didn't want to make a dill of himself; he wanted to play well.

DEAN LAIDLEY: Jason told me he wanted to tell the whole team he was retiring before we ran out onto the ground. I didn't know whether that was the right way to go because I wasn't sure our younger blokes could handle it. It was really playing on my mind, so I actually rang Mick Malthouse — I really value Mick's opinion, so I wanted to see what he thought. And he's been coaching a lot longer than I have.

I said, 'You know Jason's playing. Well, he's going to retire after this game.' I told him what Jason wanted to do and asked him what he would do.

Mick threw a few ideas around and in the end he decided: 'I'd tell them before the game.'

But after speaking to Mick, I still had my reservations about it. I finally came to the conclusion that we should just tell the core senior players — on the Friday morning after the team meeting.

The hype went to another level that night when I was interviewed on *The Footy Show*. The interview wouldn't have happened at all if the coach had had his way. Dean didn't want to set a precedent for other players by allowing me to appear on the show the night before a game. I understood exactly where he was coming from, but I had a commitment to Channel Nine at the start of the year that I would appear on the show a few times. Eddie ended up calling Dean and twisting his arm. Then he rang me and said, 'Just pop in at 7.30 — you'll be on the first segment.'

I'm glad he stepped in and smoothed it over, otherwise I would've done it and felt uncomfortable. The last thing I wanted to do was upset the coach. He had given me the opportunity to fulfil my dream. There was always the fear that we would lose, my selection would be frowned upon and Dean would wish he'd never played me.

DEAN LAIDLEY: I was initially against Jason going on *The Footy Show*. I knew it was a special occasion, but I wouldn't have let any other player go on the show the night before a game, and I didn't see why that should change. I spoke to Eddie McGuire about it. I know that Eddie and Jason have a pretty good working relationship and have worked through this whole thing together, which had been great. But in the end, I told them, 'I'm not going to say no. Jason has to make the decision.'

I was just concerned for Jason, that was all. But he handled it very well, and I suppose I should've expected that after what he'd been through.

DI LLOYD: I went with Jason to *The Footy Show*. I had an inkling that he was going to retire after the game. He always said that if he got one game, he'd be happy. And with all the arrangements that needed to be made and the fact that he was going to speak to Tony Jones from Channel Nine straight after the game, I had a feeling he would do that. I said to him, 'You're not going to make more work for me tomorrow night, are you?'

He just smiled at me and said, 'What are you talking about?'

I gave him the nickname 'Denis the Menace' because every time I thought I'd have a quiet day, something would happen with Jason that would create a massive increase in my workload.

It was a huge week trying to choreograph things for the game. We had to put together highlights packages, get hold of all the different football clubs that had been affected by the bombings and so forth. It was a hell of a week. I worked 40 hours in two days.

One of the club's assistant coaches, Robert Pyman, who, like me had played at three AFL clubs, called that night to wish me well. He said, 'You only do it once, so take your time. You'll feel yourself getting emotional but just take as much time as you want.' It was a nice touch. I also spoke to Corey.

COREY MCKERNAN: I said to him the night before, 'You didn't get to play in a premiership, but if you go out in the right way tomorrow night, it'll be bigger and better than anyone who's played in a premiership.'

The television appearance and all the other hooplah didn't stop me from sleeping like a baby that night. I woke up bursting at the seams with excitement but, outwardly, trying to be low key. I took this attitude to the club for the team meeting at 10.30 a.m. I found out that I would start the match on the interchange bench. Although you naturally want to start every game out on the ground, it didn't bother me. I'd had a feeling that would be the case anyway. I'd been around AFL footy long enough to work out the most likely scenario just from observing training and going to team meetings.

DEAN LAIDLEY: I thought it would be best if Jason started on the bench. Not knowing how he was going to come up after only a five-day break since his last VFL game on the Sunday — that was a concern. And we didn't know how he'd go adapting to the pace of the game, so we didn't want to throw him to the wolves first up. Who knows, he might have gone OK if he'd started on the ground, but we wanted to ease him into it.

TIM HARRINGTON: We thought the pace of the game might catch him out a little bit and he'd be more settled if the hurly-burly was over with and he could slot straight into it.

When the meeting finished, I addressed the leadership group of nine players — Stevo, Arch, Shagger (Shannon Grant), Adam Simpson, Leigh Colbert, Spider Burton, Sav Rocca, Brent Harvey and David King — who I'd played with the most. Referring to some handwritten notes, I also talked about the 'JUMPER' mission statement and how, if they did live by these values, there'd be no doubt they'd be successful individually and collectively. I described how those values had been a major reason for me being able to turn what wasn't much of an AFL career into a reasonable one, and how they had got me through the last eight months. 'So far, so good,' I thought. The hard part was saying that it would be my last game. I had to slow myself down a fair bit because I got a bit of a quiver in my voice. I also said, 'I haven't got a premiership medallion but, at the end of the night, I'll be satisfied, knowing that I've given 100 per cent, 100 per cent of the time, and that I'd retire with dignity and the respect of my peers.' I finished off with, 'Boys, make every post a winner — it's over sooner than you think.'

DEAN LAIDLEY: Everyone was pretty close to tears. It smacked a few blokes in the face.

ADAM SIMPSON: I actually said to him, 'What if you kick ten goals? What are you going to do then?' He said, 'Oh well, I'll go out with a bang.'

That put even more importance on the game.

ANTHONY STEVENS: I had a bit of a tear in my eye, but at the same time I wanted to talk him out of it because I thought he had a bit of footy left in him. I could see and understand what he'd been through and that he wanted to relax and make sure he got his body back to 100 per cent, but it was an emotional time. The worst thing about seeing good mates retire is wondering whether they should go on.

TIM HARRINGTON: The plan was that Jason would tell the players, then it would be 'OK, training's over, boys, see you later.' But no one left. They were all saying, 'Oh, gee, how's that? That's stunning. I wasn't expecting this.'

LEIGH COLBERT: My first thought was, 'You've worked so hard,' and I didn't quite understand why he only wanted one game or why it would be his last. But having experienced the hardships that he had, I really can understand why he retired.

A lot of the eight went and had breakfast afterwards, but I was shocked and probably more emotional than anything, so I just jumped in my car and took off home.

I just wanted to sit down on my own and think about it. It was a shock to me initially because I thought about what he'd gone through to get there.

ALLEN AYLETT: When I found out that he was planning on retiring after the game, I was disappointed — more for his own sake. But then as I analysed it, I could see where he was coming from. It took an extraordinary effort to train and play each week and it had taken its toll.

I left the club with a pile of letters, cards and faxes that had been sent to the club that week.

Mick met me at my place and I told him about my decision.

MICK MARTYN: I thought it would be a good way for him to go out. I wished him all the best and told him I hoped he had a good game and that they would win. We didn't talk much about footy though. It was just a general catch-up chat.

Mick, Paul Connors and I had lunch together. I was relaxed about the whole thing — no nerves just yet. When I got home, my family was out delivering the tickets. It was a good chance for me to settle into my usual routine — which hadn't been as regular as I would have liked — before a night game. (I hadn't played an AFL night match since 29 June 2002.) I watched a DVD — *Remember the Titans* starring Denzel Washington. It was inspiring.

The phone rang and it was Prime Minister John Howard's personal assistant. They were in Adelaide. 'I've got the PM here,' she said. 'Do you have a landline?'

'Ahh, yeah, I have,' I said, stumbling over my words.

'Well, the PM will be calling back in half an hour.'

I was shocked that the prime minister would want to have a chat with me. I didn't watch much of the movie then because I spent the next half-hour thinking, 'What do I call him? Mr Prime Minister, Mr Howard or John or what?' When he called, I settled on Mr Prime Minister. I was so taken aback that I can't even remember exactly what he said. Something about being a fine role model and showing guts and courage in the face of adversity.

NERISSA: One of the standout moments was actually Jase leaving the house. He was all suited up for the game, carrying his bag. It was like back in the old days. I gave him a big kiss and wished him the best. It was so exciting because this was the moment. It was a bit like our wedding day — so full of emotion.

On the way to Telstra Dome in Paul's car, I was reminded of the adversity I'd conquered. We put on an Eminem CD to pump me up. When the 'Lose Yourself' track came on, I turned to Paul and said, 'An Eminem song was playing in Paddy's Bar when the first bomb went off.' Hughesy reckons the song was 'Slim Shady'. In any case, it was spooky, and added another edge to my preparation.

PAUL CONNORS: It was chilling. I couldn't believe it when he said it. I didn't know what to say because I hadn't been there and I wasn't involved, so I just shut up really.

Even more chilling are Eminem's lyrics in 'Lose Yourself'. He talks about getting one shot at a lifetime opportunity, to seize the moment, and about not missing out on your chance to 'blow'. They could just as easily have related to the football match as the bombings.

When we arrived at the ground, photographers and camera operators scrambled to get shots of me. I gave a brief interview on my way into the change rooms. Once inside, I was glad to feel like one of the boys again. I wasn't in there for long though.

Normally, I wouldn't go out onto the ground until we'd done our pre-game warm-up, but I made an exception on this occasion. I thought. 'Well, I've got some time to kill, so why not?' I wandered around the Dome and tried to soak up some of the atmosphere. It was a bit of smell-the-roses time.

I looked up into the stands and, for the first time in my career, saw some banners and signs with my name on them. One said, 'JASON #5 OUR HERO', another read 'JASON THE INVINCIBLE'. They were just a couple of many. I thought, 'Bloody hell, what's happening here?' I was embarrassed that people would go to such lengths with me in mind. It completely blew my mind.

BRENDEN MCCARTNEY: There were people everywhere. I saw a few kids with Kangaroos jumpers on with Jason's No. 5 on their backs. I thought, 'This is gonna be bigger than Texas.'

TONY AUSTIN: I knew he was retiring because I'd asked him over the phone: 'Well, what if I come over next week?' He said, 'Mate, there ain't gonna be a next week.'

I bawled on the way to the ground.

NERISSA: Jan and I went to the chairman's dinner before the game. That was really special because Allen Aylett said some really nice words about Jason. Jan and I were in tears. We knew it was the start of a very emotional night.

I also reminisced about my journey — in football and, especially, in the previous eight months. 'It's all or nothing tonight,' I thought. 'Don't leave anything in the tank because after this, that's it.'

I struggled to contain my emotions — I could easily have shed a few tears. 'Come on, Jase,' I thought, 'save them for after the game.'

I almost broke up when I signed a few autographs and a little girl — she would have only been seven or eight years old — said something about being her hero. I thought, 'Oh, don't darling. Don't do it to me.'

My emotions were put on hold when I returned to the rooms and went through what had become my pre-game routine: 25 minutes of physio, then getting my ankles strapped and putting on my garments.

PAUL HAMILTON: I knew he was retiring, so I wrote him a little letter. I dropped it into his bag before the game so he could read it afterwards. I congratulated him on the way that he had handled himself throughout his whole career, not just during the crisis at the end.

DR CON MITROPOULOS: Jason did the same thing before his comeback game that he always did before every game. He came up to me in the medical room and got his Quinate, which are anti-cramp tablets. He stuck to the routine — meticulous, do your thing, no attention, no fuss. It was like any other game. It didn't feel any different and Jason didn't give any outward signs that it was such a huge game.

TIM HARRINGTON: We were keen to keep the rooms as low key and as focused as possible, which we managed to do, surprisingly. Our build-up for the game was reasonably normal because our blokes are a professional bunch. It was good to catch Jase's eye at times and give him a bit of a wink. He gave me a smile. He looked quite relaxed about it all considering he only had two hours of his AFL career left.

I tried to stay focused, which was difficult because Dad, Brenden, Steven, Hughesy, Leigh and Corey were in there. The club had been good enough to allow them access to the change rooms so they could really feel like they were part of it.

BRENDEN MCCARTNEY: It was so emotional that we were trying not to break out in tears. Blokes like Colby and Arch would come around and give Dad, Steven and me a pat on the shoulder and talk to us. They were rapt too and they said things like, 'It's gonna be a big night, boys.'

The on-ground warm-up, 40 minutes before the game, was a good dress-rehearsal for the crowd reaction and noise levels I could expect when we went out there for the real thing. It was a bit eerie though, because the lights were only at half power at the time. I ran around and got rid of some of the nervous energy that had been steadily building inside me since the start of the week.

When we returned to the rooms, I was determined not to look at Dad, Brenden or Steven. If I'd seen even a hint of emotion in their eyes, or heard the slightest quiver in their voices, I would have bawled. That wouldn't have been the greatest preparation for what I saw as the biggest game of my life.

DAVID KING: All day I was thinking, 'Better make sure we put on a good show tonight. Better make sure you get the younger guys around the place to understand how important this is because it's going to be different from a normal home-and-away game.'

Most of the senior guys know what's required, but we had to make sure that we didn't waver in any way, didn't allow our concentration to fall away at all. It doesn't always happen, but you really do want to win those special games, especially when there's such a massive crowd there on a big occasion like this one was for Jason.

LEIGH COLBERT: Pre-game, I jotted a few things down and one of them was, 'We've got to win the game,' the reason being Jason. I wrote down his qualities on a bit of paper — I generally do it on the opposition, just little things that help me get through a game or things I've got to focus on — what he meant to the place and the things he had gone through to get there. I think everyone who ran out that night was pretty much thinking along the same lines.

STEVEN MCCARTNEY: There was a lot of hype in the change rooms. I've been down in the rooms once before — when Jason was playing for the Crows — but it was nothing like that.

While they were doing the warm-ups, Stevo and David King ran past and gave us a wink and a bit of a tap because they knew what was going on. It was like they were saying, 'We're going to have a fair crack at it.' You could tell they were really pumped up.

BRENDEN MCCARTNEY: When Jase was running past, I felt like sticking my hand out. He gave Dad a tap on the shoulder. It was stirring stuff.

LEIGH HUGHES: I was with Ian, Brenden and Steven. I was lost for words. I was so happy for Jason. To think that we'd nearly lost him only eight months before.

DR CON MITROPOULOS: I shook Jason's hand before the game — I do that with all the guys who come back for their first game after a long-term injury. And Jason's recovery has got to be at the top of the list. I think Anthony Stevens has had more bad luck than anyone else I can think of: knee reconstructions, cutting nerves in his neck, etc. — he can handle anything. Glenn Archer had one of the nastiest hand fractures I've ever seen, but he played again within five weeks. These guys can play with enormous pain.

I put Stevo and Archy and Jason right up there as the most amazing people I've ever dealt with. I deal with a lot of other elite athletes, but AFL footballers, particularly these three, are just amazing. Their ability to play with pain, deformity, lack of movement or with some sort of problem, and to put it into the back of their minds and not just play footy, but play bloody good footy, is phenomenal.

And Jason's ability to cope not only physically, but psychologically, after all that trauma, was just out of this world.

ALLEN AYLETT: When I addressed the crowd at the chairman's dinner, the emotion of it all certainly got the better of me at one stage. Just knowing that Jason was going to be back — I hadn't been as excited before a match since my playing days.

Dean called us in to a little meeting room to give us our final instructions before the game started. He let Dad, Brenden and Steven in to share the experience. I couldn't look at them.

IAN MCCARTNEY: We felt really privileged. You never get the chance to do that unless you're a player. It was all very controlled and professional. There was a lot of nervous tension in there though. They were geared up to do bloody well.

Jason was pretty casual, like it was just another game. I thought he'd be more nervous than he was, or more nervous than he looked anyway.

BRENDEN MCCARTNEY: There was a coat-hanger with Jason's No. 5 facing the players. I thought, 'Laidley's gonna use it as a bit of a motivational thing in his speech.' But he didn't say anything about it. When he finished going through the game plan, he looked at the players and tapped the No. 5 about three times with a texta. Then he threw the texta on the floor and said, 'Right, let's rip into it.' The hairs stood up on the back of my neck when he did that.

It was time to get the show on the road. Corey was waiting for me outside the change rooms. We shook hands but I could only make eye contact for a second. We were such great mates I half-wished he and Mick were playing with me that night.

COREY MCKERNAN: I would've loved to have been playing alongside Jason that night. I savoured the night anyway, but it would have been even more special for me. We're so close, though, I'd hate to have seen what we would have been like. We might not have even got a kick, which wouldn't have done anyone any good.

I had a feeling Stevo would get me to lead the boys out, and that's what he did. It was typical of him — it's never about himself. He always puts his mates first.

Despite my reluctance, I led the team to the edge of the players' race, where we were forced to wait for a minute. The Richmond boys had run out first and there was a bit of confusion — 'wait, wait' and 'go, go' — so I had a quick look at the banner. The cheer squad does a sensational job with the banners and this was no exception. It read:

WELCOME BACK JASON McCARTNEY
AN INSPIRATION TO ALL

It was very touching.

When we finally set foot on the ground, I shook hands with Dad — again avoiding eye contact — and I could tell he was very proud.

NERISSA: Seeing Jase run out onto the ground was amazing. Every time I see the footage, especially when it's played to music, it gets me. It's heart wrenching — I cry every time. It was a very special moment. Jason was representing all of the people who had been affected by Bali in some way. I was proud of him.

BRAD FLOOD: I couldn't believe that he was out there after seeing the footage of him getting off the plane, to his wedding day, where he still wasn't too flash, to that night. I had to pinch myself that it was actually happening. It was a pretty moving thing.

TONY AUSTIN: I had a smile from ear to ear and tears were running down my face.

With Stevo giving me the honour of leading the side out, I felt obligated to break one of my rituals by running through the banner. I always used to run through the banner last, ever since what happened at the 1998 Grand Final. That day, it swung back and tripped me up. I landed flat on my backside. And we lost. I hadn't touched a banner since.

So I had no intention of running through the banner at my last game, but Stevo said, quiet enough for only me to hear, 'You've got to, it's your last game.'

Again I wished Corey was out there with me, because he was good at crashing through the banner. It would have made the job much easier.

Two young boys — our mascots for the night — were to run through the banner with us. Every time I thought my emotions were going to get the better of me in that electric atmosphere, I focused on the boys and made sure they were all right.

It was a tactic I learnt at my wedding when I channelled my thoughts onto my niece, Tarlie. It was a welcome distraction when everyone else's eyes were on me.

Henrietta Law: It was the first game of football I'd been to in the 15 years I'd lived in Australia. But, in my mind, I had always pictured the day that he would run through the banner. To see him do it, after all the hours and days and weeks of hard work, was very special. It was a proud moment. No matter what else happened in the match, I was already happy.

I sent a letter to the *Herald Sun*. It said:

Hope sees the invisible, feels the intangible, and achieves the impossible.

It has been a long, relentless journey that you have been through to get to this. Congratulations for your AFL comeback; you sure earned the right to this.

Your positive attitude, your determination to do the best, together with your personal strength and tremendous family support, have made therapy lead to reality. You are an inspiration to people undergoing tough times, and what you have achieved has to be celebrated.

We are very proud of you.

Kick a bag of goals, mate.

During the warm-up, I wore a new pair of gloves. But they were a bit too sticky for my liking, so I swapped them for a pair that I'd been wearing for a few weeks. I thought, 'Jeez, if I play up forward and I miss an easy goal because of the gloves, I'll be letting the side down.'

Jan McCartney: Nerissa and I went to the president's dinner and we had to run around to the other side of the ground for the start of the game. I was just amazed that we had all of our family, and behind us were a lot of others affected by Bali. They were all so happy for him. They were saying, 'He's been such an inspiration to us.' I thought, 'Well, I hope some good has come out of this because it's been so hard for all of the families involved.'

Mel and Jill from the intensive care unit at the Alfred Hospital were there. Therese Fox (who suffered 85 per cent burns) came out of hospital to the footy. One of my cousin's kids gave Therese a scarf and a hat while they took a photo of her for the newspaper.

The umpires called for Stevo to join them in the centre of the ground for the coin toss. I was stunned, and hugely honoured, when Stevo asked me to do it. It was the first time I'd been at a coin toss since I captained an under-15 schoolboys' side.

In any case, I lost the toss.

There was a buzz around the stadium and I felt their sense of mild disappointment as I jogged to the interchange bench. It was also about five years since I'd started a game on the 'pine'. I had no idea when Dean would put me on the ground — it hadn't been pre-planned — so I made sure I was physically and mentally prepared for whenever that moment arrived. I stretched constantly and went for a couple of jogs along the boundary with my fellow bench-warmers, among them Daniel Harris, Leigh Brown and Daniel Wells.

I also watched the game closely. It was played at a pace that makes VFL matches look like social games. I hoped like hell that I'd be able to handle the increase in tempo.

I was odds-on to play up forward but I knew I could be thrown into defence, especially with the Tigers boasting quality big men like Greg Stafford, Matthew Richardson and Brad Ottens, who was back for his first game of the season. Richo would have been too fast and mobile for me, but I felt capable of matching the other two. When Richmond got the first couple of goals, I thought, 'They might make a move down back now.' But even in Denis Pagan's time as coach, backmen rarely went off the ground — unless they were having an absolute shocker — because he liked to keep a solid back six. Dean operated along similar lines.

DEAN LAIDLEY: I knew it was a big game in terms of media attention and how many people were taking an interest, but I still didn't realise the full significance of it. Everyone was waiting for me to put Jason on the ground.

I knew it would give everyone a lift, not only the supporters but our players, but I had to be careful and harness all that emotion and make sure the timing was right.

By quarter time, we had clawed back to within four points and I was the only player who hadn't had a run. When you're in that position, all you can do is offer words of encouragement and pat blokes on the back. As we huddled for Dean's address, I didn't really feel part of it. I actually felt like a bit of an imposter. Strange, considering it had been built up in the media as my game.

NERISSA: The first quarter just frustrated the hell out of me. I thought, 'Why isn't he going on?' I wondered how Jason was feeling, knowing he would be getting frustrated too.

I was like a cat on a hot tin roof. 'When's this going to happen?' I wondered. 'Come on, Dean, just give me a run.' My telepathic message must have done the trick, because Dean named me at full-forward for the start of the second quarter.

DEAN LAIDLEY: The way we were structured, we thought that we needed someone who was going to be an anchor for us, so we put Jason in the goal square to get him to work and lead.

While I was apprehensive about playing in foreign territory — I'd played basically all of my footy in defence — I thought, 'This'll be OK — I can charge out at the ball without having to worry about an opponent.'

I went to take up my position at full-forward.

ADAM SIMPSON: The crowd's always a little bit in the opposition's favour at Kangaroos matches, but I think that night it was 100 per cent for Jason. When he came on the ground, there was a standing ovation.

I ran to the Coventry End, where the Richmond cheer squad was seated directly behind the goals. Like most cheer squads, they were a parochial group who I'm sure had given me plenty of flak throughout my career. To my sheer amazement, the Richmond cheer squad stood up as one and started clapping and cheering. I looked around me, thinking Brad Ottens might have been jogging behind me. He wasn't. That's when I realised they were directing it all at me. I couldn't believe my eyes. You could have knocked me over with a feather. I'd never witnessed anything like it. It certainly beat being bagged. I'd half-expected that type of acknowledgment from Kangaroos supporters but it came from most people at the ground. It was an unbelievable feeling — the rarest privilege in fact.

PETER HUGHES: That will live in my memory for the rest of my life. That signified to me that this wasn't just about the Kangaroos or Richmond. This was about Jason McCartney. It proved to me and also, I think, to the public that what he was doing was simply amazing. It was a show of pure respect.

The people who went to the game that night weren't necessarily there as Kangaroos or Richmond supporters; they were there as proud Australians.

BRENT HARVEY: I was playing in the forward line when Jase went to full-forward. When the Richmond cheer squad stood up and applauded him, I thought, 'Gee, that doesn't happen too often in footy.' That was fantastic.

I didn't have time to bask in the attention because I was there to do a job: help the Kangaroos win this important match — as much as spectators wanted me to do well, they weren't going to be able to help me get a kick.

My opponent was Andrew Kellaway — one half of the disciplined Kellaway brothers (Duncan is his elder brother) — who won the Tigers' best and fairest and All-Australian selection in 2000. He generally mixes his game up well as a defender — he can shut his opponent out of the game and create plenty of run at the same time. We were evenly matched physically — admittedly, I was a few kilograms heavier — but I was going to have a tough time winning the duel.

It didn't take long to get into the action. I'd only been on the ground for about a minute when the ball bounced along the ground towards me and I ran at it with all I had. All of a sudden, I felt like a little kid who'd never played the game before. 'I'm going to touch it, I'm going to touch it,' I thought. I touched the ball, but I didn't grab hold of it. When the ball spilled to ground, Kellaway got to it first and, in my over-eagerness to give a strong contest — forward pressure was one of our pre-game focuses — I jumped into his back and gave away a free kick.

Later in the quarter, young Drew Petrie took a mark about 65 metres from goal. I made a good lead and got a metre break on Kellaway but Drew didn't see me until it was almost too late. Just when I thought he wasn't going to kick it to me, he chipped it in my direction. It wasn't one of Drew's best kicks, as I had to stop and prop. I almost marked it anyway. But if the kick had been to Drew's normal high standard, I would've been lining up for a shot at goal from around the 50-metre line.

For the rest of the quarter, I ran around like a chook with its head cut off. My fitness had been fine by VFL standards, but sweeping across half-back for Port Melbourne was a much easier prospect than playing as a key forward at AFL level. After a few leads and contests in quick succession, I really started sucking the air in. That's why I really respect players like Wayne Carey, who play at centre half-forward and always give second, third and fourth efforts. It's bloody hard work.

DEAN LAIDLEY: I thought he looked like a fish out of water when he first went on the ground. But I still wanted to leave him on for a bit of time just to let him adjust to the pace of the game.

TIM HARRINGTON: He wasn't great. He looked a little bit rusty. But we thought, 'Bring him on again a bit later on.'

I felt slightly nauseous when Leigh Colbert went down 100 metres away after David King accidentally kneed him in the stomach in a marking contest. Colby was to miss the next eight games with a nasty pancreas injury.

LEIGH COLBERT: I argued with the doctor just before half-time, saying that I wanted to hang around. I wasn't feeling the best, but I knew what this game meant to the club and to Jason. I remember sitting in the ambulance going to the hospital and asking them if there was any chance I'd be able to get back to the ground because, at that stage, we were a couple of goals up and going all right. I thought it was going to be a good result and I wanted to be there.

It crossed my mind, for only a second, that maybe I should hold off on the retiring. I thought, 'Colby's going to be out for the rest of the year. I can't leave the club in the lurch.'

But then I thought, 'If I don't get a kick here, I'll have no choice but to retire. Otherwise, the club'll do it for me.' I hadn't even looked like getting a touch, let alone make a meaningful contribution. Maybe that's being a bit harsh because we kicked four of the first five goals of the quarter with me at full-forward. Although I didn't get a possession myself, perhaps my 'contribution' was that I had provided structure. But I wanted to do more than that.

We were 1 point down at half-time of this must-win match. I did some serious soul-searching during the break. I thought, 'Win, lose or draw, I can't come off this ground with donuts (0 kicks, 0 marks and 0 handballs). How embarrassing would that be? It would look like they gave me a game as an act of charity.' But I knew I was better than that — I deserved my spot. I wasn't there to make up the numbers. It's what I'd been building up to since November. I'd played some good footy in the VFL and it was time to step up. Time to do something.

It's amazing what some positive, proactive thinking can do. While I'm sure many people would have been thinking, 'Well, this is the last game Jason McCartney will play' — and they would have been right — I was confident that I could have an impact.

I had to wait for my chance again, as I started the third quarter on the bench. There were still some self-doubts though. 'I hope I get another chance,' I thought. 'I don't want to sit here for the next quarter and a half and come on with only ten minutes to go as a token gesture from the coaching staff. It just wouldn't feel right.'

I was relieved, and more than a little anxious, when Dean put me back on the ground just ten minutes into the quarter.

ANTHONY STEVENS: The roar when Jase came on was unbelievable. It was pretty much a full house, with supporters from all football clubs, as well as many non-supporters who'd come just to see Jase. The support from the whole football world in that stadium was enormous. When the crowd roared, I knew what it was for — it meant Jason had come on to the ground.

I went back to full-forward. I was pumped up to make my presence felt. 'This is it,' I thought. 'It's make-or-break time.'

Almost immediately, Shagger handballed to me inside the forward 50. I was under pressure on my left side — I was sure someone would be bearing down on me — but I was somehow able to wheel around onto my right foot, balance myself and have a shot at goal off a few steps. I struck it well but hooked it slightly and just missed.

After I got that touch, it felt like a concrete slab had been lifted from my shoulders. I suddenly felt free and mobile. But I was mindful of moving too far up the ground because that would have played into Kellaway's hands, as he was much fitter than me. I was to stay put at full-forward and give the forward line some structure.

Things started happening for me. I crashed into a pack and it resulted in a shot at goal for Leigh Harding — who missed amid our wayward effort of 2.7 to 2.3 for the quarter.

DEAN LAIDLEY: As soon as I put Jason back on after half-time, he had a couple of touches, had a shot at goal, and you could just see that the experience he had before half-time was enough to jolt the memory — physically and mentally.

I felt like I was 'in' the game. At a boundary throw-in a short time later, I laid a strong tackle on Darren Gaspar. Another time I cut across and spoiled a marking attempt by Stafford.

STEVEN FEBEY: When the whole crowd starts applauding a spoil, you know you're witnessing something pretty special.

NERISSA: I loved every minute of it. I just watched Jason most of the time — I didn't really watch the game. I was screaming out, 'Go, Jase.' I went through so many emotions.

At three-quarter time, we were 3 points in front and I knew I had done enough to start the final term on the ground. I had one quarter left to determine how people would remember me as a footballer. A couple of minutes in, David King grabbed the ball forward of the wing and, knowing Kingy's kicking capabilities, I made a half-lead from the goal square, up the middle of the ground.

DAVID KING: I didn't actually know it was Jason at the time, but basically I kicked it as long as I could to a tall, strong-looking target. As soon as it left my boot I realised it was Jase, and I thought, 'He's in a good position here, he's in front.'

Kingy kicked long to the hot-spot — about 25 metres from goal. Kellaway and I jostled for position and I was able to hold my ground in front. I made a lunge at the last split-second but, with Kellaway breathing down my neck, I expected him to get a fist on the ball — that's the bread-and-butter of good defenders like him. Somehow, and to my infinite surprise, he didn't get a hand on it and the ball landed in my lap for a chest mark. I tumbled to the ground with the ball in my hands as the crowd unleashed an enormous roar.

DAVID KING: Jason was strong enough and had the ability to hold off Andrew Kellaway, which is no mean feat. When he took that mark I thought, 'Well this will absolutely lift the roof off the place' — and it did. I'll never forget that.

TIM HARRINGTON: I immediately thought back to the conversation we'd had in my office a few days before. I thought, 'Can you imagine the roar if he kicks this?'

STEVEN MCCARTNEY: I missed the mark because I was up at the bar ordering a drink. Bad timing. I just heard the big roar and I looked around on the screen and, sure enough, he's got the ball in his hands. I thought, 'Oh no!' I didn't actually see that mark until we watched a replay of the game the next day.

When I walked back to take the kick, I thought, 'This is it. I can't afford to miss this one.' I hadn't had time to size up my options when I'd had my previous shot at goal, but I had plenty of time to mull over this one.

I knew I had a big audience — not only the 43,200 people at the ground either. It was Friday night footy, which always rates well on TV. I don't think too many people in the country would have been hoping for a miss — apart from Richmond supporters of course — so there was a lot of pressure on me to slot it through.

Stevo jogged over to me. He was pretty pumped up and had some words of advice. 'Mate, you said this was about us,' he said, eyeballing me, 'but this is about you. You started this, and now's your chance to finish it. Kick the bloody goal!'

As I lined up for goal — 30–35 metres out directly in front — my thoughts drifted to Mick and Denis. I remembered our game against Essendon in round 10 the previous year. We were clinging to a 2-point lead late in the final quarter when Mick kicked one of his finger-breaking punts — 50 metres up, 25 metres long — into the forward line. Everyone misjudged it except for me — I'd had enough one-on-one kicking sessions with Mick after training to work out where the ball would go — and I ended up taking an uncontested mark. I kicked the goal to seal an 8-point win.

I was also mindful of the influence that Denis had had on my career. He was the one who convinced me to have another crack at AFL football after seven unfulfilled seasons at two clubs. He showed me how to get the most out of myself and showed enormous faith to persevere with me when others were calling for my head. If it wasn't for Denis, I may well have played my comeback match in the SANFL or another competition in Adelaide.

Mick has always been a pretty good mate, but we became a lot closer after being thrown together in the crisis in Bali. And if it hadn't been for his quick thinking on the night, I wouldn't have made a comeback at all. I knew Mick and Denis would be sitting in the crowd somewhere watching the game together.

The crowd was going nuts. Although I tried to ignore it, the noise was unbelievable, like a grand final at the MCG. I knew I couldn't disappoint them.

DAVID KING: You could see the tension on all the guys' faces — they really wanted him to kick that goal. We were almost willing him to do it, like everyone else there.

I yelled out to the umpire, 'Is he on the mark or has he gone back?'

I was just making sure Kellaway hadn't crept back and I wasn't going to get too close to the mark.

I took a few deep breaths and blocked everything else out. I followed my set routine: eight steps, starting with the right, building up from a walk to a slow shuffle. Considering what was riding on the kick, I was unusually calm and methodical. I made sweet contact. It was a perfect kick.

GOAL!

I raised both arms in the air with exhilaration and relief. The goal put us 10 points up.

The roar of the crowd was special. It almost gave me goosebumps.

DENIS PAGAN: I was in a box with Mick Martyn and some Carlton people. I was certainly moved by the emotion and the way Jason played and carried himself, like most of the people at Telstra Dome that night.

STEVEN MCCARTNEY: I'd never heard such a big roar — anywhere.

TROY MAKEPEACE: I was spewing that I was up the other end because I couldn't get up there and give him a pat on the back.

NERISSA: I was so nervous, so excited, so happy, and so proud, that I just kept talking the whole time.

When he kicked the goal, I really had to control my emotions because I felt like bawling my eyes out, but I knew all the cameras were there. I'd rather do that on my own, or with Jason. I just wanted to cry and cry. I think that's why I was talking so much.

PETER HUGHES: I couldn't watch him take the kick — there was too much emotion going through me. The result of the match didn't matter to me, it was all about that kick. When it was a goal, I threw my bucket of chips in the air, which upset a few people.

JAN MCCARTNEY: I went to the toilet and when Ian met me out the front of the toilets there was a huge roar. I said to Ian, 'Jason's kicked a goal.'

He said, 'Nah.'

I said, 'Everyone's clapping, he's kicked a goal!'

We ducked down so we could see the scoreboard and there it was. We'd missed it.

The boys rushed over to celebrate. They hugged me, patted my head and shouted words of encouragement. It reminded me of how St Kilda players mobbed Jason Cripps after he kicked a goal in his comeback game in round 15, 2001. (Cripps twice snapped a hamstring tendon and had played only two games in four seasons before that game.)

Despite the euphoria, it wasn't long before I thought, 'Maybe we've celebrated a bit too much, too early here.' Richmond dominated general play for the next five or ten minutes and I didn't even get a sniff of leather.

I sensed that scoring opportunities would be scarce, so we had to capitalise, make something out of nothing.

Richmond regained the lead with goals to Andrew Krakouer and Adam Houlihan, and looked like going further ahead when David Rodan made an exciting dash inside the Tigers' forward 50. Thankfully, our first-year star Daniel Wells ran him down and laid a superb tackle. The ball rebounded, resulting in a goal to Shagger.

Only seconds later, Ottens took a big mark and put Richmond back in front.

GLENN ARCHER: I had a bit of a lowlight with a couple of minutes to go because my man (Brad Ottens) kicked a goal to put them in front. I thought, 'Bloody hell, I've stuffed it up for Jase — we're gonna lose the game.'

An opportunity presented itself shortly after. Daniel Harris scrambled a kick forward and the ball bounced through three sets of players to where Kellaway and I jostled for position at the top of the goal square. It was an awkward ball to gather, so I simply tried to trap it and keep it in front of me and hope that I could feed it off to a teammate running past. To my surprise, the ball stuck in my right hand — it must have been something to do with the gloves. There weren't any teammates close by but, although Kellaway was all over me, I had held my ground well enough to try and have a shot at goal myself. As Kellaway tried to sling me in the tackle, I tried to swing my right boot at the ball. I didn't make great contact but it dribbled along the ground towards the goal line. (It would have gone straight through if I'd got another toenail on it.) Luckily enough, the quickest player in our side, Leigh Harding, swooped on it and kicked his third goal. We led by 3 points.

TIM HARRINGTON: I thought Jason had kicked it himself, so I was jumping up and down like a madman screaming, 'He's done it! He's done it!' I probably let my emotions get away from me a bit. It was still the same result though — a goal for the team.

But then I thought, 'I'd better harness myself here because there's plenty of time left for Richmond to win the game.'

That I was able to keep Kellaway away from the ball was no fluke. We'd done a training drill that simulated that scenario.

People have asked, 'Did Kellaway take it easy on you at times?' I'm sure he's a good bloke, but no AFL footballer is that charitable. Once you cross that white line, you're regarded as being 100 per cent fit. You don't get a chance to think, 'Hang on, that's Jason; let's take it easy on him.' If the ball's there, you just go for it.

Richmond defender Darren Gaspar went down with a knee injury that later required a reconstruction. As the stretcher came out, we huddled together and discussed how we were going to approach the last few minutes. Then our runner came out and said, 'There's a minute and 30 seconds to go.'

I got the forwards in a group and said, 'Don't let this slip. If the ball comes down here, we've got to either win it or lock it in at all costs.'

As we walked to our positions, I passed young Drew Petrie and said, 'Drew, we've got to make sure we lock it in, mate, because I'm never going to play with you again. This is it.'

I didn't look at Drew for his reaction — I just said it and kept walking.

DREW PETRIE: It hit me pretty hard. There was so much going on, and I just kept saying to myself, 'We've got to win it for Jason.' Those last few minutes of the game are a bit of a blur.

The ball was kicked deep into Richmond forward line and it looked like Richo was about to mark when Arch launched himself at ball and body and created a stoppage.

Taking Arch's lead, there were some super efforts by the more senior players in those frantic dying moments. Stevo, Simmo & Co. somehow managed to hold the ball in and cling to victory.

DEAN LAIDLEY: I thought it was telling that in the last few minutes there were some very good deeds and acts of real desperation by some of our experienced players and they were the ones who knew the significance of the moment. They knew that this was Jason's last game and the younger kids just followed their example.

When the final siren sounded, the crowd roared and I charged towards my teammates with both fists in the air. It was like the premiership I never won.

ANTHONY STEVENS: Soon as the siren went and we'd won we knew that was the last game Jase was ever going to play with us as mates. That was the most emotional time.

ADAM SIMPSON: Every person in the stadium was happy. I know Richmond supporters are pretty passionate, but I think they'd cop that one.

The boys jumped all over me. It was great but after a few seconds, we were packed in so tightly that I could hardly breathe. It was like a mosh pit at a rock concert. The noise was deafening as the Kangaroos theme song was belted out over the sound system. But for all the ecstasy, there was enormous relief. We'd won. And I didn't feel like a fraud. My stats weren't startling — three kicks, one mark, one tackle, one free against and 1.1 — but, nonetheless, I played a part in the win. There wouldn't be any hard words or wild-eyed glares from Dean.

DEAN LAIDLEY: I thought Jason had a significant impact in the second half. He gave us an anchor at full-forward. We kicked it there a few times and he provided a real contest. He managed to take a strong mark, kick a goal and have a big hand in another one that turned out to be the winning goal. I didn't go into the game with any expectations about what he might do, so I was happy with his performance.

LEIGH COLBERT: A little mate of mine who comes down from Geelong every week — he's a handicapped kid — was at the game and he heard I was going to hospital, so he jumped on a train in his wheelchair and got to the hospital at the same time as I did in the ambulance, believe it or not. He had a little earpiece on his phone, so I listened to the last quarter and it was just sensational.

When Jason kicked the goal I nearly jumped off the bed. You could just tell by the atmosphere — not just the commentators but the crowd — that it was a fairytale ending.

I knew beforehand that Tony Jones from Channel Nine would interview me on the ground over the loudspeaker. It was an idea I got while commentating for 5AA when we played against Port Adelaide at Football Park in round 8. Port Adelaide's Che Cockatoo-Collins was interviewed on the ground and it was played on the scoreboard after the game, so everyone at the ground could hear it. I thought, 'If I ever get to play my comeback game, I'd love to retire like that,' because there are so many people that I want to thank publicly and the ideal place to do it is in the middle of the ground. If you do it in a press conference, the people at the ground who have ridden every bump of the match wouldn't hear it.

I told the crowd:

It's what dreams are made of. I can't thank the Kangaroos boys enough. The Richmond guys were sensational. It's just a great win ...

I think I've used up every inch of my determination through my fitness and mental effort, and I find it fitting now that I'll hang the boots up as of tonight and go out on a great note. I'm spent, it's been a tough time, but that's enough for me, mate.

Once I got selected, I knew I didn't have much more in me. It's been a huge mental battle to get to where I am today. Look, my body's still healing and it needs a rest, and mentally, it's been hard carrying the hopes of a nation, I can tell you, so I'm going to enjoy a couple of beers tonight with my family and friends. I love these guys, they've been great to me — what a way to go out.

I wasn't lying. I was spent — in every sense of the word. I'd used up every ounce of physical, mental and emotional strength I had to make it back for this one game. It was time to let my body heal properly. Time to move on to a new chapter in my life. While I was sad, I didn't get too emotional because I knew it was the right thing to do.

NERISSA: I had this big grin on my face and tears were running down my cheeks. Everyone was saying, 'You knew that, didn't you?'

I said, 'Yeah.' I was so proud. It was right up there with the wedding. It was wonderful. It was great to see Jason achieve that goal and to have been there with him all the way.

I didn't realise that I could run out onto the ground because I didn't think you were allowed to. Then when I saw Jan out there giving Jason a big hug and a kiss, I was very jealous. I would have given Jason the biggest hug in the world.

TIM HARRINGTON: When he announced his retirement on the ground, I didn't actually hear it because we were in the coaches' box, but I have since seen it on television. It was one of the great all-time speeches, not just in sport. The way he presented himself and expressed himself showed a lot of integrity. It was first-class.

GORDON MCDONALD: When he said that it had been really hard for him to play, you wouldn't have known it. He never bleated or complained. It was always more about what he didn't say than what he did say.

ROGER MOORE: It was amazing that he made it back to AFL football, yet he still didn't look a well man. All the training and hard work, and the fact he almost felt that he had to play for the people affected by Bali, made him seem dogged, like a man on a mission. He was pale and it wasn't until three or four weeks after the comeback match, when he'd stopped all the hard training, that you realised how he had taken his body right to the edge to make that comeback.

DAVID DUNBAR: I had a bit of a lump in my throat. To come back from where he was and play at the highest level is something that, both as a coach and as a person, I'll be able to talk to people about and use as an example for the rest of my life. I think I speak for everyone — Port Melbourne and the Kangaroos — when I say that we thought AFL might have been a bit beyond him. But he confounded all of us.

He's highly respected and very popular around the Port Melbourne Football Club. Even though he only played half a dozen games and a few practice games with us, he had an enormous influence on our players and the club. I can't speak highly enough of what he did for myself and the players in making the alignment between Port Melbourne and the Kangaroos work. As long as I live, I'll never forget how he helped us out.

ADAM SIMPSON: There was a bit of a wrestle about who was going to carry Jason off if we had a win, so I was taking money to see who was going to get under him. Shannon Grant was odds-on favourite — he loves that stuff.

Shagger and Drew lifted me onto their shoulders to chair me off the ground. It was quite fitting. I'm close to Shagger. He lives not far from me and he was desperate to make it back for the game because he'd missed two weeks with a hamstring injury. Not only did he make it back, but he amassed 21 disposals and kicked three goals, including our first two.

SHANNON GRANT: It wasn't planned, but when the final siren went, we ran at each other. We were both pretty happy and I just happened to be there when he was walking off, so I thought it was quite fitting that I get him up as quickly as I could.

Drew represents the new breed of Kangaroo. He's a great kid and a fierce competitor who I'm sure will be a very good player for the club.

DREW PETRIE: I feel a bit embarrassed about chairing Jason off because I'd only played with Jason for a couple of years. I thought it should have been one of the other guys. But I wasn't trying to be an attention-seeker or anything. What happened was Adam Simpson came over to me and ruckman Mark Porter and said, 'Do you guys want to carry him off?' Jason's a big guy, so it was probably a question of his size. I just grabbed him and chucked him up.

I waved to the crowd, who were unbelievably generous in their support.

JESS SINCLAIR: I must admit, my eyes weren't too dry when he was coming off, but I wasn't the only one.

Mum, Dad, Brenden and Steven were on the ground, so I got off the boys' shoulders and embraced them.

JAN MCCARTNEY: Jason said, 'Where's Nerissa?'

I pointed, 'Up there.'

I blew Nerissa a kiss in the crowd.

DR CON MITROPOULOS: I had to suck the tears back into my eyeballs when Jason's mum hugged me and gave me a big kiss on the ground after the game. She was crying and she said, 'I knew he'd do it. I knew he'd do it.'

I said, 'Yes, I'm very proud of him too.' That was when it really hit me that we'd had success. The previous several months flashed before me, and what we'd been through to get Jason up to this and it was the most emotional time for me.

Everyone says it was a fairytale ending, but fairytale endings don't just happen — a lot of people are involved, and they do a lot of hard work to achieve that result.

For volume and gusto, our rendition of the club theme song rivalled the one we belted out after the 1999 Grand Final. It matched the post-match celebrations after we beat Port Adelaide at Football Park in round 1, 2002 — after Archy's 200th game and Stevo returning from a knee reconstruction and being through hell in his personal life. This time though, the circle of players, officials and supporters was so big that the side I was on was well out of time, and tune, with the boys on the other side.

BRENDEN MCCARTNEY: Tim Harrington said, 'Get in the circle with the boys,' so we sang the theme song with them. I'm glad the camera stayed on Jason. It wouldn't have looked too good if us country boys were on TV.

I didn't realise it at the time but the Channel Nine microphone was placed under my chin so the poor people watching it on TV at home had to endure my not-so-smooth vocals. I'd been screaming a fair bit already that night, so I was fairly croaky.

While the boys did their cool-down stretching — let's face it, I had the rest of my life to get over any soreness I felt — I did a couple of interviews. The boys responded by throwing discarded tape and lollies at me. I had a chat with Eddie McGuire, who'd known on Thursday night what I planned to do but hadn't let the secret out. During the interview, Eddie said: 'It's been a fantastic night, not only for the Kangaroos and AFL football, but also for Australian society. Mate, you are a true hero — I know you don't want to hear that sort of thing at the moment — but it is one of the great stories in the history of sport.'

I mingled with the people who had been invited as my guests. When I saw Febes and Steven Armstrong — blokes from another AFL club — I thought, 'Jeez, how often would this happen? This was much bigger than just a game of footy.'

STEVEN FEBEY: I'd never been in an opposition team's rooms after a game, so to be invited there by the Kangaroos, along with blokes from other football clubs, with all the emotion of it all, was very special. Jason gave me a big hug. Look, we're not close mates but I've got enormous admiration for what he's done.

I said to him, 'Once you get on the forward line, Jase, you don't retire. It's usually when you get shifted to the back-pocket that you have to retire.' We had a laugh about that.

My wife and I talked about it all on the way home that night. Even now when it comes up in conversation, we've got something very special to talk about.

TIM HARRINGTON: We've had a lot of great wins in my time at the Kangaroos where you tell the players and the staff, 'It was a great win, boys, but don't get carried away with it. We've got another game next week, keep a lid on it.' With this one, there was none of that — the lid was completely off. We were jumping around, there were people everywhere in the rooms. I'm supposed to be in control of who's in the rooms, and I didn't know who half of them were. A lot were associated with Bali in one way or another. But everyone had a smile on their face.

GEOFF WALSH: The atmosphere in the rooms after the game is something I'll take away with me when I finish in footy and say, 'Well that was one of the very, very good things that I was privileged enough to be involved in.'

I've been lucky enough in my administrative career to have been involved in a few premierships with both Carlton and North Melbourne, but to be in the rooms that night was really something special.

ALLEN AYLETT: We had a few emotional games during the season. There was the game against Carlton in round 5 when we came up against our former coach, Denis Pagan. There was the one against Adelaide and our former captain, Wayne Carey in round 6. But they were nothing like Jason's comeback game. That was an unbeatable night for emotion. His effort is right up there with the all-time most courageous acts in sport.

GLENN ARCHER: It was right up there with the premierships I reckon. You try to treat every game the same but it's hard when you bring emotion like that into it.

It was pure elation. I couldn't believe what had happened. I was sitting there thinking back to how I saw Jason on that hospital bed to a few months later being able to do what he did. It was a bit like a grand final.

People ask me what it was like straight after the game but I can't really remember much because it's all a bit of a blur — we were on such a high.

Our results after that game weren't real good. We were having a pretty good patch through that time and probably used up a fair bit of emotion and energy that night.

Adam Simpson: It was surreal. I get the tingles down the back of my spine every time I watch it. I heard Rex Hunt doing a 'year in review' and they did a snippet on that game and the same thing happened.

It was a big thing for me and a big thing for my career to be part of that.

Anthony Stevens: There were a lot of media people going around interviewing the senior-type guys and I remember sitting next to two or three of our young guys who said, 'What are you talking about?' They had no idea until 15 or 20 minutes after the game that Jason had retired because they couldn't hear what Jason was saying on the speaker. It definitely hit them hard.

David King: It would have been so easy for Jason to have been that unlucky footballer who was caught up in the Bali tragedy and just drift away into absolute obscurity, and be someone who was never the same after it. But he didn't let that happen. He didn't want people's pity, he wanted their support. He wanted them to get on board and ride the Jason McCartney wagon back into AFL footy and show that even though this terrible tragedy had happened to him and happened to many others, you can still get on with your life and achieve the things that you need to achieve before you finish. I think it's been a great lesson for our whole club and we've really embraced it — the Jason McCartney story.

I first met Jason at the Sari Club in Bali just after he'd signed with the Kangaroos at the end of 1997. I was about to get beaten up in a bar and he came along and saved me — I'll never forget it. I was over there with former Kangaroos teammate Matty Armstrong, and a couple of blokes thought I was involved in a big blue where a couple of policemen were severely beaten when I was down at Port Melbourne in 1993. It was a pretty tense couple of moments. Jason came over and said to them, 'What do you think you're doing?'

I knew it was Jason McCartney, but I hadn't met the man, and he stepped in, along with Kane Johnson, who were both at the Crows then. I've never forgotten.

Brent Harvey: It must be the best home-and-away match I've ever played in. I've played in a premiership, but it's a little bit different to that because it's a personal game. It meant a great deal to me and I know it meant a lot to all the other guys as well.

It was perfect. I don't think he could have done it any better. He went out on a huge note, we won the game and he played his part.

If you didn't draw inspiration from what Jason did, there would be something wrong with you. His dedication to everything — not only footy, but life — is awesome.

Dean Laidley: The playing group took enormous inspiration from Jason for pretty much the whole year. It's probably the most inspirational thing that I've been directly involved in as both a player and a coach. You've got guys like Lance Armstrong (who overcame testicular cancer to regain his title as the cycling world champion) — what Jason has done certainly rates right up there with that.

I feel privileged to have witnessed such fighting spirit, to see a bloke go from being in a very ordinary condition in hospital to making his AFL comeback seven months later. That game was a good lesson for life. Even if tragedy strikes you, you can overcome adversity and, if you work hard enough, you can get back to where you were. If you will yourself to get back, you'll get good support.

TIM HARRINGTON: The whole single-minded intent to overcome that and to do it under such a huge media spotlight makes it an even bigger effort. It went beyond Jason as an individual. He ended up being symbolic of the fightback against terror. That's a huge burden for anyone to bear.

For him to physically come through all that pain and then mentally come up for that game and not only take part in it but be an integral part of it and basically win it for the team, it was a massive achievement.

He had to shoulder the burden of public expectation. I've seen that with different players who have shunned the attention because it weighed too heavily on them, it was too much of a responsibility and they didn't enjoy it. But Jason stood up in it and revelled in it.

DENIS PAGAN: Nothing surprises me with anything Jason McCartney has done. He's always had great strength of character and he has displayed it time and time again, on and off the football field, for a number of years now.

I always had enormous respect for him, but since the Bali bombings, the way he has carried himself, his courage and his composure, compassion for other people and dignity under extreme pressure has been enormous. He cared more about the people he was involved with than himself — that's a trait he possessed long before what happened in Bali.

He was the perfect guy to coach —a real role model for everybody at the club. His preparation was impeccable, second to none. It's not about how much ability you've got, it's about what you do with it, and Jason did everything he possibly could and more to get the best out of himself.

Whether he wants to be or not, Jason is really the face of the Bali tragedy, and he has taken it all in his stride. It's been a pretty special effort.

TROY MAKEPEACE: It would have to be the most memorable game I've played in. I don't remember much that happened during the game, but the things I do remember, all of them pretty much involve Jason. He didn't show any signs of holding back, he threw himself at the footy all the time. He showed everyone that nothing could beat him.

BRENDEN MCCARTNEY: Maybe I'm a bit biased, but it was a phenomenal effort. His body hadn't fully healed, but he was still able to play AFL football. A lot of the other burns victims weren't healing with 100 per cent rest, and yet here Jason was, trying to play footy at the highest level and getting belted each week.

IAN MCCARTNEY: We're very proud of what he's been able to achieve, but we're only country bumpkins. In time, it'll sink in.

STUART COCHRANE (FORMER KANGAROOS TEAMMATE, NOW AT PORT ADELAIDE): I had tears in my eyes watching it on TV. It was something that Jason really deserved. You'd hate to see anyone try their guts out and not make it. But he's got such a fighting spirit. As a player, he was always mentally strong.

I modelled myself on him because he was a true professional.

Jase would talk with anyone and he treated everyone the same. Even as a young bloke, he'd make you feel good about yourself. When he joined the Crows in 1995, I was about 16 and had gone to a pub in Victor Harbour. Jase was with Andrew McLeod and everyone was looking at them. I went up to them with a mate to say g'day and he bought us a few drinks. I thought, 'How good's this guy?' It was quite ironic because a couple of years later he ended up at the Kangaroos where I was. When he got there, I used to follow what he did.

PETER KENNEDY (FLIGHT SERGEANT, ROYAL AUSTRALIAN AIR FORCE): It was probably the second game of Aussie Rules I've ever watched in my life, and I only watched it because Jason was playing. I was pretty emotional, like the rest of the country I reckon.

We knew nothing about Jason beforehand but we really follow him now because, to us, he's a role model for everyone else that's struggling.

When Dean delivered his usual wrap-up of the game, he was clearly relieved and happy. The media pressure and all the other distractions associated with my comeback/retirement had taken its toll. So many things that happened before, during and after the game — things that he understandably wanted to control — were so far removed from usual practice that I am indebted to Dean for his flexibility and forethought, especially when you consider that he was employed to do one thing: win football matches. If my selection hadn't come off, he would have come under fire from the harshest critics.

I remember when Dean announced his retirement at the start of 1998. I'd just arrived at the club and hardly knew him, but his speech to the players made me emotional. Later, when I saw footage of Dean in a very emotional state straight after the game, with Arch and Stevo talking to him, I realised just how big — and tough — a week it had been for him.

DEAN LAIDLEY: I felt sheer relief. I was relieved that we'd won because we were on a bit of a roll at that stage. It was our third win in a row and we were playing probably our best footy of the year. I was also relieved that this game that I'd been worrying about all week was over, and that it had all gone well. It hadn't backfired on us. It was very draining though.

Talk about emotional, apparently Drew Petrie hadn't stopped crying.

DREW PETRIE: I've never experienced emotion like it. I don't reckon I've ever cried over a footy match before but when we went into the rooms, there were people everywhere — media, Jason's friends — and tears just started coming out of my eyes. I don't know why I started to cry. It was one of the biggest emotional drains I've ever felt. All of a sudden, it just hit me.

It was the most emotional game I've played in. I've never played in a grand final — that would be a massive experience — but in terms of emotions, this was the biggest ever.

I thought, 'Gee, I'm glad we didn't tell all the boys before the game that I was retiring because they might've cried all night and we might've got thrashed.'

It was really special speaking to Hughesy, Jess and her father, Billy senior, in the rooms. Hughesy was one of a very select group of people to know exactly what I had overcome to play footy again, while the Hardys came from a different perspective as people who were still grieving the loss of a loved one. To see them smile, even if it was for only five or ten seconds, made my battle all worthwhile.

PETER HUGHES: Each time he ran or played football, he was hurting. Every minute of it. I know because, like a lot of other bomb victims, I had similar injuries and I was hurting too. While Jason was being belted from pillar to post on the football ground, a lot of us were still recovering. Although he's a lot younger than I am, it's no different — it's bloody painful. What he did to get back and play in the AFL was nothing short of remarkable. Pure heroics.

It was the most inspirational thing I've ever seen. We might not see anything like that ever again. He did something that was extraordinary. I could watch that 100 times and still get the same reaction. He wasn't just a footballer, he was a real human being. And he was carrying everyone's hopes on his shoulders. It wasn't just about him, it was about us.

Not just anyone could've done what Jason did. He had to block the pain out of his mind — and he did that. Truth be known, he might tell you that there wasn't much pain, that it wasn't too bad, but I can certainly tell you that it was painful.

He not only proved something to himself but also to the criminals who were responsible for the bombs. He made a very powerful statement. In effect, he said to them, 'You might've got me on the outside, but you didn't get me on the inside.'

We all drew enormous strength from what he did. It meant a lot to everybody involved in Bali.

He lifted people that you probably don't hear about, like people out in the country somewhere that were involved in Bali. They would've sat up and watched it and said, 'Wow! If he's done that, well I'm prepared to do a bit of hard work and get well too.'

For me, it was pure emotion and respect for a person who is not only my friend, but somebody who has done a truly heroic thing. It gave me full confidence just to get up and do whatever I wanted to do. It was a sense of achievement for him but it was also a sense of achievement for me.

GARY NASH: I don't know how Jason did it. There's no way that I would have gone out there. At that stage, when I bumped my skin, it would just break down. I kept feeling every little knock. It was fantastic to see him out there — to say he's an inspiration is an understatement.

SAMANTHA WOODGATE: Just seeing Jason run out there was enough for everyone. It was amazing that he was able to do what he wanted to do in such a short time.

We were all there for him, and for each other. He'd support us in anything that we wanted to do.

It was a celebration of life and career.

People were coming up to us congratulating us on how far we'd come, and it wasn't even our night. We were proud to be part of it though.

LEANNE WOODGATE: Very few people would have had the determination or the willpower to get up and train every morning when their body's hurting so much. It was great to see him prove that terrorists hadn't stopped him from doing what he loved doing.

He's like the brother Sam and I never had. I can't even describe the connection we've got. When you've all gone through something like this together, you've got this bond.

GEOFF WALSH: Jason's story gives everyone an inward prod. It gives everyone a real sense that no matter how overwhelming the adversity might seem, you should never give up. You can achieve things that might seem out of your reach.

LEIGH HUGHES: I was playing with Peel Thunder in the WAFL. I did a dodgy on the club by telling them I was crook, so I missed Thursday's training session to fly to Melbourne. I flew back to Perth to play on the Saturday and got best on ground. The adrenalin from Jason's comeback game was still there a day later.

The only ounce of regret I have about the night was that I didn't insist that Nerissa make her way down into the rooms. It would have been special to share a few moments together in such a joyful atmosphere.

NERISSA: I wish I'd been in the rooms to soak up some of the electric atmosphere I've been told was in the room that night. But I was very proud anyway. It was an amazing, ecstatic feeling. I thought, 'You did it, honey. I love you so much!'

Jason's strength is just amazing. I can't get over how strong he is and how well he coped with the whole situation. There were a few times when he'd get really depressed and sad, and a few times where he just wanted to give up, but he never did. He just kept going and pushing himself as hard as he could. It's amazing how he remained so positive and strong and had that willingness to fight to achieve his goals.

GLENN ARCHER: It's a real lesson for us all to live each minute to the full because you never know what's going to happen. Seeing how hard he trained and worked under such stress just makes me think that if he can do it when he's 30 per cent fit, I should be working twice as hard when I'm 100 per cent fit.

LEIGH COLBERT: Jason's always been the person that the public sees now. He's always helped people and been courageous and possessed all of those sort of traits that encapsulate the man now. Everyone's saying how great a fella he is, but I knew how good a person he was before Bali. It's coming out now because he is an icon of Australia and he's really led the way for a lot of people.

I knew how well he prepared his body and how many sacrifices he made. He's a very well organised guy and he's certainly been a role model for me ever since I joined the Kangaroos from Geelong at the end of 1999.

His character's been exemplified even more because people now recognise Jason McCartney and what he's done, but I was probably lucky enough to see that prior to 2002. I've always held him in the highest regard.

After the post-match press conference, I returned to the change rooms for a shower and my regular application of creams and garments and was again the last to leave. When I got up to the Victory Room, it was like I had turned up to a surprise party. I mean, I knew it would be a big celebration — particularly if we won — but I had no idea that this big function room would be packed with people and rocking like a nightclub. I waded through the crowd to the stage and there was a sea of people cheering and chanting for me. I felt like a rock star. (Well, my middle name is Paul.)

I spotted Nerissa across the room with burns victims and those who had lost relatives. The sheer glow about them reinforced what I felt with Hughesy and Jess in the rooms. There hadn't been much — if anything — to celebrate in the previous eight months, so it was a moment to savour. It had been a great personal triumph which was made even bigger by the fact that so many people shared in it with me.

I asked the crowd to give me five minutes to catch up with Nerissa. It took me about that long to wade my way through the crowd to her. I gave her a kiss and a cuddle. They were precious minutes on an incredible night.

I spent the next hour and a half shaking hands, signing autographs and receiving back slaps. I was totally overwhelmed. The party continued at the Sports Bar at the casino until about 5 a.m. I was bursting with pride.

When we got home, I called my mate Greg Waugh, who hadn't been able to make it over for the game because his father was ill and he was flat out at work. He was wide awake — it was 2.30 a.m. Perth time.

GREG WAUGH: The phone rang and I thought my old man was in more trouble. I was pretty bloody happy that it was Jason. We spoke for about an hour and a half. I was pretty disappointed I missed out on the game. In my wildest dreams, I didn't think the match would have unfolded the way it did. And after the game, when everyone wants a piece of him, he rings me of all people. I said to him, 'With that last kick, if that had gone through, I would have told you the game had been rigged.'

BRAD FLOOD: A mate and I drove back to Adelaide after the game — I had so much work on that weekend. We'd gone through Nhill and we were probably near Keith. It was about six o'clock in the morning and Jason rang. He thanked us for coming over. I thought it was great for him to recognise that we'd made the trip over. It shows that he doesn't forget who his mates are.

I got a few winks of sleep and woke up to front and back page coverage on almost every major newspaper in the country — and all for the right reasons. Great colour photographs, glowing stories — it was terrific.

My phone rang off the hook too. Everyone wanted a piece of me. I did several radio interviews before heading to Bells Hotel in South Melbourne where TV crews from Channels Seven, Nine and Ten were waiting for me, along with newspaper journalists. When the formalities were over, it was time to relax, and reflect, with family and friends, while we watched a replay of the match.

A surprise visitor was Simon Crean, who had plenty of things on his own agenda after a challenge for his leadership of the Labor Party came from Kim Beazley earlier that week. As soon as Creany walked in, Brenden, who's a country larrikin, yelled out, 'Hey, Jase, didn't Kim Beazley throw five hundred bucks over the bar two hours ago?'

I couldn't help but laugh, and Creany took it in good humour. He had a few pots with us and put $100 over the bar before getting back to work.

SIMON CREAN: I couldn't get to the game. I had just called on a leadership challenge that week and I had to address the Queensland conference. I stayed up that night in my hotel room and watched the delayed telecast of the Kangaroos–Richmond game. I didn't know what the result was, quite frankly, because you never get any news in Brisbane about any AFL team other than the Brisbane Lions.

I only got a couple of hours sleep that night because I couldn't turn the game off.

Jason was involved in a couple of defining moments in the last quarter and it was a fairytale ending. I was quite moved by it all. He stood up for himself, and he stood up for the Kangaroos, but, most importantly, he stood up for Australia. That's what that match was all about. That's why he'll be remembered. It was the individual highlight of the football season. In a game in which everyone goes for the play of the day, the mark of the day and the goal of the day, this was the courage of the year.

It's that reinforcement of the positive attitude. It's that courage and determination. It's the strength of willpower. It's setting goals and achieving them. And it's about sparking those characteristics in other people. It's not only a great human interest story, it's a great example of what positive thinking and determination can do. It's pursuing your objectives and knowing what you want, but it's also about battling adversity. It's about taking the attitude that, 'I'm not going to let the bastards beat me.' Jason embodies that great Aussie fighting spirit, that never-say-die determination to succeed and beat your adversaries …

I flew back to Melbourne that afternoon. I rang to congratulate him and was told he was down at the pub and that he'd really appreciate it if I called in there. It was the perfect opportunity because it wasn't very far from my place. I called in on the way home. I must say that when they told me he had been there since the morning, because that's when all the TV crews had come around to film him, I thought, 'God, I don't know what sort of condition he's going to be in.' He either holds it well or he paces himself — I'm not too sure which one — but he was in good nick and we had a great yarn about proceedings from the previous night.

Jason's brothers were there and they all thought it was a hoot: the politician under pressure coming down to the pub for a beer. They were cracking jokes saying things like, 'Do you reckon Beazley would buy a shout?'

Then his family turned up. They're a lovely family … It was a great occasion.

The next morning I appeared on *Sportsworld* on Channel Seven and *The Sunday Footy Show* on Channel Nine, where I competed in a handball competition against Joel Smith. You're supposed to do five handballs with each hand, but my left hand was still fairly raw and I didn't want to embarrass myself, so I did ten with my right — as did Joel. I somehow managed to win a 68-centimetre TV, a DVD player and other prizes.

I thought, 'This retirement caper isn't a bad career move.'

27

Justice is done

There was no chance of slipping quietly out of the limelight. For a two-week period — the week leading up to my comeback match, and the week after — I became extremely popular. Someone suggested that I log on to the Internet and type my name into a search engine. It was a vain act, but I was amazed to find that over 500 articles had been published about me in that fortnight. Admittedly, a portion of the stories related to Paul McCartney, the former Beatle (funnily enough, my middle name is Paul) and some of the stories on me had been used in several publications, but you get the idea — it was a frenzy.

The *AFL Record* also published an A2-sized poster with 23 photos of pivotal moments of my comeback match and my personal commentary telling the story of the night. I was to sign hundreds of them in the following months.

To keep my feet on the ground, and keep my fitness level high, I continued to train with the Kangaroos and help the coaching staff with drills. I had worked hard to get into shape and I didn't want to have to work that hard again, so figured it was easier to maintain my fitness. I still do some form of workout three or four times a week, whether it be running, cycling or weights work. I've been active all my life and when I don't do any exercise, I don't feel good about myself. Healthy body, healthy mind. Besides, I needed to present well if I wanted to pursue a career in the media.

On that front, I walked away from a meeting with Eddie McGuire with a handshake agreement that I would serve a three-year 'apprenticeship' with Channel Nine. Hopefully, when that time is up, I'll be ready to host a show or do some football commentary.

My manager, Paul Connors, also lined up a two-year deal with ICMI, Australia's largest bureau of speakers and entertainers. Despite my limited experience of speaking in front of audiences at the time, I knew I could offer a lot in this area, particularly giving people a greater understanding of what happened on 12 October 2002 and getting across positive messages like, 'No matter what the situation, with hard work and positive thinking, dreams can come true.'

These contracts gave me great relief. After years of indecision about what I would do in life after football, I had found genuine direction. Life without football wasn't as difficult as I had imagined it would be because I was so busy. If I didn't have things in place off the field, health issues aside, I probably would have played on — or limped on — for the rest of the season.

But, on another matter, I held grave doubts. Kate Webb from the Australian Federal Police informed me that I would be required to give evidence at Amrozi's trial in Bali. By law, Kate was bound to ask me the standard question, 'Do you realise there is a travel warning on Indonesia?' While she assured me that it was a secure place to visit, I wasn't convinced. I was desperate to contribute in any way to the prosecution of Amrozi, but I was mindful of Nerissa's concerns.

NERISSA: I was scared and very upset because the last time Jason went to Bali on his own, he barely made it back. I'd been determined that I would never let him go there on his own again — it stirred up too many emotions and bad memories.

I did my best to reassure Nerissa that I'd be OK and that it was for a cause. David Bonython-Wright and Hughesy were also coming with me — Dave as emotional support and Hughesy to testify — so I relaxed a little in their company. That was until I got to Denpasar airport. It took so long for me to find my suitcase I started thinking, 'This is exactly what happened when Mick and I got here last year. I hope to God it's not a bad omen.'

NERISSA: As soon as Jason left, I lost it. I was crying all the time. I wasn't sure what would happen. Then I started receiving phone calls from friends. I thought, 'Why am I getting all these phone calls?' Then I found out afterwards that Jason had rung all these people and said, 'Call Nerissa because she's really upset.'

Peta picked me up — she's such a great friend — and we went out for a drink with some girlfriends that night. Peta was so accommodating. I'd say, 'Let's do this,' and then we'd get there, and I'd say, 'No, I don't want to do this.' So we'd go somewhere else. My mind was so scattered. I just wanted to talk to Jason the whole time and make sure he was OK.

My paranoia eased when we had dinner on the beach at Sharkey's Cafe on a beautiful Bali evening. After dinner, we went to a World Peace concert where Aussie band INXS was the star attraction. What a night! The concert was staged at Garuda Wisnu Kencana Cultural Park in Jimbaran, nestled in an old quarry near some beautiful old temples and with superb views of the surrounding countryside. It was one of the most amazing places I'd been to and, although it was my thirteenth trip to Bali, I'd never even known it existed.

I was impressed to see police everywhere and all the concert-goers scanned with metal detectors before they went in. There were about 6000 people there but not once did I fear for my safety.

We went backstage and met INXS. The then lead singer, John Stevens, is a cousin of former Kangaroos and Sydney star Wayne Schwass. We discovered we had other mutual friends as well, so we chatted for a while.

I bumped into an Australian girl who said, 'You're the footy guy, aren't you?'

I said, 'Yeah.'

'I remember you from the hospital,' she said. 'You had that big, bald guy with you.'

I remembered her then. She'd come up to me thinking I was someone else lying on a stretcher. Her mum died in the blasts.

I also met a Balinese woman who had become a widow due to the bombings. Through a translator, I found out that her husband had been a security guard at the Sari Club. Apparently, he had tried to move the bomb-van on before it exploded.

I met other widows that night and felt compelled to hand them money. They weren't asking for anything but I knew they would be doing it tough.

INXS's manager, Dave Edwards, brought out a box full of grog for us and allowed us to stand on the side of the stage while the band played. Here we were, Hughesy and I, arm in arm, beers in hand, rocking along to one of the best rock bands in the world.

NERISSA: When Peta dropped me at home, I called Jason to see what he was up to and to make sure everything was OK over there. When he answered the phone, there was a lot of noise — music and talking. He told me he was at the INXS concert. I could hear in his voice that he was really happy, which was a huge relief to me. He and Hughesy really got some quality time together. It was the perfect phone call because it just quashed all those concerns that I'd had. I was able to sleep really well that night.

Hughesy and I made sure we got plenty of rest and sleep the next night for our court appearance on the Monday morning.

Hughesy, Stuart Anstee (a bomb survivor from Tasmania) and I were briefed in the prosecutor's office at 7 a.m. I was fairly relaxed to start with but, as 'show time' approached, I became more edgy. It was similar to the way I felt before my comeback match.

There were several reasons to be anxious, not least the fact that we would be the first westerners to give evidence in a trial against terrorism. We were also about to come face to face with one of the people who played a part in killing two hundred innocent people and burning the flesh off half of my body. I wanted to throttle him. But as much as I would have had great pleasure in doing it, and as much as millions of other Australians and people around the world would have wanted me to do it, I knew it would have been a foolish move. It wouldn't bring back the people who died in the bombings and it wouldn't erase the injuries that the rest of us received.

A person in my position has to be more calculated. I had to harness my emotions — as I had done ten days before — and simply get the job done.

Stuart was the first witness called to the stand. I was up second. I watched proceedings on a TV in a witnesses' waiting room. It was surreal to see that Amrozi was only metres away from Stuart. It hit me like a ton of bricks.

Stuart gave evidence for about half an hour, during which time I made about ten visits to the toilet. It was like my pre-match routine. And, like a football match, I was about to enter a real pressure-cooker environment.

As I was escorted towards the courtroom, I noticed machine guns everywhere. If I needed any reminding that this was the real deal, that was it. It was very intimidating. I planned to have the same effect on Amrozi.

I strode into the court with purpose, almost on my tiptoes, puffing my chest out because I wanted to overwhelm him with my size. I also gave him the Glenn Archer wild stare because I wanted him to know the hatred and repulsion that I felt for him and his cronies. But Amrozi wouldn't look at me. He looked at everything in the courtroom except me. His eyes darted to the floor, the ceiling, the table, the chair. He was like a scared little boy, barely able to look over the bench. But he wasn't to be pitied.

I had to talk slowly and clearly, a couple of sentences at a time, so that the interpreter could relate it to the court in Indonesian. I actually welcomed the disruption because there was no pressure to answer quickly and it gave me time to gather my thoughts and overcome my nerves. I spoke loudly to enhance the intimidation tactics.

The hardest thing was that I couldn't say exactly what I wanted. I wanted to say, 'You might have burnt our flesh and taken lives, but our spirit is so strong that you can't beat us.' But that wouldn't have been damning evidence. I had to set aside my pride and describe how being seriously injured had affected me physically, mentally, emotionally and financially. I showed some of my burns and talked about how I'd lost income through my football career being cut short. It was all true, but saying 'poor me' isn't the Australian way. My attitude has always been, no matter what the circumstances, 'Don't waste time whinging, just get on with it.'

I was also aware that only a couple of rows behind me there were people who had lost loved ones. I can't begin to imagine how they felt. I was lucky to be alive, so I shouldn't have been complaining. But the fact was we needed to ensure that justice was done.

I told the court: 'I believe it is my duty not only to represent Australia, but the people of the world as one to take a stance against terrorism.'

On my way out of the courtroom, as Hughesy was on his way in, I nearly ripped his hand off when I shook it. I told him, 'He's scared, mate — go and get him.'

When it was over, the prosecution lawyers thanked us repeatedly for our evidence and conduct.

DAVID BONYTHON-WRIGHT: The three of them gave a very clear message: they weren't anti-Indonesian, they weren't anti-Muslim, they were anti-terrorism. Their comments hit the front page of the *Jakarta Post*, which is the major paper in Indonesia.

It was a triumphant day. We felt proud to be Australians. I must admit that I'd been apprehensive about the Indonesian judicial system before that day, but I was impressed with what I saw.

That night we went to a traditional Balinese barbecue where we mixed with some of the widows we had met at the concert, and we also met two orphaned children who had been taken in by another woman. We were surrounded by reminders of the tragedy, but it was therapeutic in a sense to speak with these people because it gave me a broader understanding of it all. I told them where I fitted in and they all broke out in big smiles when I said I was married two months after the bombings.

It amazed me that there was an outcry about how little the Red Cross had done to help Australians affected by the bombings (I think they did a good job, even if it didn't run entirely smoothly). Yet I never heard a word of complaint from these poor Balinese people who had lost their husbands, the fathers of their children, their providers, and had been given hardly anything and were struggling just to feed themselves.

I discovered that our anger towards the bombers was nothing compared to the anger of the Balinese people. They were ropeable that such mass murder had been committed and their island had been crippled by loss of tourism and business.

I asked what they would like to see happen to the bombers. Some said, 'Put them on a spit like a suckling pig.' Others wanted death by a thousand lashes.

Before we left for home, I was approached by an Aussie bloke who had an interesting story to tell about the night he met Corey in Bali — just a few weeks before the bombings.

COREY MCKERNAN: I was with a couple of my Carlton teammates, Simon Beaumont and Simon Fletcher. It was about five or six o'clock in the morning and we ran into a guy who said, 'I was at the Sari Club and I had a fight with a guy called Samudra.'

That name Samudra stuck in my mind.

The bloke lived in Bali, knew all the locals by name and so forth.

So during the period that we were there, Samudra was obviously casing the joint. It could easily have been us getting hurt or killed. They could have made their minds up that they were going to do it then.

The day after we returned home, Dave and I were off to Parliament House in Canberra to mix with the country's major political figures and propose that survivors and families of victims receive ongoing support and also throw around some ideas to commemorate the first year since the bombings. I had separate meetings with John Howard, Simon Crean, Natasha Stott-Despoja and Andrew Bartlett from the Democrats, the Department of Foreign Affairs and Trade and acting Indonesian ambassador, Imron Cotan, but the surprise of the day came when I was quietly escorted in to watch a sitting of Parliament. In acknowledging my presence, Simon Crean said, 'We salute his courage and we look forward to working with him and his colleagues in developing the positive, needed response for the victims of this tragic bombing and their families.'

Mr Howard said, '[You are] a great example of young Australian courage in adversity ... You won a lot of hearts, mate, in what you did — and that courage will always be remembered.'

Another time, Creany said, 'It's that reaffirmation, "I'm not going to let these bastards think they can do it." It's the statement for the nation, it is strength of character, determination against all the odds that we're not going to let terrorism beat us.'

Mr Howard has also said, 'It's been a terrific example of Aussie courage ... Millions of people ... admire your guts.'

DAVID BONYTHON-WRIGHT: Jason is very conscious of the other people who suffered burns or people who lost their loved ones in Bali. He's had a really strong focus on trying to use his profile to benefit other people which is, I think, a very rare quality. One of the things with sportspeople is that usually the moment of glory is all self-focused. But Jason has included a lot of other people in his journey and I think that is a really remarkable attribute.

Jason was close to death and came back for a reason. So far, that reason seems to be going to bat for lots of other people.

There are people affected by this who Jason will never know. For example, people who have suffered disfigurement who, since Jason's been public about that stuff, may be encouraged not to just stay at home feeling afraid of how the world will view them.

I think he's truly a national icon in Australia. That's a pretty incredible thing for any sportsperson to have done. But he's as capable of handling such a lofty mantle as anybody can be. At the same time, though, he's a reluctant hero.

It's also amazing that Jason's a country lad who became a footballer, who is now tackling huge issues all over the place and is doing an amazing job with it.

To top things off, I had to do what they call a 'doorstop' — a press conference on the steps of Parliament House. It was a bit out of my league because they asked a couple of curly questions. All the talk then was about whether the Australian government knew Bali was a terrorist target. I just stepped around it, saying that they couldn't have had enough information because there were three employees of the Australian Federal Police at one of the bars. If they knew there was a problem, they wouldn't have been there.

I also said that I hoped people weren't playing politics and indulging in one-upmanship on issues relating to Bali. It affects so many people I felt that politicians had to put their policies and differences aside to work together.

There seemed no end to my public appearances. The Kangaroos and Collingwood — the clubs that bookended my AFL career — struck the Jason McCartney Medal, to be awarded to the most courageous player in clashes between the two sides. It's a remarkable honour to bestow on anyone because it's not just a one-off — it's a continuing legacy.

To be honest, I was actually embarrassed when I first heard about it. I always prided myself on just being honest, reliable, hard-working and, most importantly in this instance, courageous. It was all about the team for me. I'd never aimed to win individual awards, let alone have any named after me.

I was driven on a lap of honour at Telstra Dome in front of 50,000 people, many of them clapping and waving. I marvelled at how the wheel had turned. Collingwood supporters had given me plenty since I left the Magpies, but they appeared to have changed their tune towards me. It's funny when you consider that I was never one of the most popular players in the AFL — even my own supporters took a while to warm to me — but now I am a popular person.

It was a very slow lap and it brought tears to my eyes about four times. I somehow managed to compose myself just when I thought it would be full-on waterworks.

NERISSA: I thought, 'He deserves this.' I realised how many people have actually gone on this journey with us and followed Jason's recovery through news reports. I thought it was me and Jason's family who were fighting through it, but there were a lot of other people out there fighting through it with us.

JAN MCCARTNEY: I was watching it at home in Nhill. Everyone was glued to the TV. I was so proud of him. I had a tear in my eye when I saw the crowd reaction to him — it was one of just pure respect.

Little kids were leaning over the fence and saying things like, 'You're my hero!' I thought, 'These kids aren't giving me credit for going through what I did in Bali, they're giving me credit for going through all the pain of rehab and getting back to play elite-level sport again after being written off.'

Although I think the 'hero' tag is a bit rich, I can accept it on those terms. I understand that I have given people, from elderly people to kids in wheelchairs, a great gift — hope. I also accept the fact that 12 October 2002 will be remembered as the first terrorist attack on Australians — an unfortunate distinction, but a tragedy that will be part of Australian history — and I suppose my name will be linked to it forever. I would have preferred to have faded away into obscurity, but there's no chance of that now.

I will cherish the 'J-Mac' medal as long as I live, and, when I'm gone, hopefully my kids will get the chance to present the medal.

The selection process for the inaugural winner of the medal was difficult, but my fellow judges — Channel Ten commentators Robert Walls, Stephen Quartermain and Peter Daicos — and I decided on Collingwood centre half-forward Anthony Rocca, who broke the game open with a lot of gut-busting work that resulted in a swag of strong marks, a couple of long goals and a huge Magpie win. I was particularly chuffed when Rocca, who I'd played on a few times in my career, said it was probably the biggest honour he'd received in football. That's coming from a bloke who was a star for Collingwood in the 2002 AFL Grand Final, was runner-up in the club's best and fairest in 1999 and has played a lot of big games in front of massive crowds, so it was a huge compliment.

I'm still learning to accept compliments after going through an extended patch in my career where I had the barriers up due to the negativity that seemed to come my way. The other thing is that I don't want to be seen to be getting all of the attention in regard to the Bali bombings. I don't want other survivors and family members of those who lost loved ones to think, 'Why is everyone singing his praises? We've been through hard times too.' I never forget about the other people. In my eyes, everyone involved in Bali is a hero. Except, of course, for those behind the bombings.

When I heard about the suicide bombing that killed fourteen people and injured about one hundred and fifty at the Marriott Hotel in the Indonesian capital of Jakarta on 5 August, a new door of emotions swung open. In some ways, I went back to square 1.

But when Amrozi was sentenced to death on 8 August, that door slammed shut again. I wasn't happy with the verdict, I was relieved. It proved to the world that the Indonesians were keen to take a tough stance on terrorism and set a clear precedent for others directly involved in the bombings.

Amrozi said he wanted to die a martyr, and even raised his arms and smiled like he was celebrating a soccer goal. But I know it was a front. When I saw him in court, I could tell in his eyes that he was petrified. If he wanted to die a martyr, he would have wanted to get the execution over with as soon as possible. If he wanted to die a martyr, he would have been a suicide bomber. He was more calculating than that and actually tried to get away with it. A martyr doesn't try to escape death. They die willingly for a cause. Death seems the last resort for Amrozi. He has also appealed his death sentence. Enough said.

As far as I am concerned, I couldn't care less what happened in the trials of the other people involved. Amrozi's trial set the scene for the rest to follow.

I had plenty of other things to take my mind off it all anyway. On 3 September, I received a letter in the mail from the Governor-General's office asking me if I would accept an Order of Australia Medal. I didn't need to ponder it for too long. Here I was, a normal country boy from Nhill, being asked if I wanted to have the second-highest honour an Australian can receive (behind knighthood) bestowed upon me. Jason McCartney OAM — I don't know if I'll ever get used to that. I was gobsmacked.

I didn't purposely set out to do anything special, I just did what any person would do to survive, get married on time and return to work.

The medal recognised not so much my efforts in Bali but how I've carried myself and got back to playing AFL football. It also reinforced one of my mottos: It's not about what happens to you — it's how you deal with what happens.

Another emotional event for me was the passing of young Kylie at the Alfred Hospital. The last time I saw her — a few weeks before her death — she was tired and frail but seemed well on the road to recovery from her transplants. She was about to leave intensive care. Kylie's goal was to be home in Perth by her eighteenth birthday in November. She was hooked up to a few machines and she couldn't talk because she had a tracheotomy, but she had a big smile on her face when she saw me. She passed away the day before I had planned to visit her. I had a coffee with Henrietta and we both cried. When I got home, I played a filmclip of my comeback game, turned the music up loud and bawled my eyes out. Another beautiful young life had been lost.

28

One year on

October 2003 marked ten years since my first trip to Bali. Like most milestones you tend to reflect on how far you've come, the good times and the bad, the triumphs and the disappointments. I had plenty of time to think on the flight to Bali on 8 October — just four days before the first anniversary of the bombings.

I'd been worried for most of the year that nothing would be organised in terms of an official memorial service and monument. I'd also heard reports that maybe they didn't want to recognise the one-year remembrance and that maybe the cleansing ceremony, which was held just a month after the bombings, might have been enough considering the religious beliefs of the Balinese. That would never have been enough, so I was relieved when I saw the memorial monument being built.

The general mood of the thousands who made the journey to the picturesque Garuda Wisnu Kencana Cultural Park in Jimbaran — the same venue as the INXS Peace Concert four months earlier — was a sombre defiance. There was a lot of sadness and mourning, but there was also that we're-not going-to-let-the-bastards-beat-us mentality.

The Balinese don't refer to such an occasion as an anniversary because it is not a party or something to celebrate. They call it 'remembrance'. Remembering the people who died. Remembering the acts of courage. Remembering that we have to rally against terrorists. As one.

Hughesy, Mick, Nashy and I were all together again for the first time since the bombings. We were determined to get through proceedings in as strong a fashion as possible.

I was as emotionally prepared as I could have been. It was my third journey back to Bali since the bombings and I'd been to the bomb sites and the hospital a couple of times and given evidence at Amrozi's trial, but you can never tell how you are going to react to something so powerful and moving until you actually confront it.

All of the speakers did an excellent job, including Mr Howard and in particular General Susilo Bambang Yudhoyono, the Indonesian Minister for Political and Security Affairs, who really touched me with the way he spoke.

One of the hardest jobs was performed by Ross Tysoe, a former Australian Consul-General in Bali, who read out the names of the people who were killed in the bombings. He would have had to emotionally detach himself from the situation. On the other hand, I couldn't imagine what it would have been like to hear the name of someone close to you. When Tysoe got to the Ms, I thought, 'There could have been a Jason Paul McCartney and a Michael Bernard Martyn there as well.'

JAN McCARTNEY: I got a huge lump in my throat because I thought, 'One of those names could have been Jason.'

A lady at the ceremony said that she'd lost her sister but she could accept that; she really felt for the survivors who are left to suffer with it and live with it for the rest of their lives. I thought that was a beautiful thing to say. If I was in her situation, I don't think I could look at it that way.

MICK MARTYN: It just reinforced the fact that it could have been anyone who died that night. If the terrorists did exactly what they'd planned, none of us would be here now.

Aussie music icon John Williamson had a tough gig too, singing 'Waltzing Matilda'. It was a sombre occasion and he was never going to get any real crowd involvement but he produced a heartfelt performance.

I became quite emotional during the final part of the ceremony, when we each placed a sprig of Australian wattle in the rectangular pond in front of the presentation area. I've never lost sight of just how lucky I am to be alive but that fact hit home even more then.

I saw a lot of people who'd lost family members and there was enormous pain in their faces. It doesn't all stop for them. They're reminded of their loss every day.

NERISSA: It was a moment when we held one another and thought, 'We're very lucky to have Jason and the boys here today.' My heart went out to the people who lost loved ones.

Jason's always been a strong bloke who tries to control everything that he can, but he got quite emotional. He made a beeline for Hughesy to give him a big hug.

It was really beautiful when Jase and I walked up to the pond and Hughesy and Leigh were still holding on to their flowers waiting for us. That meant a lot to me. We threw our flowers in and then we all gave each other hugs.

Jason had a good cry too, which I was really glad about because he's always been so strong and focused on other people rather than himself. We'll never take for granted the fact that Jason survived. We cherish the time we have together.

PETER HUGHES: It was a special moment — mates who already had a very special bond have been drawn even closer together. We felt so lucky to be alive. I thought I was over it all, but obviously I wasn't. It was pretty tough for everyone.

DAVID BONYTHON-WRIGHT: Jason has really progressed a long way in the past 12 months. He was able to express his emotions like a lot of other people who were at the service. I think there was a bit of relief for him and everybody else involved in the tragedy. It was good to be there with his family and stand united.

It was a very emotional day but it was a beautiful service and it went beyond any denomination, it was multi-religious and catered for everybody. It showed the world how things like this should be done.

Jason has played a wonderful role in helping the nation heal, and that's a wonderful gift to give to Australia.

I couldn't help but be upset and almost inconsolable for a while. No shame in that. It was probably just what I needed as I hadn't really had time to be upset about anything because I'd had to stay focused on things like my football comeback.

DAVID BONYTHON-WRIGHT: Jason and Hughesy have set stunning examples for other men, who wouldn't normally seek help, showing that it's OK to seek help and talk about trauma. It's all part of the healing process.

I don't think the ceremony could have been done any better. There was a lot of emotion there the whole day. I was overwhelmed with the amount of work the Balinese and the Australian Government put into making the day a success. All bases were covered.

As we walked out, photos of the dead were displayed. It was highly emotional because all of the photos captured their happy smiling faces, which made it all the more painful and overwhelming.

It was too much for me.

There was the opportunity for survivors and families who'd lost loved ones to get together for a cool drink or a coffee, but I just had to get out of there. A lot of people wanted to talk and I'm always willing to give my support to people, but I had to leave and get away from it. It was draining.

That night, after regaining my composure, I didn't make it to the bomb sites at 11.08 p.m. as I had originally intended because Nerissa and I were enjoying the fascinating company of Kadek Wiranatha, who had given us the use of one of his villas and a personal driver.

KADEK WIRANATHA: I admire Jason for giving his support to Bali and encouraging people to visit here. Slowly, very slowly, things are improving in Bali and it's because of people like Jason. He explains to people what the real situation is in Bali, and that it is a safe place to holiday. I can't thank him enough for that.

We made it to 'Ground Zero' at about 12.30 a.m. A Hindu ceremony involving a lot of prayer was in progress. A monument displaying all the names of the dead was unveiled. The monument is ideally situated because it is right between the two sites. It was a fitting tribute, but it was another reminder of the enormity of what had happened.

It really hits you when you think that 22 countries were affected by the bombings. You could go to the Sari Club on any given night and think you were almost anywhere in the world, such was the mix of nationalities among patrons. The other tragic thing was that most of the victims were so young.

But it could have been a lot worse. The Australian Federal Police examined shrapnel taken from my lower back to work out what chemicals were used to make the bomb that exploded in Paddy's Bar. They found that the chemicals had not been mixed properly and estimated that the bomb only caused a third of the damage it could have.

I didn't think there would be so many Balinese there that night, but they far outnumbered Australians. The Kuta Carnival, which had the very apt slogan, 'Celebration of Life', had just finished. There was a huge outpouring of sadness and emotion. People, including grown men, were crying openly. I held my emotions together pretty well in the circumstances.

There were floral wreaths, photos and messages on the fence of the former Sari Club site, but there was nothing at Paddy's Bar. Banana trees had been planted at Paddy's, as the Balinese believe that two cycles of fresh fruit will cleanse the site.

There was so much peace and harmony in the air. Back in March, Nerissa and I met two Balinese girls at the Bali Rock Cafe who gave us some incense to place at both sites. They remembered us and we spoke like old friends. A Balinese man approached me and said, 'Jason McCartney, Jason McCartney. I've lived in Melbourne for a while and I saw your last game of football.' Another said, 'You the football man.' There was also an old photo clipping on a tree near the Sari Club site saying, 'Jason, please help us.' For Balinese people to acknowledge me when they don't really have access to AFL football is very special. But that night wasn't about me.

When we walked on the site of Paddy's Bar, vivid recollections of that night 12 months before came flooding back. I remembered how terrible I felt in that living nightmare, and how Mick and I had run up the road through the smoke, got on the back of motorbikes and headed to the Hard Rock Hotel en route to Sanglah Hospital. It seemed such a long time ago, like three years instead of just one, because so much happened in the year since.

Then I reflected on all the hard work that had gone into my recovery to full health. I knew I'd wear the scars forever, but I felt luckier than ever. While we were wandering among the banana trees, Nerissa and I spotted Leigh Hughes and Channel Nine reporter Mark Readings. They were going to the new Paddy's Bar, which is just a drop-punt away from the bomb site. We decided to go with them. It would be a symbolic act.

When we got there, Hughesy was at the bar. I greeted him with a solid handshake.

PETER HUGHES: We gave each other a bit of a wink and thought, 'Mate, we made it, and here we are again to fight another day.'

I said, 'Right, I'm gonna have that Arak that I didn't get to finish.'

~ • ● ⬤ ● • ~

On 17 October 2003, Jason was awarded one of the nation's highest honours. He is now a proud recipient of the Order of Australia: Jason McCartney OAM.

~ • ● ⬤ ● • ~

Letters to Jason

From the time I arrived at Melbourne's Alfred Hospital on 15 October 2002 — just three days after I was critically injured in the Bali bombings — hundreds of letters, cards and faxes, expressing kind sentiments and messages of hope, started flooding into the hospital and the Kangaroos Football Club.

I extend a heartfelt thank you to the Australian public for their overwhelming support, which gave me an enormous lift during some trying times.

The following is a selection of the letters I received.

Hello, my name is Erika Rees. I live in Ballarat. I have two dogs, one cat, two lizards and chooks. I am 13 years old.

I was burnt just over four months ago. It was 20 per cent, full thickness. I put petrol on our inside fire, my dad saved my life. I was in the Royal Children's Hospital for six weeks.

I know what you are going through. I think you are very brave.

I am changing football teams from Geelong to Kangaroos.

My dad works at Mars making chocolates, he said he would take you for a tour through the factory if you would like to.

— Erika Rees

Just a short note to let you know that our thoughts are with you and your family. Looking forward to you making a full recovery and seeing you back in a Kangaroos guernsey as soon as possible. See you on the field, big fella.

— Peter and Shaun Burgoyne

On behalf of all the staff at the Indonesian Consulate-General, I wish you a quick recovery and we pray to God the Almighty that the world's situation will improve and that peace and prosperity will be enjoyed by all.

— Indonesian Consul-General Boedidojo

You won't remember me, but I remember you. About ten years ago you visited a disabled war veteran and one-eyed Collingwood supporter Gordon at Mount Royal Hospital. You came with Tony Shaw and made that delightful old gentleman so happy.

I heard of your bad burns in the Bali incident and want you to know that I'm praying for you and your family and just know you're going to be right for that December wedding.

— Pam Cotton

I am a little old lady Kangaroo member from the country, praying for your recovery and return to your family. The wonderful spirit that you display on the football field has won you so many admirers and everyone is hurting with you in this traumatic time.

It is said: 'You can do very little with faith, but you can do very little without it.'

—JOY ADDERLEY

We were saddened to hear of the bombings in Bali and it was even more upsetting to hear that you and Mick were injured. I have been a staunch North Melbourne supporter for some 40-odd years.

On 17 October 2001 I suffered extensive burns like you. My face, chest, arms and hands were charred and blackened in an electrical explosion.

I would like to tell you of my almost total recovery and if I can do it, so can you. I know what you are going through, you probably think now you won't recover, believe me you will.

You face a hard road for some time, you will have good days and bad days but the human body is an incredible thing. Take the baths, the grafts, the dressings, wear your splints, do your exercises, try not to worry and keep your family and friends close.

— PAUL BRYANT

You have been an inspiration with the courage you have shown, and such a fighter as I have found out in the occasions we went at it on the football field.

You would have been told this a number of times but I just wanted to say how much pleasure I took from seeing you play one last time against Richmond.

— MATTHEW AND LISA LLOYD

I write on behalf of the AFL Commission, our staff and the Australian team in Ireland in relation to the injuries suffered by Jason McCartney in Bali last weekend. At the appropriate time, can you please let Jason, his family and fiancée know that our thoughts are with them.

In particular, Garry Lyon and the players in Ireland along with Wayne Jackson and Andrew Demetriou would like to pass on to Jason their best wishes for him to make a full and speedy recovery.

— TONY PEEK, AFL CORPORATE AFFAIRS AND COMMUNICATIONS GENERAL MANAGER

We thought we'd send you a postcard to let you know that whilst we are away, it's been pretty hard to not think of how you've been going. We knew that when you first came to and said to the dietician that you didn't like the food that she was going to give you because it wouldn't help your skinfolds, you must be all right. It's great to hear you talking but be patient because we know what you're like. We are counting down the days until we get back and see you both.

— COREY AND ROBYN

So sorry to hear of your accident. Our daughter Karyn was in the burns ward of the children's ward at the Alfred forty years ago this year. She was in hospital for ten weeks then back for more grafts over the years.

She had a visit from Murray Weideman and she really picked up overnight. It is so important you boys do visit the sick kids as it does do wonders.

You are in good hands at the Alfred. Hoping you are feeling better, get better quickly and will be back kicking goals (not against the Pies!)

— Dawn and Ern James and family

I want to congratulate you both on the remarkable comeback by Jason. Both of you have been through a great ordeal and have faced up to it so well. It was great to see you both at the football against Richmond — Jason playing so well and Nerissa beaming with pride. I already asked God's blessing on you at the wedding but I want to do so again. May the Lord in His goodness keep you strong in love for Him and for each other.

— Fr John Herd, Millicent Catholic Parish

Well, what an amazing recovery buddy — not once did I ever doubt your comeback to play AFL football again. The courage and strength you have shown typifies the person that you are.

We talk in football terms about courage, which you always have had and always will have, but this is another courage — enduring unexpected and fearful challenges that some unfortunately encounter in life. You got through it, mate, with your great determination, love for life and support from your family, close friends and words from the caring public.

You are an inspiration to many in the world, but on a personal note I will hold you and your character so high and close to my heart — and if the going gets tough I'll think of you, mate. Friends forever.

— Stevo (Anthony Stevens)

Congratulations on a great comeback and a great career. Over the past months you have inspired so many people, I know you've already heard it but I just wanted to tell you that your courage and determination has been nothing like I have seen before.

The day I saw you in hospital I got a real shock at the extent of your burns and thought you would never play again. But watching you pick yourself up and work harder than anyone I have seen has been so inspirational to me.

When I was questioning whether to come back and play with my injury, all I had to do was look at you and my answer was simple: 'If Jason can play with all his injuries, I can play with one.' I'm sure if you take all your great qualities into the next chapter of your life, you'll be ultra successful in anything you choose to do. Well done mate!

— 'Arch' (Glenn Archer), Lisa, Madison, Abbey and Jackson

My name is Sam Marshall, I am the grandson of Bob Marshall. You may have met my grandpa at some time around the Sturt Football Club or the Adelaide Crows Football Club.

My grandpa was in Bali at the same time as you. He was with the Sturt Football Club; they were celebrating their Grand Final win. My grandpa died in the Sari Club when the bomb went off. It has been really tough for my family and me over the last months.

I have always barracked for the Kangaroos and when I was a baby my dad bought me a Carlton quilt to try to get me to change teams but it didn't work.

I watched your last game and I thought you were great. My dad and I had tears in our eyes when we saw the three Sturt players come out on to the ground with their flag. Dad and I thought it was great how you shared this night with the people who had been affected by the bombing in Bali. I knew you were doing it for all of Australia, but especially for the people who had died or were injured in Bali. I knew that goal was for my grandpa and I know he would have been really proud of you.

I love my footy and I play for Colonel Light Gardens. My dream one day is to play for the Kangaroos.

— SAM MARSHALL

I wish to take this opportunity to congratulate you on what has been a fine career. I first met you when I took Nhill U16s for training a long time ago. I remember the night well and as Floody and I put the team through their paces I was struck by the tall skinny kid who looked like he had some ability.

Since then I have followed your career with great interest. First as you found your feet at Collingwood before then accepting many challenges at the Crows. There were times during this period where I was angry at the way you were being utilised. You had to work hard to stay positive in this time but you managed to do so successfully.

This positive attitude served you well when you came to North Melbourne. You were again presented with many challenges and you always gave your best.

I know I have been proud to work with players of such great character over the past few years at our club. You have proven to be of great strength and the two best clubman awards are testament to your character.

And now in the final chapter of your career you have overcome adversity again — this time on a much larger scale as you have fought back from horrific injuries to take the field one last time. Your efforts are a triumph of the human spirit and a celebration of the power of positive thinking.

— PAUL HAMILTON

Epilogue

by Ben Collins

12 October 2003, Garuda Wisnu Kencana Cultural Park, Jimbaran, Bali. The memorial service commemorating those who lost their lives in the Bali bombings exactly one year ago has just finished and Jason McCartney, compression garments covering his burns and sunglasses shielding teary eyes, embraces his family and friends.

My wife Rebecca and I, choking back tears of our own, decide to give them the space they need to console each other. Jason has become the public face of the tragedy, so his company is in high demand. He is surrounded by other survivors, as well as families who have lost loved ones. So it is a complete surprise when he comes over to us and wraps both Bec and I in his big, strong and scarred arms. We tell him how privileged we feel to be with him on such a special day; he says he is glad we are there.

That tearful embrace was the culmination of a journey that started three and a half months earlier, when Jason and I sat down for the first of about 20 interviews that ranged in duration from ten minutes to two and a half hours. *After Bali* is the first book I've written, and it's an experience I'll treasure for the rest of my life, regardless of what else I achieve. It has been exhilarating sharing time and a common goal with Jason McCartney.

Working with Jason was easy — especially when we conducted the last of our interviews while receiving massages at the Balinese villa where he was staying. Talk about mixing business with pleasure.

Jason was a writer's dream — easygoing, honest, open to suggestions. We were both trekking new ground, but we made what I'm told can be a tedious process relatively painless. Jason understood the value of giving a warts-and-all account of some of his most personal life experiences — no question was off limits, no subject taboo.

The process of constructing this book was an insightful and emotional journey. When I first spoke to Jason's wife Nerissa, she warned me to get ready for tears. She wasn't wrong — you simply can't live and breathe Jason McCartney's story for over 100 days and not be affected by it.

But for all that Jason has endured and conquered, he remains remarkably unaffected. It must have something to do with his solid country upbringing in Nhill. The salt-of-the-earth McCartney clan welcomed Bec and I with open arms one weekend in August 2003. We went to Nhill's Commercial Hotel where several locals, mates from way back, shook Jason's hand and renewed acquaintances. To break the ice, Daryl Leyonhjelm, one of Jason's former junior football coaches, asked him, 'So, Jase, what have you been up to?'

Jason shook his head. 'Not much,' he said. He was lying through his teeth. 'Not much' translated to a full diary of appearances, meetings, treatment, training sessions, errands, favours for friends, etc. There were times during the writing of this book when I struggled to get half an hour with him. His diary is full of appointments for appearances, meetings, treatment, training sessions, errands, favours for friends and more.

While his opinion is much sought-after, Jason never pushes his opinions on others. That night in Nhill, we watched the Kangaroos play Hawthorn on the TV in the pub. Although Jason knows the Kangaroos inside out, he still listened to the views of others, even when he didn't necessarily agree with them. He wasn't above anyone else, he was just one of the boys.

He's not above making fun of his own plight either. A few days after the remembrance ceremony we were having a drink in the new Paddy's Bar, a short walk from the bombsites. A bloke walked in with a backpack on his back and Jason playfully ducked for cover behind a pylon, hands covering his ears. Another time we were in a DVD shop in Kuta when Jason spotted a movie called *Jason X*, which had a picture of a hideous monster on its cover. Jason chuckled, 'That's how I looked twelve months ago.'

Jason's a man who's just as comfortable talking to a prime minister as a Balinese hawker. He doesn't have to alter his style for different situations because he fits in well anywhere. The Balinese who know of Jason worship him. Some even called him 'Hero Man'. That is, perhaps, the most apt way to describe him.

There is a lot to like about Jason McCartney. He is the type of bloke you'd love to call a mate. I feel genuinely privileged that I now can.

Paddy's Bar, October 12, 2002 11.08 pm

Jason McCartney's recollection of the events of October 12, 2002 and beyond.

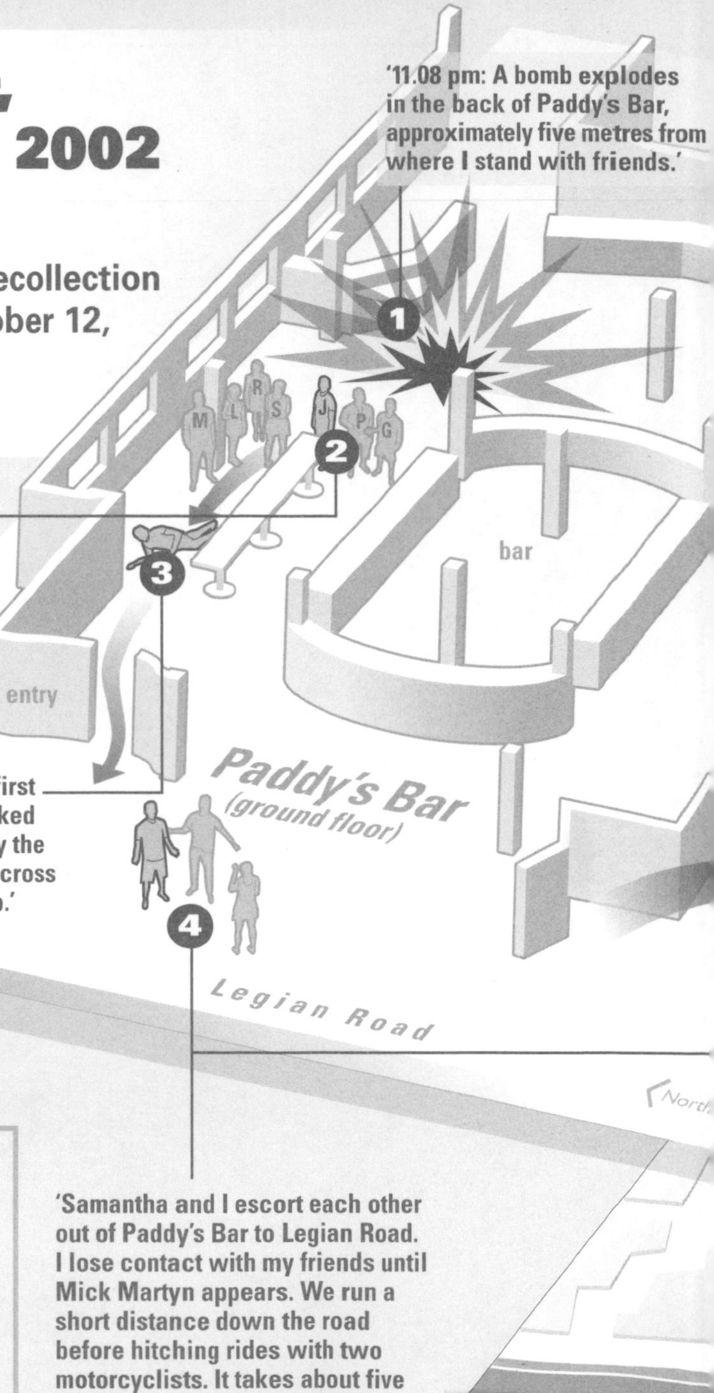

'11.08 pm: A bomb explodes in the back of Paddy's Bar, approximately five metres from where I stand with friends.'

'The blast knocks me to the ground. I grab Samantha Woodgate – the closest person to me – and we make our way towards the entrance.'

'Just seconds after the first explosion, we are knocked down again, this time by the force of the blast from across the road at the Sari Club.'

'Samantha and I escort each other out of Paddy's Bar to Legian Road. I lose contact with my friends until Mick Martyn appears. We run a short distance down the road before hitching rides with two motorcyclists. It takes about five minutes to get to the Hard Rock Hotel to see a doctor.'

M Mick Martyn
L Leanne Woodgate
S Samantha Woodgate
R Rachael Miszkowiec
J Jason McCartney
P Peter Hughes
G Gary Nash